Rethinking Security in East Asia

Studies in Asian Security

A SERIES SPONSORED BY THE EAST–WEST CENTER WASHINGTON

Muthiah Alagappa, Chief Editor

The aim of the Asian Security series is to promote analysis, understanding, and explanation of the dynamics of domestic, transnational, and international security challenges in Asia. The peer-reviewed books in this series will analyze contemporary security issues and problems to clarify debates in the scholarly and policy communities, provide new insights and perspectives, and identify new research and policy directions related to conflict management and security in Asia. Security is defined broadly to include the traditional political and military dimensions as well as the non-traditional dimensions that affect the survival and well being of political communities. Asia, too, is defined broadly, to include Northeast, Southeast, South, and Central Asia.

Designed to encourage original and rigorous scholarship, books in the Asian Security series seek to engage scholars, educators, and practitioners. Wide-ranging in scope and method, the series welcomes an extensive array of paradigms, programs, traditions, and methodologies now employed in the social sciences.

*　　*　　*

The East-West Center, with offices in Honolulu, Hawaii, and in Washington, D.C., is a public, nonprofit educational and research institution established by the U.S. Congress in 1960 to foster understanding and cooperation among the governments and peoples of the Asia-Pacific region, including the United States.

Rethinking Security in East Asia

IDENTITY, POWER, AND EFFICIENCY

Edited by

J. J. Suh, Peter J. Katzenstein, *and* Allen Carlson

SPONSORED BY THE EAST–WEST CENTER WASHINGTON

Stanford University Press • Stanford, California 2004

Published with the partial support of the
Sasakawa Peace Foundation (USA)

Stanford University Press
Stanford, California

Printed in the United States of America
on acid-free, archival-quality paper

Library of Congress Cataloging-in-Publication Data

Rethinking security in East Asia : identity, power, and efficiency /
edited by J. J. Suh, Peter J. Katzenstein, and Allen Carlson.
    p.   cm.
    Includes bibliographical references and index.
    ISBN 0-8047-4978-7 (cloth : alk. paper)—
ISBN 0-8047-4979-5 (pbk. : alk. paper)
    1. East Asia—Foreign relations.   2. Security, International.
3. National security—East Asia.   I. Suh, J. J. II. Katzenstein,
Peter J.   III. Carlson, Allen, 1968–
JZ1720.R48   2004
355'.03305—dc22   2004007832

Original Printing 2004
Last figure below indicates year of this printing:
13   12   11   10   09   08   07   06   05   04

Designed by Rob Ehle
Typeset by Heather Boone in 10/13 Bembo

Contents

Figures and Table

Contributors

ALLEN CARLSON is an Assistant Professor of Government at Cornell University. He is now revising his dissertation, "Constructing a New Great Wall: Chinese Foreign Policy and the Norm of State Sovereignty" (Political Science, Yale, 2002), for publication.

ALASTAIR IAIN JOHNSTON is the Laine Professor of China in World Affairs at Harvard University. Johnston is the author of, among others, *Cultural Realism: Strategic Culture and Grand Strategy in Chinese History* (Princeton, 1995). He is currently working on a book about socialization in international institutions.

PETER J. KATZENSTEIN is the Walter S. Carpenter, Jr. Professor of International Studies at Cornell University. He has written widely on issues of political economy and national security in both Europe and Asia.

YUEN FOONG KHONG is a Fellow of Nuffield College, and Director of the Centre of International Studies, Oxford University. His publications include *Analogies at War* (Princeton, 1992), articles on the international relations of the ASEAN region, and with David Malone (co-editor), *Unilateralism and U.S. Foreign Policy* (Lynne Rienner, 2003).

NOBUO OKAWARA is Professor of Political Studies at Kyushu University. His publications have centered on the theory of politics and the analysis of Japanese security policy.

RUDRA SIL is Associate Professor of Political Science at the University of Pennsylvania. He has written extensively on social science methods, philosophy of science, industrial relations, and the political economy of Russia and Asia. Among his publications is *Managing "Modernity": Work, Community, and Authority in Late-Industrializing Japan and Russia* (Michigan, 2002).

J. J. SUH is Assistant Professor of Government at Cornell University. His research interest includes international relations theory, international security, military alliance politics, the U.S.-Korea relationship, and Korean politics.

Preface

We started planning the project that resulted in this book when we found ourselves as colleagues teaching in Cornell's Government Department in the summer of 2001. Our complementary interest and expertise in Korean, Japanese, and Chinese security affairs made this a welcome opportunity. So did our intellectual unease with the tenor of much of international relations theory, which was seeking in East Asia a confirmation for insights and arguments that had proven less than satisfactory in Europe in the late 1980s. The September 11 attacks and the subsequent U.S.-led "war on terrorism" made a reexamination of Asian security even more timely as North Korea was labeled by the Bush administration as a member of the "axis of evil."

We first developed the idea for this book during a panel session at the 2001 meetings of the American Political Science Association in San Francisco. After this initial meeting we held a workshop at Cornell in March 2002 to discuss first drafts of the chapters that would eventually be included in this book. Together with the other authors published in this volume, we owe an enormous debt of gratitude to the insightful contributions, perceptive criticisms, and constructive suggestions of workshop participants Itty Abraham, Amitav Acharya, Muthiah Alagappa, Steven Benfell, Victor Cha, Sumit Ganguly, David Kang, David Leheny, Rudra Sil, several members of the Cornell faculty, and a number of Cornell graduate students, especially Karthika Sasikumar and Xu Xin. While authors revised their papers in light of both the workshop discussion and the unfolding war on terrorism, Rudra Sil joined Peter Katzenstein as coauthor of the introductory chapter that articulates the case for analytical eclecticism. A panel at the 2003 meetings of the International Studies Association in Portland, Oregon helped the authors to improve their drafts further in view of the constructive criticisms and suggestions they received. We are particularly grateful to Tom Christensen and David Kinsella for their helpful comments. We also thank the graduate students at Cornell for their intellectual engagement as they discussed much of the book's material in the Asian security seminar cotaught for two years by J. J. and Allen.

The workshop would not have been possible without the generous financial and logistical support of Cornell's East Asia and Peace Studies Programs, as well as the Carpenter Chair.

Muthiah Alagappa showed an early and active interest in this project for possible inclusion in the Asian Security Series that he edits, sponsored by the East-West Center and published by Stanford University Press. Muriel Bell at Stanford University Press made our task much easier than we had any reason to expect. Two anonymous reviewers also gave us useful comments that helped all authors improve their manuscripts.

In preparing the final manuscript for submission, we relied on the unfailing and efficient help of Rachel Gerber and Sarah Tarrow.

Finally, in the interest of candor, we would like to acknowledge to each other that we had a lot of fun exploring a topic that matters to us intellectually in our teaching and research, that touches on important current theoretical debates, and that is of great importance in world politics.

J. J. Suh, Peter J. Katzenstein, Allen Carlson
Ithaca, 2004

Rethinking Asian Security
A Case for Analytical Eclecticism

PETER J. KATZENSTEIN AND RUDRA SIL

Throughout the 1990s the conventional wisdom of international relations scholarship in the United States held that with the end of the Cold War and an intensification of institutionalized cooperation in Europe, Asia was ready to explode into violent conflicts. Large-scale war and rivalry were thought to be increasingly likely as an unpredictable North Korean government was teetering at the edge of an economic abyss on a divided Korean Peninsula; as an ascendant China was facing political succession in the midst of an enormous domestic transformation; as a more self-confident and nationalist Japan was bent on greater self-assertion in a time of increasing financial weakness; and as Southeast Asia remained deeply unsettled in the aftermath of the Asian financial crisis, with its largest country, a newly democratizing Indonesia, left in limbo following the debacle of East Timor and the fall of Suharto. None of these political constellations appeared to bode well for an era of peace and stable cooperation. Facing perhaps the most significant problems of any world region in adjusting to the post–Cold War era, Asia appeared to be "ripe for rivalry" (Bracken 1999; Betts 1993/94; Friedberg 1993/94).

The policies of the George W. Bush administration tend to reflect this view. Cautiously developed throughout the 1990s, the policy of engaging North Korea, for example, was put on ice after the November 2000 presidential election. Political relations with China worsened during the early months of the Bush presidency. Since

For critical comments and suggestions on prior drafts we would like to thank Ron Jepperson, David Kinsella, Audie Kotz, David Leheny, Karthika Sasikumar, John Schuessler, Alexander Wendt, participants of the PIPES seminar at the University of Chicago, participants of the research colloquium at the Free University Berlin, participants of the Cornell workshop on Asian Security, and the authors of this volume. The usual disclaimers obtain.

September 11 the war on terrorism has further strengthened the Bush administration's perception of Asia as a volatile region in which a U.S. presence is necessary to prevent conflict. The war has deepened greatly U.S. involvement in Central Asia; produced a growing military presence in Southeast Asia, particularly the Philippines, which had previously drawn little attention from the United States; and helped improve U.S. relations with China while worsening those with North Korea.

Lingering tensions over North Korea, the Taiwan Strait, and the war on terrorism notwithstanding, during much of the 1990s large-scale war was more evident in "peaceful" Europe than among Asian "rivals." More recently, it is in Europe that we witnessed the most vigorous challenges to the Bush administration's war in Iraq, raising new questions about the future coherence of NATO and transatlantic relations; by contrast, key Asian powers reacted with either official support for the United States (Japan and South Korea) or remarkable restraint (China and India). And North Korea's decision to restart its nuclear weapons program has so far been met by countries in the region with calls for dialogue rather than military intervention. This undercuts the conventional wisdom about Asian security and suggests that an alternative perspective deserves serious examination (Alagappa 2003a; Ikenberry and Mastanduno 2003). Such a perspective takes a much broader view of what is meant by the term "security." Instead of referring to military security narrowly construed, it considers also the economic and social dimensions of security. Specifically, this perspective focuses on the regionwide consensus on the primacy of economic growth and its interconnectedness with social stability, societal order, and regional peace and stability. Spearheaded by Japan and the original six members of ASEAN, this view has spread, most importantly, to China and Vietnam and, with a helping U.S. hand, also to the Korean Peninsula. Previously dismissed by U.S. security specialists as abstruse scholarly rumination with no relationship to the tough problems of Asian security, these broader, multidimensional views on Asian security have taken center stage since September 11, thus giving the alternative perspective a credibility it sorely lacked before.

The arguments marshaled in support of this view differ, however. Some tend to credit the dominant role of the United States in world politics and in Asia as the advantages of engagement are increasingly viewed as outweighing the advantages of balancing (Kapstein 1999). Others see that dominance, especially in the unfolding war on terror, as a possible source of instability and the intensification of conflict as U.S. policy and Al Qaeda are offering global frames for local grievances and conflicts (Gershman 2002; Hedman 2002). Still others have suggested that the historical experiences and normative discourses shaping states' perceptions of their regional environment make the security problems in parts of Asia less serious than is conventionally assumed (Acharya 2001, 2000a; Kerr, Mack, and Evans 1995). In light of these fundamental differences in perspective and the data to which they point, whether Asia is "ripe for rivalry" or "plump for peace" remains an open question.

Political reality we surmise is more complex than any of these perspectives allows for. This is unavoidable for the simple reason that in different parts of Asia-Pacific we find actors embracing quite different definitions of security. In Tokyo that definition tends to be broad and encompasses not only the deployment of troops in battle, unimaginable at least for the time being, but also the giving of economic aid, something that Japan does a lot of. In Washington, that definition tends to be narrowly focused on the military, which is large and powerful and dwarfs those of the rest of the world, and excludes economic aid, where the United States is exceptionally niggardly even after the promise of a doubling of the aid budget by President Bush in 2002. And in Beijing, narrow and broad conceptions of regional security remain deeply contested.

Beyond the varied security conceptions that actors hold, there are the varied lenses through which scholars analyze security. Different analytic lenses require different kinds of simplifications in how questions are posed, facts assembled, and explanations developed. Such differences, in turn, are shaped greatly by factors largely unrelated to issues of Asian security: metatheoretical considerations that define appropriate domains of inquiry, acceptable methods of analysis, and agreed-upon standards of evaluation. Although debates over such problems continue to shape research in other fields of political science and indeed the social sciences writ large (Hall 2003; Lichbach 2003; Shapiro 2002), the field of international relations in the United States has been especially affected by long-standing programmatic debates that divide "paradigms" or "research traditions" from one another. In the effort to make sense of the world, such paradigms or traditions invoke a particular vocabulary, adhere to a specific philosophical perspective, adopt a specific analytic framework, and develop a particular style of research. In noting fundamental incompatibilities between realist and Marxist theoretical perspectives, for example, Tony Smith (1994: 350) observes that "each paradigm is monotheistic, home to a jealous god." These different research traditions have become central to how we identify ourselves and others as social scientists and how we train the next generation of scholars. And they provide an enduring foundation for widely noted basic debates in the study of international affairs.

The growing interest in the existence of, and competition between, contending research traditions has not been without benefits. Indeed, one premier journal, *International Security*, has made a truly exceptional effort to present all sides of the debates, with extensive commentaries promoting or critiquing such research traditions as realism, rationalism, neoliberal institutionalism, and constructivism.[1] Similar interparadigm debates are also appearing regularly in European journals, although the tone, depth of philosophical grounding, and prevalent conceptions of world politics tend to be quite different than what one finds in the United States (Wæver 1999). This widespread attention to competing research traditions has marked international relations as a diverse field of scholarship and has contributed to increasingly nuanced articulations of theories and hypotheses within traditions. This is the sort of progress that some cite in advocating scholarship bounded within discrete research traditions (Sanderson 1987) as these contend with "the models and foils" put forward by competing traditions (Lichbach 2003: 214). This does not, however, mean that international relations research has embraced the spirit of intellectual pluralism or generated better solutions to existing problems. This is because paradigm-bound research can get in the way of better understanding as it tends to ignore insights and problems that are not readily translated into a particular theoretical language (Hirschman 1970). At the cost of sacrificing the complexity that policy makers and other actors encounter in the real world, problems are frequently sliced into narrow puzzles to suit the agenda of a given research tradition. As a result, whatever progress might be claimed by proponents of particular research traditions, there is little consensus on what progress, if any, has been achieved by the field as a whole.

The recognition of the existence of, and possible complementarities between, multiple research traditions holds forth the prospect of translating the analytic languages and theoretical insights of each in the process of improving transparadigmatic knowledge on specific substantive problems. For example, seemingly incompatible strands of liberal, constructivist, and realist thought offer different insights in different languages that can be cautiously translated and productively combined in problem-focused research. Scholars who champion the "triangulation" of methods as a promising avenue to more reliable knowledge (Jick 1979; Tarrow 1995) point the way to a different way of learning that transcends specific research traditions (Makinda 2000). Theoretical triangulation is certainly more complicated than methodological triangulation given the risk of intellectual incoherence across components of research traditions. Nevertheless, the risk is worth the potential payoffs of encouraging, in the interest of better understanding specific research problems, self-conscious efforts to selectively incorporate concepts and insights from varied research traditions.

A generation ago Anatol Rapoport (1960) pointed the way when he identified fights, games, and debates as three modal situations requiring a mixture of conflict and cooperation. Research traditions in international relations have tended to encourage conflict but have done little to foster cooperation. Fortunately, a number of international relations scholars are beginning to shun metatheoretical battles, preferring instead to turn their attention to the identification of politically important and analytically interesting problems that reflect the complexity of international life and require answers that no single research tradition is equipped to provide. In their synthetic treatment of different strands of institutional analysis, for example, John L. Campbell and Ove K. Pedersen (2001: 249) seek to "stimulate dialogue among paradigms in order to explore the possibilities for theoretical cross-fertilization, rapprochement, and integration." Similarly, others have begun to transgress the boundaries between realism, liberalism, and constructivism for the purpose of developing more integrated perspectives on particular aspects of international politics (Hellman et al. 2003). Some have been exploring the sources of "prudence" in world politics by explicitly seeking a "sociological synthesis of realism and liberalism" (Hall and Paul 1999), while others have implicitly crossed the boundaries between research traditions in exploring how aspects of political economy can produce tendencies toward both war and peace (Wolfson 1998) or how issues of status and recognition intersect with security concerns to drive weapons proliferation or military industrialization (Kinsella and Chima 2001; Eyre and Suchman 1996). These are just a few examples of works that have moved away from interparadigm "fights" in order to develop more eclectic perspectives.

This book is part of that intellectual movement. It has two purposes. First, it offers an overdue examination and partial reformulation of claims embedded in both pessimistic and optimistic perspectives on Asian regional security. Case studies examine important national security issues for key countries and regions in Asia: China, Japan, and Korea, as well as the Southeast Asian region. Our aim is to reformulate and deepen theoretical and practical insights into the security problems, arrangements, and strategies in Asia. Second, the volume seeks to illustrate the value of relying on multiple explanatory frameworks that are consciously eclectic in language and substance rather than being driven by the tenets guiding particular research traditions. Such frameworks are formulated on pragmatic assumptions that permit us to sidestep clashes between irreconcilable metatheoretical postulates, and to draw upon different research traditions and the concepts, observations, and methods they generate in relation to particular problems.

Although cast at different levels of abstraction, the book's two objectives are related. Within a particular research tradition, substantive analysis provides a firm grasp of specific logics as they work themselves out in particular aspects of Asian security. It is, however, likely to come up short in generating deeper insights into the relationships among the many factors that bear on Asian states' understandings of, and approaches to, the "security" of their region. That is not to say that everything matters, or that specific research traditions do not generate useful ideas. Borrowing from Albert Hirschman (1981), we only suggest that "trespassing" across the sharp boundaries separating different traditions allows for new combinations of problem recognition and explanation that may be less parsimonious but intellectually more interesting or policy relevant.

In this chapter we discuss, first, the pragmatic quality and problem-focused character of eclecticism in the study of international affairs. Next, we articulate a general problematique for research on Asian security that draws attention to multiple and intersecting processes that shape how Asian states understand and address their security concerns. Finally, we introduce and preview the substantive contributions that, read collectively, represent an effort to build eclectic explanatory sketches not easily subsumed within existing research traditions.

Research Traditions and Explanatory Sketches
in International Relations

Most scholars of international relations think of the theoretical universe as divided between different schools of thought to which scholars commit themselves in the belief
that they generate better explanations with greater policy relevance. What ultimately
distinguishes these schools, however, are not the substantive claims they produce but
the underlying cognitive structures upon which these claims are formulated. These
structures shape what phenomena are considered important and explainable, how research questions about such phenomena are posed, what concepts and methods are
employed in generating explanations of the phenomena, and what standards are reasonable for evaluating these explanations. Such abstract specifications reflect enduring
ontological and epistemological, that is metatheoretical, assumptions shared by members of some research communities but not others. Hence, as is true of the history of
science and social science more generally, as a field of scholarship international relations is characterized by the emergence of, competition between, and evolution or
degeneration of, discrete cognitive structures within which specific models and narratives are constructed, communicated, and evaluated.

Following Thomas Kuhn (1962), some scholars of international relations have referred to these structures as "paradigms." Paradigms are concerted intellectual efforts
to make sense of the world. When fully institutionalized, their weak links are no
longer recognized, their foundational assumptions are no longer questioned, and
their anomalies are consistently overlooked or considered beyond the purview of
specific research questions.[2] Dissatisfied with the monism implied in a Kuhnian vision of normal science, or perhaps frustrated by the absence of criteria for comparing supposedly incommensurable paradigms, some international relations scholars
have employed Lakatos's (1970) concept of "research programs" that are at least assumed to be comparable to each other in terms of how effectively the successive theories they produce deal with novel facts or anomalies over time. These scholars find
Lakatosian research programs to be "intuitively appealing and attractive" (Elman and
Elman 2003a, 2002: 253) in making sense of international relations scholarship because individual theories in the field have indeed come to be clustered around competing sets of "core" assumptions, and because debates among adherents of contending perspectives do frequently revolve around the question of whether one or the
other perspective is "progressive" or "degenerative."[3]

Although Kuhn and Lakatos represent contending epistemological perspectives,
both "paradigms" and "research programs" face limitations as units for organizing and
assessing international relations research. The persistence of divisive debates among
proponents of different approaches is difficult to square with the notion of either a
single dominant paradigm or the staying power of any one research program relative
to another. Furthermore, the overlapping of some assumptions across different ap-

proaches suggests that different schools of thought are not always mutually exclusive cognitive structures that can be evaluated according to any one standard. More importantly, although framed in different languages in different periods, the foundational divides reflected in international relations debates—for example, objectivism vs. subjectivism, agency vs. structure, material vs. ideal—represent recurrent rather than episodic problems (Sil 2000d: 9–12), suggesting that there is neither a clear sequence of normal and revolutionary science as Kuhn envisioned, nor any evidence that progressive research programs will be recognized as such by any but their own adherents. Indeed, even those who find Lakatosian research programs to be useful in assessing scholarly research differ in terms of which elements of Lakatos's metatheory are given priority, with some emphasizing the significance of sophisticated falsificationism for the resilience of conflicting theories and others focusing on the criteria for identifying progressive problem shifts (Elman and Elman 2003b). Andrew Moravcskik (2003), for example, relies on Lakatos to critique realism and advance the case for liberalism as a progressive research program, but also warns that Lakatosian thinking encourages a zero-sum competition among approaches and diverts attention from exploring the possibilities for synthesis. Even more problematic are some characteristic, often unacknowledged, weaknesses within approaches identified as research programs in international relations: proponents of research programs tend to value substantive or heuristic novelty as a measure of their scientific progress, offer multiple definitions of what constitutes a novel fact, engage in misstatements and tenacious battles that undercut tolerance and the acknowledgment of programmatic failures, and provide insufficient information to allow us to distinguish consistently between different research programs or to assign proper weights to a program's "hard core," "positive heuristic," or "protective belt" (Elman and Elman 2002: 245–52).

Because of the limitations that attend the concepts of "paradigm" or "research program," we follow here Larry Laudan's (1996, 1990, 1984, 1977) more flexible notion of competing and evolving "research traditions." This concept captures how scholars opt to identify, pose, and resolve problems in international relations research, including the vexing issues of Asian security addressed in this volume. Like Kuhnian paradigms and Lakatosian research programs, Laudan's conception of research traditions suggests long-enduring commitments that motivate and distinguish clusters of scientific research. Typically such traditions consist of two things: "(1) a set of beliefs about what sorts of entities and processes make up the domain of inquiry; and (2) a set of epistemic and methodological norms about how the domain is to be investigated, how theories are to be tested, how data are to be collected, and the like" (Laudan 1996: 83). Unlike Kuhn and Lakatos, however, Laudan offers no single model of how disciplines as a whole evolve or of how to measure their progress. He argues instead that we should focus on different research traditions as intrinsically diverse clusters of scholarship that can engender diverse theories, some more useful than others in solving particular problems. Moreover, unlike Kuhn and Lakatos, Laudan sees research traditions as potentially capable of encompassing very different types of research products involving different, at times even contradictory, explanatory propositions. This allows for the possibility that propositions drawn from different research traditions complement one another in the solution of common empirical problems, in spite of the foundational divides associated with these traditions. Since in the social sciences not all components of competing schools of thought represent elements of mutually exclusive cognitive structures and since these competing schools differ over time in their defining features and their core points of contention, it makes more sense to speak of the field in terms of more fluid research traditions rather than more rigidly defined paradigms or research programs.[4] We address the merits and limits of Laudan's reliance on "problem-solving" below, but for now we turn to the main research traditions in international relations, particularly as the field has evolved in the United States.

Although preferred labels and particular bones of contention have varied, since its inception in the early twentieth century the field of international relations has been divided by a long list of competing "isms" that may be viewed as competing research traditions. Enduring debates have existed among proponents of realism and idealism, behaviorism and traditionalism, neoliberalism and neorealism, rationalism and constructivism, and a variety of different structuralisms and poststructuralisms. In some cases, debate has revolved primarily around substantive interpretations or normative orientations; in others, around ontological or epistemological issues. Among research communities within the United States, rationalism, in both its realist and liberal variants, set the terms of scholarly debate early on. Elsewhere, the importance of ideas and identities has long been taken for granted and debates over world politics have revolved around competing understandings of the nature of "ideas" and "identity."

There are then many ways of framing competing approaches to international relations. For the purpose of defining and promoting eclectic approaches to Asian security, we rely here on the familiar triad of constructivism, liberalism, and realism as a usefully simplified way to address some foundational, conceptual, methodological, and substantive debates in contemporary international relations research. There exist variations within and across these three approaches, for example, in the extent to which a particular argument is founded on positivist assumptions or specific methodological injunctions. Nevertheless, for the limited purpose of defining and distinguishing eclectic analytic perspectives, these labels capture meaningful differences in the way scholars identify themselves and in the cognitive structures that shape how they recognize, pose, and approach the problems they seek to solve. Thus we could view constructivism, liberalism, and realism as three sides of a triangle that take for granted the centrality of some core assumptions of international life, for example, in their respective focus on identity, efficiency, and power (see Figure 1.1). At the same time, however, some variants of these traditions converge (at the triangle's corners) with one or the other research tradition's ontology, epistemology, methodology, or

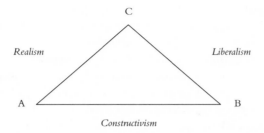

FIGURE I.I Research Traditions and Points of Convergence

normative orientations. The field of international relations thus encompasses both the practices of normal science working around shared core assumptions as well as the possibility of eclectic theorizing.

Constructivism is based on the fundamental view that ideational structures mediate how actors perceive, construct, and reproduce the institutional and material structures they inhabit as well as their own roles and identities within them. Constructivism thus highlights the significance of transformative or generative processes such as deliberation, persuasion, and socialization that, for better or worse, can lead to the transformation of identities and preferences (Johnston 2001; Wendt 1999; Finnemore 1996). Assigning epistemological significance to such processes at the individual level requires "a conception of actors who are not only strategically but also discursively competent" (Ruggie 1998: 21), something that is precluded by the utilitarian assumptions held by most liberals and realists. In constructivist analyses of state behavior and the relations between states, ideational factors and processes are expected to be important for tracing whether collective actors are likely to construct or diffuse enmity or amity between self and other. And constructivist analyses pay attention to the reproduction and transformation of collective identities as they affect the prospects for social learning and also the diffusion of collective norms and individual beliefs. Constructivists do, however, exhibit important differences in their foundational assumptions: Some identify with a "naturalist" form of positivism predicated on a scientific realism (Dessler 1999; Wendt 1995), whereas others depart from a "pragmatist" conception of social knowledge (Haas and Haas 2002), and still others adopt a hermeneutic approach consistent with the relativistic epistemology of postmodernism (Walker 2000; Ashley 1995). The first two strands are more likely than the third to share some set of epistemological assumptions that overlap with those held by most realists or liberals (near corners A and B in Figure 1.1). The "soft rationalism" embraced by pragmatist constructivists is particularly conducive to engaging realist and liberal arguments over the character and formation of actors' material and ideal interests (Haas 2001). These differences suggest that constructivist research is rendered coherent and distinctive not by a comprehensive epistemological perspective or a unique normative orientation but rather by the ontological assumption of the social construction of world politics that requires endogenizing actors' identities and treating interests as variable and thus responsive to such ideational processes as social learning, norm diffusion, and socialization.

Contemporary liberalism in its various formulations focuses largely on how rational state actors seek to maximize efficiency in an interdependent world and how, even under conditions of anarchy, this intentionality can produce cooperative arrangements and a rational aggregation of social preferences. Because of their willingness to consider the independent effects of the environments in which actors operate, some versions of liberalism can converge with some types of constructivism (around the triangle's corner B) on the significance of ideas, values, and multilateral institutions in constraining actors and reshaping their preferences (Haas 2001). Moreover, many constructivists share with classical formulations of liberalism (near corner B) a normative concern for progress predicated on the idea that the relevant actors and their interests are not fixed but variable, embedded in a wider set of social relationships and amenable to the pressure of social norms and moral persuasion (Reus-Smit 2001). More concretely, both perspectives put much stock in the possibility that international organizations can engender shared values and reciprocal understandings that can sustain, even if they do not alter, actors' identities and preferences and cooperative arrangements beyond the level one would predict solely on the basis of the strategic calculation of member states. This idea is evident, for example, in arguments about the significance of shared democratic values for the persistence of the U.S.-Japan alliance (Mochizuki and O'Hanlon 1998: 127) and the importance of shared discourses about North Korea in explaining the longevity of the U.S.-Korea alliance (Suh, this volume).

At a more fundamental level, however, neoliberals are much closer to realists than constructivists in accepting utilitarian and rationalist assumptions in the identification of the relevant actors, interests, and structures in international politics (corner C). Thus, even when contemporary liberals take seriously the role of ideas and beliefs as focal points of common concern (Goldstein and Keohane 1993), they consider these as reflections of states' experiences in the international arena or new instruments for realizing the benefits of cooperation over the longer term. They do not view ideas and beliefs as forces capable of fundamentally altering the identities or core interests of actors. What distinguishes liberals from realists is not their ontology or epistemology but their designation of the central problems that need to be investigated. This, in turn, reflects competing assumptions about the preference-ordering of states (whether they seek absolute gains or relative gains) and the causal impact of international institutions (whether, in the interest of all member states, they introduce a greater degree of predictability, transparency, and reciprocity). Liberals allow for a wider range of conditions under which absolute gains motivate cooperative state behavior, and assign greater importance to international institutions as a basis for sustaining that behavior and mitigating the effects of anarchy. Institutions may be significant for constructivists as well, but mainly as reflections of social practice or as potential sources of unanticipated consequences and major shifts in actors' identities and perceptions of interest. Specifically for neoliberals, institutions represent equilibrium outcomes of strategic interaction, reducing transaction costs, providing information, making commitments more credible, and encouraging reciprocity (Keohane and Martin 1995).

In its current formulation, realist theory is concerned with outcomes at the systemic level (usually stability or conflict among states) or, in recent neoclassical variants, in the effects of actor preferences on state behavior in different environments (Finel 2001/02). Outcomes are assumed to be driven primarily by asymmetrical distributions in capabilities, measured largely in military terms or material resources, that are required to defend one's borders, inflict harm on other states, or prevail in domestic politics. Given the centrality and objective character of the material distribution of capabilities, realists diverge sharply from constructivism's emphasis on ideational factors. At the same time, contra liberalism, realists insist that states are inescapably operating in a self-help system in which their cooperation is constrained by the objective of maximizing relative gains in the distribution of capabilities. On questions of security, the unmitigating logic of realpolitik is independently articulated by the behavior of states. Under most conditions, "institutions have minimal influence on state behavior and thus hold little prospect for promoting stability" (Mearsheimer 1994/95: 7).

This difference in problem focus and substantive interpretation does not keep realists from sharing with important strands of liberalism the view that a state's interests, identities, and ability to identify opportunities and threats are all unproblematic. This similarity permits some convergence in substantive analysis (at corner C). This is evident, for example, in arguments about how the U.S. continued military and economic engagement in Asia serves the purpose of both guarding against potential regional hegemons and provides opportunities for increased cooperation and prosperity throughout the Asia-Pacific. By the same token, weak states participate actively in international institutions in the hope of diffusing security threats posed by stronger members of those institutions. This is one reason why ASEAN member states have sought wider fora, such as the ASEAN Regional Forum (ARF), to engage Japan, China, and the two Koreas, and why multilateralism holds some promise in the attempt to resolve the conflict between the two Koreas (Khong 1997b; Kurata 1996). Furthermore, realist thought begins to converge with constructivist perspectives (at corner A) where realist behavior is viewed as a projection of particular ideas and beliefs held by state actors. This is evident, for example, in the "cultural realism" that drove Chinese grand strategy in various periods in Chinese history (Johnston 1995) and perhaps also in the symbolic significance of the Taiwan issue in the triangular relations between China, Japan, and the United States (Xu 2003; Christensen 1999).

This threefold characterization of contemporary international relations research is by no means the only way to classify research traditions. For example, the lack of deep epistemological disagreements between important variants of contemporary realism and liberalism have prompted some recent surveys of the field to refer to these schools as competing sets of claims about actors' preferences and behaviors *within* an overarching framework referred to variously as "rationalism" (Katzenstein, Keohane, and Krasner 1999a) or "neo-utilitarianism" (Ruggie 1998). Alternatively, scholars may prefer to focus on analytic subdivisions that have emerged *within* research traditions. For example, those with intellectual sensibilities that are more "reflectivist" (Wæver 1996) than rationalist, may prefer to apply the threefold characterization to disagreements among "natural" constructivists, critical constructivists, and postmodernists. Thus, no single set of metatheoretical differences distinguishes discrete research traditions in international relations. Depending on the research community in question, the operative distinctions may range from deep differences over ontological issues (for example, in the debates between rationalist and constructivist conceptions of preferences) to differences over epistemological postures (for example, in the debates between classical and structural realists or between conventional and postmodern constructivists). What matters more is that the questions and practices of scholars lead them to identify with, promote, and communicate within separate groups—as has been the case with strands of realism and liberalism for over two decades and is now turning out to be the case for constructivism as well. So long as constructivists, liberals, and realists themselves see fit to distinguish themselves from one another, and so long as the distinction produces repeated clashes over which problems are important, which variables are assigned more causal weight, and which principles more consistently guide the preference-ordering and behavior of actors, there are sufficient grounds for treating them as competing research traditions.

Another potential problem is that the distinctions sometimes get blurred when scholars deploy the rhetorical strategy of identifying their preferred research tradition with the existence of a "reasonable mainstream" that supposedly enjoys almost universal assent, or of a "conventional wisdom" that supposedly improves on and subsumes various "minority" positions. Some realists, for example, claim that institutions only matter when they reinforce preexisting common interests and thus regard neoliberal institutionalism as simply realism by another name (Mearsheimer 1995). In response, neoliberals retort that neoliberal institutionalist theory is flexible enough to subsume the utilitarian and rationalist aspects of realism (Keohane and Martin 1995). A while back, in the late 1980s, both realists and liberals could argue with some justification that critics of the mainstream had failed to produce empirically grounded research to back up their abstract claims. Over the last decade, constructivists have responded to that charge. In doing so they have opened themselves up to the opposite criticism. Some critical theorists and postmodernists have chided constructivists for having been mainstreamed by positivism (Hopf 1998; Price and Reus-Smit 1998). Such rhetorical duels are quite typical of social science debates. They cannot conceal, however, fundamental differences in a priori assumptions that guide analyses in different research traditions. In fact, the existence of such rhetoric is itself indicative of the vigor with which different research traditions attempt to establish dominance, with the paradoxical result that such efforts prevent the very monism implied by a dominant paradigm and contribute to intensified competition between the traditions (Sil 2000a).

Making the case for analytical eclecticism requires us to cut the link between research traditions and the substantive interpretations and empirical claims constructed within them. Research traditions cannot themselves be evaluated against each other. Their ontological and epistemological foundations are often too incommensurable and too abstract to produce specific methodological injunctions or substantive explanations and predictions. Nor can they be synthesized into a single unified model of scientific research. While the most doctrinaire proponents of any one research tradition will reject the need for synthesis, "even coalitions of the willing may find the going difficult as they discover the analytical boundaries beyond which their respective approaches cannot be pushed" (Ruggie 1998: 37). But what can be tested, compared, and partially recombined are the "explanatory sketches" research traditions generate. We employ this term to sidestep the ambiguity and contestation often generated by the use of such terms as theory or hypothesis, especially since these terms are often defined and qualified differently across competing research traditions. What passes for a "theory" is often little more than an empirical claim embedded in the metatheoretical structures associated with a particular school or approach. We define explanatory sketches broadly to refer to any interpretation of a set of observations that is intended to generate a causally significant understanding of specific empirical outcomes, whether these are specific historical events, patterns of similarity and dissimilarity in broad configurations, or variations across comparable processes. As such, explanatory sketches are sufficiently open-ended to encompass a wide range of empirical claims. Such claims need not be limited to a single time- or space-bound context. And they should be formulated so as permit, at least in principle, some form of validation or falsification through further empirical observation. Thus, a realist explanation for the conflict on the Korean Peninsula, a narrative interpreting the sources and significance of Japan's culture of security in the postwar international context, or a choice-based model of security cooperation in Southeast Asia during the 1990s can all be regarded as explanatory sketches. All three impute causal significance to certain facts in relation to certain outcomes. And all three draw upon logics that can be adapted to an analysis of comparable contexts.

The relationship between explanatory sketches and research traditions is the point of departure for analytical eclecticism. For the most part, an explanatory sketch is likely to be "nested" within one or another research tradition, accepting as unproblematic the ontological, epistemological, and methodological assumptions characteristic of that tradition. Conversely, research traditions are highly significant for the purpose of identifying and classifying explanatory sketches in a given field of research. They indicate which explanatory sketches accept certain assumptions as uncontroversial background knowledge; which sketches conform to established conventions governing the collection of evidence and the testing of general statements; which sketches reinforce or undermine the intellectual coherence of a research tradition; which need to be altered because they introduce unanticipated problems; and which need to be excluded entirely from the tradition because of the insurmountable challenge they pose by violating foundational assumptions. Moreover, institutional factors—ranging from the venues for publication and funding patterns to faculty hiring and graduate training—strengthen the importance investigators themselves attach to presenting their projects and findings in the form of explanatory sketches that fit easily into a well-established research tradition. These factors account for why most research in international relations over the past century can be readily identified in terms of quite familiar labels such as realism, liberalism, behaviorism, or structuralism, each of which ultimately derives its coherence and significance from the kinds of beliefs and norms that Laudan identifies as the basis for a research tradition.

Although it is true that explanatory sketches are typically "nested" in particular research traditions, for two reasons this is not necessarily so. First, research traditions vary in terms of the significance they attribute to foundational assumptions, methodological orientations, and domains of inquiry. One research tradition may be identified primarily in terms of its ontological assumptions and theoretical language, allowing for a wide-ranging domain of inquiry and a large set of methodological tools. Another may be more recognizable through the application of common methodological tools to a well-specified domain of inquiry even if groups within that tradition differ on questions of epistemology. This is evident, for example, for much of constructivism, where we find empiricist and hermeneutic approaches both sharing the assumption of a socially constructed international world and both employing the language of "discourse" and "identity" in trying to offer insights about the world. Similarly, the underlying preference for methodological individualism is a central defining feature of neoliberal institutionalism, even though some of its adherents may be game theorists testing formal models and others empiricists in search of probabilistic hypotheses. Moreover, as research traditions suggest enduring commitments, it is also likely that they will have to evolve as particular assumptions or heuristic devices become more or less valuable or fashionable over time for different generations of scholars seeking to explain similar problems in new environments. While common foundational assumptions and methodological orientations are probably sufficient to produce similarities across explanatory sketches in adjacent generations of scholarship, as the number of generations increases, differences in the character of explanatory sketches may make them difficult to recognize as part of the same research tradition, as is true, for example of work on security communities (Adler and Barnett 1998; Deutsch et al. 1957).

Second, the considerable differences *within* constructivist, liberal, and realist research traditions that we mentioned above generate significantly different explanatory

sketches that can coexist as part of a single research tradition. Some may produce substantive claims that implicitly or explicitly challenge the "normal" expectations of
their respective research traditions in spite of shared ontological and epistemological
principles. And, explanatory sketches constructed within different research traditions
can converge in their wider implications and projections, despite fundamental disagreements over foundational or methodological issues and the characterization of
specific problems. Thus, realism, regarded by some as a source of pessimistic scenarios
for Asia (Friedberg 1993/94), can also provide the basis for theories suggesting lasting
stability through, for example, the logic of nuclear deterrence (Goldstein 2001a) or a
regionally calibrated balance of power in which China's military strength is offset by
regional alliances and by the United States as an "offshore balancer" (Mearsheimer
2001: 234–66; Layne 1997). Similarly, regarded by some as inherently optimistic about
the prospects for peaceful change through norm diffusion and social learning, constructivism can be adapted to emphasize how enduring beliefs about sovereignty or
resilient images of enmity can hinder the resolution of volatile issues such as Taiwan
(Johnston, this volume) or a divided Korea (Suh, this volume; Moon and Chun 2003;
Grinker 1998). A neoliberal institutionalist sketch might interpret the growth of such
institutions as the Asian Development Bank as evidence of increasing multilateralism
across regions in an ever more interdependent world, converging with constructivist
sketches emphasizing the strength of shared norms and the socialization of particular
groups of states in overcoming historical enmities and nurturing regional alliances, for
example in the case of Southeast Asia (Acharya 2001; Johnston 1999b; Khong 1997b);
at the same time, another neoliberal sketch might view regional institutions as evidence of a more sophisticated strategy conceived by Asian states to promote their economic interests in world markets, converging with realists who view Asia primarily as
an arena of competition and conflict in the absence of a bipolar international system.
And, constructivist, neoliberal institutionalist, and neorealist treatments of state behavior may proceed from quite different assumptions and identify quite different causal
mechanisms while still agreeing on how China is likely to respond to new regional
economic institutions or how Japan's changing role in such institutions indicates a reduced willingness to rely only on its bilateral relationship with the United States.

Research traditions are not rigid doctrines that produce uniform explanatory
sketches employing similar logics. Explanatory sketches can be meaningfully grouped
in terms of the implications of their substantive claims, in spite of significant differences in their philosophical or methodological foundations and their preferred causal
mechanisms. It is thus possible to make adjustments to foundational or methodological principles to permit a more direct comparison, synthesis, or integration across explanatory sketches about similar phenomena even if these sketches are drawn from
different traditions. This may pose problems for classifying all social science and international relations research in terms of distinct and competing research traditions
(Ben-David 1978: 744–45). Yet it is precisely this flexibility in Laudan's understanding

of research traditions that opens the door to thinking about the possibilities and merits of analytical eclecticism in relation to discrete problems in international relations.

Eclecticism and Problem Solving

Analytical eclecticism detaches explanatory sketches from the competing metatheoretical systems in which they are embedded. It offers us an opportunity to draw upon clusters of empirical observations, causal logics, and interpretations spanning different research traditions. It thus permits us to take advantage of complementarities in the problems we address and the empirical claims we make. Ronald Jepperson (1998) has already alerted us to the combinatorial potential arising from several different types of complementarity. Simple complementarity, he suggests, relies on the specialization of different perspectives in different empirical domains. Additive complementarity focuses on types of effects, now often called "mechanisms," such as aggregation (choice theoretic), selection (population ecology), or social construction (institutionalism). Modular complementarity either utilizes different approaches at different "stages" of a process, or it nests arguments constructed at one level of analysis within more general arguments constructed at a different level of analysis. Finally, complementarity in problem recognition combines some sketch that isolates and describes phenomena with a newly acquired significance, with another sketch that may be adept at providing explanations for these phenomena even though it may not have recognized them in the first place.

Although specialists from competing research traditions do not view their relationship to one another in these terms, in scholarly practice simple complementarity is not unknown in international relations. Explicit acknowledgement of this fact might help in taking advantage of other forms of complementarity, for example in the definition of problems or in the development of explanatory sketches. Problem recognition complementarity, for example, can lead us to view systemic outcomes and state behavior as part and parcel of the same problem in Asian affairs; thus, China's sensitivity on Taiwan, ASEAN members' interest in a continued U.S. role, and Japan's explorations in multilateralism could be viewed as interrelated trends tending toward regional stability or conflict. This could set the stage for explanatory sketches that rely on modular complementarity in complex explanatory sketches. For example, a constructivist account of identity formation may establish variation in threat perception across states that can then be employed to understand variations in the enthusiasm with which states pursue absolute gains through open regional institutions or relative gains through strategic alliances intended to offset the capabilities of a stronger regional power (Rousseau 2002).

Analytical eclecticism does not privilege any one type of combinatorial formula or seek to build a unified theory encompassing each and every variable identified in competing research traditions. Eclecticism is distinguished simply by the articulation

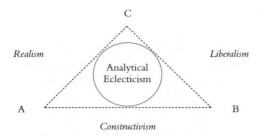

FIGURE I.2 The Possibilities of Eclecticism

of more complex problematiques that emphasize connections between outcomes stipulated in puzzles investigated in different research traditions, and by the construction of explanatory sketches that incorporate data, interpretations, and causal logics from at least two distinct traditions. That is, analytical eclecticism regards existing research traditions fluidly and is willing to borrow selectively from each to construct accounts that travel across the sides of the triangle representing constructivism, realism, and liberalism (Figure I.2).

The basic logic of eclecticism is not limited to the triad of approaches we are discussing here. For example, in research communities outside the United States rationalist analysis has occupied a less central place in the study of international relations compared to identities and other ideational structures. There the plea for analytical eclecticism might be tilted more toward integrating empiricist perspectives on international politics with postmodernist theoretical stances and text-based styles of analysis typical of the humanities. Alternatively, in a wider arena of research, eclecticism may take the form of identifying ways to bridge the gulf between the social and natural sciences, as is evident in recent creative advances in neuroscience, evolutionary biology, and the study of complexity. The point is that eclecticism is a relative construct, significant mainly as a strategy for coping with existing scholarly debate in a field in which competing perspectives may be reasonably identified as discrete research traditions. As an alternative to joining in such a debate on behalf of one or another perspective or dismissing it as proof of the fundamental incommensurability of theories, eclecticism explores new combinations of assumptions, concepts, interpretations, and methods embedded in explanatory sketches generated by competing research traditions.

The potential value of engaging in such combinatorial exercises may be understood by way of analogy to two stories about watchmaking that exhibit what Arthur Koestler dubbed "holonic principles of architecture," the relation between the whole and its parts (Mathews 1996). For Herbert Simon (1981: 200–202) the social world consists of partly decomposable systems with tight causal linkages among specific sets of factors that, loosely linked to other clusters, form a weakly linked, broader ensemble. Simon tells a parable of two Swiss watchmakers that illustrates the advantage of eclectic reasoning. Tempus built his watch from separate parts. When he was disturbed and had to put an unfinished watch down on the table, it came apart, and Tempus had to start all over again. He built few watches. Horus built his watches by assembling the individual pieces into modules that he subsequently integrated to make a watch. When he was disturbed he put down the module he was working on and thus lost less time and labor. He built many watches. A second story comes from the more recent history of watchmaking. Seiko's watchmakers revolutionized miniaturization by splitting the motor into three components and inserting them into tiny spaces between the watch's gears. Rather than thinking, as did the Swiss, of motor and gear as natural components that help in the production of the watch, Seiko engineers thought of the total product and the purpose and role of each component in relation to the whole (Mathews 1996: 27–28). Horus and Tempus, the Swiss and Seiko proceed quite differently; but, what made a difference in the productivity of Horus and Seiko was their recognition of the different ways the elements of a system could be assembled in different combinations of modules or subsystems. This, in turn, enabled them to ultimately solve problems that were not even recognized as such by Tempus or the Swiss.

Recognizing and solving problems, in fact, are at the heart of Laudan's view of scientific progress. Solved problems constitute scientific progress; unsolved problems chart areas for future exploration; and anomalous problems are those that a competing explanatory sketch may be able to solve. Research traditions and explanatory sketches vary in the kinds of problems they identify, the efficacy with which they solve these problems, and the extent to which they avoid anomalies (Laudan 1996: 79–81). The rationality and cumulation of scientific process ultimately depend less on the evolution, coherence, and status of different research traditions and more on their contribution to "problem-solving progress" (Laudan 1977: 109).

In principle, all explanatory sketches and research traditions contribute to problem solving and all have the "capacity to enable new observations of the world and thus even to generate entire new descriptive phenomenologies" (Jepperson 1998: 4). The quality of research still depends significantly on the kinds of information available and on the skills, intuition, and intellectual creativity of the researcher. Yet, in contemporary international relations scholarship constructivist, liberal, and realist explanatory sketches differ greatly in terms of the kinds of insights they offer. Some sketches get much more purchase for understanding individual choices at the micro level, others for illuminating processes at the macro level; some sketches can make us understand problems of strategic interactions among actors, others the processes by which the actors acquire and alter their identities; some sketches are well suited for contexts in which material capabilities are decisive for explaining outcomes, others in which individual beliefs are of central importance, still others in which collective norms are of primary causal or constitutive importance. These differences do not merely represent competing empirical claims. They reveal also differences in problem focus and in the capacity to solve particular kinds of problems. Relying on sketches that draw on several research traditions, without being fully beholden to any one of them, is a virtue not a vice of a problem-focused eclectic approach. Its virtue lies in a pragmatism that avoids rigid commitments to working only within existing research traditions. For example, an eclectic approach alerts us to the possibility that balance of power arguments inspired by realist theory may have connections to security community arguments following a constructivist logic, enabling us to better articulate and understand such problems as the evolution of international relations in northern Europe (Katzenstein 1996b). For Laudan, as for Chairman Deng, combining research traditions is a pragmatic move: it makes no difference whether the cat is black or white as long as it catches mice.

Attention to problem solving is necessary but not sufficient for progress in international relations research. As Laudan himself recognizes, problem and tradition are after all intertwined: by their very nature research traditions are likely to channel attention toward particular empirical issues that appear to be more readily problematized using their preferred conceptual and methodological apparatus. Moreover, there is the possibility that judgments about the problem-solving efficacy of specific research traditions may prompt some researchers to shift their tentative commitment prematurely from one tradition to another, even though such judgments presume that it is the same problem that is being explored in competing traditions and the same standard that is being used in determining whether and how efficaciously the problem is solved. How should we think about problems that exist apart from traditions and sketches? How can we even communicate a problem in a language that will be intelligible to more than one research tradition? What is the status of unsolved problems that are potential rather than actual? And, how do we form a consensus about the point at which a problem can be declared to have been solved? Realists, for example, are not likely to concern themselves with such problems as the rules governing entry into the WTO or the rate of diffusion of human rights norms across particular countries. Similarly, neither liberals nor constructivists are likely to expend much energy on problems of deterrence failure or the relative utility of offensive/defensive balances. Thus, claims that such problems have been solved are not likely to impress all students of international affairs, whether these claims are from proponents of specific research traditions or from scholars oriented toward eclecticism. In other words, research problems in international relations are not always like Chairman Deng's mice; in some cases, a cat may not even know that there is a mouse to be caught, and in other cases, the white cat and black cat may have different rules for deciding if, when, and how quickly a mouse has been caught.

Ultimately, then, the case for analytical eclecticism is dependent not on its ability to solve specific problems already identified by one or another research tradition, but on the possibility of expanding the scope of research problems beyond that of each of the competing research traditions. Following Robert Cox (1981), we might say that in contrast to theory that aims to solve problems posed within a given perspective, eclecticism is closer in spirit to critical theorizing in transcending existing analytic subdivisions and research parameters to construct a larger picture of the prevailing order and its origins. In that way our questions may come to resemble less closely stylized facts, a favorite of approaches dedicated to analytic parsimony, while resembling more the messiness of actual problems encountered by actors in the real world. Conceptual frameworks developed by competing research traditions are designed to problematize only select aspects of international life that are interconnected. Such analytic accentuation can be fruitful and is sometimes necessary in light of practical research constraints. It also poses specific risks. One is that assumptions deemed valuable for solving the kinds of problems favored by a given research tradition will be hoisted upon the analysis of other kinds of problems for which these assumptions may not be well suited. For example, neorealist explanations aiming to show that central aspects of EU politics are best captured by relative-gains calculations have failed to generate a distinctive research tradition dealing with the EU (Grieco 1990). Another risk is that explanatory sketches nested within research traditions may only pay attention to certain aspects of problems and to certain preselected variables, ignoring a wide range of factors that are potentially relevant to recognizing and solving a more comprehensively defined problem. The total silence of a voluminous literature on U.S. grand strategy on the topic of terrorism is, after September 11, a shocking intellectual failure explainable largely in terms of an overly narrow conception of security and security-relevant actors (Crenshaw 2002).

This plea for analytical eclecticism is predicated not on the rejection of research traditions or on the futility of the research products they generate, but on the hunch that there are significant intellectual gains to be had from reversing the trade-offs faced by scholars working in one or another research tradition. Following Robert Alford (1998: 9), we do not seek to dissolve or reify the tensions between different traditions and sketches, but do believe that researchers who can theorize their problems within multiple traditions are in a better position to recognize previously hidden aspects of social reality. Since no one analytic perspective can confidently claim to offer all the insights we need, "the best case for progress in the understanding of social life lies in . . . the expanding fund of insights and understandings derived from a wide variety of theoretical inspirations" (Rule 1997: 18).

Eclecticism and Asian Security: The Shrinking of "Natural Expectations"

The relevance of different research traditions to different theoretical and empirical domains cannot conceal the fact that every research tradition generates its own unquestioned, that is "natural," worldview. This worldview contains within it templates that draw investigators to certain problems at the expense of other, related ones, to specify a priori the most relevant variables in understanding these problems, and, in the process, to identify some sources of behavior among actors while discounting others. Asian security offers ample illustrations for this proposition. The totally unanticipated end of the Cold War and collapse of the Soviet Union, for example, generated not reexamination of whether and why theories drawn from the major research traditions had proven inadequate. Instead, these events yielded another round of ad hoc explanations and bold predictions that essentially served to protect the natural worldviews embedded in each of the traditions. Getting trapped in unexamined premises is as easy for the adherents of all research traditions as it is for proponents of public policy. September 11 provides an illustration for how unexamined premises can generate striking simplifications as does the stark distinction between "good" and "evil" as a rhetorical map for U.S. foreign policy in a strikingly complex international reality. This binary distinction is based on a cascading of mutually reinforcing images and the causal effects they imply: peaceful relations with prosperous, efficient states that are friends of America contrast with warlike relations with poor, inefficient states that are America's enemies. Explanatory sketches tend to be somewhat more subtle in the projection of worldviews, but the tendency toward undue simplification is still in evidence and is often debilitating to the endeavor of stating and resolving complex problems. Asian security is more complex than the unintended or deliberate cumulation of positive and negative images permits and than the natural expectations of any of the three research traditions accommodates.

For example, efforts to preserve and apply a realist worldview in the post–Cold War era initially led to overly pessimistic scenarios for Asia. Aaron Friedberg (1993/94: 7) thus argued that "in the long-run it is Asia (and not Europe) that seems far more likely to be the cockpit of great power conflict. The half millennium during which Europe was the world's primary generator of war (and economic growth) is coming to a close. For better and for worse, Europe's past could be Asia's future." We now know that the last decade has not borne out this prediction. To be sure, in the 1990s Asia had its share of military crises, and there remain numerous sources of lingering tensions that could easily lead to war. But it was Europe, not Asia, that was the scene of repeated episodes of ethnic cleansing and prolonged, bloody war. Our point is not that realist arguments must necessarily project pessimistic outcomes. Off-shore balancing (Mearsheimer 2001: 234–65) or nuclear deterrence (Goldstein 2001a) may exert stabilizing if not pacifying effects. The initial application of realist concepts to Asian security dilemmas and national security strategies required simplification for the sake of consistency with a realist worldview. And these simplifications missed important parts of the story that had relevance for real-world outcomes even if those parts of the story could not be told well in the theoretical language of realism. Although some neoclassical realists have sought to recast inexorable laws as tendencies that can be modified by the policy choices of rival states, notably the United States (Rose 1988: 171–72), in the end, such adjustments do not overcome the fundamental problem. An exclusive focus on realism, whether structural or neoclassical, privileges a particular set of problems and variables and arbitrarily precludes other lines of inquiry into potentially related domains.

Similarly unquestioned worldviews also mark liberal and constructivist styles of analysis. From a liberal perspective it seemed unquestionably true that Asia's economic miracle would continue, spurred on by the low transaction costs associated with close business-government relations, bringing another generation of prosperity. Yet, the 1990s were the decade that showed Japan, Asia's largest economy, sinking into a structural economic crisis that has generated the highest unemployment and lowest growth rates the country has seen since 1945. Another example of a mistaken liberal analysis is the IMF's excessively optimistic assessment of the economic fortunes of Southeast Asia. A conference sponsored by the Bank of Indonesia and the IMF concluded in November 1996 that "ASEAN's economic success remains alive and well. . . . The region is poised to extend its success into the twenty-first century" (International Monetary Fund 1996: 378). In an April 25, 1997 press conference, IMF managing director Camdessus remarked that the global economic outlook warranted "rational exuberance" (International Monetary Fund 1997a). And at the spring 1997 meeting, the Interim Committee of the Agreement committed itself to extend the IMF's jurisdiction to cover the movement of capital, thus completing the "unwritten chapter" of Bretton Woods, according to Camdessus (International Monetary Fund 1997b: 129). The rest, as the saying goes, was history. The Asian financial crisis began rumbling in Thailand in June 1997 and by the end of November massive speculation had forced very serious economic dislocations in Thailand, Indonesia, and South Korea and was soon to bring down the Suharto regime in Indonesia. In the following year, Brazil and Russia also fell as speculative attacks spread from Asia to the rest of the world. Now the contagion of liberal pessimism highlighted the disadvantages of the crony capitalism that marked the close relations between government and business, but also revealed the limitations of initial simplifications resulting from a liberal worldview.

Finally, constructivist analyses also make often far-reaching predictions based on unquestioned analytic premises. A theoretically innovative literature on ASEAN had extolled the emergence of a new collective identity in the early 1990s as ASEAN was moving toward an embryonic security community. ASEAN's ineffective response to the Asian financial crisis has forced some reassessment (Acharya 2003, 2001, 1999c). So has the persistence of armed rebellion in Southeast Asia and the possible links of some of the resistance movements to global networks of terror (Katzenstein 2003; Tan 2000a; Collier 1999). Constructivist scholars with a more pessimistic bent run the risk of making the opposite mistake. Thomas Berger (2000), for example, worries considerably about the force of ancient hatreds in an Asia in which race remains an acknowledged political force. Yet, compared to the early 1990s, there is no new evidence in Asian political or security affairs that gives more credence to this dark view. In both cases, a tendency to a priori privilege a particular type of identity led to simplified projections about the implications of that identity for cooperation or conflict.

None of the limitations exhibited by the application of natural worldviews, largely informed by the history of the European state system, to Asian security are especially surprising. The extension of realist insights from Europe to Asia, for example, cannot help but be incomplete. In contrast to Europe, the history of the Asian state system was shaped for many centuries by the principle of suzerainty. Furthermore, located at the European periphery, most Asian states were deeply affected by a colonial experience that was simply absent in the relations among the imperialist powers in the European core. Similarly, the nature of Asian political economies differs from that of Europe. It makes little sense to extrapolate from the political experience of the early industrializers with liberal market economies in Europe to the late industrializers with developmental states in Asia. Relatedly, in Asia the most important effect of international institutions, some of the case studies in this book suggest, is to maintain ambiguity about collective purpose while creating a sense of commonality, rather than to promote transparency of objectives while enhancing efficiency. Finally, the forming of supranational collective identities in Asia is affected deeply by having acquired national sovereignty in the recent rather than distant past. And the nature of that collective identity may be affected substantially, in ways that contemporary theories of international relations have not yet begun to analyze, by the historical experiences and legacies of the Sinocentric world, which differ in many ways from the Greco-Roman world.

Natural expectations embedded in realist, liberal, and constructivist research traditions focus on the presumed likelihood of military conflict, economic prosperity, and variants of hyper- or supra-nationalism. Yet, in light of natural expectations that have remained unmet during the last decade, the complexities of Asian security invite further thought. This invitation extends not only to assessing questions of quantity, of more or less military conflict, economic growth, and collective identity. It also suggests that we inquire into the meanings of these concepts and the debates that surround them, that is, into the very factors that shape the world of beliefs and expectations that many of our explanatory sketches hope to comprehend. Far from applying a single logic ubiquitously or retreating to Orientalist or Occidentalist arguments about a supposedly unique "Asian" or "Western" way, stripping the political reality we seek to understand of its presumed "naturalness" is an important step to enabling intersubjective understanding. The analysis of discursive politics draws attention to the fact that, by definition, political reality is always contested and needs to be understood not only in general terms but also in relation to the specific political contexts in which it occurs and, as Weber reminds us, from the viewpoint of the actors involved. This requires a theoretical multilingualism predicated on the "denaturalization" of subjects and concepts as deployed in existing research traditions.

Thus, in the analysis of the security strategies of Asian states, an important task is to articulate a problematique that acknowledges the fluidity of the meanings attached to such terms as "Asia," "state," "strategy," and "security." Asia is not simply an objective geographic boundary that encompasses unambiguously several neighboring states. It is also an enduring set of social ties that have historically encompassed some set of actors and relationships but not others, allowing for cases of both trust and mistrust, enmity and amity. Regions do not exist only as material objects. Although they have a behavioral dimension indicated, for example, by the flow of goods and the travel of people across physical space, they cannot be represented simply and succinctly by accurate cartographic depictions. They are also constructs that are imagined and thus can bend to the efforts of political entrepreneurs. Southeast Asia, as a category of geographic space became a widely accepted term only in the 1940s and its persistence is closely associated with the history of the Cold War in that region. It remains to be seen whether this region will in a few decades acquire another designation such as "Maritime China" or "the extended Pacific Rim." And the very term "Asia" has been open to many and varied attempts at political interpretation. The "Asian values" discussion, for example, had perhaps the greatest impact among U.S. academics and in U.S. policy circles although it was mainly a belated 1990s export from Singapore which deployed the concept in the 1970s as it sought to unite its ethnically divided population (Katzenstein 2000).

The origins and character of "states" in Asia should also not be taken as unproblematic. Asian states are marked by suzerainty as a long-standing institutional legacy (Oksenberg 2001). The system of tributary trade relations organized around a central power not always interested in intervening directly in the affairs of lesser powers does not have a clear functional equivalent in the conventional interpretations of the Westphalian state system. We do not understand well how that legacy affects the worldviews and behavior of Asia's modern states. While most of Asia formally acceded to the Westphalian model of sovereignty that characterizes the globalization of the Western state system in the nineteenth and twentieth centuries, it would be very surprising indeed if such a legacy would have been superseded totally by the events of the recent past. We need to leave open the possibility that Asian states embrace somewhat different expectations about the boundaries that separate domestic from international affairs as well as about the motivations and behaviors of actors located in different spaces that connect both political domains.

Moreover, in understanding the "strategies" of states, it is important to appreciate that hegemony has material and nonmaterial components requiring that the hegemon's power in its various dimensions be recognized by less powerful actors who are expected to acquiesce to the hegemonic order (Mastanduno 2003). Asian states, and in particular China and its neighbors, define their individual, institutional, and national interests, incorporating beliefs about appropriate forms of governance, with special attention to the relevance of the existing regional and social context (Alagappa 2001a: 63). For Asian security, Peter Van Ness (2002), David Kang (2003a, 2003b), and Jitsuo Tsuchiyama (2003) are all exploring the implications of a view that is predicated upon the assumption of hegemony as an important constitutive principle of international relations in Asia. This puts bandwagoning rather than balancing at the center of the analysis of Asian states' behavior. In their analyses they both draw on and undercut traditional theories of the balance of power, producing explanatory sketches that are not easily squared with the normal insights that any one of the major research traditions offers for our understanding of world politics.

Finally, compared to the notions shared widely among U.S. scholars and policy analysts, applied to Asia, the very idea of "security" needs to be understood in more comprehensive, historically contextualized terms, extending well beyond the military defense of territorial boundaries to encompass also a reasonable threshold of material welfare as well as collective understandings reflecting distinct ideational influences (Alagappa 1998a, 1998b). The latter encompass what Jennifer Mitzen (2002) refers to as "ontological security," a robust sense of collective identity embedded in a wider set of meaningful social relations. The military dimension of social life that is so central to U.S. politics is not absent in Asia. Far from it, as smoldering conflicts on the Korean Peninsula, over Kashmir, and across the Taiwan Strait illustrate. But that dimension is embedded in the dramatic economic and social transformations that have reshaped much of Asia during the past half century and continue to do so today. In the understanding of many political actors it is that transformation and not Asia's distribution of military capabilities that is the politically defining aspect of the security landscape.

In light of these considerations, the eclectic explorations featured in this volume begin with an open-ended understanding of the core subject: the "security" (broadly understood to encompass physical survival, material well-being, and existential security) "strategies" (reflecting different assumptions about actors' motivations and the character of power relationships) of "states" (which differ in historical experience and thus character from those in Europe) in the "Asian region" (as defined by the actors' own variable conceptions of the arena within which they have historically interacted with certain other actors). The "denaturalization" of the constructs that dominate perspectives on Asian security derived from existing research traditions is, however, only a first step. A second one is to open up possibilities for newly defined problems and causally significant interactions among variables normally privileged as part of distinct explanations embedded in competing traditions.

Before the mid-1990s, the theoretical discussion among scholars of international relations in the United States had concentrated almost exclusively on how to think about the relation between power and efficiency as realists dueled with neoliberals; only very recently has the crystallization of a constructivist research tradition prompted scholars of international relations to consider the intersection of issues of efficiency and identity or power and identity (Fearon and Wendt 2002; Katzenstein, Keohane, and Krasner 1999b). In Europe by way of contrast, liberal and constructivist scholars have been engaged in a long-standing theoretical debate about the relative significance of efficiency and identity, though sometimes at the expense of consideration of the continuing relevance of power. In the study of Asian international relations, an exclusive theoretical focus on either identity-driven state behavior, or regional institutions, or the distribution of military capabilities simply does not capture the complex political and analytic sensibilities triggered by different contexts. The chapters in this volume illustrate the promise of combining the insights drawn from different explanatory sketches, seeking to understand the complex ways power, interests, and identities affect each other and combine to shape Asian states' behaviors and relationships.

Thus, for some of the authors in this volume, "institutions" are not only significant for minimizing transaction costs and enhancing efficiency among cooperating actors with separate interests (as liberals would stress); they are also constructions that reflect shared identities or the distribution of power among some set of actors. Understood in this way, institutions produce shifts in actors' interests and identities, and can, in turn, be transformed by changing configurations of interest and identity. For other authors, power and wealth matter significantly, not as omnipresent and fixed determinants of behavior but as something mediated, constrained, and distorted by institutional structures and as something that is given meaning to and understood by actors in their social settings. Understood in this way, "power" may be significant not only as a means to defend borders or force others to cooperate, but also as a basis for formulas for decision making within institutions or as a way of acquiring international prestige and diffusing "ontological security." For those concerned with ideational factors, norms and identities are significant not as ever-fleeting structures of meanings, but as something that is appropriated and denied by power and as something whose influence is facilitated and embodied by institutions that constitute actors and regulate their behavior. Understood in this way, "identity" becomes almost a statement about an actor's position relative to other actors, sometimes drawing attention to asymmetries of power, sometimes shaped by historical memories involving variable levels of institutionalized cooperation, and sometimes serving as a catalyst for cooperation or conflict. Were we to adhere strictly to any one of the three research traditions, these analytic possibilities would fall by the wayside or be viewed as epiphenomenal.

Preview of Case Studies

The case studies in this volume link constituent elements from at least two, and often all three, of the research traditions discussed above in both defining a problem related to Asian security and developing an original explanatory sketch. The sketches, albeit constructed independently, all aspire to provide important insights that are helpful in the description and explanation of the security strategies of Asian states or regional security arrangements, the "dependent variable" in each of the case studies that follow. The eclectic style of analysis in each of the case studies is evident in the multiple connections revealed among "independent variables," alerting us to the existence of structures and processes that undercut the more stylized explanations privileged by any one research tradition. Put differently, the explanatory variables favored by each of the three established research traditions are partially recast in ways that emphasize the linkages between these variables as these affect different dimensions of state or regional security.

The chapters in this book take a look at different empirical problems that all feed into the larger question of Asian security, understood broadly. Is China a revisionist or status quo power? Does Japan tip the scale toward bilateral security arrangements with the United States or multilateral ones with Asia? Why does the U.S.-Korea alliance persist in the face of a North Korean regime that, compared to South Korea, has become so much weaker since the 1960s? And how have the states of Southeast Asia sought to provide for their security in an era of strategic uncertainty? These questions are politically important and analytically intriguing. They are defined in a way that does not immanently privilege the kinds of problems and explanations favored by any one research tradition. And they provide researchers with ample opportunity for developing eclectic arguments that connect variables and processes from at least two of the three research traditions.

For example, as Iain Johnston's careful empirical analysis demonstrates in Chapter 2, along many policy dimensions China has evolved into a status quo power. China's development-based grand strategy is not directed against any one country but focuses instead on the development of internal power capabilities, for purposes of legitimacy and security. Marketization and a comprehensive security strategy thus go hand in hand in consolidating a fundamentally status quo orientation in policy. On the crucial issue of Taiwan, however, this internal focus has revisionist overtones, at least in the eyes of many American policy makers. It is, however, Taiwan's democratization and Taiwanese nationalism that, together with Chinese capitalism and Chinese nationalism, are redefining the term "status quo." The established political arrangement and the appropriate political discourse to describe those arrangements have since 1995 been challenged, not by the PRC but by Taiwan. And it has, at times, looked to Beijing like U.S. foreign policy was actively supporting or, at a minimum, condoning those changes instead of adhering firmly to its traditional One China policy. In the case of China, Taiwan, and the United States, with issues of identity and power tightly fused, who is the revisionist? Johnston's analysis offers a fundamental challenge, both empirical and conceptual, to commonsensical notions, grounded in a realist research tradition, of which country in Asia is a status quo and which a revisionist power. Johnston's analysis shows how limited revisionisms can amplify each other such that both sides believe the other is a major revisionist.

For several decades many observers have insisted that it was only natural for Japan to become once again a great military power, commensurate in its military capabilities with its economic and technological standing. Yet decade after decade Japanese policy has disconfirmed those expectations. More germane than the projection of fear instilled by the past and unquestioned expectations generated from a single research tradition, is an analysis of the mixture of bilateral and multilateral elements in Japan's security policy. The conventional wisdom holds that a period of dangerous ambivalence over Japan's commitment to its security arrangements with the United States ended in the mid-1990s after the Japanese and U.S. governments reached a clear understanding of the conditions under which Japan would contribute actively in regional crises in Asia. Peter Katzenstein and Nobuo Okawara argue against that view in Chapter 3. The recalibration of bilateral and multilateral elements in Japanese policy serves not to reduce the ambiguities in its relations with the United States. Instead it reformulates that ambiguity in new terminology and expresses a long-standing Japanese objective, of wanting to belong both to the West and to Asia. The clarification of the Japanese obligations under the provisions of the U.S.-Japan Security Treaty are much clearer in English than in Japanese. Unless the Japanese home islands are directly attacked, there is nothing in the new agreements that obliges the Japanese government to any specific course of action. A very specific terminology, deliberately chosen to accommodate the different political constraints operating in Washington and in Tokyo, leaves Japan's obligations ill defined. Japanese security, U.S.-Japanese cooperation, and regional security are not necessarily undermined by ill-defined obligations; they may in fact be enhanced by them.

The persistence of the U.S.–South Korea alliance, J. J. Suh argues in Chapter 4, also presents an empirical anomaly not easily understood within any one of the three research traditions. How can we explain the disjuncture of the declining need for the alliance and its unquestioned acceptance, between alliance persistence in the face of a dramatic decline in North Korean capabilities, measured both in absolute and relative terms? The deterrent effect of the alliance may be one reason of course. But why did the South Korean government not push more actively for a minimum deterrence, Israeli style? And it overlooks important changes that have occurred on the ground over the last several decades. Suh argues that other factors may have been more important for the inattentiveness to various political signals that the North Korean government has sent at various times in possible attempts to improve relations with the South and the United States. High among these factors are the sunk costs in various institutional aspects of the alliance. Significant also are the collective identities the alliance has created over the last half century. To be sure, South Korea and the United States are not yet fully members of one democratic community. And they do not yet share fully in fundamental values. Identity does matter, however, in other and more subtle ways. Paradoxical though it may sound, the alliance derives much of its persistence from the need of the North Korean regime to maintain poor relations with its adversary to the south, so as to maintain its own internal coherence and sense of self; from the perceived political need of the South Korean government to attach itself unambiguously to the United States as the only conceivable protector against possible aggression from the North; and from the U.S. government's identity as the protector of a small and vulnerable allied nation and now as the potential victim of the policies of an "evil" state that is suspected of making available to global networks of terrorists weapons of mass destruction.

Yuen Foong Khong's analysis of ASEAN in Chapter 5 displays a different approach to combining research traditions. As is true of the U.S.-Korea alliance, ASEAN also shows the relevance of institutional analysis. Khong argues that ASEAN has created regional institutions such as the ASEAN Regional Forum (ARF) in order to reduce strategic uncertainty. Such institutions reduce strategic uncertainty by doing what liberal institutionalists say they do: providing information, lowering transaction costs, as well as frowning upon cheating. But Khong also suggests that power continues to matter: institutions like the ARF are also meant to anchor and enhance U.S. engagement in the region. The U.S. presence reassures Japan and reduces the prospect of a more far-reaching rearmament by Japan, while enhancing the prospect of a China that acts with restraint in Southeast Asia. Complementing this institutional strategy is what Khong describes as a soft-balancing strategy. Concerns about the possible withdrawal of the United States from Southeast Asia and the rise of China in the early 1990s led many of the major ASEAN states to offer the United States use of their naval facilities. Interestingly, this soft balance of power politics is couched in specific discursive conventions, such as the naming of U.S. preponderance as a constitutive feature of a regional balance of power. In sharp contrast to the importance of institutions and power, identity matters less. Nothing has replaced the ideological glue that a strong anti-Communist identity provided in the 1960s and 1970s. In the 1980s and 1990s, neither the ascendance of Southeast Asia's "economic tigers," nor the growth of a Southeast Asian "security community," nor "Asian values" have created politically equally compelling, alternative identities.

In their concluding Chapter 6, Allen Carlson and J. J. Suh underline once more that analytical eclecticism has the advantage of focusing on empirical anomalies. It helps problematize what any one research tradition may accept as "normal" or "natural." Drawing on the various case studies, Carlson and Suh drive home the argument that underlies all of them: it is only by drawing selectively and judiciously on different analytic traditions that analysis can make sense of and account for Asian security affairs in their full complexity. Despite several lingering sources, Asian governments have managed to contain potentially explosive conflicts in the region through use of formal and informal institutions and with careful recourse to a politics of naming. The future of Asia's security may hinge critically upon whether the United States as the lone superpower will remain sufficiently attuned to these features to maneuver its realpolitik in a way that does not disrupt the institutional and discursive underpinnings of Asia's security orders.

In addressing a variety of different questions, the chapters in this book share one thing in common in the answers they offer. In how they frame their questions, or dependent variables, and in the way they develop their answers, or specify their independent variables, they all combine insights drawn from at least two of the research traditions. The chapters draw on a mixture of insights from the three different research traditions, pointing to the importance of, and relationships between, identity,

interest, and power in the adaptation of Asian states' strategic behavior. This approach
will probably raise uncomfortable questions among adherents of all three research
traditions. It is also likely to yield new insights and spur further research into the in-
terplay *among* the variables or processes typically privileged by each of the traditions.

Conclusion

A problem-focused eclecticism is not cost free. In international relations research as
well as in the social sciences writ large, the flexibility required of eclectic approaches
may be too great to permit the formation of collaborations capable of mobilizing
strong attachments and enduring professional ties, crucial ingredients in often not very
subtle struggles for intellectual and other forms of primacy in the world of scholarship.
Furthermore, the theoretical multilingualism that the expanded scope of problems and
explanatory sketches requires may tax an individual researcher's stock of knowledge
and array of skills while introducing also more "noise" into the established channels of
communication, such as they are, within and across different research traditions. As a
result, to those accustomed and committed to working within particular conceptual
frameworks built on particular assumptions about social reality, the accommodation of
eclectic perspectives may be dismissed as a waste of resources (Sanderson 1987) or
merely undisciplined, "flabby" appeals for pluralism (Johnson 2002).

In light of the recurrent debates between, and inherent character of, research traditions, we are convinced that the advantages of eclecticism are well worth such
costs. Without insisting that we have any prior knowledge of how best to construct
different causal chains, we have gambled here on the intuition that analytical eclecticism can give us more purchase on interesting questions about Asian security than
can analytic monism. The most significant advantage of eclecticism is that it facilitates intellectual exchanges that deepen and extend our understandings rather than
producing the hard "truths" and "standards" of more parsimonious models addressing
questions posed simply in the unidimensional space of only one research tradition.
As Paul Diesing (1991: 364) notes, all explanations have to live with the fact that our
truths will always be plural and contradictory. This does not mean that we need to
give up the quest for explanation and it does not mean that all analytic or empirical
problems need to be considered from multiple analytic perspectives. What it does
mean is that any *shared* sense of progress in the study of international affairs depends
on a common recognition of the convergences, complementarities, and differences
across substantive claims arrived at within different research traditions; and that this,
in turn, requires a degree of methodological pluralism and analytic multilingualism
that is more characteristic of self-consciously eclectic modes of inquiry than of approaches embedded in a particular research tradition.

The analytical eclecticism we embrace proceeds from a view of social scientific research as a collective endeavor, an ongoing practice built on interdependent relation-

ships among individual researchers and research communities each with specific kinds of insights to offer in relation to particular questions cast at particular levels of generality (Sil 2000b). In this sense, analytical eclecticism has little in common with research traditions rigidly attached to core postulates, and more in common with calls for intellectual pluralism. Certainly, there are limits to how much integration can occur across approaches predicated on fundamentally incompatible foundational postulates and conceptual systems (Johnson 2002). Nevertheless, a principled refusal to "ontologize" analytic sketches offers something more disciplined paradigm-bound research cannot: it reinforces the dialogical character of international relations research and fights the tendency in scholarship to turn inward by preemptively establishing much stronger defenses of existing explanatory sketches than is warranted on intellectual grounds. For this reason, eclecticism is also principled in its opposition to the imposition of a uniform standard of scientific research practice, and, in line with current thinking among philosophers of science, it exploits the advantages and tolerates the disadvantages of inquiring into multiple truths at different levels of abstraction. Considering the diversity of approaches and the different ways of establishing what is true, as revealed in current debates in the philosophy of science, insistence on any one standard, including that there be no standard at all, undercuts the social nature of scientific conversation. If the unit of evaluation is regarded as the community of social scientists as a whole rather than the individual researcher (Laitin 1995: 456), then creating more space for eclectic approaches is virtually a necessary condition for whatever progress may be possible in social scientific research if for no other reason but that it reveals connections, convergences, or complementarities between substantive insights usually presented in different theoretical languages within different research traditions.

The adoption of an eclectic stance tends to go hand in hand with a pragmatic, "post-positivist" epistemology that is open to explore conceptual and empirical connections between approaches located at different points on an "epistemological spectrum" (Sil 2000c) spanning absolute formulations of positivism and relativism. Such a pragmatism is predicated on the refusal "to accept as hard and fast the classic oppositions between understanding and explanation, between history and science, between objective and subjective" (Alford 1998: 123). Specifically, an eclecticism predicated on pragmatism involves viewing the social world as at least partially socially constructed; recognizing the difficulties this poses for defining social facts and analyzing actors' motivations; bracketing the investigator's own subjective perceptions and normative commitments; and accepting the uncertainty accompanying the analysis of a socially constructed world without giving up on either the systematic collection and interpretation of data or the task of seeking to persuade skeptical communities of scholars. Such a perspective also calls for attention to "middle-range" explanatory sketches that split the difference between nomothetic and ideographic research, between the formalism of parsimonious models and elaborate exercises in hermeneutics or phenomenology, offering causal narratives that are transportable to a limited number of contexts without being so far abstracted from these contexts that the operationalization of concepts for each case is open to vigorous contestation (Sil 2000b).[5] Research cast at such a level of abstraction will generate neither the most elegant models for investigating a problem nor the richest narrative about any one context, but it can enable simultaneous consideration of a wider range of analytic, interpretive, and observational statements drawn from varied social contexts and cast at different levels of abstraction.

In all these respects, eclectic modes of analysis contribute to what Thomas Fararo (1989) has referred to as a "spirit of unification," the diffuse intellectual state of mind required to enable consideration of combinatorial possibilities that have frequently produced unanticipated breakthroughs and common understandings of progress in the history of science.[6] Viewed in this light, a key benefit of analytical eclecticism is not to subsume, replace, or unify explanatory sketches from different research traditions, but to foster scientific dialogue and enable communication between the different communities that produce these sketches. The skill of listening and talking knowledgeably in the languages of more than one research tradition, although requiring a large investment in time and effort and a predilection for intellectual versatility, generates an analytic multilingualism that can foster new concepts and unexpected synapses, open up new avenues for research for all research communities and last, but not least, improve the tone of the collective discussions among scholars of international relations in general and national security in particular. The discourse culture of "taking no prisoners," so prominent not so long ago, may be on the wane. The sooner it disappears altogether the better for all of us. In the analysis of Asian security, and for the social sciences more generally, scientific dialogue is the best guarantee for progress, if progress is to be had, and the accommodation of analytical eclecticism offers the best hope for furthering scientific dialogue.

Notes

1. On neoliberalism, see the exchanges between Keohane and Martin (1995), Kupchan and Kupchan (1995), Ruggie (1995), and Mearsheimer (1995, 1994/95). On constructivism, see Duffield, Farrell, Price, and Desch (1999), Desch (1998), Hopf (1998), and Wendt (1995). On rationalism, see the exchanges between Bueno de Mesquita and Morrow (1999), Martin (1999), Niou and Ordeshook (1999), Powell (1999), Walt (1999a, 1999b), and Zagare (1999). On realism, see Wendt (1995) and Mearsheimer (1994/95), and the exchanges between Feaver et al. (2000) and Legro and Moravcsik (1999).

2. Challenging Popper's gradualist theory of scientific progress as continuous and cumulative, Kuhn (1962) interpreted the history of science as a sequence of periods of normal science interspersed by shorter episodes of revolutionary science. Normal science is marked by the ascendance of a single paradigm that determines the central research questions, specifies the range of acceptable methods in approaching them, and provides criteria for assessing how well

they have been answered. Revolutionary science occurs in those brief interludes when scientific communities, frustrated by increasing numbers of anomalies, begin to focus on new problems and take up new approaches that can address these anomalies. Once a new cluster of questions, assumptions, and approaches has acquired large numbers of supporters, this may pave the way for the emergence of a new and once again dominant paradigm. Significantly, paradigms are assumed to be incommensurable, with the standards and methods employed by supporters of one paradigm judged unacceptable by supporters of another.

3. Responding to Kuhn's rejection of objective markers of continuous progress, Lakatos (1970) introduced the concept of "research program." Thus he captured more pluralistic scientific communities and left open the possibility for some limited comparisons of theories generated by competing research programs. For Lakatos, scholarship is marked by multiple research programs, some in "progressive" phases, others in "degenerative" phases, depending on whether they are still capable of producing new theories that could explain new phenomena or surpass the explanatory power of past theories. At the same time, Lakatosian research programs have a number of features—a "hard core," a "protective belt" of auxiliary assumptions, and positive and negative "heuristics"—that essentially perform the same functions as Kuhn's paradigms.

4. See Walker (2003) for a more elaborate argument about why Laudan's understanding of research traditions is more useful than Lakatos's treatment of research programs for characterizing international relations scholarship and encouraging more cooperation than rivalry among proponents of different intellectual schools.

5. This strategy for negotiating the nomothetic–ideographic divide should be distinguished from the sort of integration attempted by proponents of "analytic narratives" (Bates et al. 1998). Analytic narratives proceed from a realist, not pragmatist, philosophy of science, and the principles of explanation in each narrative are ultimately embedded in a highly abstract model of strategic rationality the core logic of which remains unresponsive to the "thick" narrative. The latter are constructed as interpretations that essentially reflect this logic but without reference to competing strands of historiography and without any possibility for generating alternative theoretical logics (Sil 2000a). A pragmatist approach to "middle-range" theorizing, by contrast, points to more modest generalizations within specified domains of inquiry, with a more dialectical understanding of the relationship between theoretical constructs and empirical interpretations.

6. Fararo (1989: 175–76) views "unification" as a series of recursive integrative episodes rather than the construction of a single theory supported by a heroic individual or a crusading group of researchers seeking to subsume everybody and everything. For example, Darwinian principles of natural selection first became integrated with the Mendelian hypothesis of inheritance through discrete genes, before a second integrative episode enabled this synthesis to incorporate principles of molecular biology. Both episodes required a diffuse state of mind that was open to consideration of facts and hypotheses from previously separate research traditions. It is this diffuse state of mind that Fararo refers to as the "spirit of unification."

2

Beijing's Security Behavior in the Asia-Pacific
Is China a Dissatisfied Power?

ALASTAIR IAIN JOHNSTON

In most aspects of its diplomacy, the People's Republic of China is more integrated into, and more cooperative inside, regional and global political and economic systems than ever before since 1949. Yet, there is growing uneasiness about the implications of "rising" Chinese power. Characterizations of Chinese diplomacy in the policy and scholarly worlds are, if anything, less sanguine of late about China's commitments to regional and international norms. Or put somewhat differently, the discourse has shifted from the 1980s. At that time there was little discussion in the United States and elsewhere about whether China was or was not part of the "the international community." From the 1990s on, however, this has been the dominant discourse— that China has been outside this community and that it needs to be pulled inside; that is has not yet demonstrated sufficiently that it will "play by the rules." The linguistic subtext is a fairly sharp "othering" of China that includes a civilizing discourse (China is not yet a civilized state) or perhaps a sports discourse (China is a cheater). Many of the harshest policy debates in the United States in recent years have been over whether it is even possible to socialize a dictatorial, nationalistic, and dissatisfied China within this putative international community. Engagers, to simplify, argue it is happening, though mainly in the sphere of economic norms (free trade, domestic marketization). Skeptics either concluded that it is not happening, because of the nature of the regime (for some China is still Red China; for more sophisticated skep-

Many thanks to the following people for their comments and criticisms: Allen Carlson, Tom Christensen, Peter Katzenstein, Bob Ross, J. J. Suh, Al Willner, and Xu Xin. Thanks as well to Michael Griesdorf, Michael Horowitz, and Manjari Chatterjee Miller for excellent research help along the way. Portions of this chapter appeared under the title, "Is China a Status Quo Power?" *International Security* 27, 4 (Spring 2003): 153–85.

tics it is flirting with fascism), or that it could not possibly happen because China as a rising power, by definition, is dissatisfied with the U.S.-dominated global order (a more power-transition realpolitik argument). A logical conclusion is that both camps view the problem of China's rising power as the primary source of instability in Sino-U.S. relations and by extension in the Asia-Pacific region. For both groups, the "problem" is China, and the "solution" lies in U.S. policy.

This chapter explores the question of China's "status quo–ness" and its implications for Chinese political-military behavior in East Asia. It asks: how should we understand the argument that China is a revisionist state? Is this best explained by the realities of a rising power, dissatisfied with the "rules of the game" that constrain its exercise of its growing power? Or is this reality in fact an illusion, a function of domestically rooted changes in perceptions of Chinese power inside major countries in the region?

The chapter begins by examining perhaps the most common characterization of China—that it is a dissatisfied, revisionist state, expressed in policies ranging from a desire to "solve" the Taiwan issue in its favor to pushing U.S. power out of the region.[1] This characterization generally draws on or hews to various realist insights into why rising powers are almost invariably interested in challenging extant institutions, norms, and power distributions. That is, the argument falls generally within a power-transition version of realism where a static set of interests—the desire to establish a regional sphere of influence—interact with changing Chinese relative capabilities to give China more opportunities to challenge U.S. power. As I will argue, the problem with this hypothesis is that it fails to understand both the status quo elements in Chinese diplomacy and the problematic status of the empirical evidence used to make this claim about revisionism. I spend considerable time in this chapter exploring this characterization of China as a non–status quo state because it is so central—if sometimes implicit—in the discourses about China in the United States and some other Asia-Pacific countries.

The second hypothesis draws from a liberal or domestic focus on internal political changes within countries in the region and how these aggregated changes affect leadership perceptions of Chinese satisfaction with regional and global order. The problem with this argument is that it exonerates, or ignores, the fact that there is concrete PRC behavior that feeds these perceptions. These domestic changes may have little to do with Chinese power or diplomacy, but Chinese power and diplomacy do have an independent effect on the intensity of these perceptions.

Thus the chapter concludes that a third, hybrid, explanation—one where China's limited revisionism, primarily on the Taiwan issue, interacts with political changes in regional perceptions creating an emerging security dilemma—best accounts for the general features of China's politico-military diplomacy in the region. That is, the "problem" for Asia-Pacific security is not China and the solution is not in U.S. policy. Rather the problem is the Sino-U.S. security dilemma. The solution therefore lies in understanding the mutual constitution of the "China threat" and the "U.S. threat."

This requires underscoring the socialization effects of security dilemmas, rather than treating them, as international relations theory has done to this point, simply as insecurity spirals into which rational unitary actors get locked in response to uncertainty under anarchy.

The approach in this chapter, then, is to denaturalize (Katzenstein and Okawara 2001/02) the phenomenon in question such that it turns into a problem to be analyzed or explained.[2] In this case, China as a dissatisfied power has become a naturalized trope in both the academic and pundit worlds. Denaturalizing it creates a puzzle: if it is generally true that China is more status quo oriented than in the past, why is this possibility essentially ruled out in the various discourses in the United States (and in some other parts of the region) about rising Chinese power? The genealogy of this trope is beyond the scope of this chapter. Moreover, it is hard to trace. As I argue here, at least some the internalization of this trope in the U.S. debates about China comes from the mutual constitution of a "China threat" and a "U.S. threat," a process of malign amplification that is not easily traced back to first causes. While this mutual constitution became much more evident after the Taiwan crisis in 1996, it has been taking place against the backdrop of deeply rooted Chinese nationalism, of an emerging Taiwanese nationalism, and of a post–Cold War American primacism. But more fundamentally, many of the individuals and institutions involved in the creation and perpetuation of this trope, in the United States at least, are wedded to an ontological and epistemological fundamentalism about the nature of international relations—namely that state interests are more or less fixed, that rising powers are more or less automatically revisionist because they are excluded from drafting the rules of the game (and that they oppose the distribution of power that defends these rules), and that these two phenomena are more or less universal across time and space. Ironically, the best insight into the weakness of this ontological and epistemological fundamentalism comes from a concept that international relations theory has long believed to be a central feature of international politics—the security dilemma. By reinterpreting security dilemmas through a constructivist-oriented lens—by viewing security dilemmas as a potential socializing experience whereby preferences and interests are changeable through social interaction—one begins to see how a more status quo oriented state might nevertheless be treated as the opposite, and thus why this orientation can itself become unstable over time.

It's China: China's Revisionism and the Power Transition Argument

A common characterization of China in the last decade or so in the United States and elsewhere is that it is operating outside of, or only partly inside, the international community on a range of international norms. In March 1997, in outlining national security policy for Clinton's second term, NSC advisor Sandy Berger referred to engagement as designed to pull China "in the direction of the international community" (Berger 1997). The Bush administration and its supporters have used similar language. In the centrist realpolitik language of the Powell Department of State, Assistant Secretary of State James Kelly remarked in congressional testimony on May 1, 2001, "We will have to see how China responds to us. It would be unfortunate if it were to renege on commitments to international standards that most of the world supports and adheres to. . . . We encourage China to make responsible choices that reflect its stature in and obligations to the community of nations" (Kelly 2001). Conservative pundits offer blunter language: Morton Kondracke suggested at the height of the EP-3 incident in April 2001 that the PRC was not a "civilized" country.[3] Others, reflecting some of the views of the primacist wing of the Bush administration, compare China's rise with the rise of other revisionist states such as fascist Japan, and especially Wilhelmine Germany (Kagan 1997; Wolfowitz 1997; Waldron 1996).[4]

The common themes in all these characterizations are obvious: China is not yet or only just becoming a constructive participant in the international community; China does not yet wholly endorse global norms of conduct; China is not yet working to build a secure international order; and China's rising power presents a potential problem to the international order established by and preferred by the United States.

There are at least two even more basic, implicit assumptions that undergird these characterizations of China and the international community. The first is that there *is* an extant international community that is sufficiently well defined such that it is obvious who is and who is not part of it. The second, and related, is that this community shares common norms and values on human rights, proliferation, trade, and so on.

But what does it mean to be a status quo or non–status quo power in international relations in the early twenty-first century?[5] Despite the centrality of the terms in international relations (primarily realist) theorizing and in discourse in the policy world, it is distressing how vague and under-theorized the definitions of "status quo–ness" in international relations theory (and in the U.S. debate) are.[6]

Morgenthau's definition is perhaps the closest one finds to both the unstated and stated definitions in the U.S. debate: "the policy of the status quo aims at the maintenance of the distribution of power as it exists at a particular moment in history."[7] A status quo policy is opposed to any "reversal of the power relations among two or more nations, reducing, for instance, A from a first rate to a second rate power and raising B to the eminent position A formerly held." Minor adjustments, however, "which leave intact the relative power positions of the nations concerned are fully compatible with a policy of the status quo" (Morgenthau 1978: 46).

Power transition theorists Organski and Kugler defined status quo states as those that have participated in designing the "rules of the game" and stand to benefit from these rules. "Challengers" (for example, revisionist states) want a "new place for themselves in international society" that is commensurate with their power. Revisionist states express a "general dissatisfaction" with their "position in the system." They have a "desire to redraft the rules by which relations among nations work" (Organski and

Kugler 1980: 19–20, 23).[8] Neither Morgenthau nor Organski and Kugler provide ways one could determine the degree to which any particular state wanted to reverse current "power relations" or desired to redraft "rules" of the game.

Randall Schweller offers a typology of revisionist and status quo states that allows for some variation in degree. This provides more nuance than some of the earlier classical realist writing. Basically, "revisionist states value what they covet more than what they currently possess. . . . They will *employ military force* to change the status quo and to extend their values" (Schweller 1994: 105).[9] Still, it is unclear what the components of the status quo are, other than the extant hierarchy of power (and prestige, assuming these are coterminous) at any given moment.

Robert Gilpin appears to be the most precise among realist scholars. He breaks down the "rules of the game" into somewhat more operationalizable components: the distribution of power; the hierarchy of prestige (which, however, tends to be coterminous with the distribution of power, for realists); and "rights and rules that govern or at least influence the interactions among states" (Gilpin 1981: 34). Thus, if one uses these three major components, then it is legitimate to ask the following questions to test for status quo–ness: how does the state speak and act regarding the specific rules of diplomacy, of arms control institutions, of international economic institutions; how does it speak and act regarding the distribution of power; and how does it speak and act regarding the hierarchy of prestige (though this should be essentially coterminous with the first test)? For Gilpin, revisionist states aim at systemic change, that is they demand fundamental changes in these three components. Anything less, it becomes problematic calling the state revisionist or non–status quo.

As is evident, for a concept at the core of IR (and specifically, realist) theorizing, it is disturbing how little thought has gone into asking precisely how one would determine across the totality of its foreign-policy preferences and actions whether a state is status quo or revisionist.[10] Perhaps because, as James D. Morrow notes (2000: 74), Nazi Germany is the paradigmatic revisionist state, international relations theory has tended to assume that we should know a revisionist state when we see one.[11] Even less thought has gone into how revisionist and status quo states are created. Randall Schweller and Charles Glaser separately make the important point that the Hobbesian features of realpolitik international relations logically require the existence of predator or revisionist states (Schweller 1996, 1994; Glaser 1994/95). Otherwise rational status quo oriented security-seeking states will prefer mostly to try to prevent getting locked into wasteful security dilemmas. But neither Schweller nor Glaser tells us where these kinds of states come from, that is, how to treat revisionism and status-quo-ism as variables themselves. I do not propose to provide a full answer to either of these questions—where does a revisionist or status quo state come from and how do we know them when we see them. In a sense, realism could provide its own answer to both questions, or at least *an* answer if it were willing to theorize more endogenously, more socially, and less linearly. Security dilemmas themselves, as I will argue later, may be a critical socializing feature of international relations that contributes to the construction of revisionist states by changing or amplifying the agents' perceptions of their interests. But before I get to this argument, let me suggest why the more orthodox rising-power-as-revisionist conceptualization does not help explain Chinese security policy in the region, and thus why it is an analytic and policy mistake to assume this model captures the process of U.S.-China political conflict in the past decade. This is the first step in showing why a security dilemma-as-socialization-process argument captures more of the variance in Chinese security behavior in the region.

As a first step, it makes sense to try to develop a more manageable set of indicators by which one can assess whether any particular actor is outside a status quo community. I develop five such indicators and group these into two sets. The first set addresses the question of how proactive a state is in challenging the major international institutions and their formal and informal rules that most other states support most of the time.[12] Here I draw from Gilpin's discussion of what constitutes the "rules of the game."

1. The actor's participation rates in the institutions that regulate the activities of members of the community are low. At its simplest, a non–status quo actor is one that could be but is not involved in the many international institutions that help constitute and mediate the relationships of the international community.

2. The actor may participate in these institutions, but it does not accept the norms of the community. It breaks these rules and norms once inside these institutions.[13]

3. The actor may participate in these institutions, and may abide by their rules and norms temporarily, but if given its chance it will try to change these rules and norms in ways that defeat the original purposes of the institution and the community.

The second set addresses the attitudes and behavior toward supposedly disadvantageous distributions of material power.

4. The actor has internalized a clear preference for a radical redistribution of material power in the international system.

5. The actor's behavior is aimed in the main at realizing such a redistribution of power.

How, then, might one "code" Chinese diplomacy along these five indicators?[14]

China's Participation Rates in International Institutions

There can be no doubt that China's membership in international institutions and organizations has increased steadily and quite dramatically in the post-Maoist period.

Figure 2.1 shows the relative number of governmental international organizations in which China belongs compared across time with a number of industrialized powers and with India, one of the most active diplomatic developing states. From the

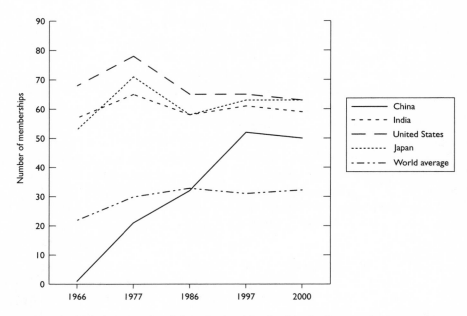

FIGURE 2.1 China's International Organization Memberships in Comparative Perspective, 1996–2000

SOURCE: Compiled from the *Yearbook of International Organizations*, 2000/01 (Brussels: Union of International Associations, 38th ed.).

mid-1960s to the mid-1990s, China moved from virtual isolation from international organizations to membership numbers approaching about 80 percent of the comparison states.[15]

Figure 2.2 provides another view of this change in Chinese participation rates. It uses level of development as a predictor of membership in international organizations for all states in the international system. The assumption here is that more resource-constrained states with fewer linkages to the global economy should be less involved in political institutions as well. High levels of development are associated with high levels of interdependence, hence with a high demand for institutions that can regulate these interactions. Thus GDP/capita can act as a proxy indicator for a demand for institutions.[16] The figure shows that over the 1990s China became increasingly *over*-involved in international organizations given its level of development. Prior to the 1990s, China's participation rates fell below the regression line. That is, for its level of development, China was under-involved in international organizations. Put differently, its demand for institutions was lower than it should have been, given its level of development. In essence, in the 1990s China moves from well below to well above the regression line.

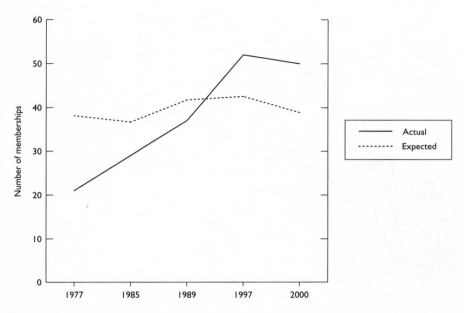

FIGURE 2.2 China's Actual and Expected Memberships in International Organizations, 1977–2000

NOTE: Based on ordinary least squares regression using GDP per capita as a predictor of memberships.

China's Record of Compliance with International Norms

Although increased participation in international institutions is a necessary or permissive "cause" of status quo behavior it is not, obviously, a sufficient one.[17] What matters is compliance with the rules, norms, and goals of these institutions. Thus a state that participates but violates the prescriptions of these institutions and its commitments to them (willfully, as opposed simply due to the lack of capacity) might still be considered a non–status quo state. In some cases it is fairly straightforward determining what international norms are. In other cases it is more difficult, thus making the question of compliance very complicated very quickly. Nonetheless I think it is accurate to code China's compliance with major international normative regimes the following way:

Sovereignty. Perhaps the most deeply internalized fundamental norm in state diplomacy is sovereignty. It is this norm that defines the key units of the international system, the key features of most international institutions (membership rules and decision rules), and the key diplomatic practices of these units. It is also clear that the meaning of sovereignty is historically contingent (Krasner 1999). Thus, China is now

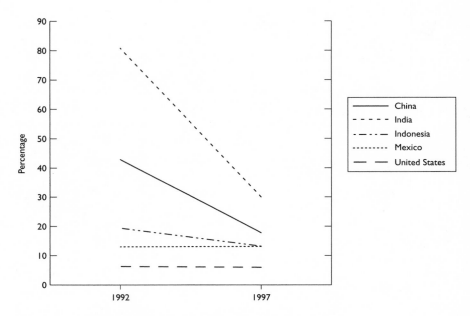

FIGURE 2.3 Comparative Reductions in Mean Tariff Rates, 1992–1997

SOURCE: World Bank Indicators, CD-ROM, Table 6.7.
NOTE: The data years are not uniform in the World Bank tables. For Mexico the data are
for 1991 and 1997, for Indonesia, 1996 and 1993, and for India, 1990 and 1997.

one of the strongest defenders of a more traditional absolutist concept, fighting as a
conservative power along with a large number of other developing countries to re-
affirm sovereignty and internal autonomy against challenges from evolving concepts
of human rights, domestic governance, and humanitarian intervention, concepts being pushed predominantly by a minority of liberal democracies and/or NGOs and
international civil society activities (Carlson 2000).[18]

Free trade. Free trade, at this point in history, is perhaps the international norm
(except for sovereignty) least contested by national governments around the world.
In the reform period China has moved generally to support norms of global free
trade outright, even though compliance with and implementation of these norms
will be difficult. In concrete terms, China's average tariff rate declined from above 40
percent in 1992 to just under 20 percent in 1997 (see Figure 2.3), the right trajectory
from the perspective of free trade norms. This will decline further with WTO membership (to an average of 9.4 percent for industrial products and 14.5 percent for
agricultural products by 2004–5). China's entry into the WTO is the clearest statement that officially China embraces the extant free trade regime. No doubt there will
be accusations of violations. But it will be very hard for China to escape international

scrutiny on this score. It will likely use many of the loopholes in WTO rules to protect politically important economic constituencies when necessary. But this is no different in kind from the arbitrary use of antidumping rules by the United States to protect important economic constituencies. Many experts also argue that China's primary compliance problem will not be so much a willful disregard of WTO commitments by the central government, but rather noncompliance by hard-to-control provincial and local economic interests (see, for example, the testimony of Donald C. Clarke 2002). Even so, at this stage the U.S. State Department has officially concluded that China made a "good faith approach" to meeting WTO entry requirements (Huntsman 2002). The Government Accounting Office recently reported that China had "shown considerable determination" to put in place the domestic legal infrastructure required by the WTO (Westin 2002).[19] Colin Powell put it bluntly: China "is no longer an enemy of capitalism" (Powell 2002).

China's gradual embrace of global capitalist institutions and, somewhat more hesitantly, the accompanying norms of free trade, open capital flows, and transparency has been a function, apparently, of the CCP's desire to enhance its legitimacy through economic development. Thus it strains logic to say, as many in the policy and pundit world do, that China is dissatisfied with the international rules of the game when these same policy analysts and pundits also say that Chinese leaders base their legitimacy in part on economic growth. Chinese leaders realize that this economic growth —hence their legitimacy—comes from integration into the global capitalist institutions, not isolation from them or attempts to alter them fundamentally.

Proliferation and arms control. On these issues judgments about China's performance need to distinguish between five kinds of behavior: actions that violate a formal multilateral treaty; actions that violate a unilateral or bilateral statement of policy but are not illegal under international law (for example, the November 2000 commitment not to assist countries to develop missiles covered by the Missile Technology Control Regime (MTCR); actions that do not violate Chinese statements of policy or international law (for example, nuclear technology transfers to International Atomic Energy Agency–inspected sites); actions that keep China outside of a treaty but that reflect shared interests with the United States (for example, opposition to the Ottawa Landmine Treaty, which calls for a global ban on the use, development, and transfer of antipersonnel landmines); and actions where China stands with a large number of other states in opposition to an isolated United States (for example, China's opposition to the Bush administration's December 2001 announcement that it would withdraw from the 1972 Anti–Ballistic Missile Treaty).

Actions of the first type are most clearly violations of unambiguous international norms. Actions of the second and third types—even though they may challenge U.S. interests—are less obviously violations of "the rules of the game." Actions of the fourth type would be hard to count as a violation of a regime, unless the regime were primarily constituted by a treaty institution. And actions of the fifth type cannot be counted as violations of international regimes.

On many arms control issues, China's performance has been hard to measure. On the question of the proliferation of weapons of mass destruction (WMDs), Chinese suppliers are not alone in transferring technology (often not formally restricted technology) to states that have major conflicts of interest with the United States. For instance, the lists of foreign suppliers for the WMD-related programs to these types of states comes from a who's who of status quo states.[20] The major exception in China's WMD behavior has been the transfer of nuclear weapons–related technology to Pakistan in the 1980s and M-11 ballistic missile components to Pakistan in 1992. Since China agreed to abide by the first version of the MTCR and the Comprehensive Test Ban Treaty, the U.S. government officially judges Chinese performance as improved, though problematic in some cases. As recently put by a senior State Department official, the Chinese are "less active traders and proliferators than they used to be" (*New York Times* 2 Sept. 2001). Robert Einhorn (2002), the Clinton administration's point person on proliferation dialogues with China, put it more specifically: "China's record on nuclear exports has dramatically improved in the late 1990s. But its record is, at best, mixed on missile-related exports."

The continuing concerns are either in dual-use technologies that China has the legal right to transfer, or in the case of missile components to Pakistan, transfers that may violate unilateral statements made to the United States rather than formal multilateral agreements. More generally, China has signed onto a number of potentially constraining arms control agreements. The Comprehensive Test Ban Treaty (CTBT) is the most notable, as it severely limits China's ability to modernize its nuclear weapons warhead designs. As yet there is no credible evidence that China has violated this commitment.

In terms of conventional arms transfers to other states, there are few intrusive regimes that China could be accused of violating. Those that have emerged are not especially strong. As noted, China opposes, as does the United States, the Ottawa Treaty banning the use and transfer of antipersonnel landmines. An international effort to establish controls on small arms trade is also opposed by the PRC, but more prominently and effectively it is opposed by the United States. More generally, although China is a major arms exporter, it has lost much of its arms market in the 1990s as countries have turned to cheaper and better-quality arms from former Soviet suppliers or to the United States and Western Europe. China's record in this regard does not reflect any dramatic new normative opposition to arms transfers, simply a loss of market share.

National self-determination. China is routinely accused of violating these norms, whether in the case of the Tibetans in Tibet or the Uighurs in Xinjiang, or the Taiwanese. Although one may personally abhor the treatment of minority populations in China, or the belligerent refusal of the Chinese regime to allow the Taiwanese people to chose formal independence from an entity called the Republic of China, the accusation that China is violating an international norm of self-determination misconstrues international norms on this question. International practice and international law, while often unclear and in constant evolution, do not recognize the absolute right of any social, political, or ethnic group to sovereign independence. International practice is ambiguous or—put more accurately—leery of unconditional endorsement of a norm of national self-determination. UN documents on decolonization and national liberation in the 1960s were clear—they recognized the right of oppressed peoples to determine their future (though not necessarily via setting up independent sovereign states), but also wanted to protect newly independent, decolonized states from further dismemberment.[21] That is, the right to self-determination has generally been only extended to those peoples who are subject to alien rule (for instance, colonialism) and who have few if any opportunities to participate meaningfully in their own governance.[22] In general, international norms concerning self-determination are designed to protect extant sovereign states, as much as we might personally prefer to see independence of particular peoples.

Second, U.S. foreign policy practice is also ambivalent about self-determination of a peoples. The United States does not support Quebec independence, even though a majority of francophones in Quebec indicated support for some form of independence in a referendum in the 1990s. The United States intervened against Serbia's suppression of the Kosovar population but did not support Kosovo independence. Indeed, initially the United States did not support Yugoslavia's break up. During the Cold War, the United States ended up defending French colonialism in Vietnam in the 1950s. It clearly does not officially recognize the right to national self-determination and sovereign statehood for Native Americans or Chechens, or indeed, even Tibetans.

Human rights. Liberal democracies and human rights NGOs routinely and accurately point out the violation of human rights in China. Two questions emerge, however. First, how are the international community's views on the human rights regime defined? One logical start would be to look at the positions taken by a majority of states toward China's human rights practices. The problem here is that in one of the key international forums for the examination of human rights practices, the United Nations Human Rights Commission (UNHCR), China has managed to put together a winning coalition of states to vote in favor of quashing every resolution critical of the PRC from 1992 to 2001 (see Figure 2.4). This simple majority (or plurality) criterion would place China inside the international community and its human rights regime. If one uses the domestic political practice of the majority of states in the international system as a criterion, however, China would be on the outside of the international community, but barely. A small majority of states in the international system function as democracies but a relatively large minority function as dictatorships or autocracies.[23]

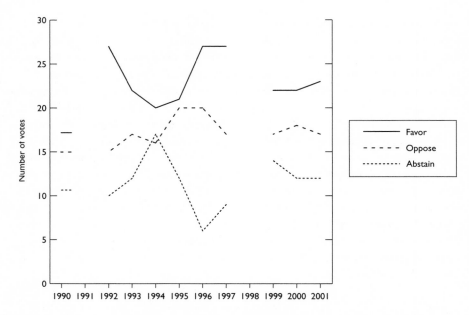

FIGURE 2.4 Voting in the UN Commission on Human Rights on No-Action Motions on Resolutions Critical of the PRC, 1990–2001

SOURCES: Kent (1999: 60–79); UN Commission on Human Rights Reports, E/1993/23, E/1994/24, E/1995/23, E/1996/23, E/1997/23, E/1999/23, E/2000/23, and E/CN.4/2001/L.10/Add.9.
NOTES: 1. A vote in favor means a vote against criticizing China. 2. In 1991 and 1998 there were no resolutions critical of the PRC.

Second, what is the content of the international human rights regime? Technically, based on perhaps the most comprehensive, authoritative consensus statement of the content of the international human rights regime—the Vienna Conference Declaration of 1993—the international community recognizes the equal status of individual political and civil liberties on the one hand, and collective social and economic rights (including the right to development) on the other. In this regard, when the United States measures China using the standard of political and civil liberties, and when China responds by stressing collective social and economic rights, both sides may be misrepresenting international community standards. There is no doubt that China's authorities, whether central or local governments, routinely violate the political and legal rights guaranteed by the PRC constitution and by the human rights agreements that China has signed. The question remains, however, is China's performance on protecting the social and economic rights of the Chinese people as embodied in the Vienna consensus equally egregious? Economic development has led to a rapid increase in the standards of living for millions of Chinese citizens. But whether this constitutes a net gain in socioeconomic rights is not so obvious. At root this becomes an ideological question, because it requires judging whether socioeconomic advances, mainly in urban China, should be counted as gains in social and economic rights for the Chinese people as a whole, or whether growing income inequality, environmental degradation, and the absence of equitable education, welfare, and health systems (mainly in rural China) violate social and economic rights. Depending on whether one is a supporter of state welfare systems or a more marketized economy, China's protection of its people's economic and social rights could be deteriorating or improving.

In sum, on a number of international normative questions, Chinese practice appears to be conforming more with an extant international community such as it is than ever before. But the discussion also highlights a fundamental problem in assessing the degree to which China is upholding or challenging international norms: these norms themselves are often contradictory. What constitutes a coherent body of international norms endorsed by a single international community when the sovereignty norm grates with the free trade norm or the evolving humanitarian intervention norm?[24]

China and the "Rules of the Game"

A third possible indicator of status quo-ness is whether a state engages in a concerted effort to change rules in ways that defeat the purposes of global institutions. That is, does it try to undermine the established rules of the game? This is hard to gauge because the term—"rules of the game"—as used both in realist international theorizing and in public debates on foreign policy is so vague. Typically when the phrase is used in the academic or punditry worlds it means something like "does the state behave in ways that the United States would prefer." Obviously this is not a social scientific criterion.

Let me suggest, however, that there are a couple of questions one might logically look at to give more analytic substance to the phrase "rules of the game":

- Does a state try to change the formal and informal rules by which major international institutions operate once it is inside?

- Does a state routinely oppose the interests of unambiguously status quo states in major international institutions?

As for the first question, one concrete indicator would be a gap between what China has proposed as rules for institutions versus what it has accepted. The gap may say something about what the rules would have looked like had Chinese leaders designed them predominantly by themselves.

In international economic institutions, at least, China has proposed very few "new rules." This is mainly because China entered most of these institutions well after their creation, and because these rules often served China's economic interests (for instance, accessing funding from the World Bank). Moreover most academic observers are generally sanguine about China's conformity to extant rules once inside these institutions. The best studies on China's involvement in the World Bank and the International Monetary Fund all suggest generally sound performance. The Chinese government has tended to meet its reporting requirements, for instance, and made no dramatic efforts to change the way decisions are made to favor China. In the WTO, the PRC has generally accepted the overall decision-making procedures and structures, and has been cautious about taking a leadership role inside the institution (Pearson 2002, 1999; Lardy 1999).

In security institutions the picture is somewhat less clear in part because China has participated in the construction of some of the more important of these institutions. Take the CTBT. Had the bargaining positions that China took into the negotiations prevailed in the design of the CTBT there is no doubt the treaty would be less intrusive and compliance less strictly monitored (assuming, of course these initial positions reflected basic preferences as opposed to opportunistic opening gambits). Moreover, states would have been allowed to conduct "peaceful nuclear explosions." On the other hand, had the Chinese bargaining position prevailed, nuclear weapons states would have had to abide by a no-first-use pledge and this would have reduced incentives to rely on nuclear weapons for security (if verified, through escrowing warheads for instance). Although a Chinese-designed CTBT would have had weak on-site inspection provisions, it would have had a very expensive and extensive satellite monitoring capacity. This would have added early-warning capabilities to the CTBT. At present the monitoring system only allows for the verification of violations after the fact. Other states, such as Canada, supported the principle of international satellite monitoring for the CTBT, but objected to the cost of the Chinese proposal.

One final point here: even if there were evidence of strong Chinese preferences to radically reorder extant economic and security institutions, it would not be easy to achieve. Sometimes the punditry literature suggests that "changing the rules" means changing the norms or ideology of an institution. In the Chinese case, invariably the pundit means China will try to weaken, rather than strengthen the constraints on sovereign state behavior. But most institutions have rules about rules; there are often procedures that govern how these norms, ideologies, and institutional purposes themselves can be changed. Thus to analyze whether China can change the rules requires understanding these procedures. And, not surprisingly, in many institutions these procedures tend to be highly conservative. They are designed to prevent actors whose preferences might change or new actors with different preferences from easily altering the purposes of the institution. The institutions themselves, if they are highly developed, with their own bureaucracies with their own sense of organizational interests and mission, will also develop decision rules and norms that prevent erosion or dilution of their power and mission. Institutions such as the WTO that require supermajorities or consensus, for example, are exceedingly hard to change. The dissatisfied actor has to put together a supercoalition or somehow overcome the veto of a single player in a consensus/unanimity system.[25]

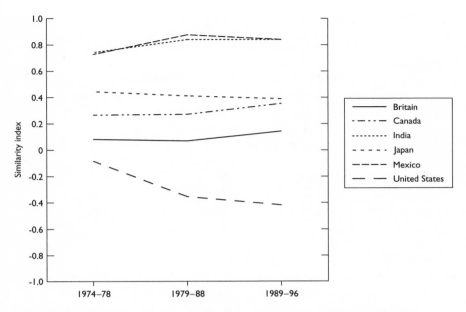

FIGURE 2.5 Mean Similarity Index with Select Countries per Foreign Policy Period

As for the second question, does China increasingly oppose the interests of other states that observers might uncontroversially call status quo states? This is, of course, an exceedingly complex question, and ideally requires inventorying a long list of economic, political, and social interests, expressed in a wide range of international forums. But one quick indicator would be the congruence of voting in the United Nations.[26] Not surprisingly, the index of similarity (essentially an index of political distance between two states) over the 1980s and 1990s is quite high between China and developing states such as India and Mexico (see Figure 2.5). The average index is lower for China and status quo developed states such as Japan, Canada, and Britain, but has increased over the 1990s in the case of the last two countries. It is lowest, by far, for China and the United States and has decreased over the 1990s. Thus, whatever growing friction there is between U.S. and Chinese interests—as manifested in UN voting—this is not an across-the-board phenomenon in China's relations with a range of other status quo states.[27] Figure 2.5 suggests, therefore, that the "problem" is not China's status quo or non–status quo behavior, but rather potential conflicts of interests with the United States, given how the leaderships in both countries have defined these interests. *These two problems should be kept analytically separate when determining how dissatisfied China is with international norms and institutions.*

In sum, using these specific definitional criteria about international institutions and normative practices, the PRC is more status quo oriented than at any time in its history.

China's Preferences Concerning the Distribution of Power

At one extreme are those who claim that China has a clear goal of establishing a regional hegemony and will go about doing so as its relative power increases.[28] These arguments variously invoke Sinocentric images of Middle Kingdom impulses, the desire to restore a tribute system, or more general historical analogies whereby China, like rising Germany and rising Japan in the past, would naturally (in realist theory terms) want to change the power and status hierarchy in Asia.

More narrowly construed are arguments that on specific issues—Taiwan and the South China Sea in particular—we can see revisionist elements in Chinese diplomacy. The corollaries to these revisionist aims are subgoals related to reducing the obstacles to changing the status quo, namely U.S. military power in the region, U.S. plans for national missile defenses, and U.S. bilateral alliances, in particular the U.S.-Japan and the evolving U.S.-ROC military relationship.[29]

There are a number of issues raised by this claim about Chinese revisionism toward regional (and global) power distributions. The first that needs to be addressed head on is perhaps the most fundamental. Can China be said to have a well thought out, cross-elite preference for establishing hegemony in the region, to push U.S. military power out of the region, and to establish some tribute system redux, or in Western IR parlance, a sphere of influence similar in essence to the Soviet sphere in Eastern Europe or the U.S. sphere in Latin America during the Cold War? This is a hard question to assess.[30] If one were to list the range of "revisionist" goals that observers believe Chinese leaders have in the East Asian region it would include, from most grandiose to least grandiose, establishing Chinese hegemony in the region at the expense of U.S. power; establishing sovereign control over territory explicitly claimed by China (for example, the Spratly Islands); and reunification of Taiwan with the mainland under the One China rubric.

Unfortunately, the clarity of the evidence for these revisionist politico-military goals in the region is inversely related to the grandiosity of the goals. We have the best evidence for the desire eventually to revise the status quo on Taiwan. There are plenty of government documents and statements, think-tank studies, and interview data about the intent to at least prevent any further drift of Taiwan toward permanent separation. There is good evidence as well that military modernization programs, training exercises, and doctrinal innovation in the PLA, particularly since 1996, are aimed to a large degree at dealing with the Taiwan issue.[31]

The evidence about the Spratlys is somewhat more speculative. Chinese diplomacy on the South China Sea question in the last five years or so has been more moderate than in the early 1990s, as China moves tentatively toward accepting some ASEAN-derived codes of conduct in the region. Some internal circulation materials do indicate, however, that the long-term intention is still to establish sovereign control over the islands. For some Chinese analysts this should occur once China has the military capacity to do so. For others it should occur through diplomatic negotiations, joint development, the use of international legal instruments, and so on, because the costs of military action are too high.[32] But in this regard China is like other claimants. Indeed no state among the claimants has a sound legal basis—whether on the grounds of discovery, occupation and settlement, extension of the continental shelf, the archipelago principle, or extension of an exclusive economic zone (EEZ)—for the claims they make. Thus China's revisionism is matched by Philippine, Malaysian, Taiwanese, and Vietnamese revisionism.

The evidence is most problematic when it comes to the goal of establishing Chinese hegemony in the region or beyond. Most who routinely make this claim infer it from particular readings of particular parts of Chinese history. Some will invoke the more ancient "middle kingdom" or the more recent Qing dynasty tribute system narratives as though the existence of these historical analogies is incontrovertible evidence for the current leadership's thinking. Others will make this inference on the basis of historical analogies from Europe (most commonly, the rise of Wilhelmine Germany). Needless to say, historical analogies are analogies, not causes or explanations. Those who use historical analogies to reason about current leadership intentions tend to commit one of two kinds of analytic errors. Either they are imprecise about how current leaders are socialized to accept the validity of some analogies (say analogies to China's tribute system or some Sinocentric IR imperial system from the past) and not others. Or they are imprecise about why Chinese conditions at *time t* that are identical to analogical conditions in *time t−n* are not corrupted, altered, or constrained by obviously new and different conditions. Why, for instance, would any similarities between Wilhelmine Germany's blustery militarism and the current Chinese leadership's obtuse politico-military diplomacy not be altered by the fact that the CCP leadership is also probably more dependent on foreign investment for economic growth (and political legitimacy) than was Wilhelmine Germany, or by the fact that in the early twenty-first century, unlike the early twentieth, the acquisition of new colonies by great powers is not a status marker of major power-hood, or by the fact that China's relative power vis-à-vis the "status quo" United States is far less than Germany's was vis-à-vis "status quo" England?[33] In short, analogical arguments such as this tend to haphazardly pick and choose the similarities to focus on while ignoring potentially important differences.

However, perhaps the more problematic element of these analogy-based claims about long-term Chinese goals in the region is the spareness of the documentary paper trail, relative to the other two revisionist goals.

One of the best pieces of evidence for these inferences about PRC intentions is the multipolarization (*duojihua*) discourse in China's diplomacy. Statements that multipolarity is an objective trend and a normative good explicitly challenge any continued U.S. unipolar status. The meaning of this discourse, therefore, needs to be examined head on because even scholars and pundits who are considered "pro-engagement" point to the Chinese preference for a multipolar world as indicative of a fundamental clash of interests with the U.S. (aka status quo) desire to preserve its global and regional predominance (Feigenbaum 2001; Gill 2001; Shambaugh 2000).[34]

On the question of global power, how important is multipolarity? The multipolarity discourse is a long-standing one. Indeed one could trace it back to Mao's evolving three world thesis, where he argued that in addition to two superpowers there were, variously comprised, a second world (capitalist developed states) and a third or revolutionary world (developing countries), and that the more powerful the second and third worlds were the more constrained the superpowers would be.[35] In the 1980s and 1990s, Chinese foreign policy discourse claimed the world was heading toward multipolarity, a more stable world of balanced power among five or so major centers (the United States, Russia, Europe, Japan, and China).[36] This was both a descriptive and normative claim. It is unclear, however, what precisely one can infer about Chinese strategic goals from this multipolarity discourse.

For one thing, the multipolarity discourse plays an ambiguous role in the policy process. There has often been a strong post hoc, faddish flavor to public Chinese commentary on broad trends in international relations (*guoji geju*). It is unclear whether the multipolarity discourse *informs* leadership decisions, *reflects* leadership preferences, or reveals a deeply ingrained victimization view of China's relationship to the world. Thus, for instance, multipolarity has in very general terms been long favored by Chinese leaders because in principle it reflects a diminution of the power of superpowers, and a relative rise in the international influence of developing states and China. But, as Thomas Christensen has pointed out, if one asks Chinese strategists if support for multipolarity means support for the rise in the relative power and strategic independence of Japan or a nuclear India, for instance, the response is often a negative or ambivalent one (Christensen 2001b: 30).[37]

Secondly, it is clear that there has been much debate over precisely what this term means. Typically from the early 1990s on the dominant claim has been that international trends showed a movement toward multipolarity and away from the bipolarity of the Cold War. What has been left understated, however, is whether the current transition period is objectively one of unipolarity, with the United States as the sole remaining superpower.[38] For instance, some conservative nationalists have argued that the world is indeed unipolar and that the official terminology is laughable. This means that China has to be cautious in the short run in challenging U.S. power, but that the long-run goal should be to develop the strategic and diplomatic alliances to do so (Zhang Ruizhuang 2001: 28; Fang, Wang, and Song 1999: 47; He 1993: 174–75).[39] Some moderate, "pro-American" voices also argue that the era is essentially one of U.S. unipolarity, but that this is not entirely to China's disadvantage.[40] U.S. hegemony is better than Japanese, for instance.[41] Moreover, it is clear that although the United States is the sole superpower, China can benefit from economic relations with the United States and from the relative global stability that U.S. hegemony affords. As one analyst put it, although China does not like an international system governed by U.S.- and Western-designed rules, it still has to admit that there are benefits from China's ability to free-ride from the provision of certain beneficial public goods (Wang 2000). Another concluded that although China supported a more just and reasonable international order, "China is by no means a challenger to the current international order. Under the current international system and norms, China can ensure its own national interests" (Zhu 2002). Still another analyst argued that China was neither a challenger nor a blind follower of U.S.-defined international order. Rather China should focus its attention on helping build international institutions and organizations, particularly among the great powers (Fan 2002). If there is policy advice from this group of moderates it is that China should use international institutions—multilateralism more so than military power—to constrain U.S. behavior (Zhang 2000b; Wang Yizhou 2001, 1999a, 1999b).[42]

Other moderates, on the other hand, continue to claim that multipolarity is still the main trend. But they do this to head off hard-liners who believe that the unipolar moment requires more vigorous balancing against the United States. Thus, for these moderates, multipolarity means that China does not need to so actively confront and challenge U.S. interests.[43] This is ironic precisely because the multipolarity discourse is used in the United States as evidence of a monolithic Chinese desire to challenge U.S. primacy.

For more centrist realpolitik voices multipolarity means, essentially, an international system based on the five principles of peaceful coexistence—hardly revolutionary or dramatically revisionist values—whereby other states will have to take China's vital interests into account.[44]

Over all, then, during the 1990s it was simply not clear that there was a consensus among analysts on precisely what the trend lines were in the evolution of polarity, nor on whether multipolarity even implies a major challenge to U.S. power.[45]

Moreover, from the mid-1990s on, after the successful projection of U.S. power in Kosovo, and in the face of the growing military capabilities gap between the United States and any and all potential contenders, many Chinese analysts have, in fact, expressed increasing pessimism that multipolarity trends are going the way the Chinese leadership would prefer. In the mid-1990s it seemed that the regime was officially hedging: it claimed that there was a long-term trend toward multipolarity, but that for a comparatively long time the system would be characterized by one superpower and many major powers (*yi chao duo qiang*) (Wang 1997: 4).[46] Most interesting in this regard was the 2000 White Paper on National Defense, compiled largely by PLA strategists. It is clear from the preamble to this document that the authors regard U.S. relative power—the gap between the United States and all other states—as remaining constant, if not actually expanding (for example, the world is getting less multipolar, not more multipolar). Chinese assessments of comprehensive national power—a composite index that weights hard power (GNP, military power, levels of education,

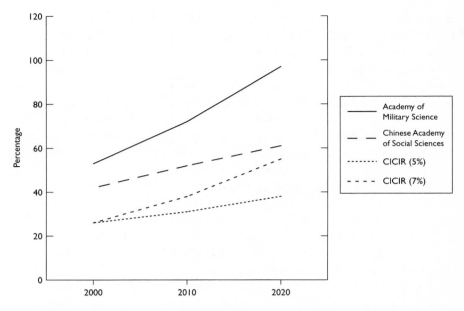

FIGURE 2.6 Chinese Estimates of Trends in Comprehensive National Power

NOTE: "Academy of Military Science" = the most optimistic estimate of relative CNP trends from a study by an AMS scholar conducted in the late 1980s and early 1990s. "Chinese Academy of Social Sciences" = a 1996 estimate from one of its subordinate institutes. CICIR (5%) = an estimate by the China Institute of Contemporary International Relations that assumes a 5 percent growth in China's CNP and a 3 percent growth in American CNP. CICIR (7%) = CICIR estimate that assumes a 7 percent growth rate for China's CNP. The CICIR estimate was made in 2000.
SOURCES: The AMS and CASS estimates are taken from Pillsbury (2000, table 10, 249). The CICIR estimates are calculated from data in CICIR (2000, 20).

etc.) and soft power (foreign policy influence, cultural dynamism, etc.) indicators used to determine relative power among major powers over the next ten to twenty years— are increasingly pessimistic about China's ability to close the gap with the United States. As Figure 2.6 shows, the estimates of Chinese CNP as a percentage of U.S. CNP seem to be declining across time.[47] For some Chinese analysts, the gap in power and in geostrategic capabilities vis-à-vis the United States means that China cannot realistically become an ocean great power (Tang 2001: 33). In practice this means it cannot realistically think of replacing the United States as the regional hegemon.

Finally, the notion that multipolarity best describes the changing structure of world politics appears most recently to be on the wane relative to new concepts such as globalization (see Figure 2.7).[48] The globalization discourse recognizes that the main factors that constrain states and state sovereignty in the future—their domestic

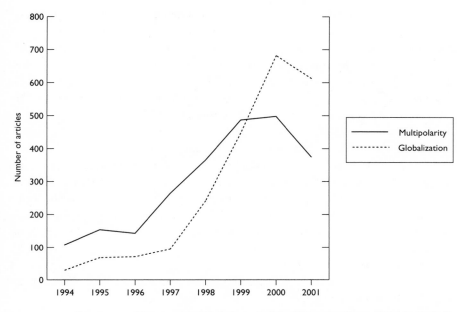

FIGURE 2.7 Frequency of International Relations Articles Using the Terms "Multipolarity" (*duojihua*) and "Globalization" (*quanqiuhua*) in Chinese Academic Journals, 1994–2001

NOTE: The frequency counts come from keyword searches of articles from the international relations and world politics subcategories in *China Academic Journals Database*, 1994–2002. China National Knowledge Infrastructure, an online service provided by East View Online Services, Minneapolis.

economic choices, domestic cultural choices, even domestic political choices, and their foreign policies—may have less to do with CNP or material power distributions and more to do with their openness to global capital, information, and technology flows. Chinese analysts mostly agree that globalization is a double-edged sword, with adverse effects for state sovereignty and autonomy in a range of policy areas (economics, culture, even domestic governance issues such as human rights) (Liu 2001: 304, 307; Huang 2000). Moreover, for many Chinese analysts, globalization does not so much replace the centrality of states in world politics as it creates a new structure of capital penetration within which states compete for the (often finite) benefits of the information and technology that capital brings with it. Globalization does not always connote a global village that replaces interstate relations, nor does it necessarily equate to integration (*yi ti hua*) nor the dissolution of the nation-state.[49]

On the other hand, the globalization trope dilutes somewhat the long-dominant vision of international politics as a struggle among states to enhance relative power in the international power structure (polarity). The metric for determining the vitality and longevity of the state and its political structures is not so much how much relative power the state controls, but how it has configured its economic and foreign policies in such a way as to tap into the transnational production of new sources of wealth, status, and economic security. What matters is not so much where a state stands in the hierarchy of material power distributions, but where it sits in the global division of labor in value-added production.[50] Some analysts push this further and argue that in a globalization framework for analysis the nation-state is no longer the primary unit of analysis, and that it is within this framework that one can talk about common global norms of behavior that transcend state interests (Wang 1995: 15–16). Implicit in some conceptualizations of globalization is the argument that national self-reliance is no longer a viable development (or security) option, particularly in the face of transnational or nontraditional security problems (drugs, crime, terrorism, ecological damage) whose appearance and virulence is related to economic and technological globalization (Liang 1999: 25; Wang 1999a: 8). Moreover, globalization transforms political relations among major powers into more complex combinations of cooperative and conflictual interactions, the relative balance of which is not so clearly determined by polarity (Wang 1999b).

In short, the multipolarity discourse is not such an unproblematic indicator of Chinese intentions these days.[51]

On the question of U.S. power in the Asia-Pacific, is China balancing? All of this discussion, however, has been in the realm of discourse about preferences. What about behavior? Is Chinese diplomacy in the Asia-Pacific region consistent with a strategic goal of establishing regional hegemony or more limited revisionist goals of defending territorial claims? Here the evidence appears more consistent with the latter than the former. The multipolarity discourse may reflect a long-term wish but it is not an especially good guide to near- and medium-term Chinese foreign policy behavior. Indeed, for all its support for multipolarity, China is not doing a great deal to encourage its emergence. In IR theory jargon, an active effort to reduce U.S. relative power and influence in the region would be called balancing. Typically, states can balance internally (mobilize economic and technological and human resources to translate into military/strategic power) and/or externally (find allies that share a common interest in opposing a stronger hegemon or dominant state). So is China balancing against the United States in the region?

There seems to be little doubt that China's military modernization program over the 1990s has been aimed in large measure at developing capabilities to deter and/or slow the application of U.S. military power in the region. But it is also clear that the immediate and medium-term issue at stake for Chinese leaders is Taiwan, not the U.S. strategic presence in the region per se nor necessarily other military contingencies such as a war in Korea.[52] That is, the PLA is tasked with minimizing the U.S. ability to defend Taiwan against Chinese military coercion. PLA modernization, at the moment, is not primarily designed to seize, for instance, the Senkaku/Diaoyu Islands or the South China Sea islands. The rate of real increase in Chinese military expenditures grew substantially in the late 1990s (18 percent in 2000). Nonetheless, it is unclear whether one should term this "balancing" in the "challenging the distribution of power" sense. For one thing, balance of power literature is extremely vague as to what kinds or levels of increases in military expenditures constitutes balancing. Military expenditures are not simply functions of external threats/opportunities, but also determined by technological innovation cycles, organizational interests, and domestic ideologies.[53] Moreover, as a percentage of GDP Chinese military expenditures do not appear to have reached a level where one could conclude the Chinese economy is being militarized and mobilized in order to balance against U.S. power.

As for external alliances, China is not trying as hard as it might to construct anti-U.S. alliances nor undermine U.S. alliances globally or regionally, certainly nowhere near the degree to which the Soviets competed with the United States during the Cold War. Although China recently signed a treaty of friendship with Russia, a treaty that embodied some of the Chinese normative vision of world politics (multipolarity, antihegemony), it would be a stretch to call this an anti-U.S. alliance. Putin and his advisors' fundamental impulse is to rely on closer ties with Europe and the United States to develop the Russian economy. Strategically, Russia's most useful role in the Sino-Russian relationship is as a source of weapons, not a strategic partner for confronting and counterbalancing U.S. power and interests in every forum. And even then, the Russian motivation appears to be an economic one—keeping Russian industries and workers afloat—not primarily an anti-American strategic one. Moreover, even those shared Sino-Russian positions that are in some sense anti-American are often positions that would *strengthen* or *uphold* the international institutional status quo, for instance, strengthening the role of the UN and preserving existing arms-control agreements such as the ABM treaty.[54]

China does not appear to be all that active in trying to pry the United States and Japan or the United States and the ROK apart. Beijing's official position has long been that foreign forces (for example, the United States, and before that the Soviet Union) should withdraw from the region. This is not new, and U.S. analysts and pundits in the 1980s generally did not take this position seriously enough to argue that China was a revisionist state at that time.[55]

More importantly, in practice the Chinese are not unequivocally against these alliances. At the moment, the primary tool in Chinese diplomacy is rhetorical—a critique of the obsolescence of "Cold War thinking" that undergirds bilateral military alliances.[56] The conceptual replacement is the so-called new security concept whereby the region would consist of multilateral institutions and stable bilateral relations based on the five principles of peaceful coexistence. This rhetoric has little appeal in the region, and is hardly a substantive challenge to U.S. alliances. We do not see (yet) for instance, the use of economic or military threats, or covert financial intervention in domestic political debates, and the like, to promote antialliance policies within Japan and Korea.[57] Indeed, the reason probably has to do with the tension between the sweeping antialliance rhetoric and the perceived interests at stake in specific alliances.

The U.S.-ROK alliance, for instance, serves Beijing's current interest in stabilizing the peninsula's division.[58] Beijing appears to believe that the ROK shares an interest in a so-called soft landing for the Democratic People's Republic of Korea (DPRK), a gradual process of domestic reform alongside greater diplomatic acceptance by the United States and Japan that help to preserve the regime as both Koreas slowly reduce barriers to trade and flows of people. Thus the ROK's interests also act as a brake on any rash U.S. attempts to engineer a so-called hard landing, the rapid dissolution of the DPRK and unification of the peninsular under the ROK's control. At the moment, China's leaders appear to prefer the geopolitical status quo—the continuing existence of an independent ROK and DPRK. It is true that since the beginning of the most recent DPRK nuclear crisis in the fall of 2002, many in China overtly blame the DPRK for regional instability (prior to this Chinese analysts only indirectly suggested that the main source of instability in the peninsula would come largely from the DPRK—a political coup, economic collapse, a missile test, the development of nuclear weapons) (Zhu 2000: 73). There is certainly no love lost between the current Chinese leadership under Hu Jintao and the Kim Jong-Il regime. Indeed, some well-connected analysts have pointedly noted that there is a difference between a change in the Kim Jong-Il regime and the collapse of the DPRK (the former would be preferred to the latter). Even so, Beijing appears to believe that stability on the peninsula can best be realized by economic development and limited marketization roughly along the Chinese model, by stable political relations among the key players—DPRK, ROK, China, the United States, and Japan (Zhang 2001)—and most recently by the complete elimination of the DPRK's nuclear weapons programs and delivery systems. By most accounts China has been relatively constructive in urging restraint in the DPRK's development of WMD capabilities and in supporting the institutions designed to ensure this restraint—the Framework Agreement of 1994, Korean Energy Development Organization, and the Four Party peace talks.[59]

For the most part, the ROK shares Beijing's interests when it comes to the DPRK, having calculated that the costs of rapid unification are excessively high (in 1998, estimates of cost of unification after a hard landing in 2000 were anywhere from $200 billion to $1.2 trillion more in government spending over an indefinite period) (Noland, Robinson, and Liu 1998). But the ROK's stake in this status quo is directly related to its sense of security from the DPRK, and the alliance with the United States serves this purpose.[60]

Beijing's one major worry is the role the alliance will play in any post-DPRK scenario. Chinese strategists are concerned that the United States intends to stay, and worse, may want to deploy forces above the 38th parallel. Chinese military exchanges with the ROK no doubt are designed to press home Chinese concerns, particularly if U.S. policy shifts more obviously to forcing a hard landing for the DPRK regime.

The PRC hopes to keep the DPRK alive because of the buffer it creates between U.S. military power and Chinese territory, and because a united Korea might divert ROK and Japanese investment from China or become an object of "greater Korea" irredentism among ethnic Koreans on both sides of China's border. It may also be that as long as the DPRK remains alive, in the context of conservative U.S. political leaders pushing for harder containment and/or roll-back policies toward the DPRK, the issue will be a source of friction between the United States and the ROK, something that is not altogether contrary to China's leaders' interests.

As for the U.S.-Japan alliance, Chinese attitudes are exceedingly complex. Since the announcement of guidelines for revising the security treaty in 1996, Chinese strategists have been increasingly worried by the possibility that this alliance will become a tool for defending an independent or permanently separated Taiwan (Qing and Sun 2001: 5; AMS 2000: 83; Yang 1999: 160; Zhao 1998: 362–63). Many Chinese analysts and leaders believe, however, that a Japan within a bilateral alliance with the United States is still better than a Japan outside of such constraints *as long as* this alliance is not used to provide military cover for an independent Taiwan. Some of the more sophisticated analysis argues that in the post–Cold War era one of the purposes of the alliance has shifted from being a "bottle cap" (*pinggai*) over Japanese power, to being both a bottle cap AND a constraint on Chinese and Russian power in the region. In other words, the bottle cap role still exists, thus implicitly so does the Chinese interest in this aspect of the alliance (Jin 2000a: 260–61, 269).[61] It is the other purpose—tying China down in an U.S.-dominated security order, particularly as it relates to the Taiwan issue—that China objects to. Thus China's diplomacy toward the U.S.-Japan alliance particularly from the mid-1990s on has been largely aimed at extracting some kind of credible commitment—so far unsuccessful—that the alliance not be used to defend Taiwan in a conflict with the PRC (Wang and Wu 1998: 33).[62] More generally, it has been aimed at suggesting ways a weakened alliance might exist alongside, and subordinate to, multilateral institutions in the region. Although this vision remains rather underdeveloped, it is still self-servingly presented in places such as the ASEAN Regional Forum.

In short, the most accurate way of describing the Chinese leadership's preferences about the U.S.-Japan alliance *at this moment* is that it return to its pre-1996 form and function, not that it disappear entirely.[63] Chinese analysts usually are careful to state that they oppose the *strengthening* or *reinforcement* of the U.S.-Japan alliance, not the alliance's existence per se (AMS 2000: 83; Jin 2000a: 258, 2000b: 205).[64]

Some Chinese strategists have also implied that China's diplomacy toward Japan in the past has been counterproductive, in part due to popular emotions concerning the history of Japan's aggression against China and in part due to an incorrect devaluation of the economic benefits of a relationships with Japan. At base, the first argument, at least, implies a recognition of security dilemma dynamics in the dyadic relationship.[65] Some have also argued that Japanese militarism is generally in check because of everything from the U.S. alliance to political change, to the inculcation of more pacific norms in the population, to the persistent economic problems Japan has experienced over the past decade, to the realism of Japanese politicians that having China as an enemy in such close proximity is contrary to Japan's interests, to the deepening economic interdependence between China and Japan (Jin 2000b: 205, 207; Zhu 1999).[66] Given these arguments, these strategists contend, China should use less-emotional diplomacy (that is, invoke the history card less frequently and vociferously) to help prevent the emergence of more nationalist and revivalist voices in Japan (Rozman 2002a: 113; Feng 2000; Zhu 1999).[67] In addition, good relations with the United States and Japan will help reduce the China element behind a strengthening U.S.-Japan alliance (Jin 2000a: 301), an interesting admission, by reverse logic, that a hard-line policy toward these two countries will have a counterproductive effect. These are hotly and publicly debated arguments.[68] Thus there is by no means a solid consensus behind them. But they appear to be the dominant arguments for the moment. This may help explain why the Chinese government shifted to what has been referred to as "smile diplomacy" toward Japan in 1999–2000. One manifestation of this was the PRC's relative quiet when Japan offered to send naval forces to assist U.S. operations against the Taliban and Al Qaeda in the fall of 2001.

Some among the Chinese public appear to agree with this more cautious understanding of Japanese power. Although Chinese citizens do not like Japan, and believe that the Japanese people and state are even more warlike than the Americans and the U.S. state, they appear not to be too worried about the revival of Japanese militarism.[69] According to the Beijing Area Study's random sample of Beijing residents in 2001 only 8 percent chose the revival of Japanese militarism as the main threat to China. Most considered domestic social unrest, Taiwan independence, or U.S. military power to be the major security threats. It is likely, however, that were Japan to participate in U.S. military operations in defense of Taiwan, the lines between Taiwan independence, U.S. military power, and revived Japanese militarism will blur, and the ethnic/racialist emotions behind many Chinese views of Japan will come more obviously to the fore.

Finally, somewhat puzzling for a balancing argument is the fact that China has become more dependent on the United States economically rather than less, even as U.S. relative power has increased after the Cold War. Chinese exports to the United States as a percentage of all of its exports has increased over time. Some argue that as the weaker state, running a large trade surplus with the United States, China's relative power benefits more from this relationship than if it did not exist. There is some merit to this argument, assuming that it is obvious how much of this net flow of economic resources to the PRC can be or has been translated into military power that can deter the United States from operating in the Western Pacific.

On the other hand, the economic relationship also creates a dependence on U.S. markets and capital for economic growth. Economic growth is, in turn, directly related to the legitimacy and longevity of the CCP rule. In 2002 the United States was

China's second largest trading partner, with about 16 percent of China's total trade.[70] China imports critical products such as aircraft and electronic integrated circuits from the United States. The United States ranked first among developed economies (excluding Hong Kong) in contracted foreign direct investment in China in 2001 (China Statistical Data, www.china.org.cn/e-company/02–06–20/web020417.htm). American foreign direct investment is critical in certain sectors of the Chinese economy such as automobiles and telecommunications. The CCP's economic development strategy creates economic, social, and technological interdependencies that—given the relative size and primitiveness of the Chinese economy compared to the U.S. economy—means that an end to these interdependencies is far more costly to the Chinese regime than to the United States.

Moreover, these interdependencies create constituencies inside the PRC that are not self-evidently hostile to the United States or supportive of all of China's external diplomacy. Economic interest groups along the coastline would be adversely affected by the militarization of East China in the event of a major conflict over Taiwan. An emerging middle class in urban China may be somewhat less supportive of strongly anti-American diplomacy than other socioeconomic groups in China, including the military. Survey data from the Beijing Area Study surveys from 1998 to 2001 show that wealth and education are positively correlated with higher levels of amity toward the United States, a lower degree of "othering" Americans, and a lower degree of nationalism. In absolute terms, the middle class tends to have a higher level of amity toward the United States than toward most other states. Middle-class supporters of free trade have among the highest levels of amity toward the United States (Johnston, forthcoming).

Relatedly, economic growth considerations, not strategic balancing, seem to dominate the PRC's reaction to Japan's economic troubles of late. If the PRC leadership were primarily concerned that Japanese economic and military power should be countered with a wide range of diplomatic and military tools, it is curious why Beijing is so worried about Japan's economic recession. A preference for pure balancing would, presumably, lead Chinese leaders to hope for continued recession because an economically weak Japan is a Japan that cannot supply the alliance goods and services that the United States is demanding from it. Instead, however, Chinese leaders, like American leaders, are worried that high public debt and banking insolvency will reduce Japan's role as a market and source of capital for Chinese economic development.[71]

In other words, under conditions of growing economic interdependence, mobilizing the economy and militarizing society to balance seriously against American power and influence in the region—with the goal of establishing a Chinese sphere of influence in the face of U.S. resistance—will create economic and social costs that, *at this point*, the regime appears unwilling to bear. This constrains China's ability to balance against U.S. power.[72] At best, one could describe China's balancing against

American unipolarity as (in the words of one astute observer), "hesitant, low-key, and inconsistent" (Deng 2001: 359).[73]

The exception that proves the rule about Chinese balancing behavior may be China's response to U.S. military power on the more limited issue of Taiwan. So-called asymmetric strategies, combined with relatively modest improvements in China's long-range cruise missile, ballistic missile, and submarine capability could slow down the U.S. response to a rapid military-political fait accompli presented to the Taiwanese government.[74] The dangers of military conflict between China and the United States over Taiwan should not be underestimated. The interaction of China's symbolic commitment to sovereignty over Taiwan and the U.S. concern about preserving the credibility of its military commitments to friends and allies is upping the political-military stakes for both sides. The spillover effects of preparations for a war with the United States and its Asian allies are, of course, not limited to the immediate vicinity of Taiwan. Thus the fallout of a war would be regionwide, even though the Chinese goal would be the geographically and politically limited one of preventing Taiwanese independence or compelling Taiwan's reunification.[75] Nonetheless, China's preparations for dealing with U.S. military power in a Taiwan conflict are not really the same thing as balancing against U.S. power writ large in the region or beyond.

Of course, the absence of clear evidence of a proactive effort to fundamentally alter the distribution of power regionally and/or globally does not mean such a desire does not exist. But the analytic problem needs to be recognized that the scope of China's revisionist claims is not obvious. More obvious are China's limited revisionist aims when it comes to Taiwan and secondarily to extend control over the South China Sea and the Senkaku/Diaoyu Islands. Here, the evidence does seem to suggest that the regime is preparing the option of using force to change the political and military "facts on the ground." Not to make excuses for China's obtuse gunboat diplomacy in the 1990s, but it is hard to generalize from Taiwan to attitudes toward long-term regional distributions of power let alone to global institutions or "rule of the game." The Taiwan issue could lead to the strengthening and expanding of more grandiose revisionist interests in China and the appearance of more authoritative evidence of such long-term goals (the defense of territorial integrity in an era of long-range high-tech precision strike means that the military operational perimeter has to expand outward and include preemption).[76] But at present, the character of China's revisionism on the Taiwan issue does not appear to be reflective of broader Chinese diplomacy elsewhere in the region or globe. It is a dangerous exception, but an exception nonetheless.

It's The Others: A Liberal Domestic Change Argument

If it is hard to find concrete evidence—apart from the Taiwan issue and its spillover effects on regional security—that China is a highly revisionist state in East Asia, there is a second explanation for the growing concern about Chinese power. That is, the primary changes have been in regional perceptions of Chinese goals, influenced by China's growing power relative to other states in the region, rather than Chinese diplomacy per se. It is regional leaders who are paying attention to power shifts and a few key watershed events (the Beijing massacre in June 1989, the Taiwan Strait crisis in 1995/6, the EP-3 incident in April 2001) and are extrapolating to Chinese strategic goals. Decision makers can often view the world as neorealists would—inferring intentions from changing relative power. Mao certainly did. There are these kinds of voices close to parts of the Bush administration.[77] This contrasts, for instance, with the "liberal" engagement-constraint arguments during the Clinton administration.

This explanation compels us to look at political and ideological changes in countries around China's periphery to explain changing perceptions of China's threat to regional stability. This would be, in many respects, a domestic political story. Political change in some countries has reduced or narrowed definitions of shared interests with China.

Political and generational change in Japan has diluted the influence of older pro-Beijing factions in the Liberal Democratic Party (LDP), and brought a younger generation into positions of political and bureaucratic power that is alienated by China's use of the history card to bash Japan; by China's apparent ingratitude for Japanese assistance for its development; by China's not-so-secret naval intelligence gathering inside Japan's EEZ, among other grievances (Green 1999).[78] With a growing role for NGOs in Japan's civil society and its foreign relations, there are now more voices inside Japan critiquing China from a liberal perspective on governance and human rights. In general, as Gilbert Rozman puts it, the contradictions between those advocating a "predominantly engagement" strategy and those supporting a "predominantly containment" approach sharpened over the 1990s. This has undermined a long-time "naïve romanticism" in popular and elite opinion, based on optimism about China's economic reform and integration and about Japan's own economic prospects (Rozman 2001).

In the United States, politics has had a large impact on perceptions of shared or competing interests in Sino-U.S. relations. After the 1994 congressional election brought a range of new conservative voices into Congress, the congressional right wing became the locus for sharp critiques of rising Chinese power, for growing political support for Taiwan's permanent separation from the PRC, and for redefinitions of U.S. interest that eliminated areas of shared interest with the PRC. Congress mandated studies of Chinese military power, of the cross-strait military balance, of allegations of Chinese espionage in the nuclear and missile technology fields. The mandate was driven by a view of the PRC as a revisionist state, a potential competitor to the United States. Moreover, for ideological reasons the conservative Republican-controlled Congress rejected a range of policy positions that the Clinton executive branch believed created shared U.S.-Chinese interests. Congress opposed the 1996 CTBT treaty, a treaty whose final form was in large measure a function of hard U.S.-PRC bargaining. Congress also rejected the Kyoto treaty, and conservatives in Congress rejected the notion that the United States and China had any shared interest in dealing with global warming as a global problem to begin with. Conservatives also opposed the ABM treaty and any restraint on ballistic missile defense, setting up a major conflict of interest with the PRC, whose nuclear deterrent, in classic free-riding fashion, benefited from the U.S.-Russian agreement. The Bush administration shared some of these congressional definitions of U.S. interest and interpretations of Chinese intentions. Moreover, whether one speaks of the Kissingerian/Scowcroft international realists or the neoimperial wing of the Bush administration, compared to the Clinton administration's understandings of the nature of international politics, both groups are more skeptical of the likelihood that rising, revisionist powers can be "socialized" inside international institutions. Thus the scope of issues on which the Clinton administration believed China and the United States had some overlap of interests has narrowed under the Bush administration.

Most recently, the scope appears to be narrowing further. One leg of the U.S.-China relationship—economics and trade—that the Clinton administration and centrist Republicans agreed was a source of stability in the overall relationship has come under some question by conservative voices close to the administration. Until recently it was only the primacist right in the Republican Party that essentially saw the economic relationship as a potential threat to U.S. power. However, the recently released U.S.-China Economic and Security Review Commission report also adopted a somewhat skeptical and conditional view of the value of economic integration. In the report's view, China's trade surplus, its access to dual-use technology, its massive inflows of foreign direct investment, its overall commercial opacity and institutionalized corruption, all mean that China's relative power may benefit from the relationship more than U.S. relative power. It is not surprising, then, that the report also concludes there are fundamental conflicts of interest between the United States and China in the region, starting with the Chinese intention of pushing U.S. power out of the region (USCC 2002). This, then, would explain a change in the inferences drawn about Chinese intentions in the region and globally. It remains to be seen how or whether the Bush administration responds to any Congressional legislation designed to "national securitize" the economic relationship, as the report appears to recommend.

Internal changes in Taiwanese politics have clearly altered perceptions of Chinese intentions. Up until the early 1990s, both sides of the strait shared one crucial vision—that there was one China (whether it was the PRC or the ROC) and that Taiwan was a part of that China. This began to change as first the ROC dropped the pretense to sovereignty over the mainland, and pursued what was known as "flexible diplomacy," expressing a willingness to accept dual recognition by other countries of both the PRC and the ROC. Democratization and rapid economic development through the 1990s contributed to a growing sense among some Taiwanese that there were large and widening differences. This sense was encouraged by deliberate government efforts, from the mid-1990s on, to create an independent Taiwanese identity, through the promotion of Taiwanese and local history and culture. The leadership in the 1990s and today, now under a proindependence president Chen Shui-bian, tried to transform a growing awareness of *different-ness* into a growing awareness of *separate-ness* from an entity called China.[79] The effort to normalize the notion that Taiwan is independent from China culminated in 2001 in a statement by President Chen that China and Taiwan were two states on different sides of the strait. He may have been describing a functional reality but this is the closest a president of the ROC has ever come to declaring that the island of Taiwan was independent from a state called China. Nothing in the PRC's Taiwan policy has compelled this discursive shift, since this policy has not changed much over the past ten years. Rather two successive presidents of the ROC are personally, ideologically committed, to developing Taiwan's separate identity and expressing it legally, politically, economically, and internationally.

American policy has evolved to the point where Taiwan is viewed as close to being the functional equivalent of a "major non-NATO ally" (MNNA). Although officially, U.S. policy has been agnostic as to whether Taiwan and China unify or not as long as it is done peacefully and with the approval of the Taiwanese people, there is a growing sense in all three capitals that the Bush administration would prefer a permanently separate Taiwan (and only because a formally independent Taiwan could not be achieved without a major conflict with the PRC).

In short, the rise of identity politics in Taiwan has contributed to the Chinese leadership's worry about the permanent separation of Taiwan, and even the formal declaration of independence from an entity called the Republic of China.[80] The manifestations of this worry are an arms buildup across the strait from Taiwan designed to deter Taiwanese from supporting independence, and stepped up diplomatic efforts to isolate Taiwan internationally. These behaviors, in turn, have contributed to arguments in Japan, Taiwan, and the United States that China is indeed a revisionist state, not only on the Taiwan issue, but on the related issue of the U.S. military presence in East Asia.

This second explanation, then, would focus primarily on domestic political changes that have redefined perceptions of Chinese interests and the purposes of its economic and military power. As attribution theory might suggest, such perceptions tend to lead to inferences about dispositions from observed behavior. That is, ideological shifts in these countries have tended to produce views of China that exaggerate the degree of unanimity inside China about what its preferences are, that discount the domestic and international situational variables to which Chinese behavior might be responding, and that tend toward bad or worst-case inferences about intentions from extant capabilities. As one example, the Department of Defense's 2002 assessment of Chinese military power notes empirically that worrisome trends in Chinese military modernization really picked up in 1999 and that modernization appears to be aimed mainly at dealing with Taiwan-crisis-related contingencies. Yet it does not conclude

that therefore PRC reactions are to domestically driven changes in Taiwan's relationship to the PRC and to the United States. Rather it imputes to these reactions
the broader long-term strategy of pushing the United States out of the region (Department of Defense 2002).

The problem with an explanation that focuses solely on political change in Taiwan,
the United States, or Japan, however, is that it completely exonerates objective Chinese behavior as a source for the threatening interpretations of its behavior. Tai-
wanization would not matter, of course, if Chinese leaders were not so heavily invested
politically in the promotion of a national victimization discourse. Taiwan's separateness
would, presumably, be less threatening if it were not viewed through the lens of
China's 150 years of humiliation at the hands of rapacious foreign powers. Chinese
leaders would not calculate, presumably, that the "loss of Taiwan" is so costly for CCP
rule if they did not also believe that Taiwan separation might encourage a domestic
domino effect. This effect would then risk the CCP's claim to preserve China's territorial and political integrity, not to mention the personal power, perks, and privileges
of the regime. This risk is, in part, a function of dictatorship and nationalism: a dictatorship that permits no open discussion about genuine autonomy for minorities in
China, and a nationalism that refuses to recognize any right to self-determination for
minorities that by most indications would prefer not to be ruled by the Han majority.

Among some emerging Japanese elites the growing impatience with and alienation
from Chinese diplomacy in the region would not be so great, presumably, if the CCP
leadership were not so crude in its playing of the history card—turning anti-Japanese
messages on and off for political leverage purposes. Only recently have some Chinese
analysts realized the counterproductive nature of this card playing (Zhu 1999).

As for the U.S. conservative attacks on the PRC's behavior, although some of this
was politically motivated by visceral reactions to the Clinton administration, and
some generated by the deeply held primacist ideology of some factions, there is of
course plenty of ammunition provided by the PRC for attacks on its human rights
performance, its military threats to Taiwan, and its more "robust" military modernization program in the late 1990s. These "facts on the ground" lend political credence
to the less credible and/or less substantiated claims about Chinese military control of
the Panama Canal (less credible), about large-scale Chinese theft of advanced U.S.
nuclear weapons designs (less substantiated), about long-term hegemonic goals in the
Asia-Pacific (less substantiated), or about rising state-orchestrated nationalism and
anti-Americanism (less substantiated).[81]

It's Everyone: An Emerging Sino-U.S. Security Dilemma?

A final explanation is basically an interaction of the first two. China's limited revisionist goals and behavior (primarily on the Taiwan issue) interact with domestic political changes/perceptions in other states. The result is growing ambivalence in China

about the structures of power and influence in the region and growing doubts outside China about the benignity of rising Chinese power. This interactivity, however, is not simple reciprocity (as in tit for tat). Rather it is a process of malign amplification, that is, cooperative actions are discounted and conflictual behavior becomes the focus of analysis, evidence of a more fundamental challenge to one's own interests. In other words, this kind of interactivity should manifest itself in arguments about the structural nature of an emerging conflict.

The evidence of this kind of interactivity requires a bit of interpretation. One should expect to see an increase in the frequency and volume of conflictual discourses; hard-liners on both sides should be making references to each other to justify an argument that the other side is threatening basic values and interests. And indeed, there appears to be a growing sensitivity in the policy discourses on both sides to what is considered to be exemplary evidence of the attitudes of the other. That is, on both sides skeptics of the status quo orientation of the other are highlighting a small number of high-profile texts that "prove" their case about the other side's underlying threat. These texts are decontextualized and turned into representations of a unitary worldview on the other side (even while the user of the text recognizes the absence of a unitary view on their own side). In essence, texts from one side that select on the dependent variable are used to inform texts from the other that also select on the same dependent variable. Metaphorically speaking, we may be seeing an echo and amplification effect from this cycle of referentiality.[82]

In the U.S. discourse about China in the policy and punditry world there are two texts in particular that are cited with some frequency to prove the dangers emanating from Chinese power. One is the nationalist screed, *The China That Can Say No*, written by a group of neonationalist intellectuals in China and published in 1996. Although it was a popular seller, it was also quite controversial, with high-profile criticisms and rebukes appearing in response (none of which informed the U.S. debate about the book) (Shen 1998).[83] Moreover the anti-American attitudes expressed in the book are not obviously representative of public attitudes toward the United States.[84] This book was brought to the attention of the policy and punditry world by U.S. news reports. It became a symbol of the evidence of growing anti-Americanism in China among intellectuals and the next generation of leaders. It was seen as the natural product of the Communist Party's inculcation of nationalist attitudes, particularly after June 4, 1989 (see, for instance, International Operations and Human Rights Subcommittee 1996). In the universe of references to the text in U.S. academic, punditry, and political discourse the text was in almost every case used to make a claim about growing anti-Americanism, nationalism, irredentism (Copper 2002), an attitude that U.S. power was a threat to China's quest for greatness or evidence of the difficulty of integrating China into the global economy (Congressional testimony of James Leech, 29 July 1996).[85] Only two authors suggested that the sentiments expressed in the book probably did not have much influence in Chinese policy circles (Pei 2001; Lawrence

2000). The book was all things to all people—engagers used it to show how U.S. policy had to be sensitive to the deeply ingrained Chinese historical memory of being
bullied; neocontainers used it to show how the government, and increasingly a core
of nationalist intellectuals, were resistant to U.S. values and desired to challenge U.S.
power and interests.

The other text that non-China experts in the policy and punditry worlds have
tended to highlight as evidence of revisionism was written by two PLA colonels
whose primary job was to write reportage about life in the military. They were not
strategists, but political officers. Their book, *Unrestricted Warfare* (Chaoxian zhan), literally "warfare that exceeds boundaries," came to the attention of the U.S. policy
community initially through *Washington Post* reporting (Pomfret 1999). What at-
tracted attention in particular was its theorizing about the tools that weak states
could use against strong states, including terrorism, violence, and electronic warfare,
among other means, to disrupt the will to fight among a state's population.

The book, like *The China That Can Say No*, was highly controversial inside China.
It was criticized in internal meetings inside the military. It was also critiqued in essays
published by the CASS Institute of World Economics and Politics (Hong 1999; Li
1999; Pang 1999; Zhao 1999) and in closed-door meetings at military institutes. The
authors apparently bought up many copies of their own book to pass out to people in
the PLA so as to increase their profile within strategy circles (Personal conversation
with PLA officers). None of this contextual information was part of the U.S. discourse, however. The book was translated quickly by the U.S. intelligence community
and circulated within the U.S. military. It has become, in many respects, the one piece
of Chinese military writing with which non-China-related U.S. military officers are
most familiar.[86] In some cases, these officers assume that it reflects PLA doctrine and
perhaps even current capabilities. Although the military intelligence community is
busy translating more authoritative strategic texts from the PLA, these have not yet
had the degree of influence on framing discussions of the PLA in policy or punditry
circles that *Unrestricted Warfare* has had.[87] In punditry circles the book is used as evidence for everything from the claim that the PLA is already controlling or will control the Panama Canal through its influence on Hong Kong shipping companies, to
the claim that the PLA is planning to engage in e-attacks on U.S. information systems,
to the claim that there are possible links, even if only ideological, between Chinese
anti-Americanism and Al Qaeda's anti-Americanism, to the more general claim that
the PLA is planning to defeat U.S. military power in East Asia.[88] Usually the distinction between military planning and strategy and the political intentions of civilian decision makers is not made, or the claim is that the Chinese civilian leadership essentially endorses the strategic preferences of the PLA. In other words, the book is prima
facie evidence of Chinese intentions to challenge U.S. power.

There are other, less obvious, "texts" that are also beginning to reinforce this discourse about China. There are terms or ways of describing and understanding Chi-

nese strategy that are beginning to play on the exotic and Orientalizing themes of an othering process. This is apparent in the treatment of a new term in the rather esoteric discourse about Chinese military and strategic concepts that the United States has to worry about. The term is *shashoujian*, translated as "assassin's mace." The term was introduced to the policy and punditry world by Dr. Michael Pillsbury, a very experienced China specialist who has worked mostly for conservative Republican administrations or members of Congress over the past couple of decades. He has argued, with great justification, that ancient Chinese military thinking has played a key role in developing current PLA strategic concepts. One term that has appeared frequently in discussions of information warfare and asymmetric strategies against the United States is this term, shashoujian. It comes from ancient folk literature and refers to a magical weapon that a righteous figure uses at just the right moment to defeat a more powerful, evil adversary. In public testimony to the congressionally mandated U.S.-China Economic and Security Review Commission, in writings for the Department of Defense Office of Net Assessment, and in congressional testimony, Pillsbury has suggested that this concept of assassin's mace is critical to understanding how China will employ exotic technologies to defeat superior U.S. power.

Much of nuance and erudition of his work, however, has been lost as the term has been incorporated into the highly charged China debates in Washington. The U.S.-China Economic and Security Review Commission report and much of the Washington policy and punditry discourse implies that shashoujian weaponry is something mysterious, inscrutable, and exotic. Rarely does this discussion ask whether the concept can be mapped onto concepts and idioms in the U.S. strategic discourse.[89] Like the two book texts, the term has been severely decontextualized. In the first place, the concept of shashoujian appears to be a relatively recent addition to the PLA's discourse on strategy. It is associated with writing on information warfare and on military organization mostly. Using a full text keyword search for the term in the China Academic Journals database—an online index for articles from over 6,000 journals—reveals that it does not show up much in Chinese military journals until after 1999. And it actually shows up more frequently (in absolute terms) and earlier in articles on economics. This suggests the term is not some deeply embedded, long-time standard way in which the PLA has always spoken about warfare, or at least not yet. Interestingly, the term is not used in Mao Zedong's major military writings.

Moreover, when used in Chinese military writings the term can refer to anything from something as "mundane" as nuclear ballistic missiles to something as technically exotic as nanotechnology. It is also used by Chinese military writers to describe certain American weapons (ballistic missile defense, for instance) and certain Russian weapons. This implies that PLA writers believe Americans and Russians can conceptualize shashoujian just as Chinese can. Often the term is cited in quotation marks to underscore that it is being used metaphorically. That is, a shashoujian could be an action, a technology, a configuration of power—anything that finally turns things one's own way. It does not necessarily literally mean a secret, high-tech weapon. Rather, it refers to any technique that one side uses consciously to turn the tide decisively in its favor. In short, it refers to anything that gives China advantage at a critical time and place in wartime, and that gives China credible deterrence power in peacetime.

The term is used a great deal in popular culture—sports, "love advice," and the like. In love advice columns and books it is used to refer to that one action or quality of an individual that finally attracts the person one hopes to attract (for instance, a subtle smile is the shashoujian to win over a prospective date). It is used in Chinese sports commentary to refer, for instance, to the really good soccer scorer who turns the tide in the game. Some Chinese analysts have termed the war on terrorism as the Republican Party's shashoujian against the Democrats in U.S. domestic politics.

Thus its use in military affairs may reflect a blending of popular culture idiom with strategic analysis in the way, say, that U.S. strategists will blend sports idioms and analogies with military analysis. It is a shorthand for talking about things, somewhat analogous to "silver bullet" in English idiom (which the *American Heritage Dictionary* defines as "an infallible method of attack or defense"). The etymology of "silver bullet" in more recent English idiom refers to the use of a magical object (silver) to defeat a seemingly overwhelmingly powerful and evil adversary (in this case a werewolf), essentially similar to the original sense of shashoujian in Chinese lore.

Of course, it is difficult to claim these texts persuaded, shaped, or dictated the direction of the policy and punditry discussion in China. For many hard-liners the texts confirmed their a priori views. But these texts helped foster a tone and atmosphere in which China policy has been discussed. The discourse has helped marginalize dissenting views, for instance, because these views could be accused of being soft on China. Or it has helped construct truisms about China (rising nationalism and anti-Americanism; rising irredentism; the blurring of distinctions between military and political intentions) that constrain how China can be talked about in Washington. But for a number of nonexperts, particularly in the military, these texts have provided an image of the "problem" that has had a causal effect on attitudes of people who heretofore had no particular views.

There is a similar process on the Chinese side. The state media and Chinese analysts, particularly those whom one might classify as hard-liners—members of China's "blue team"—are paying increasing attention to texts they believe promote "anti-China" arguments to justify the U.S. "hegemonic" challenge to China's territorial and political integrity. The highest profile of these texts was *The Coming Conflict with China*, written by two American-based journalists, Richard Bernstein and Ross Munro. The book laid out a case for viewing China as an irredentist challenge to the United States as Chinese economic power increased in the future. Although citing ancient Chinese idioms to the effect that the Chinese were sneakily biding their time and obscuring their plans and capabilities until such time that it paid off to challenge U.S. power, and quoting controversially high figures for Chinese military expenditures, the book's policy recommendations were actually rather mainstream, nothing much beyond what the Clinton administration was already doing (rebuild alliances with Japan, deter China on the Taiwan issue, be careful about dual-use technology transfers to the PRC).

Despite the relative moderation of the policy prescriptions, the book was almost uniformly viewed in China as an influential statement of the "China threat" camp in U.S. policy circles and as reflecting the post–Cold War search for an existential enemy (Luo 1997; Shi 1997: 45). Some went as far as to claim the book represented a clash between Eastern and Western cultures (Sheng 1998). Not surprisingly, more moderate voices—analogous to U.S. critics of the decontextualizing of hard-line Chinese texts in the U.S. discourse—suggested either that *The Coming Conflict with China* was not all that influential, particularly in Clinton policy, or that it reflected complex domestic struggles against the Clinton administration from within the U.S. right (Huang and Ma 1999; Tao 1998). By implication it could not therefore be used to generalize about U.S. intentions toward China.

Since *The Coming Conflict with China* was published there have been a slew of high-profile sensationalist books and reports on the threat of rising Chinese power to U.S. domestic politics and foreign policy: *Betrayal, Red Dragon Rising, The Year of the Rat, The China Threat*, the *Cox Report* on allegations of Chinese theft of U.S. nuclear weapons designs, and *Hegemon*.[90] These books have sold well, judging from Amazon sales rankings. The Chinese discourse has paid less attention to these, though one finds references to them from time to time. Mostly, the attention has been in the context of a growing interest in the impact of the *Washington Times* and its national security reporter, Bill Gertz (author of *Betrayal* and *Red Dragon Rising*), on the U.S. discourse. In the last couple of years, it appears that Chinese analysts have concluded that Gertz and the *Washington Times* help set the agenda for some U.S. politicians, help publicize some of the more incendiary China-threat claims (such as the PLA controls the Panama Canal through Hong Kong companies, that Al Qaeda has acquired weapons from China), engage in politicized leaks of material from hard-liners in the intelligence communities, and help mobilize so-called anti-China forces in U.S. politics.[91]

The blue team is increasingly viewed by Chinese hard-liners as the source of ideas and political pressure behind the Bush administration's alleged "anti-China" diplomacy, its strengthening military support for Taiwan, and its more activist strategy in trying to weaken and divide China. An example is an article written by a young Berkeley-trained IR professor from Nankai University, Zhang Ruizhuang (Zhang 2002). Zhang himself is a relentless critic of "pro-American" voices in the Chinese policy and punditry discourse, claiming that they overestimate the security-dilemma features in the U.S.-China competition, and underestimate the U.S. threat to China's existence. He, like many American hard-liners, and unlike many U.S. and Chinese moderates, views the conflict as structural, not constructed by a security dilemma, misperceptions, or the volatility of the Taiwan issue.

This structural analysis is embodied, arguably, in the Chinese hard-liners' claim that the United States has pushed a "China threat theory" (*Zhongguo weixie lun*) that now motivates much of its behavior. This claim has not always been around. It was first made in the fall of 1992 when the first article mentioning the term appeared in the *People's Daily*. The article attributed the China threat theory to efforts by the Bush administration to justify sales of F-16s to Taiwan during the presidential election campaign (*People's Daily* 10 Oct. 1992). In subsequent years, Chinese commentators added two more arguments for the China threat theory: that it was designed to whip up concern about, and thus block, China's economic development; and that it was an attempt to undermine China's relations with states on its periphery so as to preserve U.S. hegemony in the region.[92] The frequency of references to "China threat theory" really took off after the Taiwan crisis in 1996, suggesting that this event was critical in convincing many Chinese analysts of the structural nature of the conflict with the United States (see Figure 2.8).[93]

This is not to say this cycle of referencing revisionism in the other has completely dominated discourse on both sides, but there is a symmetry. Interestingly, it is possible that the range of debate in China has been wider than in the United States in the late 1990s and first couple of years of the twenty-first century. Although China as a revisionist state has been almost axiomatic in the U.S. debate, even among so-called engagers, in China there is still a lively debate over whether U.S. long-term intentions are to weaken, divide, and "Westernize" the PRC, whether U.S. unipolarity is necessarily contrary to PRC interests, and whether the Bush administration will, ultimately, follow the path of all previous administrations since Nixon and shift toward a "centrist" view of having to develop a modus vivendi with China.[94] Nonetheless, this referencing revisionism has had the effect of mobilizing the "otherers" (the hard-liners, blue teams, and primacists) in both societies.

In addition to the apparently increasing conflictual interactivity or referentiality in discursive claims about the others' revisionism, there appears to be a similar trend in behavior. There are several things one should expect to see. First, one should see greater interactivity or endogeneity in the two sides' actions. Second, this interactivity should be more than simple reciprocity. Rather, one should expect, as in the discourse, a process where cooperative moves are in some sense discounted and where conflictual moves reciprocate both cooperative *and* conflictual actions. Third, one should expect to see this more malign reciprocation become faster over time, as both sides become more sensitive to the actions of the other. That is, the lag time between action and response should shorten on average as both sides are more alert in monitoring the other side's behavior.

Unfortunately, at the moment these features of interactivity are hard to show in any systematic fashion.[95] It appears to be true, however, that after the 1996 crisis and the 1999 embassy bombing the militaries on both sides stepped up their planning and war gaming for potential conflict with the other. As a result, the U.S. relationship

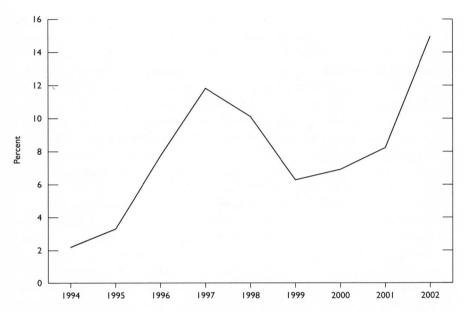

FIGURE 2.8 Articles Mentioning "China Threat Theory" (*Zhongguo weixie lun*) in the Text as Percentage of All International Relations Articles, 1994–2002

SOURCE: *China Academic Journals Database*, 1994–2002. China National Knowledge Infrastructure, an online service provided by East View Online Services, Minneapolis.

with Taiwan has evolved into a quasi-alliance as the two militaries explore everything from doctrine and operations to interoperability and satellite downlinks.[96] The pretense that U.S.-ROC relations are unofficial, maintained since 1979 by temporarily seconding State Department and Department of Defense officials to the unofficial American Institute in Taiwan (AIT), is fraying. For example, the United States will allow government officials to retain their official status while they serve in the AIT. The recent *Quadrennial Defense Review* (QDR) is perhaps the clearest statement that the U.S. military believes rising Chinese power is the major long-term military challenge to U.S. power (Department of Defense 2001).[97] On the Chinese side, internal-circulation publications on PLA operational doctrine mostly seem to posit— without saying so directly—that the main military adversary the PLA needs to plan against is the United States.[98]

Some cooperative actions are viewed as variants of noncooperative behavior. There is often a skepticism on the Chinese side about even relatively benign U.S. overtures. A concrete example of how Chinese skepticism of U.S. motives has led to a fundamental misperception is the reaction to the proposal of Admiral Blair, commander in chief, U.S. Pacific Command (CINCPAC), for setting up a security community in

East Asia. The proposal comes directly from readings in constructivist arguments about how security communities emerge such that members come to accept the impossibility of violence in interstate relations, ideas that were promoted by one of Blair's advisors, John Hanley. Such a proposal and the philosophical foundations for it are in a certain degree of tension with the realpolitik ideology of the Bush administration and U.S. hard-liners on China policy. Yet one Chinese analyst promptly took this proposal and called it part of more malign U.S. policy to deal with a rising China.[99] On the U.S. side, China's multilateral diplomacy in the ASEAN Region Forum and in various other security dialogues is almost uniformly viewed as directed at undermining U.S. alliances and U.S. power in the region, as is China's new interest in regional economic integration in the form of the ASEAN+3.[100]

The timing and substance of much of this interactive discourse and behavior is consistent with the argument that the Taiwan crisis of 1996 had a galvanizing effect on hard-liner opinion on both sides. The crisis was a product of a Chinese military response to Taiwanese efforts to establish a more independent identity and stature in international politics. In response to a high-profile visit by then-president Lee Teng-hui to the United States in the summer of 1995, China ran a series of large-scale military exercises and missile tests in late 1995 and early 1996 to signal to the ROC and the United States that the Taiwan issue was still one of war and peace, and to signal to Taiwanese voters prior to the presidential election in March 1996 that there would be a cost to pay for supporting proindependence politicians. China's coercive diplomacy in this regard increased regional ambivalence about the long-term intentions of a rising and possibly revisionist China. Although China-threat arguments existed before the Taiwan crisis of 1996, Chinese actions crystallized and mobilized a range of opinion within the United States and Japan in particular, alerting even those who supported engagement to the possibility that U.S. commitments to Taiwan would require the United States to eventually fight Chinese forces. During the latter half of the Clinton administration, the U.S. Department of Defense in particular initially pressed for closer military coordination with the ROC—including more transfers of hardware (arms sales) and software (doctrinal and planning exchanges)—because it believed it better to understand and control Taiwanese military responses to PRC military pressure (Goldstein and Schriver 2001). Later, under the Bush administration, this coordination has been pushed not only by this calculation, but also by an ideological affinity with the ROC, by astute Taiwanese lobbying among in Congress, and by concerns in the primacist wing of the Republican Party about the Chinese challenge to American power in the region.

This worry about the malevolence of China's intentions in the region translated into concrete military-political steps to hedge against Chinese power. Although the U.S.-Japan treaty revision guidelines were initially conceived in the early 1990s to prevent Japanese defection in a Korean crisis, after the Taiwan crisis there is little doubt that China is one of the foci of the revisions. The military relationship with

Taiwan under the Bush administration has evolved into a quasi-alliance, surpassing the level of coordination reached under the Clinton administration. As a result, the credibility of U.S. alliance commitments elsewhere in Northeast Asia, in Washington's eyes, rests increasingly on its commitment to Taiwanese security.

In some cases, this worry about China's revisionism translates into concrete military-political steps to hedge against Chinese power. The Chinese leadership picks up these hedging signals and interprets them in malign ways (discounting the carrots while focusing on the sticks). The Clinton administration's engagement strategy, for instance, was sometimes termed a "soft-containment" strategy. An influential voice in the Bush administration has explicitly called for a mixed engagement/containment strategy, but he is basically at a loss as to how to reassure Beijing that engagement is not subterfuge or strategic deception (Khalilzad et al. 1999). So it is not surprising that a hedging strategy is viewed in Beijing as more sinister and less driven by uncertainty about Chinese power than its proponents in the United States claim.

We know this phenomenon well—it is a security dilemma, a cycle of growing distrust and malevolent interpretations of behaviors among more-or-less status quo oriented (and/or mildly opportunistic) actors that then leads to reactions that encourage these interpretations of intentions and capabilities. Thus it may well be that China's diplomacy is in some objective sense more assertive and decreasingly confident that the current distribution of power and influence in East Asia serves Chinese interests as defined in Beijing. But a powerful reason for this changing estimate of the value of the status quo in the last few years is the perception that other states are becoming more assertive in challenging what the Chinese leaders believe are their legitimate interests. The long-term value of cooperation and/or restraint for China appears to be uncertain because of perception of the behavior of others (for instance, the U.S. violation of its 1982 arms sales commitments to Taiwan; the U.S.-Japan alliance taking on roles in defense of Taiwan; national missile defense [NMD] designed to undermine China's deterrent, and so on). However, the U.S. violation of its 1982 commitments, and the growing China focus of U.S. strategic policy in East Asia is, in part, a function of China's politico-military efforts to constrain U.S. intervention in a Taiwan crisis. And so on.

The presence of security dilemma dynamics does not mean that conflicts of interest do not exist. But security dilemma dynamics do mean that the severity and "zero-sum-ness" of conflicts of interest are variable, and are determined to a large degree by the language of diplomacy across states. That is, conflicts that may have been viewed as negotiable at time t are seen as nonnegotiable at time $t+1$ because of inflammatory rhetoric. What kind of rhetoric will have this kind of effect? "Identity" blaming, language that generalizes about the nature of the "other side" and about one's own side, where the other is solely responsible, and morally so, for conflicts. That is, "the Chinese" are like X, "we" are like Y, where X is a quality or attribute that carries a great deal of moral opprobrium, and Y is a quality or attribute that carries great moral value. There is interesting evidence, for example, that "real" interethnic conflicts in U.S. neighborhoods are accentuated because of perceptions that others are blaming one's own in-group for the problems. Blame rhetoric, in other words, has an independent and destructive effect on intergroup relations, regardless of the nature of the "real" conflict of interests at stake (Romer et al. 1997). A striking feature of the 2003 U.S.-China Economic and Security Review Commission report is this kind of generalized identity language, where "China" is sharply "othered," and where stark, generalized (often Orientalizing) differences between the way the "Chinese" think and the way the "United States" (sometimes "the West") thinks about strategy and global order are presented as truths about each side. Chinese official rhetoric also routinely reverts to overly generalized (Occidentalizing) characterizations of "the West" and its aggressive intentions vis-à-vis China and its culturally rooted peaceful orientation. This convergence in rhetorical type and polarization in rhetorical content needs to be watched carefully. As it moves to extreme levels on both sides it may serve as an early-warning indicator that the leaderships in both countries have given up searching for cooperative solutions to conflicts of interest. But as it moves to extremes it may also have a more important impact in framing definitions of interest and threat.

If indeed security dilemma dynamics explain the evolution both of China's level of dissatisfaction *and* of regional perceptions of China's revisionist goals, then Joseph Nye's famous statement about the self-fulfilling nature of the "China threat" is basically correct.[101] Similarly, so is the statement by Beijing University scholars Ye Zicheng and Feng Yin: "If China only looks at the actions of anti-China forces in the United States, and views every U.S. move as an adversarial one and consequently adopts tit-for-tat methods, then the likelihood that China and the United States will mutually turn into enemies increases dramatically" (Ye and Feng 2002). This kind of argument has had less appeal among both the more traditionally realpolitik and the overtly primacist schools in U.S. foreign policy because it requires policy makers to accept that definitions of interest are dynamic, and because it implies a degree of shared responsibility for the deterioration of relationships. Similarly, security dilemma arguments rarely have had appeal inside China because they require a recognition that China's own behavior has been counterproductive and has undermined its own security.[102] Thus Chinese and U.S. perceptions feed security dilemma dynamics precisely because leaders on both sides tend to ignore or downplay the existence of these dynamics.[103]

A security dilemma explanation links the more empirically accurate end of the first explanation—that as best as we can observe in East Asia China's strongly revisionist goals are primarily limited to Taiwan—with the second explanation—that domestically driven political changes in some key regional players have reduced the perceived degree of shared interests with China. The responses to Chinese power have reinforced two worrisome elements in Chinese diplomacy in the region: perceptions that the United States and its allies and friends present a more fundamental challenge to Chinese interests than was thought early in the 1990s; and perceptions that there may be a limited time frame or window of opportunity to prevent worst-case outcomes on issues that matter—in particular the Taiwan issue.[104]

Conclusion

This chapter has argued that in most respects Chinese diplomacy is more accepting of extant international institutions, international norms (such as they are), and U.S. dominance of the international and regional power structure than at any time since 1949. The most obvious and dangerous exception to this status–quo–ization of Chinese diplomacy is the Taiwan issue. Here China reserves the right to use force to change the political and military "facts on the ground" in an effort to defend its symbolic claim to "name" the island of Taiwan. In an effort to stake this claim Chinese leaders have taken military measures that have raised doubts outside of China about the overall status quo orientation of Chinese power in the region. These doubts have been magnified by changes in political ideologies and definitions of interests in some key capitals—Washington, Tokyo, and Taipei in particular.[105] Their responses, in turn, have magnified doubts in Beijing that these three other players will accept China's self-perceived legitimate interests on questions of sovereignty and territorial integrity. The militarization of security interactions among these four players, this mutual construction of adversarial images, is best explained by security dilemma theory, not by some simplistic characterization of Chinese revisionism or American hegemonism.

The limited U.S.-Chinese counterterrorism cooperation after September 11 has not changed these dynamics much. The tenor of Sino-U.S. relations improved somewhat after 9/11 as Chinese leaders realized that both countries shared an interest in defending sovereign states against violent nonsovereign state actors. There is, according to press reports, some limited sharing of intelligence. In addition Chinese leaders were helpfully low-keyed about Japan's unprecedented decision to send a small naval force to assist the United States in the Arabian Sea. The United States and China share an interest in seeing a multiethnic, more or less secular, Afghanistan. China and the United States also have every interest in seeing Pakistan survive as a unified, moderate Islamic state. There has been relatively close coordination recently in trying to convince the DPRK to abandon its nuclear weapons program.[106]

But precisely because so much of the U.S. perception of other states' level of cooperativeness will be viewed through the 9/11 lens (for us or against us), the potential for speeding up security dilemma dynamics, perhaps even for transitioning China's interests into more overtly revisionist ones, is there. If the United States allows states to choose from a wide menu of actions in support of the war against terrorism, then China can offer intelligence or assistance in tracking the terrorists' financial networks. These will be less demanding tests of China's cooperation. A narrow menu of choice will be a tougher test, one that makes it more likely that China may "fail." In light of the ongoing debate over the nature of Chinese power, a failure will have added weight in determining that China is a fundamentally revi-sionist state. A Chinese "failure" will also contrast sharply with any Taiwanese sup-port for the U.S. war on terrorism, however symbolic that support may be.

Even though it does not appear to be asking for any explicit or short-term quid pro quo for cooperation thus far, the Chinese leadership has to expect that the United States should become more sympathetic to China's "legitimate" interests. Yet the U.S. policies that worry the Chinese leadership most—arms sales to Taiwan, closer U.S.-Taiwan political and military relations, National Missile Defense, the China-directed elements of U.S. bilateral alliances in Asia, among others—are issues for which there is strong support in Congress and the Pentagon. Domestic critics of any strategy of cooperation with the United States will certainly be looking for, even while not ex-pecting, U.S. concessions on these issues. The absence of any substantial U.S. overtures will be used as evidence of the failure of a conciliatory approach to U.S. power.

This leads to my next point. It should be noted that the decline in revisionist in-terests in China does not mean their elimination nor the impossibility of their reap-pearance. For China, "globalization"—a headlong, relatively unregulated, rush for short-term benefits under the rubric of the open door policy—has created vast in-come discrepancies. These can be sustained with relatively high rates of absolute growth across socioeconomic groups. But it is not hard to imagine social unrest lead-ing to political preferences that are at odds with status quo interest in the current economic "division of labor" within China and between China and other states. China moved from being a revolutionary "revisionist" state to a "status quo" one in forty-odd years. It is not implausible that a more fundamental "revisionism" might emerge from disillusionment with marketization, or from problems of internal seces-sion, or from the domestic effects of Taiwan's gradual reconstruction as a U.S. ally in the containment of China. Indeed, because of security dilemma dynamics and the negative effects of unrestrained marketization, in retrospect we may see the 1980s and 1990s as a period of relative Chinese "status quo–ness," sandwiched by Maoist revi-sionism and some post-Jiang quasi-fascism.

This leads me to my final point. That security dilemma arguments may best char-acterize the changing nature of the interaction between China, the United States, Japan, and Taiwan is not a theoretical breakthrough. In the policy and punditry worlds, however, this *is* a controversial argument because of the pervasiveness of at-tribution errors in in-group worldviews. To argue in the policy world for a security dilemma explanation is to argue that all actors are more or less status quo oriented or at least would prefer to minimize conflict in the relationship, and that there is at least some moral equivalence in the actions that promote tensions. This argument is po-litically unacceptable in the U.S. government (even as, ironically, more and more peo-ple are making it tentatively in the PRC).[107]

In the theory world, the dynamics of security dilemmas are left fairly under-theorized. It is assumed that they can be produced by two basic "facts"—states want to maximize their security, and states operate under conditions of uncertainty.

But, in fact, these two assumptions are loaded theoretically, and empirically often wrong. They are theoretically loaded because, as Glaser and Wendt have pointed out from two very different perspectives, there is nothing natural about a security dilemma. For Glaser it requires rational security maximizing actors to believe that it is cheaper to achieve security and to reduce uncertainty through an open-ended arms buildup rather than through the exploration of a codifiable modus vivendi. Why they would believe this—why state leaders would believe that security is more certain in an arms buildup than in the search for ways to institutionalize the status quo—when history suggests that often this belief is empirically wrong, speaks to the question of why bad lessons are relearned by rational actors in IR. That is, why are realpolitik lessons of various stripes so persistent when it is clear that only rarely does a truly revisionist state come along? For Wendt a security dilemma requires the prior construction of a Hobbesian or a Lockean culture of anarchy. Moreover, its dynamic is such that it can create revisionist actors where there once were none. Standard security dilemma theory assumes that the goals, desires, and level of satisfaction of actors do not change much. Scholars speak of security dilemmas of status quo states (a stag hunt gone bad) or security dilemmas of opportunist states (a prisoner's dilemma). They do not tend to talk about security dilemmas where the interaction shifts from stag hunt interests to prisoner's dilemma interests or worse, deadlock interests (in the latter case, the conflict is no longer a security dilemma). We know that shifts can go in the other direction, as experiments in iterated prisoner's dilemma play have shown (Alker 1996).

Thus the fact of a security dilemma, and the possibility of an intensifying one, in Sino-U.S. relations requires an explanation, and it does not come naturally from assumptions of fixed state interests and the inherent uncertainty of anarchy. This particular security dilemma—its timing, and the issues that are most salient in propelling it forward—have a lot to do with Taiwan's status in modern Chinese nationalism, domestic developments in Taiwan, and Taiwan's place in Sino-U.S. interactions over the last fifty years. These are ideational and historical factors that various stripes of realism and an exclusively domestic-politics-focused theorizing do not have much room for. We need, then, to theorize about the kinds of issues that are salient in security dilemmas. In particular, does variation in these issues explain variation in the intensity of a security dilemma? And to what degree does the social history of a security dilemma actually change interests in a way that would not have happened absent the security dilemma? One might expect the literature on enduring rivalries to help here. But it does not since it too posits a fixed-ness in state interests through the entire history of the rivalry. This is odd, since presumably one of the reasons for an *enduring* rivalry is the construction over time of images of self and other (hence definitions of the interests of self and others) that are dynamic, not static. The China case

suggests that the degree of dissatisfaction may be in flux and may be related to the issue at the heart of this particular dilemma.

This leads to an interesting implication for security dilemma theorizing. I think international relations theory typically considers a security dilemma as falling within a
defensive realist ontology—it is, according to this kind of realism, a real phenomenon
of uncertainty under anarchy when states are security seekers. Thus, security dilemmas
are a reason for the reproduction of realpolitik practice, and this is why realists can be
confidently ahistorical and a-cultural in their claims about realpolitik practice. Anarchy plus (more or less) status quo states creates security dilemmas. Other realisms (offensive) claim that the presence of revisionist or status quo states (the balance of interests) is the source of realpolitik practice—revisionists pursue realpolitik and status quo
states have no rational choice but to respond with realpolitik practice.[108] But the
emerging U.S.-Chinese security dilemma suggests something a little different, a synthesis of these two realisms that only a socialization perspective can understand—
namely, that security dilemmas can change state interests in "hard realpolitik" directions. One needs to think a bit more endogenously. That is, security dilemmas create
features of a Hobbesian anarchy. Security dilemmas may be a critical (though not the
only source—ideology is clearly another) in creating some kinds of non–status quo
states. These states, in turn, accentuate or sharpen the features of Hobbesian anarchy.

Even Robert Jervis, the most perceptive analyst of security dilemmas, strongly
implies that in security dilemmas interests remain fixed. There is no security dilemma
when one state is so dissatisfied with the status quo that it is willing to risk survival
to change it (an aggressor state). But he does not suggest that security dilemmas can
in fact create these kinds of actors. It is necessary to view security dilemmas as social
interactions—socializing experiences—in order to understand this change in fundamental interests. Enduring rivalries are enduring because the security dilemma features in the early interaction of these actors creates mutual dissatisfaction with the
status quo, hence a willingness to take greater risks in trying to eliminate the other
rival. Or put differently, the level of concessions required to reassure become so great
that no side is willing to make them.

Charles Glaser hints at the possibility of security dilemmas creating more revisionist states out of less revisionist ones through a process of increasing the adversary's
"interest in expansion." This interest in turn is a function of a growing perception
that the first state is not a status quo state, but a revisionist (or greedy) state. This perception can be formed by particular kinds of military buildups by the first state, or by
a self-perception of oneself as clearly status quo oriented. Thus the other side's
buildup can only be aggressive, since one's own motives are so clearly not a threat to
the other side (Glaser 1997). This captures some of the dynamics in the U.S.-China
dilemma, but it does not capture the question of changed interests. True, U.S. and
Chinese decision makers, or important sectors of them, view the other as aggressive
because they view themselves as inherently peaceful or status quo oriented. But

adding to this dynamic is that the security dilemma may be leading to an ideational devaluation of the payoffs from status quo behavior in other areas in the relationship. In other words, there is a spillover effect.

The only major student of war in U.S. IR who conceptualizes security dilemmas as socializing processes is John Vasquez. But even Vasquez is ambivalent about whether security dilemmas change preferences of actors, or change the political power of actors with realpolitik preferences. He suggests the latter—that security dilemmas create domestic conditions that are not conducive to the victory of ideas for cooperative strategies. Hard-liners win out in the marketplace of ideas. He does not address the possibility that cooperators actually change their conceptualization of the adversary as well. There is evidence this may be happening in the U.S.-China case. Engagers in the United States have not just been under attack from primacists for being soft on China. But due to this and Chinese behavior (for instance, in the EP-3 incident) some engagers are rethinking their conceptions of Chinese intentions. Many propose now with certainty that China wants to fundamentally alter the balance of power in the Asia-Pacific, yet they cling to the notion that engagement can perhaps constrain the pursuit of this goal. This creates considerable tension in their arguments and probably weakens their voices politically.

But there is nothing particularly inevitable—certainly nothing inevitable derived from anarchy per se—about security dilemmas. The U.S.-China security dilemma is in large measure a function of the Taiwan question. How can one best understand the salience of Taiwan in this security dilemma? As a function of specific and politically powerful claims about Chinese, Taiwanese, and American identity: The political forces in these three countries most active in supporting behavior that accentuates the security dilemma are Chinese nationalists with a bias toward military solutions, Taiwanese nationalists with a bias toward de jure independence instead of satisfaction with de facto independence, and American primacists who understand the world in power-transition terms.

This does not mean one should be overly optimistic about the ability of "agents" to "construct" more peaceful and stable Sino-U.S. relations. I try to avoid tea-leaf reading. But here I would agree with Aaron Friedberg's pessimistic conclusion about the future of relations despite the recent improved tenor in the post–9/11 world (Friedberg 2002). We disagree about the reasons for this pessimism, however. His have to do with the dominant ontology and epistemology that has helped create the trope of a rising, dissatisfied China—mentioned at the start of the chapter—namely, an ontology and epistemology that accepts that rising powers are inherently dissatisfied because the "rules of the game" (and the "distribution of power" that reinforce them) are set by dominant powers. My pessimism comes from the possibility that the level of dissatisfaction with the rules of the game (to the extent these exist and are identifiable) can be rooted in issues that are nonstructural, that have little to do with distributions of power or rules of the game per se, but have a lot to do with how the concept of "rising powers are inherently dissatisfied" itself becomes a lens through which these issues are analyzed.

In short, the China case suggests that security dilemmas can turn nonstructural conflicts into perceived structural ones: the socializing experience of security dilemmas consists of the amplification of threats and threat perceptions such that one side begins to only look for confirming evidence of the other's predisposition to threaten. The China-U.S. case suggests security dilemma theory needs to go more micro, to abandon unitary rational-actor assumptions, and look at the political, societal, and ideational implications of treating others as adversaries. By combining the notion of socialization and the possibility of endogenized changes in interests with the concept of a security dilemma, we come to a better understanding of the dynamics of Sino-U.S. relations in the post–Cold War era by problematizing the notion of a "rising" China's dissatisfaction with the "rules of the game."[109]

Notes

1. For one of the few public scholarly debates over the status quo–ness of Chinese diplomacy see the exchange between Xiang Lanxin (2001) and David Shambaugh (2001).

2. I take "eclectic theorizing" to mean, in part, the denaturalization of a phenomenon such that it turns into a problem to be analyzed or explained. In this case, I think it is fair to say that China as a dissatisfied power has become a naturalized trope in both the academic and pundit worlds. Denaturalizing it creates a puzzle—the topic of the chapter—and a potential characterization of the relationship between China and other major actors in the Asia-Pacific. On denaturalization as a part of eclectic theorizing see Katzenstein and Okawara (2001/02).

3. On "Fox Special Report with Brit Hume" (9 Apr. 2001, 18:45 ET).

4. William Kristol, one of the most prominent voices in the primacist wing, has used the term "neo-imperial" to describe its views.

5. For an effective summary see Zhang Biwu (2002).

6. For example, E. H. Carr (1940) mentions the term "status quo" state at least twelve times in his classic, *The Twenty Years Crisis, 1919–1939*, without providing a definition.

7. Morgenthau (1978: 46). See also his criteria for determining whether a state has an imperialist (aka revisionist) foreign policy (p. 74).

8. There is some tension between Morgenthau's definition and the one used by Organski and Kugler. The power transition definition sees the status quo partly in terms of intentions, not just capabilities. Does the rising power intend to or want to change the rules as its relative power increases? Morgenthau's definition emphasizes simply a change in the distribution of power (which is presumably followed by a change in the rules). For Morgenthau, any rising state is by definition a revisionist one insofar as it wants to increase its power and change the global distribution. For Organski and Kugler, only rising states that want to change the rules as the power distribution changes are non–status quo powers.

9. Emphasis mine. By Schweller's definition, China would not be a revisionist state if it used economic development as a way of increasing its political influence in the Asia-Pacific.

10. For a sophisticated summary of definitions of revisionism in international relations theory see Lyall (2001).

11. Kissinger (1957: 1–2) uses Nazi Germany to define a "revolutionary" (read revisionist) state—a state that is dissatisfied with international order. He does not outline generic indicators of what this dissatisfaction looks like. But inferring from this example, it would mean substantial dissatisfaction with low power, territorial control, economic losses in the current global economy, imposed restrictions on its relative power by institutions, and perhaps some vaguer notion of lack of respect or status.

12. Behavior is not necessarily a good indicator of intentions or preferences. But behavior that is, across different contexts, persistently and consistently similar to what one would expect if preferences were of a particular kind is one place to start, especially when analyzing a decision-making process that is inordinately opaque. There is good reason for assuming that participation in international cooperative institutions is likely a reflection of intention and motivation of the foreign policy decision makers rather than some unintended, or low preference, response to external constraints. Starting with realist assumptions, there is no obvious reason why a state would be forced by its weakness to join. It could simply remain outside, and still serve the interests of the powerful state or states that set up the institutions. Or it might join but in a perfunctory fashion, essentially hiding or acting passively once inside. It is unlikely that an avowedly revisionist state would join many of these institutions, given the likelihood that they would be dominated by status quo powers. More likely, states join institutions because of convergent interests with them or because of the domestic status and legitimacy acquired from joining. In other words, they join because they are motivated by their preferences to participate. In the Chinese case, there is fairly good evidence that the post-Mao Chinese leadership—reversing years of intention and practice—initially joined some of the main economic institutions because it believed these capitalist institutions, though dominated by the United States, served its interest by improving China's economic well-being and shoring up the legitimacy of the regime. In other words, there is no evidence that joining these institutions was (1) compelled by U.S. power, or (2) motivated by a desire to undermine capitalist institutions once inside. In short, the move into economic institutions in particular reflected the growing convergence of the Chinese leadership interests with the ideology and interests of these status quo institutions.

13. This indicator assumes, of course, that these norms and rules are obvious. As I will note, one analytic difficulty is that in some cases there is no plausible international community standard to follow. This complicates, but does not wholly undermine the endeavor to measure status quo-ness, however.

14. Zhang Biwu's (2002) important analysis of Chinese images of the United States is one of the few other studies to try to develop criteria for measuring the level of China's status quo orientation. It uses U.S. domestic and foreign policy behavior as a benchmark for the status quo and observes Chinese attitudes toward these benchmarks to determine how much distance exists between the United States and China. I find the use of the United States as the benchmark problematic because although U.S. power defines the polarity criteria, U.S. power and interests are not always coterminous with international norms and the normative purposes of international institutions. Thus the United States as a benchmark for the first three criteria becomes problematic.

15. This pattern is similar in the history of Chinese treaty accessions as well. For example, in the early 1970s, China had signed onto 10–20 percent of the international arms control agreements that it was eligible to join. By the mid-1990s, it had signed on to 80 percent of the treaties it was eligible to join. These data, in a sense, capture the willingness of China's leaders to participate in institutions.

Prior to 1971, the PRC was not in the UN, so it is unclear how one should code its memberships before this point. That is, even if China had wanted to join many international institutions it would have been excluded from doing so by insisting on the One China principle. However, technically one could argue that this was a choice made by China's leaders, and thus the low level of participation prior to 1971 should be coded the result of a conscious policy choice. My thanks to Al Willner for making this point.

16. I used GDP/capita as a predictor for the number of IGO memberships for each state for which both sets of data were available, and entered these data into an OLS regression equation for the years listed in Figure 2.2. The R^2 ranged from 0.16 to 0.23 and all were statistically significant below the 0.01 level.

17. A state could in principle "hide" or isolate itself, and thereby not challenge the status quo. But if it is a potentially powerful or important state on some issue of regional or global importance (for example, it is a major transboundary polluter, or a major source of some key economic good or a large failed state whose very failure destabilizes its neighbors), then hiding may in fact undermine the purposes of status quo institutions.

18. Under the Bush administration's conservative unilateral impulses, U.S. and Chinese policies were more convergent in defense of a traditional definition of sovereignty than was the case for most of the 1990s.

19. For the full report see GAO (2002).

20. As of 1998, suppliers of nuclear-related technology to Iran include companies from such countries as Argentina, Belgium, France, Germany, Italy, Switzerland, the U.K. and the United States as well as China and Russia. See Koch and Wolf (1998). One could argue in the Chinese case that given the authoritarian nature of the regime the government could, if it had its normative and budgetary priorities right, crack down on these shipments. In contrast, for Western status quo states these suppliers tend to be hard-to-monitor private companies.

21. On conditional norms of national self-determination see Freeman (1998) and "Competing Claims" (2000). See also the "Declaration on the Granting of Independence" (1961). This document places self-determination in the context of anticolonialism. This context has evolved over time to open the possibility of self-determination to peoples who are subject to systematic discrimination based on such things as race, creed, and ethnicity. It is unclear, however, how this condition is to be determined, particularly in nondemocracies where everyone suffers from political discrimination, and in the China/Taiwan case where Taiwan is not subject to this discrimination in the first place. See Epps (1998).

22. For an analysis of the problems in applying international norms of self-determination to Taiwan see Tzou (1992: 70–85).

23. In 1999, 55 percent of states scored a 5 or more on the Polity IV index for overall level of democratic institutions. Sixty-four scored 1 or more on this index. The index runs from -10 (autocracy) to 10 (democracy).

24. Indeed, Thomas Weiss (2001: 423–24) calls for banishing the term "international community" on the grounds of its intellectual vacuousness.

25. On how decision rules can protect the ideology of an institution see Downs, Rocke, and Barsoom (1998).

26. Here I use the index of similarity developed by Kurt Signorino and Jeff Ritter (1999). The S index is basically a spatial model measuring the distance between country A and B on one or more policy dimensions, and is a more accurate indicator of congruence in roll call voting than the traditionally used tau B. I am grateful to Erik Gartzke for providing his similarity (Affinity) index data set. Period one (1974–78) starts with the beginning of the data set and goes through to the end of the Maoist era. Period two (1979–88) runs from the start of the

Dengist reforms through to just prior to June 4 crackdown. Period three (1989–96) runs from Tiananmen through to the end of the data period.

27. Using a different measure of congruence in UNGA voting on resolutions of importance to the United States, Erik Voeten (2002) finds that from 1991 to 2001 there is virtually *no change* in the "distance" between the United States and China on these resolutions. China's distance is the largest of all the other major powers, but over the past decade there has been an *increase* in the voting distance/incongruence between the United States and other status quo states such as France and Britain. These data suggest that relatively speaking China and the United States demonstrate quite substantial conflicts of voting interest in the UNGA, but that there has been a trend toward convergence in Chinese and other major power positions on these issues. That is, all other majors are distancing themselves from the United States.

28. The U.S. Department of Defense's annual Report to Congress Pursuant to the FY2000 National Defense Authorization Act on Chinese military power states that "China also wants to become the preeminent Asian power by generating enough 'strength' so that no major action will be taken by any other international actor in Asia without first considering Chinese interests. . . . China seeks to become the preeminent power among regional states in East Asia" (Department of Defense 2001). This is taken to be axiomatic by many commentators. See Friedberg (2000) and Wortzel (1998: 16).

29. There are two broad clusters of arguments that one could invoke to explain this hypothesized revisionism and proponents of this characterization of Chinese goals will often invoke all of them. The first is domestic political change arguments. Here there are three subarguments: The CCP regime faces legitimacy problems and has been willing to play the nationalist card domestically, including appeals to historical notions of Chinese greatness in the region. Relatedly, nationalist messages are combined with militaristic and mercantilist conceptions of how to achieve security, giving relatively more influence in the policy process to hard realpolitik voices. Finally, the CCP leadership has historically been committed to reasserting regional hegemony but until this point has lacked the capabilities to do so. Economic growth over the past twenty years is creating the resources for a more assertive foreign policy. The second cluster would focus on international structural changes. In particular, the collapse of Soviet power and emergence of the United States as hegemon directly threatens Chinese security. Thus China's leaders, security-maximizing rational actors, are balancing against U.S. power as neorealist theory suggests they ought to.

30. This is a separate question from whether or not Chinese leaders and elites would like to see China as a great power with interests and influence beyond its immediate boundaries. Proponents of hard realpolitik in Chinese foreign policy undeniably see the behavior of other major powers as giving China a mandate to develop global interests and enforce these, when necessary, with military power. Many Russian and French citizens wish the same for their own countries. In the absence of a clear concept of the kinds of institutions, norms, regimes, actors, and redistributions of territory and power that a state's leaders believe ought to occur, this kind of hope is not particularly strong evidence of proactively revisionist preferences. Moreover, it is unclear how widespread these sentiments are.

31. On the importance of preventing Taiwan's independence see Christensen (2001a) and Finklestein (2000: 5–6).

32. As one study put it, China's policy of "putting aside differences and jointly developing" the area (*gezhi zhengyi gongtong kaifa*) is a "stratagem not a goal" (Lu 1996: 311). For an argument in favor of diplomacy over military force see Zhang and Wu (1996: 267). Canadian diplomats have noted that privately specialists in regional security in the Chinese Ministry of

Foreign Affairs have acknowledged that the existence of the ASEAN Regional Forum (ARF) and other multilateral relationships with states in the region have reduced the probability that China might use force to resolve its claims. (Interview with Canadian diplomat involved in regional security dialogues, Oct. 1998).

33. For a pithy critique of this and other analogies to describe a rising China see Goldstein (2001b: 862). Moreover, "revisionist" Wilhelmine Germany spent its first decade trying to balance *with* England—the alleged status quo actor—not *against* it.

34. Often analysts in the United States will point to PLA writings as evidence of revisionist claims, for example, evidence of the use of preemption, power projection, and offensive operations, the desire for a blue water navy, and so on. There is no doubt these concepts are increasingly informing how the Chinese military prefers to fight military conflicts should it be given the political go-ahead. However, inferring a desire for political and diplomatic dominance from a military operational claim is problematic. Military operations and politico-strategic decision making by civilian leaders are not the same thing. No one would infer the foreign policy preferences of the U.S. president or the executive branch solely from an analysis of the DoD's Joint Vision 2020 or the doctrinal manuals of different service branches. Of course, military operational requirements, once established, can spill over into, and constrain, diplomatic commitments (U.S. relations with Saudi Arabia are a case in point). But in this regard, currently the best evidence for a conscious design to pursue regional hegemony does not come from the capabilities and operational doctrine being developed by the PLA. Rather the evidence suggests that the PLA appears to hope to keep the U.S. Navy and Air Force far enough away from the Chinese coastline such that the U.S. cruise missile and long-range strike advantage is neutralized; realistically this is likely to be along the boundaries of the so-called first island chain (Japan, Ryukyus, Taiwan, Philippines). Hence the lower-than-expected interest in logistics support and long-range power projection (for example, aircraft carriers) and long-range amphibious landing capabilities. Others argue that the PLA envisions relying less on the navy to keep U.S. naval power at bay in the region than on long-range missiles (both cruise and ballistic). These capabilities are not the kind that necessarily allow for the creation of a Chinese "lake" in East Asia. See the summary of a C.N.A. conference on PLA naval strategy in (Allen 2001: 6). At the moment they are primarily designed to give the political leadership credible options for compelling a unification outcome acceptable to the PRC, probably sometime in the 2005–10 timeframe.

35. Wang Jisi (1997: 1) traces it back to Mao Zedong's concept in the 1940s of an intermediate zone between the USSR and the United States.

36. For a thorough summary of this discourse see Pillsbury (2000: 3–61).

37. A well-known conservative Chinese strategist, a major and early proponent of the multipolarity concept, also impressed upon me once that he personally supported a U.S.-China alliance against Japan, a position that is in considerable tension with the argument that Japan should become a separate pole in a multipolar world (author conversation 1996). This points up an important methodological point, made by Berger and Luckman (1966: 13), that the Chinese foreign policy field has tended to miss—namely, that in understanding the "deep structure" of collective understandings and desires, official worldviews may be less insightful than the "commonsense ideas" that come out in contextualized questioning of these worldviews. Simply put, one has to engage interlocutors in discussion about real-world scenarios and the choices they believe they would face under those conditions.

38. For a subtle but devastating critique of his own leadership's tendency to view every era in IR as a "transitional period" with little explication of the content of these transitions see Wang (1998: 302).

39. Those who prefer a more proactive anti-American balancing strategy are, not surprisingly, leery of China's growing dependence on global capital and markets. Thus they are also critical of China's decision to enter the WTO. Since this is Chinese policy, however, this suggests that the hard balancers are not the dominant voices at the moment in the foreign policy decision-making process. I will come to this question of balancing in more detail in a moment.

40. See, for instance, Zhang Yunling's analysis of the strength of American unipolarity (2000a: 24–30). He implies that even if one refers to the current system as "one superpower and many major powers" (*yi chao duo qiang*) as a somewhat more politically correct way of referring to U.S. unipolarity, of these "many major powers" a number of them are close American allies, part of American power (p. 30).

41. See Wang Jianwei's (1999) study of Chinese elite attitudes in the early 1990s. In the 1998 Beijing Area Study randomly sampled poll of about 700 Beijing city residents, those who believed that U.S. power would increase over the next ten years held far higher levels of amity toward the United States than those who believed that U.S. influence would decline (ANOVA $F=29.01$ $p=0.00$). The same pattern holds in attitudes toward China's influence over the next ten years. Those who believed it would increase had a lower level of amity toward the United States than those who believed China's influence would remain the same or decline (ANOVA $F=3.05$ $p=0.048$). More interesting is that the small number of respondents who believed that U.S. power would strengthen while China's would not also held extraordinarily above-average levels of amity toward the United States (75 degrees on a 100 degree feeling thermometer versus the sample average of 63 degrees). These findings would suggest that a strongly pro-American posture is associated with a descriptive and normative preference for increased U.S. power.

42. Zhang Yunling (2000a: 31) notes that where potential balancers against U.S. power are U.S. allies, one should not overestimate the emergence of a more powerful Europe, for instance, as a constraint on U.S. power. Rather, under these conditions the two major constraints on U.S. power are markets and international organizations. Another moderate analyst, Shen Biru (1999: 383), argued even at the height of fears of U.S. interventionism during the Kosovo war that building multipolarity and opposing U.S. unipolarity cannot be accomplished through traditional great power conflict, but through the construction of a new world order.

43. See, for instance, the critique of one "new thinker's" (Shi Yinhong) views by one of the more prominent nationalist intellectuals, Wang Xiaodong (1999: 3–20).

44. See Yan Xuetong's (1999a: 349–55) vision of a multipolar world in 15–20 years where the five principles of peaceful coexistence reign, where China is a more powerful defender of developing world interests (why China would still be a developing country after its rise as a pole is unclear), and where "Eastern" values of collective and national interest are stronger relative to "Western" values of the individual as more important than the state or group.

45. This diversity of views is a point made by Michael Pillsbury (2000), but one that is lost on many of the users of his research in Washington.

46. This was a characterization that China's "new thinkers"—those less worried about American unipolarity because China benefited from some of the institutions created by U.S. power—were happy to live with. Interview with senior think-tank specialist (Beijing, Dec. 1998).

47. See Deng Yong's analysis of China's debate over multipolarity. Deng aptly describes the normative preferences of the Chinese leadership as "China's utopian multipolar world" (2001: 344). For an insightful assessment of the estimates of China's relative weakness vis-à-vis the United States, and the cautiousness this has induced in Chinese diplomacy in the region, see Finklestein (2001).

48. Qian Qichen (2000), the former minister of foreign affairs and still a key figure in for-

eign policy making, recently listed some of the key issues in international relations research for China. First on the list was the "information society." Second was the question of globalization. Multipolarity was not among the topics.

49. For one of the few secondary analyses of the concept of globalization in China see Moore (2000).

50. Appropriately, then, some Chinese analysts argue that traditional realist theory is no longer as useful for understanding international politics as liberal and institutional theory. See, for instance, Wang Xueyu (2000: 52).

51. This point was missed by the recently released U.S.-China Economic and Security Review Commission report. The report seemed to take the multipolarity concept as prima facie evidence of a consensus in China that U.S. unipolar power was on the wane. As is clear from more recent debates over multipolarity in China, the report's conclusion was out of date before it came out. See USCC (2002).

52. Another important general goal for the Chinese military is to protect China's "economic center of gravity" as this has shifted from the hinterland in the Maoist and early Deng periods to the coastal areas. The capabilities useful for this purpose are similar to those required to keep the U.S. military away from the Chinese coast in the event of a war over Taiwan. See Finkelstein (2000: 17–18).

53. This is a point made, ironically, by those who believe that the U.S. NMD is not provocative to the PRC because, due to these various factors, China is likely to build up its nuclear forces regardless of U.S. actions. See Payne (2001).

54. For an insightful study of the motives for and limits on Sino-Russian strategic cooperation, see Lukin (2001).

55. For a more recent statement of this hope from one of the leading realpolitik analysts in China, see Yan Xuetong (1997: 288). Yan calls for the gradual reduction in foreign forces in the region, to be replaced by commitments of regional actors not to join alliances aimed at third parties, and for an extensive multilateral structure that includes early warning mechanisms, increased military transparency, and a proactive preventive diplomacy committee, among other measures.

56. Minor diplomatic offensives in places such as the ARF have been aimed at constraining U.S. bilateral alliance activity. These have been unsuccessful, however, in undermining these alliances in the eyes of other states in the region. One such effort in 1997—to get the ARF to agree to voluntarily invite observers to joint military exercises (which the United States and its allies conduct, and which China does not)—reflected PLA preferences more than MoFA preferences, and ran into heavy criticism from other ARF delegations. The PRC ultimately shelved the proposal (Interviews with various Chinese, Canadian, and American diplomats, analysts, and/or military officers 1996, 1997, 1998).

57. This does not exclude the likelihood, of course, that in the lead-up to an imminent war with the United States over Taiwan, China will threaten Japan with military retaliation for its intervention on the U.S. side. Some in the PLA contend that it would be a political mistake to attack U.S. targets in Japan (Comments to author by senior PLA officer, Nov. 2000).

58. For sophisticated analyses of Chinese interests on the Korean Peninsula, see Tang (1999) and Goldstein (2002).

59. To the extent that the DPRK used *potential*, as opposed to deployed, WMD capabilities as a tool for extracting economic and political benefits from the ROK, the United States, and Japan, it is not entirely clear that at least some DPRK extortion was contrary to Beijing's interests in the past. Since early 2003, however, the Chinese government believes that nu-

clearization could lead to some of China's worst security nightmares—war on the peninsula and/or the nuclearization of Japan.

60. On China's relatively relaxed view of the U.S.-ROK alliance, see Yu (1999: 10–11).

61. Even some PLA analysts imply that the United States intends to use the alliance both to control Japanese power and to deal with China and Russian power. See AMS (2000: 81).

62. Beijing wants a statement excluding Taiwan from the scope of the U.S.-Japan treaty revisions (AMS 2000: 83).

63. As Christensen (2001b: 30) points out, this contingent view of the alliance is consistent with the Chinese practical preference that Japan not emerge as an independent pole in a future multipolar world.

64. There is actually a very subtle, moderate, security-dilemma–sensitive argument for increasing the relative importance of regional multilateral institutions, an argument that is not simply anti-American or Taiwan focused. That is: because the relative power shift between a rising China and a stagnating Japan will be so dramatic, China has an interest in reassuring Japan. The U.S. alliance, of course, could do this, but at China's expense. Thus the alternative is a credible multilateral institution that channels Chinese power in ways that reassure Japan. For the outlines of this kind of argument, see Tang and Zhou (2001).

65. See, for example, the opinion piece written by a PLA officer prominent in regional security policy, Sr. Col. Zhu Chenghu from the National Defense University (Zhu 1999). See also Feng (2000: 12). On the unconstructive *interactivity* in the relationship, see Feng (2000: 15) and Jin (2000b: 207).

66. Normally fairly realpolitik on regional security issues, Yan Xuetong does not list Japan among the region's major military powers (China, the United States, Russia). See Yan (1999b: 39).

67. For an interesting analysis of China's Japan specialists and their arguments, see He Yinan (1998). He's analysis is somewhat dated, ending in 1997, just as Chinese concerns about Japan's role in Taiwan scenarios began to rise. Still the arguments she notes in this literature about the potential constraints on Japanese militarism still persist among those who recommend a less emotion-laden diplomacy toward Japan.

68. For example, some PLA analysts are worried that Japanese public opinion is no longer a constraint on Japanese military expansion. See Yang (2001). Others want to retaliate for Japan's alleged lack of contrition on historical issues by shifting economic linkages away from Japan and toward Europe and the United States. See Feng Zhaokui's critique of this view (2000: 12).

69. According to the Beijing Area Study, a randomly sampled survey of about 700 Beijing residents conducted by the Research Center on Contemporary China at Peking University, the mean temperature towards Japan on a 100 degree feeling thermometer has dropped from 51 degrees in 1998 to 36 degrees in 2001. The mean level of warlikeness on a 1–7 point peaceful-to-warlike scale attributed to the Japanese people in 2001 was 4.2, to Americans 3.7, and to Chinese people, 1.5. For a summary of a study of Chinese history textbooks and their images of Japan, see Rozman (2002a: 119–20).

70. I am grateful to Robert Kapp of the U.S.-China Business Council for providing these data.

71. That some realist theorists might respond with the argument that Chinese leaders are taking a long-term view of their balancing strategy—supporting Japanese economic revival for the economic benefits to long-term Chinese power—instead of a short-run view of the strategic benefits of a weak Japanese economy only underscores the indeterminacy of mainstream realist theory.

72. Some concrete policy advice—admittedly from one of the "new thinkers" in the in-

ternational politics analysis community—for promoting multipolarity includes: diversifying China's economic interdependence to include Europe, but doing so in a way that does not damage economic relations with the United States and Japan; improving relations with a diverse range of (status quo) influential middle powers such as Australia, Brazil, Turkey, and Egypt; joining a strategic dialogue with the United States and Japan so as to pressure them to improve their transparency; becoming a more prominent voice in regional security issues; actively joining important multilateral institutions, including the G-8 so that China's voice is heard. See Wang Yizhou (1998). Wang is careful to note, however, that a more active and leading role in multilateral institutions in the Asia-Pacific region does not mean that China should oppose all multilateral activities in which the United States takes the lead or controls the process (Wang 1999b). These suggestions hardly constitute a radically destabilizing challenge to the global distribution of power. Rather they would fall under what Morgenthau might call "minor adjustments which leave intact the relative power positions of the nations concerned." These, he writes, are fully compatible with a policy of the status quo (1978: 46). Indeed Wang notes that China must convince the world that its call for multipolarity is not a simplistic opposition to the extant order. Rather China should only support multipolarization that is gradual and stabilizing.

73. The U.S. Department of Defense hedged in 1998 by claiming that "Although China has no plan to lead a faction or bloc of nations in directly challenging U.S. power its international political activities and certain of its economic and military policies are designed to achieve the same result" (Department of Defense 1998).

74. See, for instance, Christensen's (2001b) argument about a Chinese limited blockade strategy against Taiwan.

75. Japan would likely be committed to supporting U.S. operations in defense of Taiwan. The United States might also put pressure on Australia to participate in some form. The spillover effects would, of course, be affected by the scope (for instance, whether Taiwan and/or the United States would strike mainland targets), duration, and severity of a war.

76. Historically, in the Cold War-era for the United States the seamlessness of credible commitments to allies required a global military reach that, in turn, required political acquiescence and deference from a wide range of countries. The expansion of American power in the Cold War, therefore was to some extent a function of a conservative geopolitical goal of containment combined with offensive military requirements dictated by the preservation of a global alliance system.

77. Paul Wolfowitz, among others, has endorsed power transition arguments about China, using historical analogies that underscore the virtually inevitable of a clash of Chinese and U.S. power (while holding out some possibility for avoiding collision). These may not be the dominant views in the National Security Council (NSC) or the State Department, but they have been more prominent in the Department of Defense, particularly after Bush took power. It is not surprising that many of the so-called "China hawks" in the Department of Defense (Rumsfeld, Wolfowitz, Rodman) are associated with the Project for New American Century, the main primacist institute in Washington. See the Project's Statement of Principles (www.newamericancentury.org/statementofprinciples.htm).

78. That in the eyes of political leaders in the ROK and Russia rising Chinese power is not as much of a concern in their politico-military policies as it is for Japan, the United States, and some Southeast Asian states, even though in material structural terms they ought to be more worried about relative power imbalances, underscores the problems with a neorealist explanation for regional responses to Chinese power. On the relatively low level of concern about Chinese military power in the ROK and Russia, see Allen (2001: 16) and Cha (1999).

79. There are two hypotheses here. One is that democratization meant that Taiwanese politicians had to respond to public opinion, which was spontaneously evolving toward a greater sense of identity separation from mainland China. The other is that Taiwanese politicians were entrepreneurial in this regard, pushing public opinion along, "normalizing" the notion of Taiwanese separateness. This is not the place to test these hypotheses, but according to one study of cross-strait interaction, the most "provocative" discursive signals from Taiwan, in the PRC's view, come mainly around election times. This suggests that the entrepreneurial argument may carry more weight. See Su (2000).

80. On trends in Taiwanese identification and the discourse of identity, see Su (2002). For examples of the use of the identity card by Taiwan nationalists, see "Taiwan's Identity Crisis," BBC Report (17 May, 2002), http://news.bbc.co.uk/1/hi/world/asia-pacific/1993608.stm; and "Identity Crisis Eats at Nation: Lee," *Taipei Times* (8 June 2002), www.taipeitimes.com/news/2002/06/08/story/0000139436; "Editorial: Taiwanese Must Make A Choice," *Taipei Times* (5 June 2002), www.taipeitimes.com/news/2002/06/05/story/0000139047.

81. In the U.S. political punditry world, the conclusions about rising Chinese nationalism and anti-Americanism come mostly from anecdotal evidence provided by Western journalists in China. I conducted an analysis of U.S. newspaper articles from October 2000 to July 2001 that mentioned Chinese nationalism. In the fifteen papers that had such articles, almost 30 percent of the citations were to interviews with non–randomly selected Chinese students, while another 22 percent were to younger Chinese professionals. Only 12 percent were to U.S. (non-PRC) China specialists. If this were the sample used for an analysis of U.S. popular attitudes toward China, we would rightly be cautious about how much one could infer from such interviews. The Beijing Area Study polls do not show a clear trend line, with declines in the degree of amity toward the United States in 1999 and 2001, but increases in 2000 and 2002. There is also sufficient variation in attitudes toward the United States across socioeconomic status, levels of education, and clusters of attitudes on other public issues to make any generalizations about an overall rise in anti-Americanism problematic. As for nationalism specifically, the BAS 2002 survey asked questions about the degree of loyalty/attachment to China. Again, there are variations in the level of nationalism depending on these same socioeconomic control variables. Younger respondents were not necessarily more nationalistic than older ones. Nationalism has always been central to the legitimacy of the CCP, before and after the disillusionment with Marxism-Leninism of the Maoist period. Some of the themes are new to the 1990s—themes that stress the greatness of traditional culture, for instance—but the core element of modern Chinese nationalism—a victimization discourse—is certainly not new to the 1990s. And the periods of decline in amity toward the United States among the population—judging from the Beijing Area Study—are largely sensitive to major crises in U.S.-China relations. They do not track closely with post–June 4 efforts by the regime to shore up its legitimacy.

82. In the past there were occasionally texts that had a nontrivial effect in creating impressions of China in U.S. policy circles—Mao's Red Book and Lin Biao's famous 1965 essay, "Long Live People's War," which Dean Acheson called China's *Mein Kampf*, being the most obvious. But in general, particularly in the Dengist era through to the early 1990s, we have not seen this phenomenon of a popular text plucked out of the Chinese context and dropped into U.S. policy debates. In part this reflects the confluence of a growing commercialization in Chinese publishing and a growing political space for hard-line voices in the public sphere. Note the following is not a discussion of changes in popular images of the other. One needs to note, however, that in both countries public-opinion polls show a declining level of amity over the past few years toward the people of the other side.

83. As one example of the tendency of U.S. punditry and political discourse to "select on

the dependent variable," there has been virtually no coverage of another best-selling book, written by Qian Ning, the son of senior foreign policy figure Qian Qichen, on life in the United States and China (Qian 1997). According to both American and Chinese readers, this book was considered a balanced, fair treatment of images of the United States that were often contrasted positively with images of China. See, for example, the report from the U.S. embassy in Beijing on the book, www.usembassy-china.org.cn/sandt/webqiann.htm.

84. At least one of the authors of the book had worked on a nonscientific readers' poll published by the *China Youth Daily* in 1995 that purported to show a huge majority of respondents disliked the United States more than any other country. Yet, according to the randomly sampled survey of Beijing city residents conducted by the Beijing Area Study, in 1998 on a 100 degree feeling thermometer, the average level of amity toward the United States was highest of all thirteen countries about which these feelings were measured.

85. My deep thanks to Yan Xiaojun and Manjari C. Miller for their excellent assistance in searching for references to *The China That Can Say No* in U.S. academic journals and books, congressional speeches and testimonies, and Washington-based news magazines and political journals (*Newsweek, New Republic, Weekly Standard, The National Interest*, and others) through to 2002.

86. Author e-mails with U.S. military officers. In the list of readings on doctrine at the Air War College the major reading on Chinese doctrine is *Unrestricted Warfare*. See www.au.af.mil/au/awc/awcgate/awc-doct.htm. See also Hawkins (2000: 16).

87. There are differences of opinion inside the military and the intelligence community on the impact of *Unrestricted Warfare* in these communities. Some claim that although it was hotly discussed for a year or so after it came out, there is less attention being paid to it now. Others claim that the book and its authors are still cited in military discourse about Chinese strategic thinking. The majority of those whom I surveyed (about fifteen people from both communities) believe the book has had a critical impact in framing what nonexperts in the U.S. military believe is known about how the PLA thinks about strategy, despite the fact that there is little evidence the book reflects mainstream PLA thinking about strategy.

88. As unsubstantiated by U.S. intelligence community as the claim regarding the Panama Canal is, it has been pushed by influential "blue team" congressional staffers and former staffers (Al Santoli and William Triplett), think tanks (for instance, the Center for Security Policy), and Unification Church–funded media outlets such as *Insight Magazine* and the *Washington Times*. Indeed, this text, more than *The China That Can Say No*, has been played up by the far-right media and congressional staffers and politicians as evidence of Chinese strategic intentions.

Regarding claims of possible links to Al Qaeda, see Senate testimony on U.S.-China cooperation against terrorism, 25 Oct. 2001. See also the article by another "blue team" member, Richard D. Fisher, Jr. (2001).

The claims about the Panama Canal and Al Qaeda are not backed up by the U.S. intelligence community. The claims about e-attacks and a PLA desire to deter through denial American intervention in a Taiwan war are most likely accurate.

89. The U.S.-China Commission report does use the term "special silver bullet" to describe shashoujian. But the tone of the report drops this parallelism between U.S. and Chinese idioms in favor of a more generalized othering of Chinese strategic thinking.

90. Almost all of these, incidentally, were published by Regnery Press, a far-right press that in its early days published John Birch Society material.

91. For examples of the recent attention being paid to the *Washington Times* and Bill Gertz, see "Meiguo xin zhengfu de dui Hua zhengce qingxiang" [Trends in the new American government's China policy], *Xiandai guoji guanxi* [Contemporary international relations] 1 (2001):

19; "Wo waijiaobu yanzheng boxi *Huashengdun shibao*" [China's Foreign Ministry sternly refutes the *Washington Times*], *Qingnian cankao* [Youth reference news] (27 Dec. 2001), www.cyol.net/gb/qnck/2001-12/27/content_363058.htm.; "*Huashengdun shibao*—zai duan Zhongguo de xinxiang" [The *Washington Times*: Again sullying China's image] (21 Dec. 2001), www.peopledaily.com.cn/GB/junshi/20011225/634306.html; "Caifang Meiguo fan Hua xiaobao" [Visiting America's anti-China paper] (20 May 2002), www.peopledaily.com.cn/GB/guoji/25/95/20020520/732076.html.

92. See the authoritative "Observer" article (1995). Usually "observer" articles in the *People's Daily* reflect the views of a substantial portion of the Politburo, but are not quite as authoritative as a *People's Daily* editorial.

93. The data in Figure 2.8 suggest that despite a somewhat improved tenor in Sino-U.S. relations in the last year or two, particularly with cooperation in the war against violent Islamic fundamentalist groups and on the North Korean nuclear issue, many Chinese analysts still appear to believe that China threat discourse is a prominent feature of U.S. policy.

94. Only in late 2002 did a Bush administration official challenge the characterization of China as a revisionist state. Richard Haass, head of the State Department Policy Planning, argued in a speech in December 2002 to the National Committee on U.S.-China Relations that China was for the most part "in" the international community and that the analogies to imperial Germany were inappropriate. It is unclear, however, how representative Haass' views are. See www.state.gov/s/p/rem/15687.htm.

95. There is no single reliable events data times series that goes up through to 2002 and that could be used to test these hypotheses. The two main available data sets are the Kansas Events Data Set (KEDS) and the Integrated Data for Events Analysis (IDEA). KEDS has data from 1987 to 1997, while IDEA has data from 1991 through 2000. Combining these two data sets is problematic, however, because there are some obvious disparities in what events they have recorded and coded. For example, in 1991–96, KEDS data show a slightly declining trend line in monthly average amount of cooperation from China directed toward the United States, while IDEA shows a discernible increase in the average monthly level of cooperation. If one had a reliable times series the next step would be to employ a statistical technique used in economics to analyze interactivity or endogeneity—vector autogression (VAR). VAR is complex and its results are often highly sensitive to heteroskedasticity. The procedure identifies the amount of lag time between actions taken by one actor and the reactions taken by another and determines the degree to which actions by A at time *t* are causally related to reactions by B at time *t+1*, where B's actions at time *t* are also hypothesized to partially "cause" its reactions at time *t+1*. Preliminary VAR tests on both the KEDS and the IDEA and an integrated data set yield complex and hard-to-interpret results. On the one hand, there appears to be greater volatility in U.S. and Chinese actions toward each other over time. For instance, the standard deviations in the monthly level of cooperation increase in the post-1996 Taiwan crisis period. There is also statistically some lagged interactivity in the U.S.-China relationship, a connection that appears in particular after major crises points in the relationship (1989, 1992, 1996). However, the IDEA data show little interactivity in the late 1990s up to 2000. What the raw scores show, of course, is high-profile cooperative events such as the Jiang-Clinton summits of late 1997 and the summer of 1998, plus the improvement in official government-to-government relations in late 1990 through 2000 with the passage of permanent normal trade relations (PNTR). These, combined with U.S. efforts to assuage China after the 1999 embassy bombing, skew the data in relatively cooperative directions (despite the highly conflictual signaling from China after the bombing). The data stop at the end of 2000, thus they are unable to capture much of the conflictual interactivity after the May 1999 embassy bombing crisis and none

after the Bush administration came to power in 2001. My deep thanks to Michael Horowitz's excellent work on inputting the events data and running a large number of VAR tests. It is unfortunate that the data were so hard to work with.

96. On satellite downlinks see "U.S. to 'Conditionally' Share Military Data with Taiwan" (7 Oct. 2002), www.taiwansecurity.org/AFP/2002/AFP-100702-1.htm. As for interoperability, the U.S. House of Representatives has pushed for this in defense appropriations legislation, though as of this writing the Bush administration is reluctant to put this requirement into law, preferring instead a quieter and more controllable increase in military-to-military coordination.

97. The QDR outlined a broad strategy of redistributing U.S. forces in Asia to make the application of military power more flexible, rapid, and less vulnerable ("places not bases") to coercion from China (though China was not explicitly mentioned). In the post–9/11 era similar arguments about redeployments are being made in terms of fighting terrorism and dealing with instability from Central Asia through to East Asia. But the current arguments are being made by the same people in the DoD who used China to justify redeployment arguments in the QDR. According to a couple of close observers of the DoD, the China focus of these proposals remains (along with the new post–9/11 reasons), but for diplomatic reasons it is not politic to mention it.

98. This is an overarching theme even when the immediate scenarios are military operations against Taiwan, for instance. See Wang and Zhang (2000).

99. For a recent statement of Blair's proposal, see Blair and Hanley (2001). They explicitly cite Emanuel Adler and Michael Barnett's work on security communities (1998). For a Chinese critique of the security community proposal, see Song (2000: 12–13).

100. This is not to say that for some in the PRC anti-American motives are not reasons to support the ARF or the ASEAN+3. But this conclusion is far too simplistic and misses some of the history of multilateralism in China. To be brief, the push for more activism in the ARF in the mid-1990s came largely from the Asia Division of the Ministry of Foreign Affairs, which has developed a more "promultilateralist" organizational mission than the PLA. The interest in the ASEAN+3 seems to be largely driven by China's economic reformers, such as Zhu Rongji, not strategists whose primary consideration might be to constrain U.S. power in the region.

101. As is clear, my claim about security dilemma dynamics in China–East Asian relations is not a novel argument. In addition to Nye's famous comment, see also Christensen (1999). Some of the components of a security dilemma argument are found even earlier in Eikenberry (1995).

102. There is a small number of IR "new thinkers" in China, however, who are well aware of the security dilemma effects of China's own behavior on its own security. See Ye and Feng (2002); Qin (2001); Tang (2001: 30); Shi (2000); and Zhang (2000b). In a security dilemma, the tragedy is often that without high-level political protection those who understand this dynamic are delegitimized because they are seen as too soft, naïve or, worse, threatening national security. Quite specifically, these individuals and others are precisely those whom the United States should prefer to see influencing public debate in China. But their credibility is not helped by U.S. diplomacy toward China. Needless to say, the situation in the U.S. public debate about China has its parallels.

103. As Jervis (1978: 181) puts it, "the dilemma will operate much more strongly if statesmen do not understand it." This is failure of empathy. In large part the end of the Cold War came about because Gorbachev and his new thinking consciously recognized security dilemma dynamics the U.S.-Soviet relationship. This allowed him to experiment with unilateral, de-escalatory signaling and limited demilitarization of Soviet foreign policy. See Evangelista (1999) and Wallander (2002).

104. Jervis (2001) hints at a counterfactual test to see if there might be a security dilemma

at work. Could one plausibly imagine that both actors could be content with the extant nature of the other regime, with the current distribution of power, with current spheres of influence, and with institutionalized linkages that raise the costs of political conflicts *if* both were in principle reassured that the other was not a threat to their vital interests (in China's case Taiwan, in the U.S. case its military posture in East Asia or possibly its counterproliferation interests)? Certainly one could be more confident that this might be true in the U.S.-China than in the U.S.-Soviet case.

105. I have not discussed Southeast Asian views mainly because the major politico-military question in China–Southeast Asian relations—the South China Sea—is not an especially prominent issue at the moment (except for the Philippines). Yuen Foong Khong (in his chapter in this volume) suggests, however, that ambivalence and uncertainty about China's revisionist intentions have compelled Southeast Asian states to engage in "soft balancing." If so, this would add to the puzzle of why so many countries do not perceive any major status quo reorientation in Chinese diplomacy over the years. Based on interviews with regional specialists and policy makers in Singapore in 2003, my sense is that the underlying analytic structure for many analysts in ASEAN (the Philippines, and to some degree Indonesians, being the primary exception) still differs from that of the hard-liners in Washington. That is, many ASEAN analysts believe China's diplomatic trajectory is responsive or reactive to how other states treat China. Thus they endorse Joseph Nye's axiom about the self-fulfilling prophecy of treating China as an enemy. This implicitly, and sometimes explicitly, means endorsing a security dilemma framework. When they agree with Washington hard-liners it is usually about worst-case scenarios—the rise of aggressive nationalists in Beijing, a Taiwan conflict (though Singapore analysts, for instance, expect this to occur after a "provocation" by Taiwan independence forces), economic collapse in China, and so on. These are seen as potential *deviations* from the current trajectory in Chinese diplomacy, not necessary as the current trajectory itself. As insurance, an American military presence in East Asia makes sense. Thus the analytic framework behind soft balancing is different from that behind hard balancing, "congagement," or containment arguments that one hears in Washington.

106. Arguably, however, as of this writing (July 2003) the U.S. strategy here has been to underscore to Beijing that if it does not press the DPRK to its fullest capacity, the United States may have no choice but to use force against the DPRK, leading to some of the worst outcomes for China. This kind of strategy may be effective, but not necessarily conducive to the development of mutual trust or deep cooperation.

107. Jervis (2001: 43) notes that this kind of argument in the Cold War—that the Soviet Union and the United States were both imperialist powers—though rarely made was also politically incorrect in both states.

108. For a clear statement of this distinction, see Rynning and Guzzini (2001). One version of offensive realism, Mearsheimer's (2001), rejects the existence of status quo states all together. All major powers are revisionist all the time, since they are never secure unless they are the unchallenged hegemon.

109. Is the theorizing in this chapter "eclectic"? Initially I was worried that the term could easily be viewed as an excuse for theorizing and empirical work that was too inclusive, too haphazard and inattentive to fundamental incommensurabilities across different research traditions, a kind of slack competitive hypothesis testing where the explanatory results are "all of the above." But I am more worried by another implication. In my view, the characterization of eclectic theorizing by Katzenstein and Sil (in their chapter in this book) ends up creating a very fine line between moving away from paradigm fights on the one hand and trying to subsume or appropriate core elements of other paradigms on the other. By arguing that the interaction

of Chinese and Taiwanese nationalism in the late twentieth century creates a valuation of a piece of territory that leads to behaviors that encourage a particular U.S. interpretation of Chinese preferences and from there to U.S. behaviors that in turn lead to new and more malign interpretations of U.S. preferences in China, am I moving away from constructivist-versus-realist paradigm fights by acknowledging that constructivist notions of mutual constitution of preferences and interests on the one hand and a realist concept of a security dilemma on the other can usefully be combined to understand the dynamics of a real world problem? Or am I trying to subsume realist expectations about state behavior (conflictual, realpolitik) within a constructivist (the mutual constitution of adversarial identities) paradigm, to show the fundamental explanatory strengths of the latter? Is it an effort to show how ideational and identity variables help us understand the origins of realpolitik and conflictual behavior (joining language and concepts from two different research traditions) or an effort to fix a gaping hole in constructivism's theoretical and empirical edifice, namely the explanation of realpolitik behavior, and by doing so further undermining materialist realism's monopoly on explanations for this kind of behavior? Simply put, is eclectic theorizing a stealthy way of trying to subsume competitive research traditions? Frankly, I do not know. On the one hand, to worry about this is to reify tribalism in IR based on an "analytical eclecticism"–versus–"analytic monism" bipolarity. Thus, perhaps one should not worry. On the other hand, perhaps we should worry about the sociological effects of this bifurcation for the IR field, just as eclecticists worry about the effects of the traditional divisions in IR. Following from social identity theory, are we creating a new tribalism—reifying a group of analytic eclectics who are positioned in opposition to analytic monists (who may or many not exist)?

3

Japan and Asian–Pacific Security

PETER J. KATZENSTEIN AND NOBUO OKAWARA

Extolling, in the abstract, the virtues of a specific analytic perspective to the exclusion of others is intellectually less important than making sense of empirical anomalies and stripping notions of what is "natural" of their intuitive plausibility. With specific reference to Japanese and Asian–Pacific security affairs, this chapter argues against the privileging of parsimony that has become the hallmark of paradigmatic debates. The complex links between power, interest, and norms defy analytic capture by any one research tradition. They are made more intelligible by drawing selectively on different traditions—that is, by analytical eclecticism, not parsimony.

We illustrate this general point with specific reference to Asia-Pacific, an area central to security affairs since the end of the Cold War. The precise meaning and geographic scope of "Asia" and "Asia-Pacific" are highly controversial. Geography is a subject of both material reality and political construction. For the purposes of this chapter, we have chosen Asia-Pacific as the most general concept that encompasses

An earlier version of this chapter appeared under the title, "Japan, Asian–Pacific Security and the Case for Analytical Eclecticism," *International Security* 26, 3 (Winter 2001/02): 153–85.

Without saddling them for any of the remaining errors of commission and omission, we would like to thank for their criticisms, comments, and suggestions on earlier drafts of this chapter: Amitav Acharya, Steven Benfell, Thomas Berger, Robert Bullock, Allen Carlson, Tom Christensen, Susanne Feske, Michael Green, Walter Hatch, Brian Job, Chalmers Johnson, Alastair I. Johnston, Robert Keohane, Kozo Kato, Stephen Krasner, Ellis Krauss, David Leheny, T. J. Pempel, Richard Samuels, J. J. Suh, Keiichi Tsunekawa, Robert Uriu, members of seminars at UC San Diego, Cornell University, and Aoyama Gakuin University, and participants in the Cornell Workshop on Asian Security: Alternative Analytical Perspectives (28–30 Mar. 2002). We are also very much indebted to a large number of Japanese and Chinese government officials and policy advisors for generously sharing their scarce time with us.

U.S. relations with Asia and that also describes security affairs in East and Southeast Asia (Hemmer and Katzenstein 2000; Lewis and Wigen 1997). In the first section, we question briefly what is supposedly "natural" or "normal" about Japan. In the second section, we analyze the formal and informal bilateral and embryonic multilateral security arrangements that mark Japanese and Asian-Pacific security affairs. Next we argue that styles of analysis that focus exclusively on either material capabilities, institutional efficiencies, or norms and identities overlook key aspects of the evidence. In the last section, we argue that analysis of discursive politics, an important aspect of Japanese and Asian-Pacific security affairs, is served best by analytical eclecticism. We conclude with some general reflections on Asian-Pacific security affairs after September 11.

What Is a "Natural" or "Normal" Japan?

Perhaps the most important advantage of analytical eclecticism is to put into question some of the basic presuppositions of different explanatory sketches (Midford 2002; Kawasaki 2001; Heginbotham and Samuels 1998; Uriu 1998a, 1998b). Because they constitute actors and define their interests, constructivism, for example, takes as normal that identities and norms are of overriding importance; it regards as second-order phenomena raw material power and institutional efficiencies. Liberalism takes for granted the centrality of social interests and institutional efficiencies as the engines of most important political developments; typically it neglects, however, material capabilities and actor identities. Finally, realism focuses its attention on relative capabilities and the security dilemmas they create; it pays scant attention to factors that are not "real," including institutions and identities. A first important step that analytical eclecticism requires is to strip us of the preconceptions of what is natural or normal that are built into the explanatory sketch that the analyst finds suitable for the task at hand.

Contemporary analyses of Japanese security policy illustrate the tenacious grip unquestioned presuppositions hold on our imagination. To many observers, U.S.-Japan security arrangements and Japan's passive stance on issues of defense are unnatural, to be superseded sooner or later by an Asia freed from the shackles of U.S. primacy and a Japan no longer restrained by pacifism. We disagree on both empirical and analytic grounds. Based on the evidence, we argue that an eclectic theoretical approach finds that there is nothing "natural" about a multipolar world with U.S. primacy and nothing that is "normal" about a Japan without the institutional legacy of Hiroshima and defeat in World War II.

According to one group of Asia experts, the ongoing presence of U.S. forces in South Korea and Japan prohibits the restoration of a regional balance of power as the "natural" course of events in Asia-Pacific. Chalmers Johnson, for example, argues that U.S. policy has a stranglehold over Japan that carries an exorbitant cost to both the United States and its regional partners (2000a, 2000b: 4). Far better, Johnson argues, to recall the U.S. military and let Asians be in charge of Asia. With the end of the

Cold War and the disintegration of the Soviet Union, the United States no longer needs its far-flung empire, military or otherwise. China's high-growth economy, the eventual reunification of North and South Korea, and a Japan that overcomes its self-willed form of political paralysis are all natural developments that U.S. policy makers need to recognize. According to Johnson, only by bending to the natural course of history will the United States escape from the mounting cost of empire blowback at home that he suggests threatens the very fabric of American society.

Our main empirical finding points to a different conclusion: The continued U.S. presence in Asia appears to be beyond doubt for the short to medium term, that is, for the next three to ten years. Formal and informal bilateralism is thriving in Asia-Pacific, while an incipient multilateralism is beginning to take shape. The parallel to economic developments is striking. After the debacle of the 1999 World Trade Organization Ministerial Conference in Seattle, the Japanese government, seeking to forestall isolation, wasted little time in beginning to negotiate bilateral free-trade arrangements with Singapore, South Korea, and Mexico, with the intent of eventually building a free-trade area in Asia-Pacific that would supplement the WTO (Munakata 2001; Scollay and Gilbert 2001: 1–4). Whether this incipient multilateralism will become sufficiently strong and durable to offer a partial complement to traditional balance-of-power politics, as evidently has happened in Western Europe, remains an open question. But in the short to medium term, most of the governments in Asia-Pacific will continue to welcome the U.S. presence. As has been true in Europe since 1989, in Asia-Pacific the United States is seen as more distant and more benign than other regional powers, such as Japan and China. The period of U.S. security reassurance, to be sure, may well be limited to a few decades. But in Asia-Pacific, there is nothing natural about incipient multilateralism or the tendency to balance power. History is not a series of deviations from a "natural" state of stable or unstable affairs. Rather it is an open-ended process in which the accumulation of events and experience from one period alters the contours of the next. Nothing about this process is "natural" unless we permit our analytic perspectives to make it so.

Another group of Asia-Pacific analysts takes a different, more threatening view of Japan that also cuts against this article's analytic and empirical grain. According to this view, Japan is once again becoming a "natural" major power. It is spending more money on developing its military prowess and power projection capabilities. Japan's military is beginning to equip itself with both shield and spear. By passing the International Peace Cooperation Law (which authorized the Japanese military to participate in United Nations' peacekeeping operations); purchasing modern fighter planes such as the F2; and moving to acquire airborne refueling capabilities, develop spy satellites, and adopt a theater missile defense system, the Japanese are signaling their intention to play a more active role in regional security.

Also according to this view, Japan's domestic politics is increasingly revealing traits that mark the return to a "normal," right-wing nationalism. The Japanese military is no longer viewed as a pariah and is evidently experiencing a process of normalization (Frühstück and Ben-Ari 2002; Interview 10-00, Tokyo, Jan. 14, 2000). In both houses of the Diet, panels were set up in 2000 to debate a possible revision of the 1947 Constitution, and the war-renouncing Article 9 has been one of the items at the center of the debate. In 1999 the Diet enacted legislation to implement new defense guidelines giving the Japanese military broader missions. Moreover, the Diet passed an anti–organized crime law that allows wiretapping of citizens' telephones and electronic mail. And it curtailed the civil liberties of members of Aum Shinrikyō, the religious cult that organized the 1995 sarin nerve gas attack in the Tokyo subway, by passing a law that allows law enforcement to monitor the cult's activities. In addition, in 1999 the Diet officially recognized the sun flag as Japan's national flag and a song that celebrates the emperor's reign as its national anthem. In October 1999 a newly appointed parliamentary vice minister of defense, Shingo Nishimura, claimed that the Diet ought to consider arming the country with nuclear weapons. This and his subsequent resignation created a furor that, in the words of Howard French (2000: A6), "laid bare deep fault lines in the new and politically shaky coalition government." In May 2000 Prime Minister Yoshiro Mori made a public statement evoking the spirit of Japanese nationalism in the 1930s. In April 2001 controversial junior high-school history and social studies textbooks that downplay Japanese aggression in Asia, and are tinged with nationalistic sentiments, passed screening by the Ministry of Education. In December 2001, in its first naval engagement in half a century, Japan's coast guard sank a North Korean fishing vessel with a crew of fifteen suspected of spying inside Japan's exclusive economic zone (Brooke 2001). Prime Minister Koizumi's visit to the Yasukuni war shrine in April 2002 was a bow in the direction of conservatives and nationalists (French 2002). And in May 2002, Chief Cabinet Secretary Yasuo Fukuda hinted to reporters that, if shifts in the international situation and public opinion occur, Japan could reconsider its ban on nuclear weapons. In sum, this more threatening view seems to suggest that there is ample reason to bemoan the stubborn ignorance with which U.S. policy makers and media continue to deny obvious historical parallels between contemporary Japan and Japan of the 1930s.

The above news items are like dots that we can connect to create an image of a Japan readying itself to strike militarily once again. But these dots can be connected in many other ways. Paul Cohen (1997: xiv) reminds us that historians do not only reconstruct the history people made. History is also experienced and mythologized. "Experiencers are incapable of knowing the past that historians know, and mythologizers . . . are uninterested in knowing the past as its makers have experienced it." How we go about drawing connections thus depends largely on the implicit analytic lenses we use to interpret Japanese politics. Because it regards as "natural" the displacement of a 1960s' style liberal pacifism by a 1930s' style militant nationalism, a pessimistic interpretation of the evidence neglects many facets of Japanese politics and society that may be worth consideration. But none of the political movements on the left or the right is "natural." Instead they influence one another in a process of historical evolution that is likely to be combinatorial in creating unforeseen outcomes. The kind of nationalism that will shape Japanese politics remains largely unknown. Falling back on past events to make sense of snippets of current news is a mistake. Instead our analysis should focus on the institutional norms and practices that Japan's political and other public leaders use to evolve novel forms of politics and policy (Katzenstein 1996a; Katzenstein and Okawara 1993).

This line of reasoning applies to all cohesive visions of Japan. Take the notion of Japan as a "peace-loving trading state" that is at the core of many liberal and constructivist explanations. The break in Japan's trajectory after the end of the Pacific War was sharp; but it is not irreversible. Things could have turned out differently than they did, and they might in the future. Constructivist and liberal analyses would be wrong in denying that possibility. No polity remains frozen in time, and none returns to its "natural," historical origin. Obviously, it would be wrong to rule out the emergence of a new kind of nationalist politics in Japan. Here and elsewhere in Asia-Pacific, historical animosities and suspicions run deep. Thomas Berger (2000: 405–6) may therefore be correct in looking to ethnic and racial hatreds as the most likely source of future military clashes in Asia-Pacific. Yet liberal and realist analyses are correct in pointing to the improbability of such a development, in light of the international balance of power and Japan's institutionalized domestic politics of security. It is most reasonable therefore to suggest that the combined legacies of Japanese nationalism and internationalism, and militarism and pacifism are likely to produce new political constellations and policies that will resist analytic capture by ahistorical conceptions of a "normal" Japan. Real life is both more complicated and more interesting. In approaching a political problem such as Japanese security, analytical eclecticism moves us beyond familiar presuppositions that give us a false sense of what is normal and natural.

Bilateralism and Multilateralism in Japanese and Asian-Pacific Security

Ever since the Meiji restoration Japan has tried to square the circle between being both a part of Asia and a part of the West. In the late nineteenth century Japan's concerted modernization drive was predicated on the notion that Japan had to "leave Asia." By the 1930s Japan's military aggression in China and Southeast Asia occurred under the ideological banner of "Asia for the Asians." Although policy swings have become less extreme since the end of the Pacific War, they have persisted. The foreign policy line of Prime Minister Yoshida and his successors leaned heavily on the United States and lasted well into the 1970s. Since the mid-1970s, Asia's importance has once again been on the rise without replacing, however, the United States as the main anchor of Japanese security.

This convergence is one illustration of the "comprehensive" character of Japan's security policy encompassing its economic and social dimensions as well as political and military ones (Pyle and Heginbotham 2001: 77–82; Soeya 1998; Katzenstein 1996a). Threats to Japanese security are conceived in broader than conventional military terms. Defending Japan's "internal" security, for example, was an integral part of the mission of Japan's Self-Defense Forces (SDF) in the 1950s and 1960s when Japan's conservative political coalition and the United States viewed left-wing groups in Japan's major metropolitan areas as offering potential staging areas and sources of mass support for external agents smuggled into Japan to destabilize the Japanese polity. The deployment pattern of the SDF, around Japan's major cities rather than close to the beaches, indicated the expected battle area. With the SDF serving as a backup to the police, which after 1960 honed their tactics for controlling mass protests, the rise of left-wing violence in the 1960s and 1970s found a government ready to engage internal threat with a restrained policing strategy. Finally, Japan's comprehensive security policy goes beyond threats to the country's national and internal security to encompass also economic development, technological autonomy, and social stability both at home and abroad. What the United States has discovered only since 9/11 has been clear to Japanese policy makers for decades. Security does not only deal with issues beyond the water's edge. In developing the doctrine and practice of comprehensive security, Japan is far from unique. Other states have similar conceptions suitable to the specific security threats they face. Japan's, however, is noticeable for the clarity with which it has been enunciated since the late 1970s, the comprehensiveness of its vision, and the contrast with the U.S. approach that it offers.

Japan's comprehensive definition of security enjoys broad social and political support. It is embedded so deeply in domestic institutions that political actors in the foreign policy establishment, the national security apparatus, the police, and the economic bureaucracy regard it as normal and acceptable. What is normal in Japan, however, is not normal in Washington. And as the junior partner in the security arrangements between the two countries, Japan's approach to security thus needs to be multidimensional. Mike Mochizuki (1997a: 37 n2) has noted that attention to the nuances of language matters on this vital point. The Japanese government translates the term *takakuteki* as *multilateral*, but it could also be translated as *multidimensional*. The latter translation conveys that Japanese policy aims at embedding its bilateral security ties with the United States in a broader, multifaceted set of security relations rather than moving some distance from bilateralism toward multilateralism. Bilateralism, multilateralism, and the relation between them thus go to the core of Japan's security policy as it complements its vitally important ties to the United States with an Asia of increasing economic and political relevance, and relates the military security concerns of the United States to a more comprehensive Japanese conception of the same term.

Compared to the United States and Europe, Japan's security policy thus has a distinctive cast. The United States has command of the full register of multilateral, bilateral, and unilateral policy instruments in its arsenal. Europe takes pride in having overcome unilateralism and bilateralism and is a champion of multilateralism as the constitutive principle of modern statecraft. Japan's approach, finally, differs from both. Because it lacks the social purpose and the necessary capabilities, Japan devalues strongly unilateralism. It prefers instead bilateral arrangements, both with the United States and also its partners in Asia-Pacific and other parts of the world. Yet general developments in the international society of states as well as in the Japanese polity have created an embryonic multilateralism during the last two decades that has begun to complement rather than substitute for Japan's traditional, bilateral approach (Okawara and Katzenstein 2001/02).

Bilateralism

In the early years of the Clinton administration, growing bilateral trade conflicts, Japanese uncertainty about U.S. strategy in Asia-Pacific, and an increasing emphasis on Asia-Pacific in Japanese foreign policy all pointed to the possibility of a loosening of bilateral ties between Japan and the United States. Despite these potential signals, a series of reevaluations of strategic options in both Tokyo and Washington culminated in the April 1996 signing of the Japan-U.S. Joint Declaration on Security and the September 1997 Revised Guidelines for Japan-U.S. Defense Cooperation. The joint declaration calls for a review of the 1978 Guidelines for Japan-U.S. Defense Cooperation, and the revised guidelines spell out the roles of the U.S. military and Japan's Self-Defense Forces in the event of a crisis. The latter refers specifically to "situations in areas surrounding Japan that will have an important influence on Japan's peace and security" as the context in which the two governments could provide each other with supplies and services (Defense Agency 2000: 236; *Gaikō Forum* 1999: 134–35, 141. See also Hosoya and Shinoda 1998; Gourevitch, Inoguchi, and Purrington 1995).

In the context of modern warfare, the expanded regional scope of the new Japanese-U.S. defense cooperation arrangements has somewhat diluted Japan's traditional postwar policy against the use of force in the absence of a direct attack. SDF operations, for example, will no longer focus solely on the defense of the Japanese home islands (Interview 03-99, Tokyo, Jan. 12, 1999). In a future crisis, this may make it difficult for the Maritime Self-Defense Force to delineate Japan's defense perimeter (Interviews 12-99 and 13-99, Tokyo, Jan. 14, 1999). The 1995 revised National Defense Program Outline (which calls for the SDF's acquiring the capability to cope with situations in areas surrounding Japan that could adversely affect its peace and security) and the Defense Cooperation Guidelines have effectively broadened the mission of the SDF (Araki 2000). The mission of Japan's military is no longer simply the defense of the home islands against a direct attack, thus securing Japan's position in a global anti-Communist alliance. In the eyes of the proponents of the revised mission of the SDF, Japan's military is also committed to enhancing regional stability in Asia-Pacific and thus, indirectly, Japan's own security.

In the wake of the attack on the United States on September 11, 2001, the mission of the SDF has expanded further. In October 2001 the parliament passed the Antiterrorism Special Measures Law, which authorized the SDF to provide logistical support to American and other militaries engaged in antiterrorist operations anywhere in the world, although the SDF was to operate only in noncombat zones and only with the consent of the foreign countries in which the SDF was operating. Furthermore, in July 2003 parliament passed the Iraq Special Measures Law. Effective for four years, it authorized the SDF to provide humanitarian relief to Iraq and logistical support to American and other militaries operating in that country. The law limited SDF operations to noncombat zones, but allowed the forces to transport weapons and ammunition for other militaries. The Director of the Defense Agency gave dispatch orders to the SDF in January 2004. The two new laws enacted to adapt to the post-9/11 world have expanded the geographic scope of Japanese-U.S. military cooperation in a way few people thought politically possible before September 2001.

The importance of bilateralism is not restricted to Japan's security relations with the United States. As an example, senior Japan Defense Agency (JDA) officials met annually between 1993 and 1997 and again in 1999 with their Chinese counterparts to discuss a variety of issues of mutual concern.[1] In addition, Japan has initiated regular bilateral security talks with Australia (since 1996), Singapore (since 1997), Indonesia (since 1997), Canada (since 1997), and Malaysia (since 1999) (Bōeichō 2000: 187). With the tightening of U.S.-Japan security relations after 1994, Japan has become more self-conscious in developing a broad set of bilateral defense talks and exchanges that both complement its persistent dependence on the United States and cement the U.S. presence in the region. By 1999 Japan had committed to about ten regular bilateral talks, too many for the two officials assigned by the JDA to this task. India, for example, was interested in commencing bilateral defense consultations, but Japan stalled, not for reasons of policy but simply because of resource constraints. In brief, the JDA is increasingly engaging Asia-Pacific in a broad range of bilateral security contacts (Interviews 10-00 and 13-00, Tokyo, Jan. 14, 2000).

Informal bilateralism has been Japan's most important response to transnational crime. Combating problems such as illegal immigration, organized crime, money laundering, the distribution of illegal narcotics, and terrorism remains almost without exception under the exclusive prerogative of national governments. Nevertheless, Japan's National Police Agency (NPA) has begun systematic cultivation of contacts with law enforcement agencies in other Asian-Pacific countries in an effort to increase trust among police professionals throughout the region. In so doing, the NPA hopes to create a climate in which Japan's police will be able to cooperate more easily with foreign police forces on an ad hoc basis (National Police Agency, International Cooperation Division, International Affairs Department 1998: 62; Keisatsuchō 1997: 95–99; Katzenstein 1996a: 68–71; Donnelly 1986: 628).

The NPA seeks this cooperation primarily by encouraging the systematic exchange of information through the development of personal relationships with law enforcement officials from other countries. This is especially true of Japan's bilateral contacts with Burma, Cambodia, China, Laos, Taiwan, Thailand, and Vietnam. In the view of the NPA, bilateral police relations are good or excellent with the members of the Association of Southeast Asian Nations (ASEAN), Hong Kong, South Korea, and the United States. High-level police contacts with law enforcement authorities in Taiwan are good, but Taiwan's ambiguous diplomatic status severely constrains cooperation at lower levels.

Japan's relations with China are difficult because of the strong central control that China's vast Public Security Department bureaucracy exercises over its localities, such as Fujian Province, where drugs are produced and shipped to Japan. The department's insistence on strict observance of its rules and procedures seriously undermines bilateral police cooperation (Interview 06-99, Tokyo, Jan. 13, 1999). The NPA remains nonetheless eager to strengthen its contacts with police officials from Fujian (Interviews 09-99 and 10-99, Tokyo, Jan. 13, 1999). For example, the NPA funds projects that send Japanese researchers to northeast China. These researchers investigate the local conditions that permit China's crime syndicates to operate in Japan. They also develop closer ties with provincial police forces (Interview 04-00, Tokyo, Jan. 12, 2000). Even more significant are recent joint operations between the Japanese and Chinese police. For instance, in 1997 the NPA helped Japan's prefectural police departments in contacting the police in Hong Kong, Guangzhou, and Shanghai. International police cooperation resulted in several arrests in 1997–98 (Interviews 08-99 and 10-99, Tokyo, Jan. 13, 1999; Hirano 1998: 45–46). In addition, NPA officials met with their Shanghai and Guangzhou counterparts, having already established ties with the Hong Kong police before 1997 (Interview 10-99, Tokyo, Jan. 13, 1999).

Multilateralism

The 1990s also witnessed the gradual emergence of a variety of Asian-Pacific multilateral security arrangements involving track-one (government to government), track-two (semigovernmental think tanks), and track-three (private institutions) dialogues (Green 2001: 193–227; Wada 1998; Stone 1997). Differences in the institutional affiliation of national research organizations participating in track-two activities, however, confound efforts to draw a sharp distinction among different tracks. They vary from being integral to the ministries of foreign affairs (the two Koreas, China, and Laos), to being totally (Vietnam) or partly (Japan) funded and largely (Vietnam) or moderately (Japan) staffed by the ministry of foreign affairs, to having very close proximity to the prime minister (Malaysia), to exhibiting high degrees of independence (Thailand and Indonesia) (Interview 04-00, Tokyo, Jan. 12, 2000). For most Japanese officials, whatever the precise character of these dialogues, they involve semiofficial or private contacts that are useful to the extent that they facilitate government-to-government talks; however, they have no value in and of themselves. Track-two institutions thus tend to support rather than undermine the state. There are instances when we should think of them not as nongovernmental organizations (NGOs) but as governmentally organized NGOs or GONGOs. In many states in Asia-Pacific, the divide between public and private is easily bridged. Prominent businesspeople and scholars, nominally in the private sector, are often linked informally to politicians and bureaucrats whose attendance at track-two meetings in their "private" capacity is polite fiction. Hence the choice between the multilateralism of different tracks can be a matter of political convenience for governments (Interview 01-00, Tokyo, Jan. 11, 2000; Stone 1996: 9–25).

The trend toward security multilateralism in Asia-Pacific is reflected in several track-two dialogues. Since 1993, for example, Japan, seeking to enhance mutual confidence on security, economic, and environmental issues, has participated with China, Russia, South Korea, and the United States in the Northeast Asia Cooperation Dialogue (NEACD). In addition, since 1994 a Japanese research organization (the Japan Institute of International Affairs) has cosponsored with its American and Russian counterparts (the Center for Strategic and International Studies and the Institute of World Economy and International Relations, respectively) the Trilateral Forum on North Pacific Security, which is regularly attended by senior government officials from all three countries. Furthermore, since 1998 Japan has conducted semiofficial trilateral security talks with China and the United States (Fukushima 1999b: 36; Naito 1999; *Asahi shimbun* 1998d; Sasaki 1997).

Important track-two talks arguably occur in the Council for Security Cooperation in the Asia Pacific (CSCAP) (Job 2000; Interview 04-00, Tokyo, Jan. 12, 2000; Simon 1998: 207–9; Wada 1998; Stone 1997: 21–25), whose predecessor was the ASEAN-affiliated Institutes for Strategic and International Studies. In the early 1990s, the institutes played a crucial role in encouraging ASEAN to commence systematic security dialogues. And with the establishment of the track-one ASEAN Regional Forum (ARF) in 1994, the track-two activities of these institutes have grown in significance. For example, they prepare studies that may be too sensitive for governments to conduct, and they organize meetings on topics that for political reasons governments may be unwilling or unable to host.

Track-two activities shape the climate of opinion in national settings in which security affairs are conducted. They can also help decision makers in articulating new ideas. They may also build transnational coalitions of elites with considerable domestic influence. Over time, they may socialize elites either directly or indirectly to different norms and identities. In brief, they have become an important feature of Asian-Pacific security affairs.

An embryonic multilateralism is also evident on issues of internal security. Since 1989 the NPA has hosted annual three-day meetings on how to combat organized crime. Funded by Japan's foreign aid program, these meetings are designed to strengthen cooperative police relationships (Interview 06-99, Tokyo, Jan. 13, 1999). Also, confronting its third wave of stimulant abuse since 1945, Japan convened an Asian Drug Law Enforcement Conference in Tokyo in the winter of 1999 (Haraguchi 1999:

30, 36–37; Jo 1999; Masaki 1998b). Ironically, at that meeting the director of the United Nations Drug Control Program chastised the Japanese government for its limited commitment to multilateral efforts to curtail regional trafficking in methamphetamines (Friman 1999). The NPA attended as an observer a May 1999 meeting in which the five Southeast Asian–Pacific countries (Burma, Cambodia, Laos, Thailand, and Vietnam) and China formally approved a policy strategy to deal with international drug trafficking (Haraguchi 1999: 36–37). And in January 2000, the NPA organized a conference, attended by officials from thirty-seven countries, to discuss how police cooperation could stem the spread of narcotics (*Asahi Evening News* 2000).

Because terrorism is a direct threat to the state, it has been an item on the internal security agenda of the multilateral Group of Seven/Eight meetings since the mid-1970s. More recent summit meetings in Ottawa (December 1995), Sharm al-Sheikh (March 1996), Paris (July 1996), Denver (June 1997), and Cologne (June 1999) reflect the concerns that this threat continues to generate. Since the September 11 attacks on the World Trade Center and the Pentagon, these concerns have catapulted to the top of the security agenda of the United States and the G-7/8. Over the last few years, Japan has sought to create similar regional collaborations in Asia-Pacific. In June 1997, for example, the NPA was instrumental in helping to create the Japan and ASEAN Antiterrorism Network, which seeks to strengthen ties among national police agencies, streamline information gathering, and coordinate investigations when acts of terrorism occur. Following up on an initiative taken by Prime Minister Ryutaro Hashimoto during his travels through Southeast Asia in January 1997, the NPA and the Ministry of Foreign Affairs (MOFA) jointly hosted in October 1997 a Japan-ASEAN Conference on Counterterrorism for senior police and foreign affairs officials from nine ASEAN countries (Gaimushō 1999: 103–4; Keisatsuchō 1999: 231; Interview 07-99, Tokyo, Jan. 13, 1999; National Police Agency, International Cooperation Division, International Affairs Department 1998: 53; Hishinuma 1997). Generally speaking, however, on the issue of internal security the absence of multilateral regional institutions in Asia-Pacific remains striking. A recent inventory of transnational crimes lists several global institutional fora in which these concerns are addressed but, besides CSCAP's working group on transnational crime for Asia-Pacific, there is only one other regional forum: the ASEAN ministry on drugs (Shinn 1998: 170–71).

Bilateralism and Multilateralism

Asia-Pacific's entrenched bilateralism and incipient multilateralism need not conflict (Tsuchiyama 2003: 11–12, 18–19; Capie, Evans, and Fukushima 1998: 7–8, 16–17, 60–63, IV/3–4, 7). Amitav Acharya speaks of an interlocking "spider web" form of bilateralism that compensates in part for the absence of multilateral security cooperation in Asia-Pacific (Blair and Hanley 2001; 2000b: 18; 1990). In the 1960s and 1970s, for example, a commitment to anti-Communism provided the rationale for joint police operations and cross-border "hot pursuits" of Communist guerrillas (for example, between Malaysia and Indonesia and between Malaysia and Thailand). And as Michael Stankiewicz (1998: 2) observes, efforts in the 1990s to deal with the North Korean nuclear crisis illustrated "the increasing complementarity between bilateral and multilateral diplomatic efforts in Northeast Asia." Equally interesting, improvements in bilateral relations in Asia-Pacific, occasioned by the conflict on the Korean Peninsula, are fostering a gradual strengthening of multilateral security arrangements such as the NEACD and the Korean Peninsula Energy Development Organization. Thus the potential for a flash-point crisis between North Korea and its neighbors has been a source for strengthening nascent multilateral security arrangements in Northeast Asia. The April 1999 creation of the Trilateral Coordination and Oversight Group by Japan, South Korea, and the United States to orchestrate policy toward North Korea is but the most recent example of this trend (Tainaka 2000; Interviews 02-99 and 05-99, Tokyo, Jan. 11–12, 1999).

Japanese diplomacy thus is beginning to make new connections between bilateral and multilateral security dialogues (Interviews 02-99 and 05-99, Tokyo, Jan. 11–12, 1999). This policy accords with the argument of the Advisory Group on Defense Issues (1994: 16) in its report to the prime minister that "the Japan-U.S. relationship of cooperation in the area of security must be considered not only from the bilateral viewpoint but, at the same time, also from the broader perspective of security in the entire Asia/Pacific region." According to a member of that advisory group, Akio Watanabe: "I don't feel it's a question of choosing one framework or the other. From my standpoint, the issue is the necessity of redefining the Japan-U.S. security relationship within the new international conditions of the post-cold-war era" (Igarashi and Watanabe 1997: 36). Takashi Inoguchi (1996: 37) agrees when he writes that "the Japan-U.S. relationship could develop into an arrangement having multilateral aspects" (see also Alagappa 2000: 6–7).

Japan's government takes a pragmatic approach: It views multilateralism as a complement to rather than as a substitute for bilateralism. The informal exchange of information on a range of difficult issues around the edges of official talks enhances predictability and helps build trust. Although multilateral dialogues do not solve problems, they can make the underlying system of bilateral security arrangements in Asia-Pacific operate more smoothly (Interviews 01-00, 02-00, 03-00, and 04-00, Tokyo, Jan. 11–12, 2000). Given this sense of pragmatism, it is not surprising that, as Paul Midford (1998) notes, Foreign Minister Taro Nakayama's July 1991 proposal for a new multilateral security dialogue in Asia-Pacific did not resemble the European-style multilateralism that John Ruggie (1992) has analyzed: Nakayama's proposal excluded socialist states such as the Soviet Union; it was implicitly discriminatory by according the United States and Japan special status as major powers; and it did not advocate diffuse reciprocity but recognized instead the role of the United States as a security provider in Asia-Pacific and the circumstances of Japan as operating under domestic legal restrictions.

With Japan's active support, Asia-Pacific in the 1990s began to develop an embryonic set of multilateral security institutions and practices. But compared with the scope and strength of both its formal and informal bilateral arrangements, Asia-Pacific's achievements in multilateralism remain limited at best. Even ASEAN's long-standing and relatively successful multilateralism has encountered serious setbacks since Asia's 1997 financial crisis. The multilateralism Japan has traditionally supported has been modest. In sum, formal and informal bilateral approaches, supplemented by nascent forms of multilateralism, are defining both Japanese security policies and Asian-Pacific security relations. As we show in the next section, analytical eclecticism is particularly well suited to the task of analyzing the fluid politics of Japanese and Asian-Pacific security.

Analytical Eclecticism in the Analysis of Japanese and Asian-Pacific Security

A robust bilateralism and incipient multilateralism in Japanese and Asian-Pacific security affairs are typically not well explained by the exclusive reliance on any single analytic perspective—be it realist, liberal, or constructivist. Japan's and Asia-Pacific's security policies are not shaped solely by power, interest, or identity but by their combination. Adequate understanding requires analytical eclecticism, not parsimony.

Analytically interesting questions of Japan's security policy also matter politically. The indeterminate direction of the Asian balance of power, the size of and rate of increase in Japan's defense budget, the normative foundation of Japan's alliance with the United States, the relative inefficiency and lack of transparency in the security arrangements with the United States, the limitation in the emergence of a collective ASEAN identity, we argue below, are all substantive political issues that highlight the advantages of analytical eclecticism over parsimonious realist, liberal, and constructivist explanations. Furthermore, Japan's attempt to constrain China through a policy of engagement, the institutionalized and deliberate ambiguity with which the Japanese government has approached the issue of Taiwan, cooperative security approaches, and informal dialogues as ways of institutionalizing acceptable standards of behavior, illustrate politically important developments, we argue below, that analytical eclecticism captures well.

Disadvantages of Parsimonious Explanations

Strict formulations of realism, liberalism, and constructivism sacrifice explanatory power in the interest of analytic purity. Yet in understanding political problems, we typically need to weigh the causal importance of different types of factors, for example, material and ideal, international and domestic. Eclectic theorizing, not the insistence on established research traditions, helps us understand inherently complex social and political processes.

Realism. Realist theory has various guises. Drawing on an increasingly rich literature, Robert Jervis (1999), for example, operates with a twofold distinction (between
offensive and defensive realism). Alastair Johnston (1999a) favors a more complex
fourfold categorization (balance of power, power maximization, balance of threat, and
identity realism). Although they formulate their analyses somewhat differently, they
and other realists share many insights—the most important being the effects of the security dilemma on state behavior. Realists such as Kenneth Waltz (2000) underline the
brevity of the unipolar moment that the United States has enjoyed since the end of
the Cold War and the disintegration of the Soviet Union. For them, however, the
magnitude of current U.S. capabilities is less important than the policy follies—such
as interventions in areas of the world not directly tied to the national interests of the
United States—that squander it. Hence "the all-but-inevitable movement from
unipolarity to multipolarity is taking place not in Europe but in Asia. . . . Theory enables one to say that a new balance of power will form but not to say how long it will
take" (Waltz 2000: 32, 30). Though distinctively his own in style of argumentation,
Waltz's analysis is in broad agreement with other types of realist analysis that consider
factors besides the international distribution of capabilities, such as absolute security
needs and threats. Japan and China are rising great powers in Asia-Pacific. In view of
a large number of potential military flash points, the security dilemma confronting
Asian-Pacific states is serious. Between 1950 and 1990, one study reports 129 territorial disputes worldwide, with Asia accounting for the largest number. Of the 54 borders disputed in 1990, the highest ratio of unresolved disputes as a fraction of total
contested borders was located in East and Southeast Asia (Huth 1996: 32). In this view,
Asia-Pacific may well be "ripe for rivalry" (Betts 1993/94; Friedberg 1993/94). For realists, balancing against the United States as the only superpower, currently by China
and in the near future by Japan, is the most important prediction that the theory generates (Mochizuki 1997b).

Realist theory, however, is indeterminate. It cannot say whether Japan will balance
with China against the United States as the preeminent threat or whether it will balance with the United States against China as the rising regional power in East Asia
(DiFilippo 2002; Armacost and Pyle 2001; Green 2001: 77–109; Rozman 2001). This
limitation is not restricted to realist analysis of Asian-Pacific security affairs. In strict
analogy, realism was unable to specify whether at the end of the Cold War European
states would balance with Germany against the United States as the remaining superpower or with the United States against a united Germany as a potential regional
hegemon. Balance-of-power theory predicts that a withdrawal of U.S. forces from
East Asia would leave Japan no choice but to rearm. Alternatively, balancing theory
can also support a very different line of reasoning in which Japan, though wary of
China, might recognize China's central position in Asia-Pacific and stop far short of
adopting a policy of full-fledged remilitarization (Interview 04-00, Tokyo, Jan. 12,
2000). To infer anything about the direction of balancing requires auxiliary assump-

tions that typically invoke interest, threat, or prestige—all variables that require liberal or constructivist styles of analysis. Moreover, it is unclear whether a united Korea will balance against Japan (with its powerful navy that might ultimately control the sea-lanes on which Korean trade depends so heavily) or against China (with the strongest ground forces in Asia and with whom Korea shares a common border) (Cha 2000). Thus realist theory points to omnipresent balancing but tells us little about the direction of that balancing.

Nor do military expenditures alone yield a clear picture of the geostrategic situation in Asia-Pacific. Asia's 1997 financial crisis slowed Asian-Pacific arms rivalries and lowered military spending. Taking account of weakening currency values, defense spending (measured in U.S. dollars, 1997 prices) was cut in 1998 by 39 percent in Thailand, 35 percent in South Korea, 32 percent in the Philippines, 26 percent in Vietnam, and 10 percent in Japan—if measured in yen, this represents the first reduction since 1955 (Ball 2000; Umbach 2000: 12–17; Huxley and Willett 1999: 16; National Institute for Defense Studies 1999: 33–35; Asagumo shimbun-sha 1998: 263–67; Richardson 1998). Since the end of the Cold War, Japanese defense expenditures show rates of increase that are much smaller than those of China. Between 1990 and 1997, while China's defense spending increased 45 percent from $25.1 billion to $36.5 billion, Japan's defense budget increased only 18 percent from $34.3 billion to $40.8 billion (1997 exchange rates) (Bessho 1999: 35; Asagumo shimbun-sha 1998: 267). Thus instead of worrying about escalating arms rivalries, some defense experts began to express greater concern over potential risks created by possible imbalances in military modernization and financial strength. After 1997, countries less affected by the financial crisis—such as China, Japan, Korea, Singapore, and Taiwan—appeared to be much better positioned to harness sophisticated technologies to enhance their military strength (Richardson 2000).

Liberalism. On its own, liberal theory also encounters serious difficulties. Some analysts have suggested that the U.S.-Japan alliance can last only if it articulates common values. Mike Mochizuki and Michael O'Hanlon, for example, have advocated that the alliance should become as "close, balanced and principle-based as the U.S.-U.K. special relationship." Not a common military threat but common interests derived from shared democratic values, Mochizuki and O'Hanlon argue, are the best guarantor for sustaining the U.S.-Japan alliance (Mochizuki and O'Hanlon 1998: 127. See also French 2001; Armitage and Nye 2000).

What would happen, however, if the United States or Japan were no longer a member of the "free world"? Liberal analysis is hindered by the theory's underlying assumption that identities are unchanging. Do liberal values really constitute both the United States and Japan as actors? This is implausible. The promotion of democracy as a positive value, for example, is handled very differently by the U.S. and Japanese governments. The philosophical assumption informing U.S. policy is that democracy and human rights should proceed hand in hand with economic development. In con-

trast, Japanese policy assumes that economic development is conducive to the building of democratic institutions. This difference in philosophy leads to an equally noticeable difference in method. The United States operates with legal briefs, economic
sanctions, and "sticks." Japan prefers constructive engagement through dialogue, economic assistance, and "carrots" (Takeda 1997). Such systematic differences in approach
undercut a liberal redefinition of the U.S.-Japan alliance. To Japan they make the
United States appear high-handed and evangelical, while to the United States Japan
seems opportunistic and parochial. These differences point to the importance of collective identities not shared rather than of democratic institutions that are shared.

An alternative neoliberal analysis of the U.S.-Japan alliance focuses not on shared
values but on efficiency (Inoguchi and Stillman 1997; Kahler 1995: 80–81, 107–16).
For example, after the 1993–94 missile crisis on the Korean Peninsula, policy makers
in Japan and the United States became convinced that their bilateral defense guidelines needed to be revised to enhance the efficiency of defense cooperation. The 1960
Mutual Cooperation and Security Treaty and the 1978 Guidelines for Japan-U.S. Defense Cooperation had left unclear the role to be played by Japan in regional crises.
Specifically, they left undefined both the extent to which Japan would provide logistical support and whether the U.S. military would have access to Japan's SDF and
civilian facilities. The 1997 revised defense guidelines reduce these ambiguities and
thus helped to prepare Japan for potential participation in both possible U.S. and UN
operations undertaken, in the eyes of the proponents of the revised guidelines, in the
interest of regional peace and security. This is an instance of government policies
seeking to lower transaction costs and enhance efficiencies through institutionalized
cooperation (Council on Foreign Relations Independent Study Group 1998: 20–26).

The revision of the defense guidelines was, however, a central feature of Japanese
security policy in the last decade that eludes neoliberal explanations. It extends the
scope of the U.S.-Japan security arrangement under the provisions of the treaty for
the maintenance of peace and security in "the Far East" to include "situations in areas
surrounding Japan." The operative understanding of "the Far East" in Article 6 of the
security treaty was geographically defined by the Japanese government in 1960 as
"primarily the region north of the Philippines, as well as Japan and its surrounding
area," including South Korea and Taiwan. The revised guidelines explicitly state that
the phrase "situations in areas surrounding Japan" (short for "situations in areas surrounding Japan that will have an important influence on Japan's peace and security")
is conceptual and has no geographic connotations. In situations when rear-area support may be required, these areas are not necessarily limited to East Asia. The political leadership has denied, however, that "situations in areas surrounding Japan" involve
no geographic element whatsoever. Prime Minister Keizo Obuchi claimed before the
Lower House Budget Committee that the "Middle East, the Indian Ocean, and the
other side of the globe" cannot be conceived of as being covered by the new guidelines. According to this interpretation, even though an interruption of oil supplies

from the Middle East would constitute a potentially serious threat to Japan, that threat insofar as it is located in the Middle East or the Indian Ocean, would not be covered by the guidelines (*Asahi shimbun* 1999a; Interview 01-99, Tokyo, Jan. 11, 1999).

This ambiguity has given rise to much debate in Japan and beyond. Under the revised guidelines, U.S.-Japanese cooperation in combat is obligatory only when it involves the defense of Japan's home islands. In the view of revision advocates, problems may emerge in a crisis not involving an attack on Japan—including any that arise in the Asia-Pacific region—but that would require general defense cooperation with the United States in the interest of regional stability and security. For some, the revised defense guidelines free Japan to provide logistical and other forms of support to the United States, falling short of military combat, as long as the crisis is politically construed as constituting a serious security threat to Japan (Interview 03-99, Tokyo, Jan. 12, 1999). Adopting a less flexible approach, the Ministry of Foreign Affairs director of the North American Affairs Bureau stated in May 1998, before the Lower House Foreign Affairs Committee, that "situations in areas surrounding Japan" were restricted to those occurring in the Far East and its surrounding areas (*Asahi shimbun* 1998a, 1998b, 1998c).

In the future, the clash between more or less flexible interpretations of the scope of U.S.-Japan defense cooperation will be shaped by changing international and domestic political conditions. The ambiguity that lurks behind conflicting viewpoints and temporary victories of one side or the other is central to how Japanese officials adapt security policy to change. According to the government's official interpretation, it is the specific security threat at a specific time that in the judgment of the cabinet and the Diet will determine whether that threat will be covered by the ambiguous wording of the revised guidelines. Thus the scope of the areas surrounding Japan is variable and depends on a functional and conceptual, rather than a geographic and objective, construction of Japan's changing security environment.

The ambiguity in the notion of "situations in areas surrounding Japan" has been increased by a law, enacted in June 2003, that gave the government the powers it saw as necessary in coping with military emergencies. It covers not only an actual military attack or a situation in which attack is imminent, but also a situation in which attack is "expected." The government has claimed that the latter can also be a "situation in areas surrounding Japan." Such an interpretation gives the Japanese government a broader range of options in dealing with a regional crisis than if it adhered to the strict distinction, maintained in the new guidelines, between "situations in areas surrounding Japan" and "an armed attack against Japan." But the notion of "situations in areas surrounding Japan" has become even more ambiguous.

Neoliberal explanations of the U.S.-Japan alliance cannot explain the deliberate ambiguity in the definition of the term "surrounding area" in the revised defense guidelines. This ambiguity undercuts efficiency because it leaves unspecified the contingencies under which the Japanese government might choose to participate in regional security cooperation measures. Yet for the guidelines' advocates, ambiguity, by deflecting criticism in Japan, may well increase U.S.-Japanese defense cooperation. In seeking to create flexibility in policy through a politics of interpretation and reinterpretation of text, ambiguity is a defining characteristic of Japan's security policy (Katzenstein 1996a: 59–130).

Constructivism. Parsimonious constructivist analysis of Japanese and Asian-Pacific security also lacks plausibility. International security institutions in Asia are relatively weak. And they are of recent origin. By themselves, their effects on actor identities, interests, and policies cannot be very strong simply for lack of time. The ARF, for example, was founded in 1994 and thus is only a decade old. It would be very surprising to find transformative effects of the kind that constructivist theory stipulates.

Contrary to claims by neoliberals, multilateral institutions do more than facilitate the exchange of information. ASEAN processes of trust building, for example, appear to be well under way (Acharya 2000a, 2000b, 1999a, 1998, 1995: 181–82, 1991; Khong 1998, 1997b; Simon 1998). The ARF is more than an intraorganizational balancing of threats and capabilities. Yuen Foong Khong writes that it is the only "mechanism for defusing the conflictual by-products of power balancing practices" in Asia-Pacific (Khong 1997b: 296). It is thus understandable why governments are eager to adjust regional security institutions to new conditions rather than to abandon them altogether. Exclusive reliance on balancing strategies of the kind favored by realists appears to Asian-Pacific governments to be fraught with risk (Acharya 1999a).

In three carefully researched case studies dealing with relations between Malaysia and the Philippines between the 1960s and 1990s, ASEAN's policies after Vietnam's 1978 invasion of Cambodia, and the period of strategic uncertainty after the end of the Cold War, Nikolas Busse (2000, 1999) has shown that ASEAN norms have noticeably influenced government policy. In the 1990s, specifically, ASEAN members did not balance against the destabilizing possibilities of U.S. disengagement, Japanese reassertion, and Chinese expansion. Instead member states sought to export the ASEAN way of intensive consultation to East Asia through the ARF and the Workshops on Managing Potential Conflicts in the South China Sea that Indonesia has convened since 1990. More recently, the ASEAN+3 meetings have provided a forum for discussion of security issues involving ASEAN members, Japan, South Korea, and China (Interview 01-00, Singapore, June 7, 2000; Kurata 1996: 132–38). And in 2000, the ARF officially accepted North Korea as a member. Busse's research points to the importance of the legitimacy, success, and prominence of norms of informal consultations; consensus building; and nonintervention for Asian-Pacific security. In brief, ASEAN's strategy made China, the United States, and Japan part of ongoing security dialogues that replicate three important ASEAN norms: informal diplomacy, personal contacts, and respect for the principle of nonintervention.

The redefinition of collective identities, however, is a process measured in decades, not years. The accomplishments of various track-one and track-two security dialogues in Asia-Pacific remain limited. Bilateralism and multilateralism, as Acharya (2000b: 18) has pointed out, are less threat and more uncertainty oriented. Collective identity is therefore less directly at stake than are trust and reputation. Skeptics have joked that the bark of the ARF is worse than its bite. The ARF has sidestepped the most pressing security issues in Asia: conflicts on the Korean Peninsula, across the Taiwan Strait, and in the South China Sea. North Korea's nuclear and missile programs have become a major source of instability in Asia-Pacific (Hughes 1996). Hoping to defuse this crisis, the United States, Japan, China, and South Korea are all engaged in complicated, interlinked diplomatic initiatives that exclude both ASEAN and the ARF. The same is true of the smoldering Taiwan Strait crisis. With China declaring the status of Taiwan a domestic matter, the ASEAN norm of nonintervention has prevented the ARF from playing a mediating role in this crisis. This is not an exception. All Asian states either voted against or abstained from voting on the September 27, 1999, United Nations High Commissioner for Refugees resolution calling on the UN secretary-general to establish an international commission of inquiry into violations of international law in East Timor (Foot 2000: 20). Finally, in the South China Sea the ARF has been slightly more engaged while still falling well short of seeking the role of active mediator between clashing state interests (Interviews 08-98, 01-00, and 07-00, Beijing, June 21, 1998, June 13, 2000, and June 15, 2000).

The restricted scope of ARF activity is reflected in its minuscule organizational resources. Since its first meeting in 1994, the ARF has modeled itself after ASEAN. It has "participants" rather than "members," thus signaling the premium it places on a lack of permanency and formality. ARF has no headquarters or secretariat, and it is unlikely that either will be established (Interview 07-00, Tokyo, Jan. 13, 2000). Although there are a number of intersessional working groups, the ARF itself meets annually for one day only (Bōeichō 1999: 187; Gaimushō 1998: 31; Masaki 1998a).

The ARF has been weakened further by three developments in the late 1990s. First, Asia's financial crisis has put new strains on relations among several ASEAN members (including Malaysia and Singapore) and has illustrated, in the words of former prime minister of Singapore Lee Kuan Yew, that "we can't help each other" (Rüland 2000: 439; Acharya 1999a: 3, 26; *Economist* 1994: 44). Second, the ARF was unable to act in a politically meaningful way in the 1999 crisis in East Timor. The United Nations, not the ARF, was the central international arena and actor to which Indonesia turned. Third, there are some indications that, according to Michael Leifer, the accession of Cambodia, Laos, and Vietnam to ASEAN is leading to "revisionary fragmentation," with the three governments meeting separately at times from the older ASEAN members (Leifer 2000: 4). In addition, the United States is putting increasing emphasis on bilateral diplomatic and military relationships. Since 1996, for example, it has strengthened its links with Japan and Australia and has expanded its military access to ASEAN members such as Singapore, Malaysia, Indonesia, Thailand, and the Philippines (Acharya 1999a: 2).

The Taiwan problem has imported the ARF's track-one problems into track-two talks. The ARF has not admitted Taiwan as a participant. After China joined CSCAP in 1996, Taiwanese participation in working group discussions occurred only by special invitation that had to be vetted informally by China (Brian Job, personal communication, July 1, 2000; Interviews 01-98 and 02-98, Beijing, June 12, 1998; Fukushima 1999a: 149, 155, 197; Hoshino 1999: 181; Terada 1998: 361). Procedural and political controversies thus lurk just below the surface and tend to hamper progress in CSCAP. Its working groups are typically staffed by relatively young researchers given to a relatively free and informal style of exchanging views. The Chinese representative, however, is often unwilling to participate in these discussions except to stop them whenever they veer toward the politically sensitive issues of Taiwan's status or sovereignty disputes in the South China Sea. In the context of the working group discussions, some Japanese participants interpret China's role as bordering on systematic obstructionism of the track-two process (Interviews 01-98, 02-98, and 07-00, Beijing, June 15, 1998 and June 15, 2000; 04-00, Tokyo, Jan. 12, 2000; 09-00, Tokyo, Jan. 13, 2000).

The self-blocking tendencies of security multilateralism require much patience and reinforce, in the eyes of Japanese policy makers, the advantages of bilateral approaches to security issues (Interview 04-00, Tokyo, Jan. 12, 2000). The Japan Institute of International Affairs (JIIA) is the undisputed center for Japan's active involvement in a broad range of track-two activities (ibid.). Founded in the late 1950s and well connected in Japan, Asia-Pacific, and throughout the advanced industrial world, the JIIA has acted as the coordinator and secretarial office in Japan not only for CSCAP (since 1994) but also for the Pacific Economic Cooperation Council (since 1980), and for the Northeast Asia Cooperation Dialogue (since 1998) (Bōeichō 1999: 189–90, 422; Fukushima 1999b: 31; Interviews 02-99 and 04-99, Tokyo, Jan. 11–12, 1999). Bilateralism marks the activities of JIIA. Based on a decade-long tradition of bilateral meetings with think tanks, universities, and international affairs institutes in North America and Western Europe, regular bilateral exchanges with Asian-Pacific countries have increased sharply only since the mid-1980s—for example, with the China Institute of International Studies (since 1985), the South Korean Institute of Foreign Affairs and National Security (since 1986), the North Korean Institute for Disarmament and Peace (since 1990), the Vietnamese Institute for International Relations (since 1992), and the Indian Institute for Defense Studies and Analysis (since 1995) (Interview 04-99, Tokyo, Jan. 12, 1999). The self-blocking tendencies of multilateral security institutions and the persistence of bilateral approaches do not deny the importance of informal diplomacy, personal contacts, and respect for the principle of nonintervention that a constructivist perspective highlights. They do, however, underline the limits of a perspective that blocks out the effects of variables emphasized by liberal and realist theories.

Advantages of Eclectic Explanations

Compelling analyses of empirical puzzles can be built through combining realist, liberal, and constructivist modes of explanation. Realism and liberalism together, for example, can generate powerful insights into the mixture of balance-of-power and multilateral politics. A soft form of balance-of-power theorizing, for example, informs the 1995 Nye report that provides a rationale for continued U.S. military engagement in East Asia (Nye 2001; Bandow 1999; Council on Foreign Relations Independent Study Group 1998). At one level the report is about increasing trust, communication, transparency, and reliability in a U.S.-Japan relationship marked by complex interdependence, thus seeking to stabilize the alliance and enhance predictability and stability in the region. But it is also about maintaining U.S. primacy. The 1997 Revised Guidelines for Japan-U.S. Defense Cooperation spell out the operations that Japan would be expected to carry out in a regional crisis, and thus ensure that in such a crisis potentially hostile states could not drive a wedge between the United States and Japan; Japan's support of U.S. forces would be sufficiently robust to prevent a backlash in the U.S. Congress against either the alliance or the forward deployment of U.S. forces in Asia-Pacific; Japan's defense posture would continue to be guided by alliance planning; and finally, the United States would be able to win decisively in a possible military conflict with North Korea without shouldering excessive costs (Michael Green, personal communication).

In this realist-liberal perspective, the United States remains militarily and economically fully engaged in Asia-Pacific, thus reassuring Asian-Pacific states against the threat posed by Japan's present economic preponderance and potential military rearmament. Japan emerges as a potential economic and political leader contained within well-defined political boundaries. This double-barreled U.S. approach is rounded out by hopes for a unified and peaceful Korea and an economically prospering China increasingly engaged with the West, Japan, and the rest of Asia-Pacific (Auer 1998).

Japan's China policy also reflects a mixture of realist and liberal elements (Interview 03-00, Tokyo, Jan. 11, 2000). Just as Germany avoids at all cost having to choose between the United States and France, Japan avoids having to choose between the United States and China. Without risking its primary security relationship with the United States, Japan since the 1970s has consistently sought to engage China diplomatically. This entails an element of balancing as Japan seeks to constrain China, a potential opponent, through a policy of engagement. From Japan's perspective, countering China is possible only through alignment with the United States. Because China's military does not currently pose a serious threat to the region, and because military modernization is a costly and prolonged process measured in decades rather than years, the military aspects of the Japan-China relationship are relatively unimportant. Instead Japan's diplomacy aims at a slow, steady, and prolonged process of encouraging China to contribute more to regional stability and prosperity. On several

issues—such as China's growing involvement in the ARF, an officially unacknowledged but nonetheless evident policy of seeking to enhance stability on the Korean
Peninsula, and the somewhat greater flexibility with which the leadership in Beijing
has addressed encroachments on China's sovereignty on issues of political authority
and economic independence (as opposed to those involving territorial integrity and
jurisdictional monopoly)—Japanese patience is being rewarded (Carlson 2000; Christensen 1999: 69–80; Interviews 01-98, 04-98, 05-98, 07-98, and 09-98, Beijing, June
15, 16, 19, 20, and 22, 1998). The settlement of virtually all of China's continental border conflicts, its acceptance into the World Trade Organization (WTO), and its far-
reaching domestic reforms all point to a general political climate conducive to
Japan's policy of engagement. A mixture of realist and liberal categories is also better
than either alone to capture the combination of balancing and engagement characteristic of the diplomatic strategies of many Asian-Pacific states. Even though some
Southeast Asian states (such as Indonesia, the Philippines, and Vietnam) are wary of
China because of past or current territorial disputes, they nevertheless seek to engage
it in multilateral institutions such as the ARF. And even though Japan is the overwhelming power in Southeast Asia, its relations with states in the region have been
good and are getting better in the wake of the Asian financial crisis (Interview 02-
00, Tokyo, Jan. 11, 2000).

A combination of constructivist and realist styles of analysis also has considerable
heuristic power, as David Spiro (1999) and Alastair Johnston (1995) have argued. The
volatile issue of Taiwan, potentially the most serious trouble spot in Asia-Pacific, illustrates this analytic possibility (Christensen 1999: 62–69). The use of the term "surrounding areas" rather than "Far East" in the revised guidelines creates ambiguities,
but they have been acceptable to both U.S. and Japanese defense officials for instrumental reasons. The United States has an interest in enhancing the deterrent effect of
its alliance with Japan against China; Japanese officials have an interest in leaving undefined Japan's response to a possible crisis over Taiwan. The advantages of ambiguity on Taiwan are widely acknowledged inside the Japanese government (Interviews
02-99, 05-99, 11-99, and 13-99, Tokyo, Jan. 11–12 and 14, 1999), as are the risks (Interview 03-99, Tokyo, Jan. 12, 1999). In the 1979 Taiwan Relations Act, the United
States combined its diplomatic recognition of the People's Republic of China with a
commitment to Taiwan's defense. Japan, however, has kept its stance on Taiwan as
ambiguous as possible. Japanese insistence on the domestic nature of the conflict between Beijing and Taipei, however, may not suffice in future crises. More than any
other issue, Taiwan's status potentially confronts Japan and the United States with serious difficulties in defense cooperation should China seek to resolve this issue
through military means (Interviews 02-99 and 13-99, Tokyo, Jan. 11 and 14, 1999).

A combination of constructivism and realism also offers historical insights. John
Fairbank (1968), for example, has offered a broad interpretation of East Asian international relations. For many centuries, Asian international relations were institution-

alized as a suzerain, rather than as a sovereign, system of states in which the central power did not seek to subordinate or intervene unduly in the affairs of lesser powers within its ambit (Kang 2003b: 169–73; Feske 1997: 18–19). China was the center of a system of tributary trade in which polities emulated and aligned with the central power. Focusing on systems with a preponderant source of power, Randall Schweller (1994) speaks of "bandwagoning for profit." Less material objects than profits narrowly construed were involved, however. In Asia tribute was not only trade. It was also an institutional transmission belt for collective norms and identities in Chinese culture. Power, trade, and culture were central in defining the political relationships between the Middle Kingdom and its neighbors.

The Sinocentric world order was anarchic and organized around the principle of self-help. Power and geographic location mattered, just as realism leads us to expect. Yet Chinese diplomatic practices also facilitated cultural emulation, thus yielding a system with a distinctive mixture of hierarchy and equality. In this Sinocentric world, discrepancies between norms and practice were common, as is true of the Westphalian system of sovereign states. But as Michel Oksenberg (2001) observed, the nature of the misfit was different, so that certain ambiguous solutions of the past concerning territorial disputes over Taiwan, Tibet, and Hong Kong are today rendered more intractable (see also Krasner 2001). Christopher Twomey (2000), Michael Green (2001), and Seng Tan and Ralph Cossa (2001) also seek to enrich realist balancing theory with constructivist insights. Twomey's analysis of Japan as a "circumscribed" balancer, Green's analysis of Japan as a "reluctant realist," and Seng Tan's and Ralph Cossa's "cooperative balances" unfortunately are too inattentive to various aspects of socialization and identity to exploit the full benefits of analytical eclecticism. Amending his own published work, Robert Jervis (1999: 61–62) goes further than they do and usefully underlines a theoretical point that many realists and neoliberals discount unduly: the dynamic and unanticipated consequences that institutions can have for preferences over outcomes, especially through affecting in domestic politics "deeper changes in what the actors want and how they conceive of their interests."

Liberalism and constructivism can also be combined to good effect. This decade, for example, has witnessed the growth of formal and informal multilateral security arrangements in Asia-Pacific. "Cooperative" approaches focus on military and nonmilitary dimensions of security, seek to prevent the emergence of manifest security threats, and are inclusive in their membership. Dialogues and various confidence-building measures are crucial to the creation of mutual trust (Kamiya 1997: 21–22). These seek to lower the costs of making political contacts, facilitate the exchange of information, enhance transparency, and strengthen trust between governments (Interview 13-99, Tokyo, Jan. 14, 1999).

Multilateral security institutions can enhance efficiencies and over time alter underlying preferences and thus redefine interests (Gourevitch 1999: 137; Jervis 1999: 58–63). The analytic difference between these two effects is mirrored in the attitudes of Japanese officials between a more skeptical and "realistic" stance on Asian security institutions on the one hand and a more enthusiastic and "pacifist" one on the other (Interview 04-00, Tokyo, Jan. 12, 2000).

Over longer periods, multilateral security institutions can do more than create efficiencies in the relations between governments. They can redefine identities and acceptable standards of behavior and thus reduce or increase fear and hostility or the collective pursuit of economic prosperity and political cooperation. Scholars who have written on the ARF, for example, have made a strong case for the importance of informal and formal dialogues as ways of creating not only more transparency but also arenas of persuasion and a partial change in preferences and interests (Busse 2000, 1999; Acharya 1999a, 1999b, 1998, 1995; Johnston 1999b; Khong 1998; Simon 1998; Cheng n.d.).

Analytical eclecticism offers distinct advantages. Whether they stress materialist or ideational factors, rationalist analytic perspectives such as realism and liberalism are enriched when employed in tandem. And they are also enriched greatly by the incorporation of constructivist elements.

Discursive Politics: Bridging the Gap between Words and Action

Analytical eclecticism can also enrich our analysis of discursive politics or the politics of naming (Fierke 2002; M. Katzenstein 1998). Many American observers and policy makers tend to downplay the importance of discursive politics, even to dismiss it altogether as "cheap talk" or "mere rhetoric." Allen Carlson and J. J. Suh argue in the concluding chapter that this can be a big mistake. They offer a useful taxonomy that helps illuminate how, in the analysis of Japan's security policy, discursive politics matters. Discourse may be strictly instrumental, reflecting either genuine beliefs or willful misrepresentation. For example, American lawyers who have spent years in trade negotiations with Japanese bureaucrats want to "cut the talk" and get to the core of contentious issues. Besides being part of purposeful action, discourse is, however, also a means for communication and persuasion to arrive at collective understandings. This is what lawyers try to do in court and law professors try to do in class. Finally, discourse can be constitutive. It can create the very reality that an instrumentalist perspective takes for granted and that a communicative view sees as open to renegotiation. By naming a thing we bring it into existence. By insisting, for example that nuclear weapons are the main symbol of great-power status we make the possession of nuclear weapons more attractive. In this view discourse imbues a material world with meaning. In the creation of meaning, discourse draws on and resonates with existing symbols and perceptions widely shared in society. Ideological hegemony exists when discourse and social presupposition have melded so powerfully as to be thought of as a "natural" depiction of the world.

Analytical eclecticism shields the observer from taking any of the three types of discourse—instrumental, communicative, and constitutive—to be "natural," that is, beyond question. It is attuned instead to the fact that discourse can, as Carlson and Suh argue in the conclusion, "move" between different types, over time, and across different political domains. In our analysis of Japanese security policy, we find each of the three faces of discourse as an unending and deeply institutionalized process of producing, stabilizing, and reconciling different meanings. William Riker (1996) has called this process "heresthetic." It is a form of rhetorical action that relies on a form of public argumentation that draws on the commonsensical understandings of an audience as a resource to develop argumentative strategies, sometimes backed by persuasion, to prevail over political opponents and elicit the consent of the public (Jackson n.d.: 41–43). We thus view discursive politics as occurring in a public site where actors debate the meanings of power, interest, and identity.

Scholars navigate between explanatory sketches, politicians between words and action. Discursive politics (M. Katzenstein 1998), the politics of naming, is a politician's way of dealing with the inevitable tensions between the two. In domestic politics, discursive politics builds on a foundation of collective understandings that remain open to contestation. In international politics, discursive politics occurs in an environment in which contestation typically outweighs collective understandings. There actions often speak louder than words. If in the 1990s Japan had spent heavily to acquire a broad range of power projection capabilities this would undoubtedly have influenced international assessments of ambiguous Japanese pronouncements. However, measured in constant 1995 dollars, Japanese defense outlays increased by less than 7 percent between 1992 and 1999 (Ball 2000: 4). Japan's discursive politics thus was sufficiently synchronized with behavior for most governments in Asia-Pacific not to question seriously Japanese intentions.

Yet it remains true that since they carry different meanings in different national contexts words are easily misunderstood in international affairs. In domestic politics many Japanese accept the distinction between a literal reading of words and their interpretation. In international affairs such acceptance is much more limited. For what is said in one context often means something quite different in another. Discursive politics at home is often heard abroad as mere double-talk, deliberately deployed to obscure rather than inform.

"Talk" as an avenue to trust is distinctive of Asian regional security more generally. Informal security dialogues in Asia have proliferated and now number in the dozens. In the second half of 1995 one study reports forty-nine track-two dialogues, compared to thirteen governmental ones. And by early 1996 at least eighty multinational conferences, symposia, and workshops had been scheduled for the year to discuss security developments in Asia-Pacific. Although many are one-time affairs, a 1995 survey identified forty institutionalized fora in East Asia alone seeking to promote political, economic, and security discussions (Evans 2003, 1994; Cossa 1996: 25). The number of regional dialogues was so large that an Asia-wide regional commit-

tee has been set up to improve coordination among them (Shirk 1994: 6). The ARF
provided the forum for the European security discourse of common or cooperative
security that the Social Democratic parties of New Zealand and Australia as well as
Mikhail Gorbachev and the Canadian government introduced in Asia (Wiseman
1992: 42–43). Such discourse enhances transparency and predictability in an uncertain world by giving states more information. Over time such security discourse may
also affect how Asian states conceive of their relations with others in the evolution of
regional security orders.

Japan's discursive politics offers numerous examples important for an understanding
of Asian-Pacific security. The situational rather than geographic denotations of the
concept of "surrounding area" in the revised guidelines, discussed earlier in this chapter, for example, would be an explosive issue in an armed conflict between China and
Taiwan. To take a second example, the Japanese are deeply divided over the meaning
of their national anthem. "The government is tying itself in knots reinterpreting the
words to mean just about everything but what they seem to" (Kristof 1999). In another
example, the Japanese government has claimed since the 1950s that the constitution
does not prohibit the possession of purely defensive nuclear weapons. Such interpretation of the constitution has led to fears both at home and abroad that the Three Nonnuclear Principles enunciated in 1967 might be abandoned amid international tensions
(Lim 2002). And addressing specific domestic audiences whose collective understandings are at odds with those of audiences outside of Japan, Japanese politicians over
decades have acquired a reputation for "misspeaking" or being "misunderstood."

Article 9 of Japan's peace constitution illustrates with particular clarity the importance of discursive politics, of national security policy by interpretation. While
guiding Japanese defense policy in important ways, Article 9 has also functioned as a
legal and political cover that could be altered while leaving both political actors and
observers unclear when and where the constitution was stretched through reinterpretation or revised in practice. Repeated alterations have, to some, smacked of a
hypocritical opportunism and a rhetorical smokescreen to conceal bad intentions.

But the difference between "rhetorical" and "real" is often problematic and normally politically defined. Michael Green (1998: 13) asks rhetorically "what will happen when the Japanese people are really afraid?" and argues that the "real story" of
multilateral security arrangements such as the ARF will become apparent once we
know whether they are more than mere "'talk shops'" (Green 1998: 38). In a similar
vein, Mike Mochizuki (1997a: 5–40) argues that the United States and Japan should
transform their security arrangements into a "true alliance" marked by "a more equal
partnership in which Washington truly consults with Tokyo." Unreal fear and talk,
however, and untrue alliances and consultations are important parts of a discursive
politics that helps define the identities and interests of actors. In their interaction
with institutions they deserve to be taken seriously along with capabilities and information. From this vantage point security policy by constitutional reinterpretation is

an institutionalized way of adapting to change without throwing to the wind deeply institutionalized constitutional values and political practices. Article 9 is not a "meaningless" scrap of paper. A security policy that proceeds by a politics of constitutional reinterpretation illustrates how power and interest matter, shaped by the instrumental, communicative, and constitutive aspects of a discursive politics.

Championed by Japan since the late 1970s and developed further by ASEAN in the 1980s, the terminology of "comprehensive security" was broadened even further in the 1990s as it was increasingly accepted by Chinese officials to discuss Asian-Pacific security affairs (Capie, Evans, and Fukushima 1998: 25–30, IV/7–8; Interviews 08-98, 01-00, 03-00, 04-00, Beijing, June 21, 1998, and June 13, 2000). Throughout most of the Asia-Pacific region, the Asian financial crisis has reinforced the belief that security must be understood in "comprehensive" terms (Interviews 03-98 and 04-00, Beijing, June 15, 1998, and June 13, 2000). In the case of Japan, the concept of comprehensive security includes both external ("national" or "international") and internal ("societal") dimensions. Both are bringing Japan's Defense Agency, the Maritime Safety Agency, which is a part of the Ministry of National Land and Transportation, and the National Police Agency closer together. By exchanging information and developing new forms of cooperation the Ground Self-Defense Force, the Maritime Self-Defense Force (MSDF), and the police are attempting to meet what to the government looks like novel threats to Japan's security including incursions into Japan's coastal waters, acts of terrorism, and guerrilla attacks on airports, nuclear power plants, and harbors (Interview 10-00, Tokyo, Jan. 14, 2000).

The concepts of "confidence and security building measures" (CSBM's) and "preventive diplomacy" also illustrate the importance of discursive politics. Widely used by Japanese officials, they illustrate that meanings can be both roughly similar in different cultural contexts and also subtly different (Interviews 01-00, 07-00, 10-00, 11-00, Tokyo, Jan. 11, 13–14, 2000; Capie, Evans, and Fukushima 1998: 2, 33–6, 66–7, IV/10, 18). CSBM's refer to the enhancing of trust through words such as security dialogues or the publication of national white papers on defense. Few if any Japanese policy makers think of CSBM's as including the monitoring of maneuvers or the mutual inspection of military bases as would be quite common in Europe. The concept of preventive diplomacy also has acquired a specific meaning that differs from its European origin. Asian-Pacific governments have had a strong commitment to the principle of nonintervention. Until the July 2001 ARF meeting in Hanoi, in the CSCAP interstate conflict had been understood to be not part of the concept and practice of preventive diplomacy (Agence France Press 2001; Interview 09-00, Tokyo, Jan. 13, 2000; Ball and Acharya 1999). With the changes adopted at the Hanoi meeting, the intrastate conflicts would continue, however, to remain excluded from ARF's preventive diplomacy.

Discursive politics is at the center of the domestic basis of Japan's changing security policy. Security policy planning in Japan's MOFA focuses not on identifying real or potential international threats but on the persistent effort to convince the Diet of the necessity of the U.S.-Japan security relationship (Interview 07-00, Tokyo, Jan. 13, 2000). The government, however, does not dictate the terms of public debate. In the words of one Japanese defense official, "we must follow public opinion" (Interviews 01-99 and 11-00, Tokyo, Jan. 11, 1999, and Jan. 14, 2000). And public opinion is often shaped by Japan's mass media (Krauss 2000). Depending on the specific public interpretations of particular crises, the new guidelines thus could enhance or diminish policy flexibility (Interview 12-99, Tokyo, Jan. 14, 1999). Hitoshi Tanaka, a MOFA official involved in the writing of the new guidelines, argues that "there are always things that are left undefined by law, not only in the field of security but in every area. To begin with, what sort of development falls under what category of situation is a matter of judgment. . . . But I do think that we have to create a firm and clear legal framework for the mechanism by which the country reaches these decisions" (Ina 1997: 32).

The 1997 defense guidelines, implemented by a 1999 law laying down such a legal framework, remains open to discursive politics. The guidelines created the image of no more than an incremental domestic adjustment of Japan to the changing security environment in Asia-Pacific (Kato 1999: 17–18). That adjustment has occurred, according to its proponents, *within* the existing frameworks that the constitution and the U.S.-Japan Treaty of Mutual Security and Cooperation provide (Council on Foreign Relations 1998; Council on Foreign Relations Independent Study Group 1998: 2–4). In the words of Mike Mochizuki (1997a: 7), "bilateral military cooperation is to be strengthened by working within the existing policy parameters." An increasingly open domestic debate about the desirability of constitutional revision did not sway the Liberal Democratic Party (LDP) leadership from the path of incremental adaptation. The LDP's fear of opposition from their erstwhile coalition partners, Social Democrats and New Party Harbinger, the domestic public at large, and Japan's Asian-Pacific neighbors was simply too strong.

Discursive politics marks the debate over preemptive strikes. In 1956 the Hatoyama cabinet made a statement to the effect that taking minimum measures, such as attacking enemy missile bases, to defend against enemy attack is legal (Asagumo shimbun-sha 1998: 523). The statement did not elaborate on the conditions under which attacking enemy bases is permitted by the constitution. On March 18, 1970, the head of the Cabinet Legislation Bureau (CLB) specified three conditions before the Budget Committee of the Lower House. (1) A preemptive attack (defined as initiating an attack when there is a substantial risk of armed attack by an enemy) does not constitute the exercise of the right of self-defense. (2) The exercise of the right of self-defense is justified when an enemy attack has actually occurred and even before actual damage has been incurred. (3) The launching of an attack by an enemy constitutes the occurrence of an enemy attack; the identification of the occurrence of an attack is affected by specific circumstances.

Enunciated in 1970, this policy has persisted. On March 3, 1999, the head of the

Defense Agency, Hosei Norota, reportedly expressed before the Lower House Security Committee the view that the threat of a missile attack from North Korea was sufficiently grave that the Japanese government should consider the constitutionality of a preemptive strike against North Korea (Nakamoto 1999; *Wall Street Journal* 1999). In fact Norota expressed the view that "it is legally possible to exercise the right of self-defense and attack enemy base, even at a point in time when no actual damage has been inflicted on Japan" (www.shugiin.go.jp/index.nsf/html/index. htm). This was consistent with the second and third of the conditions of the CLB director's 1970 statement. The media's misinterpretation of Norota's statement and possible political misunderstandings among some members of the Diet and foreign governments led to an express reconfirmation of the 1970 statement by both the CLB and the JDA (Interviews 05-00, 11-00, and 12-00, Tokyo, Jan. 12 and 14, 2000; *Asahi shimbun* 1999b).

Discursive politics also marks the government's traditional position that the constitution prohibits all use of force except when Japan is under direct attack. In writing a bill dealing with the provision in the new guidelines committing Japan to cooperate with the United States in ship inspection based on UN Security Council resolutions, one of the main points of contention has been whether to allow the SDF to fire warning shots. The bill that eventually passed the Diet in November 2000 did not authorize the SDF to engage in such action (http://law.e-gov.go.jp/cgi-bin/idxsearch.cgi). While adhering to such a position, the government developed, in the context of the Gulf War of 1990–91, a doctrine defining the scope of the SDF's legitimate logistical support operations. The doctrine was to apply to situations that did not involve a direct attack on Japan. The SDF's logistical support operations "integrated with" use of force, whether it be American, UN-sponsored, or otherwise, are unconstitutional (Mochizuki 1997a: 20, 31–2). In the new guidelines and the law passed on May 25, 1999 to implement them, the government introduced the term "rear area." This was to avoid the integration of SDF operations with American military operations. "Rear area" refers, in the words of the guidelines, to "Japan's territory" and "high seas and international airspace around Japan which are distinguished from areas where combat operations are being conducted." The SDF's logistical support for the U.S. military is to be restricted to such areas. Furthermore, also to avoid SDF operations getting integrated with American use of force, the SDF is neither to provide the U.S. military with SDF-owned weapons and ammunition, nor, according to the new law, to refuel or rearm U.S. jet fighters about to strike enemy targets. Similarly, the Antiterrorism Special Measures Law of 2001, referred to above, excludes combat zones from the area in which the SDF may operate. The law also prohibits the SDF from providing American and other militaries with weapons and ammunition, and refueling or rearming jet fighters preparing to take off for combat. And when the government decided in November 2001 against sending a high-tech Aegis destroyer to the Indian Ocean, one important reason was the fear that the sharing of real-time battle data with U.S. counterparts might integrate its operations with American use of military force (*Asahi shimbun* 2001b).

Thus the new missions that the revised guidelines and the new law mapped for the SDF were, in theory, compatible with the government's traditional interpretation of the constitution and existing doctrine concerning logistical support. However, whether SDF operations in the "rear area" may actually avoid integration with combat operations in the context of modern warfare is open to serious question. The MSDF's chief of staff stated in a press conference after the revision of the guidelines that, taking long-range weapons into account, it is difficult to draw a line separating "rear area" from the area where combat operations are being conducted (*Asahi shimbun* 1997). To the extent that this is true, the sharp distinction between logistical support operations that are not integrated with the use of force, and those that are—and thus constitute, for example, a collective self-defense effort or participation in UN-sponsored military operations—has now been blurred.

Complications induced by changes in weapons technology are not a recent development. They have bedeviled Japanese security policy for years. Since the early 1980s, for example, advances in missile technology have made it impossible to defend against incoming missiles close to Japan (Interview 10-00, Tokyo, Jan. 14, 2000), thus leading to an increasingly expansive definition of the concept of "self"-defense. The United States and the Japanese public by and large have supported, or acquiesced to, a gradual change in Japanese policy. The process by which this has happened is shaped by the instrumental, communicative, and constitutive aspects of a discursive politics that exploits, tolerates, and reflects legal ambiguity (Katzenstein 1996a: 132–38).

The 1990s have posed this old dilemma with renewed urgency. The planned deployment of Japan's own military reconnaissance satellites and the planned acquisition of midair refueling capabilities by the Air Self-Defense Force (ASDF) are good examples. In 1969 the Diet passed a Resolution on the Peaceful Use of Space that permitted the SDF to use satellite technologies already in use for commercial purposes while prohibiting the militarization of space. The two satellites deployed in 2003 and the two to be deployed after 2004 are the outgrowth of a commercial venture that started around 1980 and meets the requirements of that policy as its capabilities will be similar to those of IKONOS (a satellite launched by an American firm for taking and merchandizing high quality aerial photos) (Interview 05-00, Tokyo, Jan. 12, 2000; Richardson 2000). A Cabinet Satellite Information Center was created in 2001 to plan the taking of aerial photos and to analyze them (http://news.tbs.co.jp/part_news/part_ news38743.html). Even though Japan needs to buy some technologies and parts for the new program from U.S. vendors, it is clear that the new satellites may eventually serve direct military purposes, for example, in cueing for upper-tier theater missile defense. Although there was some discussion about this in the United States, the Department of Defense has acknowledged the importance of Japan's independent capacity to gather information and the desirability of a mutual sharing of information. And

Asian-Pacific countries have not voiced any serious criticism of Japan's new policy (Interview 05-00, Tokyo, Jan. 12, 2000; *Asahi Evening News* 1999).

Acquisition of midair refueling capabilities has been a controversial issue since the 1970s. In December 1999, the government decided to include the procurement of air-to-air refueling aircraft in the 2001–6 Mid-term Defense Plan (Iitake 1999). And in December 2001, the government decided to make an initial deposit on the first plane during FY 2002 (*Asahi shimbun* 2001d). The government maintains that the program is consistent with the new National Defense Program Outline and a report issued in 1994 by the Advisory Group on Defense Issues, a blue-ribbon commission appointed by Prime Minister Hosokawa. Although it is true that offensive capabilities are strengthened, from the perspective of Japanese defense officials the new technology needs to be combined with others that Japan lacks to create offensive capabilities such as jamming capability to protect aircraft from SAM attacks. There have been few negative responses from Asian-Pacific countries. There was no discussion with the United States about the inclusion of the program in the next Mid-term Defense Plan since the United States regards it as uncontroversial; the F4, F15, F16, and F2 all can be refueled and twenty-five countries, including China and Singapore, have refueling aircraft (Interview 05-00, Tokyo, Jan. 12, 2000). But in this instance, too, technological change is having the effect of expanding Japan's definition of "self"-defense. Japanese policy makers thus seek to make compatible the contradictions between the historical legacies of pacifism and the dynamism of technological change. What to foreign observers looks simply like deliberate deception is often a complex amalgam of taken-for-granted Japanese policy assumptions and instrumental exploitation of rhetorical ambiguities.

Discursive politics brings together the disparate worlds of words and action. At home it bends the, for realists, "natural" forces that should propel Japan to become a "normal country" seeking power projection capabilities and nuclear weapons to counter an emerging threat from China. Yet an analysis of Japanese defense policy demonstrates that the offensive and defensive character of weapons is not determined technologically as much as it is constructed politically (Katzenstein 1996a: 131–52). In a Chinese context, and for different reasons, Thomas Christensen (1999: 64) argues similarly that "the usual argument about the offense-defense balance and the security dilemma applies poorly." Discursive politics is an important mechanism through which political actors move between word and action. Rather than stressing any one of its instrumental, communicative, or constitutive functions to the exclusion of all others, it is better to see how several of them interlace in the production of discursive structures. Such an eclectic approach will probably give scholars more analytic leverage on the multilayed and complex connections between power, interest, and norms than insistence on a more parsimonious approach.

The discursive politics of Japanese security matters. We have argued here that in Japan it creates ambiguity not clarity, for example, in the renegotiation of the security arrangements with the United States. This ambiguity expresses political strategies that may seem odd to Americans, such as embedding apparently antithetical bilateral and multilateral elements of policy in a "multidimensional" frame. This is not the kind of ambiguity that rationalist theory of bargaining has built into deterrence theory. In the Japanese case ambiguity has sources other than instrumental rationality.

This argument receives support from a decade of experimental work in the field of cultural psychology. The results point in a direction that is uncomfortable for the universalist aspirations of a rationalist cognitive psychology. East Asian patterns of cognition value context, U.S. patterns object. The geography of thought that Richard Nisbett (2003) maps looks very different in East Asia than it does in the United States.

The instrumental, communicative, and constitutive aspects of discourse appear in different forms in realist, liberal, and constructivist approaches. Generally speaking, realist and liberal approaches stress the instrumental aspects of discourse while constructivism highlights its communicative and constitutive features. But this distinction is only useful as a first cut. Truly hegemonic, uncontested, and uncontestable hegemonic discourse makes the world so unproblematic that the difference between realism and constructivism vanishes. Similarly, the emphasis liberal explanations place on the importance of information for signaling, updating of beliefs, and bargaining is rarely included in constructivist analyses. Yet information is an important aspect of communication and persuasion. It thus would be a mistake to draw too sharp a line separating liberalism from constructivism. Put differently, an analysis of discursive politics is served best by analytical eclecticism.

Conclusion

The American war on terrorism has had little influence in changing the trajectory of Japan's security policy in Asia. The sense of vulnerability that Americans experienced so viscerally and for the first time on September 11 has been with the Japanese since August 1945. That sense of vulnerability has given a very broad scope to the Japanese definition of the concept of security and helped define the basic principles of Japanese security policy for more than half a century. Reliance on the U.S. security guarantee and a cautious and gradual adjustment to changes in its security environment have been central to Japan's approach (Katzenstein 1996a). In contrast to the United States, far from rupturing, September 11 has reinforced Japan's traditional approach to problems of security.

This is not to deny that 9/11 was, if not the beginning of a new "war," as for the Bush administration, still a "big event" (Katzenstein 2003). It prompted quick adjustments in policy and paying close attention to the actions of Japan's most important ally. The adjustments, however, occurred along familiar lines charted since the Gulf War. They aimed at increasing Japan's readiness to participate in U.S.-led multinational security operations, short of assisting the U.S. military in combat. They did not lead to a reevaluation of Japan's approach to its internal security. On balance, then,

Japan's response to September 11 resembled closely those with which it matched the many serious security crises it has encountered over the last several decades: Japan's policy was carefully measured and cautiously incremental.

An important reason for this continuity in approach is the obvious fact that Japan evidently does not feel threatened directly by Al Qaeda. September 11 presented to the Japanese government a political opportunity to show resolve and to preempt the criticism of being a do-nothing power. Prime Minister Koizumi quickly committed Japan to a seven-point emergency plan in support of possible U.S. countermeasures in Afghanistan. Pictures broadcast around the globe showed units of the Japanese navy accompanying the USS Kitty Hawk and other ships as they left, seemingly, for the Arabian Sea. Furthermore, in April 2002 the government submitted to the Diet a bill granting it what it saw as badly needed powers in case of an enemy attack. The absence of such legislation had been a long-standing source of complaint of conservatives as well as military officials. Enacted in June 2003, the legislation introduced the concept of "situations in which armed attack has come to be expected," which the government, by interpretation, links to the inherently and deliberately kept ambiguous concept of "situations in areas surrounding Japan." More relevant for the immediate crisis was the fact that under an emergency law quickly enacted by the Diet in October 2001, the Japanese military is now empowered to give logistical support to U.S. and other military forces engaged in antiterrorist missions countering the attack on September 11 anywhere in the world. Specifically, the Japanese navy has provided support for U.S. forces in the Indian Ocean since December 2001, mostly by refueling ships of the U.S. navy. Further, under a law passed in July 2003 the SDF is authorized to provide logistical support to foreign militaries operating in Iraq. The Air Self-Defense Force planes have transported supplies for American and British militaries since March 2004. The two new legislations have broadened the geographic scope of Japanese-U.S. military cooperation. These changes are significant but not revolutionary. As was true before, the SDF is prohibited by law from positioning itself in combat zones, providing the U.S. or other militaries with weapons or ammunition, and refueling or rearming allied aircraft prior to takeoff for combat missions. In sum, the reaction of the Japanese government to 9/11 has consolidated policy changes during the 1990s that have pushed Japan into playing a more active role in dealing with Asian regional security issues as a junior partner of the United States.

It is far less clear, however, whether Japan has done anything since 9/11 to enhance its capacity to deal with the threat of terrorism. This is very much in keeping with the government's tepid response to the threat that Aum Shinrikyō posed in the 1990s, culminating with the sarin gas attack in the Tokyo subway in 1995. The debates on legislation submitted to the Diet since September 11 have not made much of the fact that the war on terrorism has begun to spread to Southeast Asia, with Singapore and the Philippines as the initial battle sites. It is far from clear that the current terrorism in Southeast Asia is closely linked to global networks. Although some links exist, demon-

strably in the case of cells arrested in Singapore in January 2002 and possibly in Indonesia and perhaps Malaysia, the importance of Al Qaeda arguably lies in providing
a global frame of reference for local or regional grievances rather than in providing
operational guidance for terrorist acts. Yet this may be less relevant than the fact that
the United States in fighting a war on terrorism may be informed by a variety of political motivations that seek to further U.S. interests in Asia that are unrelated to that
war. For example, such a war is a convenient way of reinserting the U.S. military into
the Philippines, at the request of the Philippine government. And it provides a convenient pretext for the Bush administration's get-tough policy toward North Korea.
For reasons unrelated to global developments, local or regional terrorist networks in
Asia thus might become targets of an American policy. Despite Japan's low-key approach to international affairs and its low international profile, as America's most
prominent ally in Asia-Pacific, Japanese embassies, businesses, and tourists might become inviting targets for terrorist attacks. In this way the American war on terrorism
might pose or intensify new security threats for Japan. Yet Japan continues to work
for peace with a shrinking foreign aid budget that is more clearly focused on helping
settle some of Asia's most difficult civil wars, for example, in the Philippines, Sri
Lanka, East Timor, Afghanistan, Cambodia, and Indonesia (Brooke 2002).

To date, however, the United States has largely been an important part of the solution to the security dilemmas that Japan has faced in Asia-Pacific for the last half
century. Japan's political caution so far has always succeeded in minimizing the risk
of being drawn into the far-flung and occasionally imprudent military actions of the
U.S. government in Asia. The war on terrorism raises this familiar prospect once
again. In the record of Japanese policy since September 11 there is little indication
that Japanese caution will be exhausted in the near future. There is no reason to believe that the analytical eclecticism that serves us so well in understanding the multifaceted character of Japan's security policy during the last half century will be less
helpful for an analysis of the cautious stance that marks Japanese policy since 9/11.

Notes

1. The 1998 hiatus was most likely occasioned by the adoption of the revised U.S.-Japan
guidelines. Interview 13-00, Tokyo, Jan. 14, 2000.

2. The following month, the government dispatched two supply ships and three
destroyers to the Indian Ocean. Replacements were made in February 2002 (*Asahi
shimbun* 2002a, 2001a, 2001c). Between December 2001 and early May 2002, the supply ships refueled U.S. ships sixty-five times and British ones three times (*Asahi shimbun* 2002b). The cabinet decided in May 2002, November 2002, and May 2003 to
continue with the operations for another six months (*Asahi shimbun* 2003, 2002c,
2002d).

4

Bound to Last?

The U.S.-Korea Alliance and Analytical Eclecticism

J. J. SUH

The last two decades of the twentieth century represented an extraordinary period for the "German Democratic Republic" ("GDR") and "Federal Republic of Germany" ("FRG"). The Cold War confrontation, which seemed so entrenched that no political scientist had anticipated its end, all of a sudden disappeared. The two arch adversaries who seemed determined to pursue their confrontation to the end decided to terminate their enmity. The détente was accompanied by a gradual but unmistakable power shift at the systemic level, which by the end of the twentieth century transformed the international structure from bipolar to unipolar. With the political rapprochement between the United States and Soviet Union—not to mention the latter's disappearance in short order—and with the transformation of the international structure came the political momentum to move beyond the East-West divide in "Europe." Numerous meetings, including a summit, were held between the "GDR" and "FRG," and it seemed almost certain that "Germany" would finally overcome the division imposed on her by outside powers at the end of World War II. A couple of years into the new millennium, however, the two "Germanys" are as frozen in their Cold War division as ever. There are very few contacts and fewer exchanges—cultural, humanitarian, or otherwise—across the dividing line. Lest we forget that the "Germanys" are still in the state of war, the "German" militaries occasionally clash near the border and exchange fire. The clashes predictably roll back the

I would like to thank the following for their criticisms, comments, and suggestions on earlier drafts of this chapter: Amitav Acharya, Steven Benfell, Allen Carlson, Victor Cha, Tom Christensen, Avery Goldstein, David Kang, Peter Katzenstein, Chong-Sik Lee, Ian Lustick, Chung-In Moon, Rudy Sil, members of seminars at Cornell University, and participants in the Cornell Workshop on Asian Security: Alternative Analytical Perspectives (28–30 Mar. 2002).

little political rapprochement the two "Germanys" have made. Seen in the context of sea changes at the global and regional level, "divided Germany" looks like "a Cold War island in a sea of détente."

The "GDR" and "FRG" in the above story, of course, are not the real Germanys but pseudonyms for South Korea and North Korea. I use the pseudonyms to bring to relief the remarkable difference between Germany and Korea. Seen in this comparative light, the continuation of the Korean division—and of the U.S.-Korea alliance whose existence is predicated on the division—into the twenty-first century makes for a dramatic nonevent. This chapter analyzes the nonevent and presents an explanation for it. This nonevent, politically significant as it is in itself, presents a fertile ground for testing different analytic perspectives. I argue that analyses that rely on one perspective to the exclusion of all others fall short of capturing the complex link between power, interest, and identity that lies behind the nonevent under study. It is only by drawing selectively and judiciously on different analytic traditions that the analyst can fully understand the nonevent in its full complexity. Analytical eclecticism frees the analyst from the intellectual straight-jacket of monocausal paradigms, and enables her to concentrate on explaining empirical anomalies rather than focus on battling contending paradigms.

I illustrate this argument by examining the U.S.-Korea military alliance in a way that draws on insights made by realist, institutionalist, and constructivist styles of analysis. My purpose is explicitly to explain a political phenomenon and not to demonstrate the supremacy of a particular analytic construct—be it material capabilities, institutional features, or ideational factors—or of a particular paradigm—be it realism, liberalism, or constructivism. My problem-focused research, with its openness to different analytic approaches, leads me to a theoretical model of institutional persistence that is informed by interparadigm debates in the field but is not driven by a prior commitment to a particular side to the debate. In the first section, I demonstrate that analyses that rely exclusively on material capabilities miss key aspects of the evidence. In the second section, I argue that the institutional features, which the U.S.-Korea alliance has produced, enhance the efficiency of the alliance's operation but that its continuation is not justified on the grounds of efficiency. Next I make the counterintuitive argument that the alliance is grounded on interdependent identity needs among South and North Koreas and the United States despite the apparent fact that there is more commonality between the first two than between Korea and the United States. In the last section, I argue that alliance persistence is best explained by a model that synthesizes insights made by realist, liberal, and constructivist styles of analysis. I conclude with reflections on the implications of my argument for the future of Korea's security and the U.S. role in the Korean Peninsula, particularly in light of 9/11 and its aftermath.

Why Is the U.S.-Korea Alliance a Puzzle?

As Katzenstein and Sil argue in Chapter 1, one of the advantages of analytical eclecticism lies in its power to enable the analyst to problematize what seems normal and to unpack what looks like the natural order of things. Analytical eclecticism is particularly useful in analyzing "nonevents" because by definition they seem "natural," and hence elude the analyst's attention. Nonevents hide behind the status quo to preempt analytic investigation; they offer conventional wisdom to stifle scholarly inquiry. Continuation of a political institution constitutes one such nonevent. A political institution, be it a state, a central bank, or an alliance, may emerge out of a political competition or confrontation but, once established, it frames political discourse and channels political behavior, making the institution look like part of political normalcy. It is then within the political institution that not only "normal" politics but also political conflicts are framed and carried out—until of course political entrepreneurs begin to challenge it. An institution is part and parcel of "normal" politics. Analytical eclecticism offers a useful and effective tool to put normal politics under scholarly scrutiny. In the effort to problematize and explain such normalcy, I put under the lens of analytical eclecticism the continuation of the U.S.-Korea military alliance.

In this section, I offer a definition of alliance persistence, my dependent variable, and show why the persistence of the U.S.-Korea alliance constitutes an anomaly that defies monocausal analyses. I unpack persistence into three different components as a way to show that a single explanatory framework blinds the analyst to some aspects of reality. The Korean nonevent represents an anomaly for a number of analytic traditions that focus on one variable to the exclusion of others. Realists argue the alliance exists because of power or threat disparity; but they remain oblivious to changes on the ground. Liberals argue the alliance has created institutional features that enhance efficiency; but they overlook the fact that the continuation of the alliance has little to do with efficiency. Constructivists argue that shared norms and identities can lead to the establishment of a security community; but they have little to say about the alignment pattern that cuts against shared identity.

In my chapter, I adopt Kegley and Raymond's definition of alliance: "formal agreements between sovereign states for the putative purpose of coordinating their behavior in the event of specified contingencies of a military nature" (1990: 52). First, this definition provides the rigor necessary to differentiate alliances from similar phenomena, such as alignments. An alignment is a relationship that is more general, less formal, and possibly more encompassing than an alliance. It is defined by actions, rather than formal treaties, and often extends into political, economic, and cultural spheres (Morrow 1991; Ward 1982). Second, and more important for this study, the formal definition allows for assessing alliance persistence.

There has been a considerable amount of research and theoretical debate about the purposes of alliances. Political scientists in general group these purposes into two categories: power balancing and bandwagoning. Historical studies, however, have shown that, to protect their integrity, states engage in much more variegated behavior than balancing and bandwagoning, including "hiding" and "transcending" (Deudney 1995; Schroeder 1994a, 1994b; Schweller 1994). It is not my intention here to participate in the debate on the purposes or origins of alliances. I take it as unproblematic that alliances are formed for various purposes and reasons, and limit my research to defensive alliances formed to "balance power." My purpose is to use realist predictions, the most rigorous theoretical articulations of alliance formation, as a baseline against which to test one empirical case. The argument I develop in this chapter, nevertheless, should hold as well for the persistence of alliances formed for purposes other than power balancing.

An alliance is said to "persist" when it is renewed or continued even after the initial conditions that gave rise to it have disappeared or been so transformed as to eliminate the original need. Since a defensive alliance is formed to counterbalance a power distribution deemed unfavorable to a state, the alliance is viewed as persisting if it continues after that power has been so redistributed as to give the state a capability equal to or greater than its adversary. It is not easy to determine precisely when a state's needs for an alliance have expired, not just because it is difficult to ascertain the correlates of forces but also because alliance practices, as I argue below, are implicated in the assessment of the "objective reality" of military balance. Although it may be technically infeasible to pinpoint the time of a power-balance reversal and politically implausible to anticipate an alliance's termination as soon as the reversal occurs, it is reasonable to expect to observe a few years, even a decade, of uncertainty and confusion, parallel with the changes in power distribution, when political entrepreneurs are engaged in activities and debate in support of or opposition to the goal of alliance preservation. If the actors perceive little change in the caliber of the threat despite the power redistribution, and thus make few efforts to reformulate the alliance, however, then this is a clear case of alliance persistence. Also if the actors are cognizant of the power shift but show no willingness to consider changing the alliance, this too qualifies as alliance persistence.

Another difficulty in determining alliance persistence concerns role substitution: an alliance, formed to counterbalance country C, may be reconfigured to balance country D. The issue is complicated because it is possible that the role substitution might have come about to justify the continuation of the alliance, a clear case of alliance persistence where role substitution is used as a tool of persistence. But it is equally plausible that power has been redistributed in such a way that the same allies are compelled to remain allied against a new adversary. The latter may be considered a special case of alliance persistence that takes advantage of existing institutional arrangements.[1] The question of how to distinguish one from the other can only be answered by closely analyzing each case, bringing in historical and comparative cases to bear upon the arguments put forth for the role substitution.

I argue that the U.S.-ROK alliance is persisting in the twenty-first century. The alliance was formed in the 1950s to counterbalance the power superiority of North Korea over South Korea. The U.S.-South Korea alliance was justified on the grounds that U.S. power was needed to restore the imbalance caused by Pyongyang's power edge, which was amplified by the alliances North Korea had forged with the Soviet Union and China. Throughout the intervening decades, however, there have been such profound and unmistakable shifts in power distribution that by the beginning of the twenty-first century the North's power advantage has been neutralized, if not replaced, by the South's superiority (Beldecos and Heginbotham 1995; Hayes 1994, 1991; Yi Yŏng-Hŭi 1992; Goose 1987).[2] And yet the U.S.-ROK alliance lives on. On the basis of capabilities alone, capability-based theories would expect North Korea to forge new alliances, yet one observes the opposite: it is losing its traditional allies, Russia and China. Despite the North's declining power and growing international isolation, there has been little noticeable change in the political actors' perception of the power transition and few observable efforts, by either the South Korean government or oppositional social movement groups, to bring the alliance in line with the power shift (Cha 1997; Cumings 1997; Bandow 1996).[3] To most in South Korea the alliance looks like the natural order of things. To them a Korea without the alliance is "unthinkable."

This summary statement, however, shortchanges realist theories and conceals an important aspect of the phenomenon. For there is a crucial difference between the beginning and end of the 1990s in the vitality of the alliance. In the early 1990s the U.S. government decided to begin the process of military drawdown from Korea and the South Korean government seemed to begin to prepare for a Korea without U.S. military support. The U.S.-Korea alliance began to decline in the face of a declining threat, just as realists would predict. The U.S. Congress passed on July 31, 1989 the Nunn-Warner revised resolution that called for a reduction of the U.S. Forces in Korea (USFK); a few months later, in 1990, the Bush administration adopted the East Asia Strategic Initiative, a three-stage plan to reduce the size of the American military presence in Korea. As the first major step, the 802nd Division of the U.S. Army Corps of Engineers was dissolved in February 1992. By early 1992, the U.S. government was well on its way to completing the first stage of the reduction whereby 5,000 noncombatants would be withdrawn from its ground forces in Korea. The Department of Defense went so far as to suggest in its report to the Congress in May 1992 that it would decide whether or not to *dissolve* the Combined Forces Command on the basis of its assessment of the North Korean threat. In the most significant step, the Bush administration withdrew all U.S. tactical nuclear weapons from South Korea in 1991.

The series of events in this period seemed, therefore, to signal realism's triumph:

the end of the Cold War and the decline of North Korea's power began to bring about changes in the U.S.-Korea alliance in line with realist expectations. Given that the power and threat changes were already unmistakable by this time, these moves corroborate realist insights. Although the two allied governments never explicitly suggested they were contemplating the termination of the alliance, the dissolution of the Combined Forces Command would have in effect ended the alliance. And the fact that the governments showed their willingness to consider the end of the Combined Forces Command (CFC) suggests that they recognized the profound power shifts warranted a modification of the alliance structure. In line with the direction of the power transition, they began to reduce the alliance's military capability.

These policies of drawdown, however, were all reversed in the following years and led to the entrenchment of the alliance by the end of the decade, confounding realist expectations. The process of reversal began with the Twenty-third Security Consultative Meeting (SCM) in 1991 where the allies "agreed to postpone the second stage of USFK troop cuts, originally scheduled to begin in 1993" (Ministry of National Defense 1993: 143). At the Fourteenth Military Committee Meeting (MCM) the following year, top officers from the U.S. and Korean militaries agreed to recommend to their respective governments the resumption of the Team Spirit exercises in 1993 and the suspension of the second stage of Bush's withdrawal plan. At the Twenty-fourth SCM the next day, the two governments approved the two recommendations made by the MCM, and furthermore reconfirmed that the United States would extend its nuclear umbrella to South Korea.

Following the Twenty-fifth SCM decision in November 1993 to suspend the second stage reduction, the U.S. Department of Defense put the final nail in the coffin by issuing its 1995 posture statement, *U.S. Security Strategy in the East Asia Pacific Region*, that declared the number of U.S. troops stationed in Korea would no longer be reduced as part of the new plan to maintain the total number of U.S. soldiers in Asia at 100,000. The posture statement in a single stroke effectively killed Bush's reduction plan, the Nunn-Warner resolution, and Department of Defense's plan to study the feasibility of a CFC dissolution. The U.S.-Korea alliance would face no further reduction of forces and no more changes in its structure; it could now go on practicing "alliance as usual."

The reversal is particularly troublesome for realist theories because the balance of power and threat on the Korean Peninsula tilted even further in favor of South Korea throughout the rest of the 1990s. Since the allied governments, recognizing the favorable power transition, began the process of alliance reduction in the beginning of the decade, realists would expect them to, if anything, accelerate the process. Changes in the power distribution at the end of the 1980s brought about the corresponding reduction in the allied military power at the start of the 1990s; bigger and more profound changes should cause a faster and larger reduction, if realist insights are right. What we observe instead is the opposite. North Korea's material capabilities continued to decline in absolute and relative terms through the 1990s; yet the U.S.-Korea alliance not only persisted but also increased its military capabilities.

It is easy to see that this disjunction between the capabilities and the alliance represents an anomaly for analyses that focus exclusively on material capabilities. North Korea's economic and military capabilities have declined relative to South Korea's at least for the past thirty years; and they have declined in absolute terms also for the past ten years or so. If in the 1950s South Korea and North Korea were more or less on a par in terms of their GNP's, the South's GNP began to outstrip the North's in the late 1960s, exponentially widening the gap ever since. By 1995, the South had an economy about forty times as big as the North. During the 1960s, Pyongyang had outspent Seoul on the military, but Seoul soon caught up and began to surpass Pyongyang in 1972, and the gap widened throughout the rest of the 1970s and the 1980s, resulting in a cumulative difference of $38.7 billion by 1990. In 1997, the South's defense spending was $15 billion, more than seven times as much as the North's $2 billion. These macro power indicators display a clear, consistent trend: North Korea's economic and military power was superior to the South's in the 1950s, but these sectors grew at a slower rate than South Korea's and were overtaken by those of the South in the 1970s. The power gap between the two Koreas continued to widen throughout the 1980s and 1990s (Hamm 1999; Dunnigan 1993). Yet there has been no change in the military alliance between South Korea and the United States.

Despite North Korea's weakness in aggregate economic indices, it is at least conceptually possible that it possess the military capability to successfully invade the South. Some indicators indeed show that the North Korean People's Army (NKPA) enjoys an overwhelming numerical superiority over the South Korean Army (ROKA) in manpower and every weapons category. The North's army is estimated to total 930,000 soldiers, outnumbering the 575,000 troops in the South Korean army by about 1.6:1. The North outnumbers the South in tanks and mortars by roughly 50 percent. The NKPA has more than twice as many artillery pieces as the ROKA while enjoying a 4-to-1 superiority in self-propelled artillery and a 16-to-1 supremacy in multiple rocket launchers (International Institute for Strategic Studies 1997).

There are a couple of problems with these seemingly robust facts, however. First, if these accurately reflect the actual fighting capabilities, they may explain the continuation of the alliance but cannot account for the early 1990s efforts to draw down the allies' military. If these numbers justify the alliance in the twenty-first century, they certainly called for the same, if not a higher, level of military readiness a decade ago. But despite these robust numbers, Bush's Republican administration decided to reduce its military presence in Korea and even considered disbanding the Combined Forces Command. This suggests that these "bean counts" might not have been the only, or even primary, power indicators the decision makers relied on.

Second, and related to the above point, the ROKA's alarming numerical inferiority may not accurately reflect its fighting capabilities since the "bean counts" conceal a number of crucial qualitative differences. Most of the South's military equipment is more advanced and more capable than that of the North's. For example, the North's main battle tanks, the T-54/55 and the T-62, were introduced in 1949 and 1961 respectively while the South's main battle tanks, the K1–A1, were produced in the 1990s. Of the North's 860 combat aircraft, 460 are MiG-17s and MiG-21s (and J-7s, a Chinese version of the MiG-21), Soviet fighters designed in the 1950s, while 260 are yet older vintages. Twenty-four MiG-29s represent the only modern fighter aircraft in the North's inventory whereas the South's main combat aircraft consists of F16s, which are superior to MiG-29s (Department of Defense 1990; Dunnigan 1988).[4] By combining quantitative and qualitative factors, some analysts have suggested that the South has an overall military capability superior to the North while others make a somewhat less bold estimate that it possesses the capability at least to deter a North Korean attack or defend itself if the deterrence should fail (Hamm 1999; Suh 1999a; O'Hanlon 1998; Hayes 1991; Goose 1987). Both groups' analyses draw a consistent and mutually reinforcing conclusion that the South's military has the capability, without American support, to thwart a North Korean blitzkrieg. Not only the aggregate measures of power but also Weapons Effectiveness Index/Weapons Unit Value (WEI/WUV) scores and simulations show that the South does not need outside assistance to counterbalance the North's military power. Furthermore, these serious analyses have faced few challenges or rebuttals. And yet the alliance goes on as if it by the end of the 1990s had become blind to the more sophisticated analyses of power that it seemed to see only several years earlier.

In the 1990s, moreover, Pyongyang lost its traditional military allies and Seoul picked up the very same countries as new friends. The North's defense treaty with Russia expired in 1991 and was replaced almost a decade later with a "Treaty of Friendship, Good Neighborliness, and Cooperation" devoid of the provision of "automatic military intervention in case of a contingency" (BBC 2000). Moscow and Beijing, Pyongyang's traditional allies, who had maintained their distance from Seoul, entered into diplomatic relationships with Seoul in 1990 and 1992, respectively. Moscow has embraced its new partner enthusiastically, not only holding *ten* summit meetings by 1999 and enlarging its trade but also sending to the South its most advanced weapons systems, such as T-80Us, that it did not even sell to the North. Taking a more nuanced approach, Beijing seems to be engaged in an equidistance policy, treating the North more or less on the same footing as the South. Beijing made it known that maintaining peace on the Korean Peninsula was its priority. There is no question that this new international configuration represented a sea change from the previous arrangement in which the Communist countries, the Soviet Union and China, had been South Korea's "enemy states" and appeared to be ready and eager to assist the North's military adventures. In the 1970s and 1980s, South Korea might have been able to fend off a North Korean military offensive, an assessment upon which Presidents Nixon and Carter seemed to have based troop withdrawal decisions. At that time, however, one could not rule out the possibility, indeed the likelihood, of the North being assisted by its allies, a scenario that was used to oppose American disengagement and to support alliance maintenance. By the 1990s this scenario was no longer a serious possibility. Clearly neither Russia nor China was interested in supporting any adventuristic moves by the North. The international power configuration made the U.S.-Korea alliance irrelevant. Yet there was no change in the alliance.

By the summer of 1994 Pyongyang's nuclear programs became the central security concern of the alliance to the point where the Clinton administration seriously considered taking military measures to destroy the North's nuclear facilities. Realists might cite the North's nuclear capability as a palpable material factor that justifies the alliance, and this at first sight looks plausible. As I elaborate later in the chapter, however, the "nuclear crisis" is not so much a material fact as a social reality. Even if North Korea is armed with nuclear weapons, the material capability alone cannot explain why it is that the North's bomb is perceived as a threat while Chinese or American bombs are not. The answer lies in the *social* structure of enmity, the "Hobbesian culture" as Wendt (1999) calls it, that exists between the alliance and North Korea. The North Korean bomb is a threat because the North is—just as U.S. bombs are not a threat because the United States is not. As Weldes (1999) argues with respect to the "Cuban missile crisis," facts on the ground (and at sea) lend themselves to multiple interpretations and are perceived differently by actors who understand the world in different terms. Just as the events on and around Cuba in 1962 were seen as a crisis by a United States that understood the world through the Manichaean prism of the Cold War, so were the events in North Korea in 1994, and again in 2002–3, perceived as a security threat by a United States and South Korea that were locked in a Cold War–like enmity with the North. All of this suggests that material capability indicators have some explanatory power but *by themselves* fail to account for the existence of the threat and hence the U.S.-Korea alliance in the twenty-first century.

A plausible way to salvage the power-balancing theory is to suggest that there has been a substitution of the threat against which the alliance is balancing. The most likely new threat would have to be China. Yet throughout the Clinton administration China was characterized as a "strategic partner"; under the Bush administration it has become a "strategic competitor." The two countries have been engaged in a complex strategic tango in which they push and pull each other, gauging the "partner's" or "competitor's" strength and intentions. But it would be a stretch of the imagination to argue that the U.S.-Korea alliance has been reconfigured to counterbalance China. Likewise, although there have been discussions among policy makers and analysts from Korea and the United States about a possible reconstitution of the alliance against a new threat, there is no consensus yet as to who is the new threat: some, particularly from the United States, point to China whereas others, especially from Korea, to Japan. "Strategic uncertainty" seems to be the uneasy compromise, but the allied governments do not even quibble about this as they share a unanimous view that the alliance must be maintained against North Korea.

Another way to salvage balancing theory is to add a perceptual variable to argue that the alliance continues to counterbalance "threat." Walt (1987) notes that Waltz's theory of balance is an indeterminate systemic theory that is inadequate to explain state policies. He argues that a state's decision to ally against another state can be explained by adding a variable of threat: states balance against threat. The level of threat is measured in terms of geographic proximity and aggressive intention among other factors. Given that aggressive intention is the only variable in the Korean case, Walt's argument can be operationalized in terms of Pyongyang's aggressive intention: the greater its aggressive intention, the greater the need to maintain an alliance.

Even Walt's modified realist theory, however, does not fare well in explaining the persistence of the U.S.-Korea alliance. Beginning with the nonagression pact that Pyongyang signed with Seoul and the nonnuclear declaration in 1991, Pyongyang has engaged in its version of "Glasnost." In the nonagression pact, Pyongyang publicly pledged that it would not initiate aggression. The North dramatically increased its peaceful interactions and exchanges with the South, and repeated in various statements that it had no intention or desire to attack the South or to reunify the country by force.[5] North-South trade ballooned more than 3,000 percent from $19 million in 1989 to $724 million by 2003, involving 581 South Korean businesses. By the end of January 2004, Pyongyang had allowed over 600,000 South Koreans to visit North Korea as tourists; the number of nontourist visitors jumped dramatically from 183 in 1990 to 12,825 in 2002 (Ministry of Unification, n.d.; Korean National Tourism Organization, 2004). A number of South Korean businesses were building or operating factories in the North, all with Pyongyang's blessing.

As Pyongyang was increasing peaceful exchanges with the South and toning down its belligerent rhetoric, it made numerous and consistent peace proposals and gestures toward the United States throughout the 1990s: to sign a peace treaty, to end hostilities, and to normalize its relationship with Washington. A content analysis of Kim Il-Sung's New Year's addresses shows that the United States was cast in more favorable terms in the 1990s than in previous decades and that Pyongyang was more interested in peaceful engagement with Washington than in confrontation.[6] Combined with a shift in the power balance, these moves suggest that there was a decline in the North's "aggressive intention," as defined by Walt (1987). The balance of threat, measured in these terms, has moved in favor of the South. Yet there is no change in the U.S.-Korea alliance.

I am not arguing that North Korea is a peaceful country that harbors *no* aggressive intention, but rather that there was a decline in the indicators that one would use to measure "aggressive intention." At any give moment there are other contradicting indicators that show "aggressive intention," such as the forward deployment of its military forces, intermittent clashes along the border, or occasional bellicose re-marks.[7] It also adds to perceptions in the United States and Japan of the North as a rogue state that has been engaged in weapons trade, kidnappings of unarmed citizens, and drug smuggling. In the history of confrontation between the two Koreas, how-ever, these represent a constant. North Korea has always maintained a large conven-tional force near the Southern border; small-scale military clashes are the order of the day; and flamboyant rhetoric of war represents a hallmark of North Korea's state-ments. What has changed is the emergence and increase of peace gestures, initiatives, and measures—particularly in the 1990s. Since the late 1980s, Pyongyang has said and done a number of things that should have reduced the threat perception: the North-South Denuclearization and Non-Aggression Declaration, the Geneva Framework, the North-South summit, and others. Since states can change their policies and since their declarations and agreements can turn into a mere scrap of paper, I do not ex-pect these things to completely eliminate the threat perception. But I do expect them to decrease the threat perception. And the balance of threat theory would lead us to expect the U.S.-Korea alliance to reduce its military readiness. What we ob-serve, however, is the opposite. Walt's balance of threat theory fails to explain why the alliance continues on and even strengthens in the face of a declining threat.

A residual threat may still save the balance of threat theory. Just as some realists ex-plain NATO's persistence in terms of the lingering Russian threat, one can argue that North Korea, despite all the decline in its power and reduction in its threats, still represents a mortal threat that warrants the continuation of the U.S.-Korea alliance. This argument, however, overlooks the obvious possibility that the residual threat at a reduced level can be met with a lower level of military capability. After all, NATO continues on but at a much lower level of military power: the United States has pulled out large segments of its military from Europe; European members of NATO downsized their militaries; and NATO reidentified itself as a democratic community concerned with stabilizing and democratizing neighboring countries. Just like NATO, the U.S.-Korea allied governments did try to draw down the military preparedness early in the 1990s—*before* Pyongyang began to take threat-reducing measures. But those initiatives were all reversed, unlike NATO, *after* Pyongyang's glasnost. This pres-ents an anomaly that defies the residual threat explanation.

The above discussion illustrates not only the inadequacies of balancing theories but also the need to complicate our understanding of alliance behavior. For it raises questions about institutional and discursive contexts within which power/threat bal-ancing is carried out. Military balance can be measured by a number of indicators, yet one particular measure is privileged; aggressive intention can be assessed with ref-erence to different factors, yet a particular set is weighed more. The fact that a par-ticular representation of power or threat is privileged over others suggests that meas-uring balance is not so innocent or objective as measuring the size of a book. A balancing act is done within discursive and institutional contexts that skew the relative weights of power/threat indicators in a particular way. Balancing is implicated in a discursive tug of war. And the institution of the alliance brings its weight to bear upon the tug of war. For example, the more sophisticated power analyses, which represent a closer approximation to the real fighting capabilities, are relegated to the sidelines, if not the outside, of the public debate as a result of discursive politics. Allied government officials and officers, when discussing the alliance, make references only to the bean counts, which are then processed and reproduced by media and academia. Thanks to their power over public debate, the bean counts are recognized and named as the true representation of the military balance. The bean counts reign in the public debate. As a result of the politics of naming, the public debate on Korea is dominated by the discourse of a superior North, notwithstanding the evidence to the contrary. Analytical eclecticism problematizes the complex ways in which power balancing is done, and illustrates the intimate ways in which a balancing act is implicated in institutional and discursive imbalancing acts.

Institution and Efficiency

In *After Hegemony*, Robert Keohane brings in the institutional context of state action to explain the continuation of existing international institutions even after the conditions that prompted their creation have disappeared. Institutions are created as a result of the distribution of power, shared interests, and prevailing practices; they persist, however, because they are valuable to states. And they are valuable, according to Keohane, "because they perform important functions and because they are difficult to create or reconstruct" (1984: 14). Hence an international institution that states have created generates an incentive structure that promotes its persistence. Applying Keohane's theory to NATO, neoliberal scholars such as Duffield and Wallander advance a functionalist explanation for its persistence and adaptation after the end of the Cold War (Wallander 2000, 1999; Duffield 1994/95).

Their work captures an aspect of forces that prolong an alliance's life, notably the way an outcome of state action can provide a context that constrains later choices by the state. Their work, however, describes only the demand side of the story. To see why such a demand is met, one needs to look—as Walt (1997) does in his study of alliance collapse/endurance—at the domestic as well as the international context of state action. I argue in this section that an international institution creates an institutional context for state action at both the domestic and the international levels and that such a context facilitates the persistence of the institution. The impact of war making on state making has been extensively studied not only in the European context but also in non-Western regions. Much as war making influences the state-building process so does alliance operation impact the structures of the state and society. More precisely, alliance practices transform allies' states and societies so as to produce what I call "alliance asset specificity" and "alliance constituency." Also, an alliance's imprint on the state and society, namely these alliance asset specificity and constituency, produces an incentive structure and pressure to prolong the alliance even in the face of its obsolescence.

Borrowing a concept Oliver Williamson (1987) articulated to explain the emergence of economic organizations, I argue that alliance operations generate asset specificity: durable investments that are undertaken to complete alliance commitments, and that would incur higher opportunity cost than best alternative uses or alternative uses if the original alliance should be terminated. Just as asset specificity gives economic actors an incentive to bind themselves in a governance structure, usually in the form of a firm, the alliance asset specificity gives security providers an incentive to bind themselves in the alliance structure. Although alliance asset specificity can be classified into four types—equipment, process, human asset, and location specificity —I focus here for the purpose of illustration only on the ways the U.S.-Korea alliance has resulted in equipment specificity.

Allies make durable investments in military hardware to ensure the interoperability of weapons systems, platforms, and infrastructure between the allies' militaries. Equipment specificity refers to these durable investments, which embody a large sum of opportunity costs that could have been invested in alternative weapons systems. If an alliance is terminated, the equipment specificity would impose a heavy loss because some portion of the investments are specific to the alliance and would be lost in any other security arrangement. Thus, durable investments, together with their potential replacement costs, set up a barrier to alliance change and facilitate the continuation of the existing arrangement.

The U.S.-ROK alliance displays an unusually high degree of equipment specificity. The ROK Army (ROKA) was established with arms supplied by the United States, and has relied on the United States for the continued provision of arms, ammunition, parts, and upgrades. As a result, nearly all of the equipment of the ROKA is of American origin, making weapons interoperability practically a nonissue. Not only do the ROKA and U.S. forces share the same U.S.-made weapons systems, but the weapons systems that South Korea produces are also based on U.S. designs and use U.S.-made parts. In addition, Korean-designed weapons systems are so configured as to be compatible with American ammunition and petroleum, oil and lubricants (POL), and conversely, Korea's ammunition and POL are designed to fit American weapons systems. Airports, ports, roads, and railroads are designed, built, and maintained for American as well as for Korean use. The level of equipment specificity and its binding effects are recognized by Yu Chun-Hyŏng, vice president of the Korea Defense Industry Association:

> After the Korean government was established in 1948, its army was equipped with U.S. weapons systems, was trained according to American doctrines, and carried out operations in accordance with American strategies and tactics. As almost all of Korea's major weapons systems are comprised of American ones that it has received as military assis-

tance from Washington, it is not easy now to shift its American weapons systems to other, European ones (1990: 3).

Even though Korea started diversifying the sources of its imported weapons in the early 1990s, over 85 percent of its weapons imports in 1995 still came from the United States (Ku 1998; Hartung 1994). As a result, the American and Korean militaries face few difficulties in maintaining the interoperability of their weapons systems. For example, in what Peter Hayes describes as the "fusion of South Korean and U.S. nuclear warfighting forces," the American military had plans to use *Korean* artillery tubes to fire *U.S.* nuclear projectiles.[8] This would not have been possible if the two forces had not maintained interoperability between Korean cannons and American shells or between their communications equipment. Likewise, it would have been much more complicated if the two militaries had not achieved a high level of integration in command structure. Indeed, more than integration, there was control: the arrangement whereby the commander in chief of the Combined Forces Command, who had operational control of South Korean military forces, was a U.S. army general, enabled the CFC commander to use Korean detachments for nuclear operations and yet, as nuclear commander, answer only to U.S. authority, not to Korean (Hayes 1991).[9]

Equipment specificity leads to specificity in weapons production because the allies are engaged not just in weapons transfer/sales but also in joint production/development, license production, and technology transfer, as the M-16 production program shows. The Memorandum of Understanding for the M-16 Rifle Production Program stipulated that the South Korean government would contract with American firms "for the license, proprietary rights, documentation, production equipment, components, raw materials, and technical assistance required to initiate and implement the program" and "all components of complete M-16 rifles assembled in the Republic of Korea . . . will be procured from United States sources." The South Korean government "will take necessary steps for such production engineering, tooling control and maintenance, *as will ensure the operational and logistic interchangeability among the M-16 rifles and components being produced in Korea and in the United States* [emphasis added]." The M-16 program led to a separate memorandum of understanding concerning the ammunition requirements, which regulated the receipt, storage, transportation, accountability, inventory, surveillance, demilitarization, maintenance, and security of the ammunition. As this simple case shows, the equipment specificity resulting from weapons interoperability spins off a whole array of connections between the two militaries and societies.

Yet the M-16 program represents just one of many licensed productions that include M-101 and M-114 howitzers, M-19, M-29, and M-30 mortars, 20 mm Vulcan cannons, M-60 machine guns, M-113 armored personnel carriers, M-48 tanks, and F16 fighters (Bruce 1996; Baek, McLaurin, and Moon 1989; Morrocco 1989; Nolan 1986; Ha 1984). There are well over 140 defense items that Korea produces under U.S. license.[10] The need for weapons interoperability, generated by the alliance, results in equipment specificity while it also widens and deepens the transnational ties between the two states and societies. These ties sometimes take the form of an organization, such as the U.S.-ROK Military Industry Conference, which actively participates in policy debates on the alliance as an advocate of cooperation between American and Korean military businesses (U.S.-ROK Military Industry Conference 1990). But the value of weapons imports can hardly be limited to the issues of interoperability and asset specificities, as Nolan notes. "Importing U.S. material has symbolic and military importance, reaffirming close security ties with the United States. As long as the United States continues to provide relatively liberal access to coproduction and coassembly arrangements and continues to support Seoul's objectives, the costs of actions that risk terminating the relationship likely will outweigh any apparent benefit" (Nolan 1991: 51–52). Hence equipment specificity raises the cost of terminating an alliance or switching sides in multiple ways. First, should a member withdraw from an alliance, it would have to find a new ally or develop its own arms, a classic alliance-versus-arms question (Conybeare 1994; Sorokin 1994). Keeping the existing ally appears to be cheaper than finding a new one because equipment specificity provides the current ally with the first-mover advantage. Second, arming oneself includes the costs that could be incurred by the termination of coproduction and/or coassembly arrangements, by problems in the supply of maintenance parts, or by the increase of license fees. Thus specificity militates heavily against changing the alliance.

A weapons sale involves more than an exchange of weapons for cash. It includes, in many cases, technical and logistics services, personnel training, and the design and construction of supporting infrastructure. For example, when the Bush administration decided in 1992 to sell F15s to Saudi Arabia, the Saudis agreed to set aside one third of the $9 billion package to build facilities specifically designed for the American planes' use. Although they would be built for the F15s that the Saudis were buying, they could be used by all American fighters. And thus the Americans were in effect using Saudi money to construct an infrastructure that would be available to U.S. forces, a fact frankly admitted by Carl Ford, undersecretary of defense: "many of the infrastructure developments that have occurred in the facilities, air bases, were done with an eye to the possibility that the U.S. Air Force . . . might have to come into Saudi Arabia at some point" (Ford 1992: 28). Hence a weapons sale, facilitated by an alliance, produces specificity not just in the allies' equipment but also in their infrastructures.

Just as alliance operations produce asset specificity, so do they lead to the establishment of an "alliance constituency," a set of domestic groups that are born out of the necessities of the alliance and that depend for their existence on the alliance. They include officer corps who work for the alliance and weapons producers and other civilian groups, and usually form a transnational or transgovernmental network among themselves. Alliance constituency results at least partially from a special kind of asset specificity: the team specificity that obtains as a result of alliance practices that place allied personnel in a team configuration that, in the case of the U.S.-Korea alliance, ranges from the Security Consultative Meeting to the Combined Forces Command headquarters to various military units to task-specific committees.[11] Not only does the alliance relationship promote the proliferation of a vast network of transnational and transgovernmental ties at various levels, but also it itself is further bound by these diffuse and dense networks of governmental, corporate, and private teams. This web of ties is specific and partial to the alliance, privileging it over other possible security relationships at contract renewal time.

There is a multiplicity of "teams" involved in the alliance operation starting with the ROK/U.S. Military Committee at the top. Providing political and strategic guidance to it is the Security Consultative Meeting (SCM), held annually since 1969, where the U.S. secretary of defense and the ROK minister of national defense lead their respective delegations that include senior defense and foreign affairs officials. The SCM reiterates in its joint statement every year that "the combined US-ROK forces . . . should continue to maintain and develop combined readiness, tactics, doctrine, professionals, training and interoperability" (Security Consultative Meeting 1997). The SCM has under it a number of subcommittees on policy review, logistics cooperation, security cooperation, and defense technology and industry cooperation. A U.S.-ROK Military Committee Meeting (MCM), instituted in 1979, over which the chairs of the respective joint chiefs of staff preside, is also held annually.

Although the SCM and the MCM represent permanent teams instituted to guide and manage the alliance, there are a number of ad hoc or temporary teams created to deal with specific issues that arise from time to time. For example, the USFK-MND Brigadier General Contentious Issues Task Force was created to discuss some of the more thorny issues between the allies: the use and return of facilities and areas granted to the USFK, the return of the Tongduch'ŏn training area, the Status of the Forces Agreement (SOFA) revision process, and the relocation of the Camp Hialeah. Establishment of a joint operation facility is usually accompanied by the creation of a team to coordinate the use of the facility and to resolve problems that may arise. For example, when the Taegu Operation Facility was established, a Joint Coordinating Group (JCG) was created to "maintain close interaction and coordination to insure that the spirit and intent of this agreement are maintained and to resolve problem areas" (*Memorandum of Understanding* 1981). Also, weapons production, particularly a licensed or joint production, leads to a formation of a team of experts and officers from the two countries to manage the project. The M-16 rifle production agreement, which was mentioned above, for example, obligated the U.S. and South Korean governments to "designate a Liaison Officer to monitor and coordinate the M-16 rifle production program."

Training—essential to any military—provides another mechanism by which an alliance constituency is created. Between 1950 and 1970, South Korea had the largest number of military officers trained in the United States, having sent 21,063 officers to U.S. military academies for training, compared to 23,878 officers from all Latin

American countries trained in the U.S. during the same period. By 1989, 36,000 Korean officers, NCOs, and enlisted soldiers had received training through the U.S. International Military Education and Training (IMET) program (Graves 1989: 19). The three presidents who ruled South Korea from 1960 to 1992 were all retired generals who had been trained in the United States, and two of them had even served under an American commander in the Vietnam War. As a result of this training, not to mention the daily interaction within the Combined Forces Command, Korean and American officers have developed professional and interpersonal ties that are specific to the alliance.

The huge influx of U.S. weapons has also resulted in a large contingent of officers needed to deal with it. The Procurement Headquarters employs 138, including 44 officers. A disproportionately high number of military attachés are sent to the United States: 13 in the United States, compared to 1 each in Britain, Germany, France, and Russia as of 1997 (Kwon 1998; Procurement Headquarters 1996). The Procurement Headquarters trains its officers at the Korea Trade Association on trading practices (and in English) and sends a limited number them to the Institute for Foreign and Security Policy. It annually sends two officers to the United States for training at the Security Assistance Agency and Logistics Management School. It also operates a language laboratory and administers foreign language evaluations twice a year. Defense industries have also been involved in coproduction arrangements, have formed joint committees, and have held annual conferences, all of which facilitate the development of personal ties and social networks among arms producers.

Major U.S. arms export deals have what Michael Klare (1984) calls a long "prehistory," lasting anywhere from several months to five years or more. The prehistory includes a series of informal discussions, exchanges of information with foreign governments, demonstration of specific equipment for representatives of the potential purchasing nation, and reviews by the State and Defense Departments, the National Security Council, and other executive branch agencies. All these activities generate a powerful political momentum behind a sale. Hence a sale involves more than a simple exchange of hardware and money; it generates an intimate web of connections among the involved officers, officials, and businessmen, who learn through these contacts organizational and personal idiosyncrasies: a team specificity.

Team specificities are not limited to the military but extend more broadly into society. For example, equipment specificity, a spin-off of the hardware requirement of the alliance, leads to intimate connections between Korean and U.S. arms manufacturers. At the Security Consultative Meeting in June 1988, Korea and the United States signed a Memorandum of Understanding on Defense Technology and Industry Cooperation (DTIC) and established a DTIC Committee as one of the key teams under the aegis of the SCM. The DTIC is made up of defense industry representatives from the two countries as well as concerned officers, who provide an official channel of contact and communication between powerful actors in the two societies. Defense contractors themselves have also taken the initiative in promoting team specificity in their sector. The Korea Defense Industry Association (KDIA) and the American Defense Preparedness Association (ADPA), for example, have held the annual U.S.-ROK Defense Industry Conference since 1986 as a forum to exchange views and coordinate lobbying. They moved the degree of their team specificity one step further by establishing in 1987 the Korea-Oregon Defense Industry Committee with the Korea Defense Industry Association and the Oregon Chapter of the ADPA as its members.

No less important are the civilian ties whose birth is midwifed by the militaries. U.S. soldiers marry Korean nationals at a rate of some 2,000 per year (Taylor 1989: 115). By the end of the 1970s there were 60,000 such marriages and by the end of the 1980s nearly 100,000 (Yuh 1999; Lee 1997; Joyner 1983). There are also U.S. veterans' groups that represent those who fought in the Korean War or had their tour in Korea, including the American Legion, American Veterans Committee, Chosin Few, Korean War Veterans Association, Second Division Association, and Veterans of Foreign Wars. American participation in the Korean War also resulted in the formation of groups of families who lost members in the war, including the Association of Korean War Families, and the Coalition of Korean War Families.

The effect of equipment specificity is not limited to one side of an alliance although there may be differences in the degree of the binding power over the alliance members. In other words, if weapons imports impact South Korea for obvious reasons, they also affect the exporter, the United States. South Korea is one of the biggest consumers of U.S. military hardware, with imports totaling, for example, $4.8 billion in 1999 and $3.6 billion in 2001.[12] An analysis prepared for the American League for Exports and Security Assistance estimated that recent and prospective sales to Saudi Arabia could generate over $80 billion for U.S. contractors and their communities and over 1.5 million man-hours of employment over a twenty–year period (*Defense Monitor* 1991). Since the value of American sales to South Korea is comparable to that of Saudi Arabia, a similar argument can be made about the impact arms sales to Seoul might have on American society. Defense contractors and their trade associations such as the Aerospace Industry Association and the Aerospace and Defense chapter of the American Chamber of Commerce remain a powerful constituency supporting the alliance. In short, equipment specificity not only brings the two militaries closer because of the interoperability of weapons systems, platforms, and infrastructure, but also makes the two societies, or at least some societal sectors, more interdependent.[13] This makes the termination of the alliance or a switch in alignment costly to the United States as well as to Korea even if the former would find it less painful than the latter. There may be a difference in the degree of "vulnerability" to an alliance termination between the two countries, but both would nonetheless suffer a loss.

We have so far considered how specificities are created by normal alliance operation and the extent to which alliance specificities are entrenched. These specificities, an unintended but natural byproduct of alliance practices, in turn affect the life span of the alliance in two ways. First, they affect security costs for the allies: they lower the costs of alliance maintenance while they raise the costs of an alliance termination or switch. And second, the specificities, by generating an "alliance constituency" that benefits from the status quo and would suffer losses in case of an alliance termination, ensure that there will be political actors who favor maintenance of the alliance. In the face of a diminishing threat or an improving power balance, which present material conditions for alliance termination, we expect the alliance constituency to assert its influence to protect its interests tied to the alliance, that is, these actors will oppose the termination and act accordingly. Also we expect them, and others, to argue that cost calculations favor alliance maintenance. In this way, the two mechanisms whereby asset specificities cause alliance persistence have a snowballing effect, one strengthening the other.

Neoliberals would happily stop here, concluding on the basis of the foregoing that the functionalist imperatives, generated by the asset specificity and the transnational ties, *must* explain the alliance persistence. There is an interest to serve; therefore there is an institution. These expectations are only partially met, however. Although the alliance constituency was not insignificant in terms of its size and its influence, its contribution to alliance persistence was not decisive. For despite some instances where its economic interests overrode national security considerations and despite some actions that it took to protect its interests, particularly in the early 1990s, the level of its activities was not anywhere near what would have been expected if its interests had been fatally threatened. Immediately after the fall of the Berlin Wall, there was a flurry of activity: a number of articles appeared in monthly journals that emphasized the need to keep up the level of defense spending; the Korean defense industry refurbished its publicity campaign; and Defense Ministry officers and weapons researchers voiced their concerns about potential weakening of the alliance. The alliance constituency soon realized, however, that neither its own existence nor the alliance's existence was threatened by the end of the Cold War.

Maintaining an alliance is not without cost. It demands an allocation of material resources and attention. In a world of scarce resources and many demands for attention, maintenance of an alliance can and often does lead to a competition for resources. Thus, on the way to the persistence of an institution, we expect to observe debates, competition, or even conflicts over attention and resources. We have seen that kind of debate in the struggles over the best institutional arrangements for post–Cold War Europe, with a number of institutions competing for a majority share of resources: NATO, the Organization for Security and Cooperation in Europe (OSCE), the Western European Union (WEU), European Union (EU), and European Security and Defense Identity (ESDI). In post–Cold War Japan also, political entrepreneurs proposed different security arrangements, of which the U.S.-Japan alliance was just one, while some passionately opposed extending the alliance. We do not observe that kind of debate or competition with respect to the U.S.-ROK alliance in the 1990s, however. The absence of the competitive or conflictual process in U.S.-ROK alliance persistence needs to be recognized and explained.

The absence is particularly puzzling since conditions were more conducive to public debate and competition in the 1990s than in any previous period. Korea was more democratized than ever; the end of the Cold War removed many of the obstacles to open discussion of national security issues. Now that the Korean Parliament had a number of activist-turned-politicians who once advocated the removal of the U.S. military, one should expect to have seen at least a debate about the alliance in the Parliament. Since maintaining an alliance is not costless and keeping foreign troops is not frictionless, we should expect to see a rise in public debates about the utility of the alliance, in the face of which the alliance constituents would rise to justify the alliance and lobby for its maintenance. What is interesting about Korea, however, is there was actually a decrease in public debate about the American military and in anti-U.S. activities throughout the 1990s. There was no such debate in the Parliament, in contrast with the Philippines, whose senate passed a resolution asking the U.S. military to leave and whose legislature amended its constitution with an explicit provision prohibiting the stationing of foreign military.

Liberal and neoliberal theories provide a useful framework that accounts for an aspect of the alliance that eludes realist theories. Yet they fail to capture the absence of debate within which the alliance persists. Explanatory frameworks that rely on efficiency factors and domestic actors exclude the possibility of taking the absence as a "fact" that makes up part of the phenomenon and as a puzzle that requires explanation. As I illustrate in the next section, identity politics makes up an integral part of alliance politics and provides an enabling condition for the alliance constituents to realize their interests without invoking efficiency arguments. Analytical eclecticism helps the analyst move beyond the exclusive efficiency domain and inquire how institutions/efficiency and representations/identity interact.

Identity and Alliance

Identity-based theories seem at first sight to offer little insight into the pattern whereby South Korea is allied with the United States—with which it has few commonalities—against North Korea, with which it makes one nation. The alliance presents a puzzle to constructivists who view a common identity as a basis for a security community or an alliance (Adler 1998; Barnett 1996; Risse-Kappen 1995). Not only do North and South Koreans share a common identity as a nation but also the Korean nation is so thoroughly naturalized that they take it to be an objective entity. Even if it is an accepted wisdom in academia that a nation has no prediscursive, primordial existence and that a nation is an "imagined community," this represents, to

Koreans, one of the most difficult propositions to accept. To them, Korea is objectively and unmistakably one nation. The Korean nation is a concrete object that has existed for over five thousand years on the Korean Peninsula and that shares a common language, culture, and history. To the average Korean, the Korean nation is an objective reality to which he or she naturally belongs. More sophisticated Korean intellectuals may acknowledge that other nations such as the French or the Germans are imagined communities. Even to them, it is a blasphemy to suggest that the Korean nation is an imagined community constructed out of various social practices. Despite the high degree of a shared and accepted common identity, however, the two Koreas not only fail to form a security community or an alliance but are arch enemies, against which alliances are maintained.

Despite few commonalities, on the other hand, South Korea and the United States have maintained one of the longest surviving alliances—for almost half a century—confounding identity-based theories. The origin of the alliance cannot be accounted for by identity; nor can its maintenance, at least until the end of the 1980s, be explained in terms of a shared culture or political system. The absence of ideational or social glue was overcome by the security imperative that South Korea faced immediately after the 1950 war: to counterbalance the power imbalance on the peninsula. The multitude of social differences between Korea and the United States was swept aside by the need to maintain the balance of threat on the local and regional levels. If the alliance in its early years fell squarely in the realist territory where power trumped efficiency or identity considerations, Korea has since then developed a number of asset specificities that strengthen its institutional bond with the United States. Since the mid-1980s it became more democratic and "Americanized," perhaps laying a foundation for an alliance based on a common political or even cultural identity. If the process of homogenization continues, the alliance may be reconstituted as a community of democracies in the future. It would be premature, however, to suggest that the alliance continues on in the first years of the new millennium thanks to shared identity.

Although identity-based theories fail to account for the alliance from its origin until the 1980s, they can help shed light on its persistence in the 1990s if we understand the military alliance as a political practice central to state identity. Such an understanding begins with the recognition that a significant portion of an alliance's activities consists of discursive practices that help constitute social reality. Allied officials and officers, for example, issue a number of statements, findings, directives, announcements, and so on, that "identify" threats and define security. The representations they produce then become a primary source for reporters, civilian analysts, scholars, and politicians, who proliferate these representations in different forms. These representations as a whole form a discourse about the world and its inhabitants. Because the institution of alliance is considered authoritative in security matters, the discourse it spawns is privileged over other discourses, becoming a preferred framework that policy makers and the public turn to in order to understand the world. The alliance discourse provides the conventional matrix of interpretations within which some states are identified as allies and others as adversaries: alliance practices are accompanied by the simultaneous construction of "us" and "them" (Campbell 1992; Neumann and Welsh 1991; Said 1978).

This is not to suggest that alliances create a fiction. Before they produce representations, there must be "facts on the ground"—that is, an actor taking actions deemed hostile or a state uttering words suggesting aggressive intentions—that many reasonable minds agree can constitute a security threat. Nonetheless, words and deed, except for rare extreme cases, carry a degree of uncertainty since an actor's intention is never crystal clear and his mind may change tomorrow. What seems benign behavior can turn out to be a deception; what is construed as aggression may have resulted from mistakes or confusion. Except in rare occasions where a state is undoubtedly revisionist, as Nazi Germany was in the 1930s, there is usually a degree of uncertainty about a state's identity and intentions. And the degree of uncertainty is narrowed by social practices that impute meanings to uncertain material reality. Alliance discourse constitutes a perceptual prism through which societal members understand an actor's capability, words, and deeds as benign or malign.

Alliance theorists working in a rationalist tradition have observed the "identity effect" that alliances have upon interstate relations (Snyder 1997; Liska 1968).[13] They have pointed to an important dimension of alliance politics but stopped short of delving into discursive processes of identity reproduction. As they have pointed out, states—in forging an alliance—identify who is the ally and who the adversary, but they do more. Through alliance practices, they also *discursively* constitute social identities, particularly in the area of national security. Not only do alliances contribute representations to a particular discourse that enframes social reality, but they also privilege the discourse over alternative possibilities. As a result of discursive practices, the alliance discourse can achieve a hegemonic status, establishing the alliance as the natural order of things. Within the hegemonic alliance discourse, the ally is seen as the natural, permanent partner, parting company with whom is unthinkable, while the adversary is viewed as the constant, immediate, and eternal danger, reconciliation with whom is unimaginable. Once the alliance discourse becomes hegemonic, the alliance itself is privileged over other alternative security arrangements because the alliance is seen as a natural framework. The discourse has rendered a particular constitution of identities natural, permanent, and hegemonic, setting it in the realm of what Bourdieu called "doxa" (Bourdieu 1997).

A poll conducted in South Korea in early 2001 is indicative. Sixty-one percent of the respondents thought North Korea's military capability was still superior to South Korea's, indicating the wide gulf between perception and objective power indicators. About half of those who believed the South had superior power thought that it was nevertheless likely that North Korea would attack South Korea if no U.S. military were stationed in the South. North Korea's image as a threat was so entrenched that it was viewed likely to attack even if it was weaker. Interestingly, 53 percent had never thought of the possibility that there might not be a U.S. military presence in the future, and of those who responded that the U.S. military was needed, 55 percent said they would find it problematic if the foreign military was not the *U.S.* military. This suggests that the U.S.-Korea alliance might be based not only on the naturalized threat perception but also on a hegemonic conception of the United States as a natural ally.

A hegemonic discourse, however, is not instantiated by a single founding act but rather continuously reproduced by an ensemble of social practices. And a change in material conditions calls for different practices to produce the same discursive effect. The new material conditions into which the U.S.-Korea military alliance was precipitated in the 1990s—the end of the Cold War, the change in the brute power balance, and the decrease in the North's aggressive intentions—necessitated different representational practices and institutional adjustments so that the discourses about North Korea and the United States might be hegemonized despite all these changes. Below I turn to what Katzenstein and Okawara in this volume call the "politics of naming," which imputed a particular meaning to the North Korea of the 1990s: a new threat that necessitated maintaining the alliance in the last decade of the twentieth century and into the twenty-first century. Thanks to the success of these discursive practices, the hegemonic status of North Korea's identity as a "menace" was preserved, contributing to the persistence of the U.S.-Korea alliance.

The post–Cold War security environment is now constructed in opposition to "proliferation threats," against which the alliance must guard. The "proliferation threats" consist of nuclear and missile proliferations, both of which are now represented as primary threats to the national security of the United States and Korea. Ever since the early 1990s, when the U.S. Central Intelligence Agency (CIA) made public its suspicion that North Korea was engaged in a nuclear weapons program, "proliferation threats" have headed the security challenges that the U.S.-Korea alliance has had to face (Sigal 1998; Suh 1996). North Korean missiles are the primary threat against which the United States is currently building its missile defense and from which South Korea and Japan are scrambling for protection. The nuclear issue brought the alliance and North Korea to the brink of war in the summer of 1994, and the situation was only temporarily defused with the signing of the Geneva Agreed Framework in October of the same year. Indeed proliferating are symbolic and linguistic representations of "proliferation threats" to identify and hegemonize North Korea's identity as a "danger" to U.S. and Korean security (Mutimer 1997). The discourses of proliferation threats predispose those actors who operate within them to ignore inconvenient facts about Pyongyang's missiles and to zero in on confirming facts surrounding North Korea's nuclear program, reinforcing their prior conception of the North as a danger. The discourses of proliferation threats predispose the actors to remain disinclined to consider the possibility that the North's actions, dangerous as they may be, are a defensive measure taken in response to what it perceives as a threat posed by the alliance. The discourses constitute an ideational context within which the alliance considers its own actions defensive and the North's offensive, unwittingly and unknowingly reproducing a security dilemma.

Naming an object is a crucial first step in governance, as Confucius noted thousands of years ago. A name places the object in a particular location in a social order of things, imputing a status and a meaning to it, a consequential act that enables social actors to understand how to deal with it. The consequential nature of naming can be seen in the "politics of naming" that was vividly played out immediately after Pyongyang launched a rocket at the end of August 1998. U.S. intelligence immediately called it a "missile test"; this was then picked up and circulated as a "fact" by the media. Government and military officials then cited media reports to explain what Pyongyang had done and what they were about to do in response. These official statements lent more credence to the media reports of the "fact." Added to this were assessments by foreign policy experts and North Korean observers as to possible motives behind this "missile test." Some argued that it demonstrated yet once more Pyongyang's dangerous aggressiveness while others suggested that it was designed to extract more concessions from the West. Security specialists chimed in with their analyses of the security implications this "missile launch" might have: Japan was now under immediate danger of a direct attack from North Korea; even the United States was seen as within the range of the North's missiles. These specialists busily debated the best means to counter this new threat: whether to deploy Patriot batteries, to develop theater missile defense, to employ preemptive measures, and so on.

Amidst all these reports, statements, analyses, and speculations, it became accepted as a "fact" that the North fired a missile. Not only did all these significations coalesce to produce what Stuart Hall calls the "reality effect," but the "reality" also triggered real responses, which in turn had the effect of entrenching the "Hobbesian culture"—to use Wendt's apt phrase—between the North and its neighbors (Wendt 1999). The Japanese government immediately took punitive measures, such as cutting airline travel to North Korea and freezing KEDO funding. The United Nations Security Council adopted a resolution condemning the North's missile test fire. The U.S. Senate passed a resolution tying U.S. funding for heavy oil to the president's certification that Pyongyang did not export missiles. The U.S. House cut off KEDO funding.

Four days after it fired the "missile," Pyongyang caught everybody off guard by announcing that it had launched a satellite. With unusual candor, it went so far as to provide a detailed description of the satellite's orbit. On September 14, U.S. State and Defense spokespersons publicly acknowledged that it had indeed been a satellite launch, but one that had failed to put the satellite in orbit. By then, however, the symbolic struggle over this event was already over. It had become reality that North Korea fired a missile over Japan. And it had been taken for granted that the North's missile test had undermined peace and stability in the region. By then, the missile was even given a name, Taepodong (Big Cannon), by Western experts despite the fact that the North Koreans themselves named it Kwangmyongsong (Bright Star). The Japanese even coined a new term to describe the shock they felt when the "missile" flew over their heads: Taepodong shoku.

In this example, the politics of naming was played out after North Korea fired a projectile into space in 1998, yet the same politics was repeated a year later even *before* an action took place. Again, as before, U.S. intelligence picked up indications that the North was preparing to fire a "missile"; this was then dutifully reported by the media as a fact. Then policy makers and analysts acted on this fact, issuing statements, producing analyses, and implementing policy measures. South Korean, Japanese, and U.S. officials expended a considerable amount of political capital to persuade the ASEAN Regional Forum (ARF) chairman to issue a statement criticizing North Korea's "missile" test-firing. They also worked assiduously to convince the Chinese government to jump on the bandwagon. These diplomatic maneuverings had immediate political implications, of course, but it is notable that a considerable amount of work had to be done to make certain everyone on the bandwagon saw the same reality. At a deeper, discursive level, these statements and diplomatic gambits added another layer of reality to the "reality," multiplying the "reality effect."

In order to grasp the full significance of the establishment of this "reality," we need to juxtapose it with other possible, less threatening realities. There is, of course, the North Korean official "reality" that the North Koreans had launched a satellite. This reality was consistent with the available data about the projectile's trajectory, and was conceded by the U.S. government. To the extent that the North Koreans did have a projectile to place in orbit, this reality was credible. Since there is little technological distinction between a satellite launch and a missile test fire, however, this reality may not have made much difference in terms of its security implications. Whether or not the North had placed a satellite in space, it demonstrated to the world that it had the scientific know-how, technical prowess, and political will to produce a projectile that it could use for a military purpose. What mattered the most to South Korea and the United States then was that they believed Pyongyang intended it to be a military device with which to undermine the peace and stability of the region. This concern was well reflected in all the official statements and analyses that repeatedly and pointedly called the North's "missile test" a threat to peace. U.S. secretary of state Madeleine K. Albright put it quite bluntly: "We stressed that another long-range missile launch, whether it is declared to be a missile test or an attempt to place a satellite in orbit, would be highly destabilizing and would have very serious consequences for our efforts to build better relations" (Agence France Press 1999).

Even if it had been a missile, there would have been various possible meanings, but government officials produced a stream of significations to privilege one meaning over others. South Korean president Kim Dae-Jung and U.S. president Clinton warned in their summit in July 1999 that if North Korea test-fired another missile it would "pose a serious obstacle to peace" on the Korean Peninsula. U.S. secretary of defense Cohen said after meeting Japan's Defense Agency director general Hosei Norota, "another missile test by North Korea would create an element of instability and uncertainty in the region." U.S. secretary of state Albright, ROK foreign minister Hong Soon-Young, and Japanese foreign minister Komura Masahiko, who met trilaterally on July 27 in Singapore to coordinate their respective policies on the DPRK, agreed that this action "would adversely affect peace and stability on the Korean Peninsula and beyond." And they called on North Korea to "choose to build a positive relationship with its neighbors by foregoing such testing" (U.S. Department of State 1999). This series of statements, produced by those who had powerful, privileged access to the public discourse, established the perimeters of a reality that was then taken for granted. North Korea's "dangerous missile" has become the natural order of things.

However, other "realities" are possible—at least conceptually. First, the North's missiles may be a bargaining chip, as Leon Sigal suggests:

> If North Korea is determined to develop, deploy and export longer-range ballistic missiles, as some in Congress believe, it should have been testing and perfecting its No Dong, Taepo Dong-I and Taepo Dong-II missiles for several years. Yet the North did not conduct any tests from May 23, 1993 until August 31, 1998. Again, that is a strange way to develop new missiles. It suggests that North Korea is restraining itself somewhat in the hopes of conducting a missile deal with the United States. Pyongyang has been expressing interest in such a deal since 1992 (Sigal 1999).[14]

Alternatively, the missiles may be a conventional deterrent. The North's missiles are so inaccurate that a few hundred of them would have to be fired to destroy one meaningful military target such as a command center or an airport runway. Since North Korea has fewer than 100 missiles, a missile offensive would not be a very efficient use of its limited arsenal (International Institute for Strategic Studies 1999: 194).[15] The North Koreans might be trying to terrorize the South and the United States to gain concessions, as suggested by Sigal and David Wright, but their intention might instead be to terrorize their opponents enough to deter an attack. Under the condition of its strategic inferiority, the North may be holding the missiles as a weapon of deterrence, much as U.S. and Russian missiles serve as deterrents (Suh 1999b). *Jane's Defence Weekly* reported that American intelligence and military officials acknowledged as much. According to a briefing by CIA, Defense Intelligence Agency (DIA), National Reconnaissance Office (NRO), and air force high officials in April 1997, the Rodong 1 missile is less suitable as a strategic offensive weapon than as a weapon of terror, because of its low accuracy and absence of a guidance system (*Jane's Defence Weekly* 28 May 1997).

It may turn out that neither of the two alternative realities is accurate. Nevertheless, they are consistent with known attributes of the "missile" and explain Pyongyang's motive at least as well as the dominant discourse does. All three could therefore have been given more or less equal footing in the public discourse, producing lively, healthy debate. The debate never transpired, however, because only one alternative was given the access, a privileged one, to the discourse and was thus accepted as *the* reality. Entangled in the missile crises were both the "politics of naming" and the politics of security. More precisely, the two politics of naming and security are caught in a recursive cycle, the outcome of one producing the outcome of the other and vice versa: security concerns about the North's projectile produced the reality of the North's "missile threat," which then produced such security measures as missile defense and the sale of missile-site-buster missiles, which then generated Pyongyang's hostile reaction, which then reinforced the "dangerous North" reality, ad infinitum.

The same kind of recursive cycle can be seen in how the alliance and North Korea are now caught in a nuclear crisis. If the "missile" politics showed a discursive tug of war between Washington's and Seoul's charges and Pyongyang's denials, however, the nuclear crisis has been the product of both parties' behavior and rhetoric that has bound them in a tightening security dilemma. In launching its nuclear program, Pyongyang may have believed that it took what it deemed an evidently defensive measure because it was facing an aggressive revisionist opponent in the Bush administration. But its action was in turn seen as hostile by the U.S.-Korea alliance, which held the mirror image of the identities: the United States and South Korea as status quo states and North Korea as revisionist. In the nuclear politics, furthermore, one side may be seeking to deter the other by convincing the other of its willingness, as well as capacity, to inflict unacceptably costly damage. But this type of rhetorical tactic and behavior only end up adding to the view that it is truly aggressive and revisionist. Both sides' words and actions reinforce the Hobbesian culture of enmity, within which the alliance and the North reproduce the vicious cycle of insecurity.

There is another important way the nuclear crisis is different from the "missile" politics. Although the nuclear politics is a higher-stakes game, its short history—from the early 1990s—contains episodes not only of confrontation but also of negotiation. While this suggests that it may be possible for the alliance and the North to escape from the insecurity dilemma, it also shows the extent to which Hobbesian culture can complicate and even derail their attempts to escape. In 1991, Bush senior's decision to withdraw tactical nuclear weapons from South Korea was reciprocated by Kim Il-Song's signing of the North-South Denuclearization Declaration and the Safeguards Agreement with the International Atomic Energy Agency (IAEA). This quid pro quo began to deescalate the tension and unravel the Hobbesian culture, ultimately contributing to the summit meeting between the two Koreas and the exchange of highest level officials between Pyongyang and Washington in 2000. Despite some ups and downs caused by suspicions about the other, the process seemed to be leading to a final breakdown of the insecurity dilemma by the end of 2000.

The end of the global Cold War enmity probably contributed to the loosening of the local enmity on the Korean Peninsula, which was promoted by the regional rapprochement early in the 1990s when China and Russia became more favorably disposed toward South Korea and Japan. The single most important event that triggered the whole train of events, however, was the change in American behavior: namely, the U.S. withdrawal of tactical nuclear weapons from Korea. Also critical to the process was that Pyongyang did not take advantage of the American action by launching a surprise attack on the South—as in a realist's "worst case scenario"—but reciprocated with its own disarming moves. Washington's quid was returned by Pyongyang with its quo, initiating a virtuous cycle of security enhancement that helped the alliance and the North to begin to break the vicious cycle of insecurity. Quickly taking advantage of the opening, the two Koreas held a series of exchanges—reunions of separated families, cultural performances, and sports events—propelling the virtuous cycle ultimately to the summit in 2000. In a series of negotiations with Pyongyang, Washington too came close to resolving many issues of concern. Clinton's visit to Pyongyang at the end of 2000 was supposed to put an end to the Hobbesian culture of enmity and open a new chapter in the history of the two countries.

Subsequent events are history. The virtuous cycle was halted in 2001 when Bush junior ordered a review of his predecessor's engagement policy. In his 2002 state of the union address, President Bush restored the North's identity as an "evil" that must be removed, thereby effectively ending the virtuous cycle. Bush's name-calling was angrily returned by Pyongyang, which labeled the United States the "empire of the devil." It is important for analytical eclecticism to recognize that no obvious changes in material power condition triggered such vitriolic exchanges. It was a change in the actors' social understanding that broke the virtuous cycle. The new Bush administration brought to American decision making its Manichaean understanding of the world where the North, together with Iraq and Iran, constituted the axis of evil that spreads the danger of terrorists, missiles, and nuclear weapons. Not only did the verbal exchanges reflect the new understanding of the actors' identities but they also provided the ideational context within which Washington and Pyongyang took actions that restored the vicious cycle. Because the former could not trust the "intransigent North" to honor the Geneva Framework Agreement, it halted the shipment of heavy oil; because the latter feared "aggressive Washington," it restarted its nuclear programs. Within the restored Hobbesian culture, the other was always a suspect that compelled one to take defensive measures. Within the enmity, such defensive steps were perceived as a reneging, an aggression, or a preparation for an attack. Thus the vicious cycle of insecurity was restored with vengeance.

The social structure of enmity serves as a perceptual prism that privileges an interpretation of facts and uncertainties about the North's nuclear program as a dangerous source of proliferation. It discounts the possibility that the North, as well as the United States, is caught in a security dilemma; it amplifies the possibility that the North lies, cheats, and deceives. It skews the discursive space in such a way as to dismiss as a deception Pyongyang's offer to negotiate while accepting its rhetoric of war as true. Its denial of a weapons program is a lie; its admission a truth. The enmity constitutes the ideational context within which realists have it both ways. What is striking about the nuclear crisis is the ease with which many of the uncertainties and facts about the North's nuclear program have been assumed away or disregarded. Alternative interpretations have been quickly brushed aside as the threat of the "North's nuclear weapons" established itself as reality.

At the beginning of the twenty-first century when North Korea's conventional military threat was increasingly coming into question, the reality of "the missile threat" and "the nuclear threat" added another layer to the master narrative, "the dangerous North." Because that master narrative had existed ever since Korea's division in 1945, it made it all the easier to return to the familiar reality. The relative ease of restoring the vicious cycle and the relative difficulty of maintaining the virtuous cycle provide evidence that the discursive playing field was skewed in favor of the North's dangerous identity. If the alliance's perception of the North as dangerous had been heavily influenced by the global Cold War enmity, since the 1990s the reality of "the dangerous North" was reproduced through the articulation of "the nuclear threat" and "the missile threat." Alliance practices produced a constant articulation of danger to the national security of the allies. The "danger," through these practices, has become part of the social reality within which the alliance understands the North and the world.

This is not to suggest that North Korea's nuclear or missile threats are nothing but lies fabricated by intelligence officers. I am not arguing that their perception of threat has no material basis or that their interpretation of material facts is so out of touch it borders on fantasy. It is undeniable that there are "stubborn realities." For example, it is a well-established fact that North Korea has a nuclear reactor and a reprocessing facility; it is also a fact that it fired a projectile into space in 1998. As the North has been engaged in aggression, guerrilla infiltration, and other brutal acts, Pyongyang's past behavior warrants caution and suspicion. At the same time, however, there are other possible interpretations that explain the same "stubborn realities" as well as the conventional wisdom. The alternative interpretations have the advantage of marshaling novel facts that do not fit the conventional discourse and that support the alternatives. If the public space were a "level playing field," therefore, one would expect at least a debate between different discourses. But one observes none. The fact that there were no meaningful public debates between different views shows that the playing field was not level. Policy debates, to the extent they existed, were carried out only within the discursive space demarcated by the alliance discourse; and policies that were not predicated on the same understanding of North Korean identity were excluded from the debates themselves. It is this skewed nature of the discursive playing field—the hegemonic status of North Korea's identity as "a danger"—that I am pointing out.

North Korea's identity is so entrenched that even defenders of Clinton's engagement policy and Kim Dae-Jung's sunshine policy abandoned efforts to render understanding of the North more complex by making its "danger" less central and highlighting its conciliatory gestures. Breaking away from previous, more confrontational policies, these two administrations planned to increase peaceful contacts with the North. No sooner had they announced the new policies, however, than they came under attack by Republicans in the United States and by opposition party members in Korea. The critics' jobs were made easy by the naturalized status of North Korea's identity because its seemingly indisputable status as a "threat" facilitated criticism of any conciliatory move. On the other hand, defenders faced the challenge of having to realign the hegemonic discursive practices of the "Northern danger." What is remarkable about the Clinton and the Kim Dae-Jung administrations is that their officials did not even attempt to face up to the challenge; instead they succumbed to the constraining effect the dominant discourses had on those who advocated a more conciliatory approach. Whether they were promoting an engagement policy or humanitarian aid, they justified or defended their preferred policy within the confines of the hegemonic identities. The following statement by Charles Kartman typifies their defenses. Kartman, who as "special envoy for the Korean peace process" and deputy undersecretary of state was mainly responsible for implementing Clinton's engagement policy, unequivocally laid out his administration's understanding, one that reflected and reinforced the hegemonic identity of the North:

> Let me make clear that, in these as in past negotiations, the U.S. approach was one of seriousness with respect to the security risks at stake, coupled with deep skepticism. Let me be clear, we do not trust North Korean intentions. It remains *indisputable* that North Korea represents a major threat to peace and stability not only in northeast Asia, but also in other volatile areas in the region (Kartman 1998; emphasis added).

The location of U.S. military bases in downtown Seoul, which emerged as an issue in the 1980s because of a counterhegemonic project initiated by the Koreans, became a nonissue again at the height of the nuclear crisis in 1994. The representational practices of the alliance, which successfully brought about the reality of the "nuclear danger," defeated the efforts to represent the United States as "the enemy." With this victory in the struggle over how to define the identities of North Korea and the United States, the alliance restored and stabilized a familiar reality: that of the "dangerous North" and of the "security-providing alliance." The image of North Korea as a "nuclear danger," an effect of the politics of signification, was beginning to make its presence felt in policy choices. In the face of the nuclear threat, the Department of Defense put on hold its plan to reduce the U.S. military presence in Korea.

In order to achieve this, the governments of Korea and the United States have collaborated closely. The two countries' defense ministers foresaw a problem in their alliance at the "twilight" of the twentieth century: the North Korean threat was in decline and reunification even seemed possible, two worst-case scenarios that would threaten the raison d'être of the alliance. Hence, at the twenty-fourth U.S.-ROK SCM of October 1992, they directed RAND and the Korea Institute of Defense Analyses (KIDA) "to assess whether and how the United States and the ROK can maintain and invigorate their security relationship should North Korea no longer pose a major threat to peace and stability on the Korean peninsula" (Pollack and Cha 1995: iii). The study unequivocally laid out one of the principal challenges confronting the United States and the Republic of Korea at the time: "developing and articulating a logic for future security collaboration, assuming diminution of the North Korean threat and the ultimate unification of the Korean peninsula" (p. xv). Now the cart was squarely placed before the horse: the need to maintain the alliance preceded the need to deter or defend against the North!

Hence, the "threat" persists, independent of real intentions the North may hold and independent of material capabilities it may have. For North Korea's material capabilities and intentions are embedded in discourses, and are seen and understood only in such discursive terms. The persistence of the "threat" is then used to justify the continuation of the alliance that had been "born in blood, forged in the crucible of war" (*International Herald Tribune* 2000). The hegemonic status of the "threat" precludes debates about the need for the alliance or about alternative security arrangements. According to General Thomas A. Schwartz, commander in chief of the CFC, "North Korea remains the major threat to stability and security in northeast Asia and is the country most likely to involve the United States in a large-scale war" (Schwartz 2000). As long as the "North as threat" identity "remains indisputable," it is only natural for the alliance to go on, to persist into the twenty-first century, as the following joint communiqué shows: "Secretary of State Cohen and I [Minister Cho] reconfirmed our common position of building on our undeviating alliance of half a century. The security situation on the Korean Peninsula still remains fluid. . . . We agreed to further strengthen the Korea-U.S. combined defense posture based on this assessment" (Security Consultative Meeting 1999).

Although the continuation of the alliance into 2003 largely confirms my argument about the durability of the alliance, Korea in recent years has provided two difficult tests: the 2000 summit that showed the North's identity, hegemonic as it may be, can be changed in a quid pro quo process; and the anti-U.S. demonstrations at the end of 2002 that showed the South's perception of the United States as its defender is not impervious to change. If change had continued without resistance or problems to the point where the new identities were accepted as natural, that would have been a strong disconfirmation of my argument that the social identities had a staying power independent of material conditions or institutional framework. By the summer of 2003, however, the changes in the identity of the North and of the United States were repelled and their original identities restored, displaying the resilience of the hegemonic discourse. The two episodes nonetheless provide an insight into how the actors, caught in the vicious cycle of insecurity, could transform it into a virtuous cycle of security.

Before the September 11 terrorist attack, the two Koreas had made historic strides in overcoming the Cold War enmity and in starting to build a community based on amity. At the first ever summit in 2000, Kim Dae-Jung and Kim Jong-Il laid the groundwork for further exchanges, dialogues, and political rapprochement and even agreed that their reunification policies shared a common ground. Groundbreaking as it was in its political and economic ramifications, the summit brought about as significant a change in the discursive dimension. Now Koreans began to think the unthinkable and to talk the untalkable. *Chujok* (the "main enemy"), as South Korea's Defense White Paper had designated North Korea, disappeared. No longer was Kim Jong-Il the head of an antistate organization bent on wiping out the South Korean state, as defined by the National Security Law. Nor was North Korea the other, in opposition to which South Korea defined its identity. Gone was the self-other divide that had been the core of the North-South division. A so-called Kim Jong-Il syndrome swept South Korean society. For six euphoric months after the summit, the hegemonic discourse of the North as the other looked like anything but hegemonic. This probably represented the culmination of the process set off by Bush senior's decision to pull nuclear weapons out of Korea. But the Koreans brought the process to its culmination by sidestepping the intractable national security issues and focusing instead on activities that would draw on and arouse the nationalist identity deeply felt in both North and South.

A year later, however, Bush's "axis of evil" speech and Pyongyang's visceral "empire of devil" retaliation sent a chill over the Korean Peninsula. The naval clash in the West Sea (Yellow Sea) between the two Koreas several months later provided the "facts on the ground" that only added credence to the "evil" rhetoric. Amidst the war of words and the skirmish of the navies, the political rapprochement, spearheaded by Clinton's "Perry process" and Kim Dae-Jung's "sunshine policy," came to an abrupt halt, restoring the North's identity as the other and sending the two Koreas back to a confrontation reminiscent of the 1950s' Cold War. The U.S.-Korea alliance renewed its life once again.

If Kim Dae-Jung's policies and the North-South summit pose a difficult challenge to my argument, the events of late 2002 and 2003 present the most challenging test yet. South Korea, one of the most loyal of America's allies, became highly critical of the U.S. military presence, and hundreds of thousands of its citizens poured into the streets to protest the acquittal of two American soldiers accused of killing two Korean students. Former human rights lawyer Roh Moo-Hyun rode the wave of anti-Americanism into the presidential office in the December election by appealing to the public's anger over the acquittal. He had the right credentials: in his activist lawyer days, for example, he had advocated the withdrawal of U.S. troops. Also he appealed to the public's nationalist sentiment by criticizing politicians who visit the United States mainly for a photo-op session with the American president. More importantly, his campaign was aided by the general apprehension of the Koreans that the Bush administration might undermine the South's security. Many Koreans feared that if the U.S. military struck the North's nuclear facilities according to its policy of preemption, the South would be at the receiving end of the North's tens of thousands of cannons. Whether a candidate, when elected, could stand up to Bush and oppose his unilateralism became the litmus test for many voters. In the end, a major-ity judged Roh to be the right choice. The rise of anti-American protests and the election of an anti-American president combined to produce the perception that South Korea had become implacably anti-American. This raised the possibility that the alliance had lost its hegemonic status. It seemed to be heading for trouble: the re-siliency of the social identities was in question.

Events following the election, however, suggest otherwise. Anti-American demon-strations quickly died down although none of the protesters' main demands were met. The acquittal stood, no official apology was offered, and no tangible change was made in the Status of the Forces Agreement, the mother of all the agreements and one that many Koreans deemed deeply unfair. Yet in 2003 the famous candlelight vigils failed to draw the public's attention, much less a crowd. The end of the protests was precip-itated by Roh who, as soon as he was elected, made a direct appeal to the public to stop the demonstrations. Roh, elected as a president who could say no to the United States, no sooner took office than he caved in to the pressure of the alliance, pleading for a continued American military presence and weakening, if not abandoning, his opposition to military strikes against the North. Taking a cue from the president's wa-vering, the Korean Ministry of National Defense in its 2003 guide to military educa-tion singled out North Korea as "the most significant enemy that constantly threatens our survival and well-being," a designation much stronger than "chujok" (the main enemy) that had been used prior to the adoption of the sunshine policy. Hence the perception of the North as *the* threat was restored with a vengeance, sustaining the dis-cursive foundation of the alliance, on which it found a renewed life.

Realists might argue that such a change is attributable to a material factor: North Korea's nuclear weapons. Given the number of measures that Pyongyang took with regard to its nuclear programs and given the number of claims it made about its "nu-clear deterrent," North Korean nuclear weapons became much more real and palpa-ble in 2003 than ever before. Thus the realist argument does capture an aspect of the reality. Its account, however, is not so much wrong as incomplete because the pres-ence of nuclear weapons themselves does not constitute a threat. Only when the ma-terial factor is contextualized within a social relationship does it become a meaning-ful social fact such as a threat. As Wendt (1999) pointed out, the hundreds of nuclear weapons that the British possess do not pose a threat to the Americans while a few nuclear weapons that the North Koreans may acquire constitute a threat because the United States is embedded in different social relationships with these countries.

To the South Koreans this was not a hypothetical intellectual exercise. The ques-tion they were dealing with in 2002 and 2003 was precisely what constituted a threat when both the United States and North Korea wielded nuclear weapons. In the midst of the anger about American soldiers' crimes late in 2002, many in the South felt that the Bush administration, which contemplated a nuclear preemptive strike against the North, represented a bigger threat. In a dramatic sea change in the perception of

American identity, a majority of South Koreans believed, for the first time since the Korean War, that the United States actually had become a source of their insecurity (Woo-Cumings 2004).[16] This dramatic development was aided by a more benign perception of their Northern brethren to which the 2000 summit and subsequent exchanges had contributed. That perception was, however, standing on a weak foundation as it went against the more entrenched view based on the Hobbesian culture of the previous fifty years. It was easily turned and yielded to the traditional, more dominant discourse, as the events of 2003 revealed.

I have thus far demonstrated how constructivist insights on discourse and identity can help explain the persistence of the U.S.-Korea alliance into the twenty-first century. It must be borne in mind, though, that constructivism by itself is not adequate in capturing the puzzle. If identities are shaped only at the discursive level, as many constructivists suggest, then such an analytic framework blinds the analyst to the possibility or reality that behavior creates "stubborn realities." In other words, North Korea's identity as a threat is hegemonic not just because of the discursive and representational practices of the alliance but also because of the North's behavior and rhetoric. Discursive politics is carried out in the form of the politics of naming or a war of words; but naming or words gain credence and acceptance when they demonstrate a clear connection to "stubborn realities" that themselves may be constituted by behavior or past practices of discursive politics. There is an intimate and recursive interaction between representational practices and "facts on the ground." By focusing on how representational practices constitute social identities, constructivists tend to fail to note the interaction. By bringing in behavioral contexts of discursive politics, analytical eclecticism corrects a constructivist blind spot.

Also the institution of the alliance functions as an active producer of representations and as a powerful participant in discursive politics. Constructivists may sometimes overlook the privileged power and resources that an official institution enjoys in the politics of naming. The institution of a military alliance creates an "alliance constituency," which is accompanied by institutional arrangements created to support it, and which is allocated a significant amount of resources to carry out its activities. All of these factors coalesce to strengthen, and possibly to hegemonize, the alliance discourse. The alliance gives these national security managers a privileged position in representational practices because they almost monopolize access to primary sources. Discursive politics is not carried out in a vacuum but within a political sphere shaped by institutions and actors with different power endowments. In the 1990s, the alliance asset specificities reasserted their power as a conservative force that advocated "business as usual"; in the same decade new social practices were invented to make the new material conditions *seem* "business as usual." The former was made possible by the latter. Analytical eclecticism enables the analyst to capture this interface between institutions and discursive politics and between efficiency and identity.

Conclusion: Power, Efficiency, Identity, and Alliance Persistence

More generally, analytical eclecticism captures a complex interaction among power, efficiency, and identity. As Katzenstein and Sil lay out in Chapter 1, the three variables complement each other in complex ways rather than exclude or subsume others. My study of the U.S.-Korea alliance illustrates one such complementarity as it shows the intimate and inseparable relationship among power, institution, and identity. Power, perceived through the lens of identity, generates allies and enemies; efficiency, seen within a particular framework, represents an advantage. Institutional choice is facilitated by identity; identity formation is strongly affected by power at a certain point, but it can in time become autonomous. State identity is constituted by discursive practices, which are carried out by institutions and which have emerged as a tool of power balancing. States are engaged in a balancing act, using the tool of institutions, within the social context constituted by identity. Institutions are created as a tool of power management; they are maintained within the discursive space opened and constrained by identity. Alliance persistence or termination represents the outcome of the resultant integration of three powerful, mutually interdependent variables.

The beginning and the end of the 1990s present striking contrasts. In the earlier years, the U.S.-Korea alliance looked ill, perhaps terminally. Faced with challenges from within and without, the allies implemented measures to reduce the visibility of the alliance within society and took the first steps in a seemingly irreversible course toward its termination. Changes in the distribution of power were bringing about corresponding changes in the international alignment in Northeast Asia, as realists would expect. By the end of the decade, however, the alliance was anything but ill. The allies had nullified previous measures and stepped backward to their original positions. Power redistribution had accelerated in favor of the South, yet despite realist expectations of the alliance's progressive weakening, the passing of the decade saw only the restoration of the alliance. The U.S.-Korea alliance, which was limping toward its deathbed in the early 1990s, was at the end of the 1990s bigger and stronger than ever.

The alliance constituency, a domestic coalition of officers, officials, and merchants whose existence stemmed from and grew through the alliance, had an existential interest in bringing about this reversal of the alliance's fortunes. And as one would expect, the constituents made a number of moves to salvage the alliance from the challenges of the early 1990s. My explanation for the alliance persistence, however, does not end on this functionalist note. At this point I have made a constructivist move to explain the ease with which the alliance constituents won the persistence. Their easy victory was made possible by the discourse that identified North Korea as the threat of the 1990s, and their practices were as significant for their discursive effect as for their immediate political outcome. Alliance constituents operated in an environment embedded in the discourse of danger; at the same time they participated in reproducing and hegemonizing the North's identity as the danger. The hegemonic discourse perpetuated the identities of North Korea as the "irrational, dangerous other." No matter what North Korea said or did, its words and deeds were viewed as part and parcel of its grand revisionist desires. And that hegemonic status of the "dangerous North Korea" made it possible for the alliance to win the war of survival without fighting a battle.

It is not surprising that the alliance constituents would be beneficiaries of the return to the status quo ante. From that one might be tempted to turn to a functional logic to explain the return: instrumental rationality of the alliance constituents might be at work. But it is not so easy to complete the demand-driven logic with supply-side evidence. We observe instead the "malign amplification" of threats exacerbating insecurity, which rejuvenates and strengthens the bond of the alliance. Instrumental rationality operates, if it ever does, behind the cloak of discursive politics; at the minimum it is a passive beneficiary of identity politics in the short run.

In my conception of alliance, the end of the Cold War, or the mid-1990s at the latest, represented a contract renewal time for the U.S.-ROK military alliance because changes in power distribution rendered its defensiveness questionable. I view the alliance as persisting in this decade because it was maintained, not only as the cheapest possible alternative, but also as the only option because no viable alternatives were present in the political or discursive space. I explain the alliance persistence in terms of the transformations that alliance practices have brought about in the corporate and social constitutions of the allies' identities. I started out by accepting the conventional assumptions that state identities exist and are stable, that power distribution exists and is knowable and known independently, and that external danger exists and is known on the basis of the power distribution. In the second step, I relaxed the first assumption a little, and examined in terms of asset specificity how the security practices implemented to buy security impact the corporate identity of the state and society, and how the affected identity in turn has a binding effect on the alliance. In the final step, I turned the inquiry upside down, and questioned how alliance practices constitute the subjectivity of security. The socially constituted subjectivity, and the corporate identity that is also a product of alliance practices, are caught up in a positive loop of self-reinforcement, leading to alliance persistence.

The basic causal arrows in my model are presented in Figure 4.1. I explain the phenomenon of alliance persistence in terms of the transformation that alliance operations bring about in the ways the corporeal and social identities of states are constituted. At a hypothetical time, T_1, after states are joined in an alliance, they develop, on the level of "material identity," the condition of "asset specificities" as they carry out the terms and obligations of the alliance. On a discursive level, or on the level of "social identity," the alliance relations produce social practices and representations about "security" and "threat" that affect the allies' state identities. At a later time, T_2, the asset specificities privilege the alliance by creating a cost barrier to alliance termination/replacement and by generating a domestic constituency that advocates al-

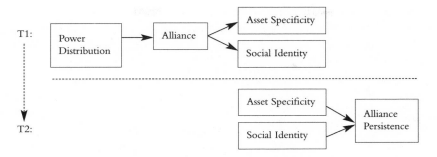

FIGURE 4.1 Causal Arrows of the Institutionalist Theory of Alliance Persistence

liance maintenance. The state's social identities become hegemonized in such a way as to overextend the alliance. Hence the alliance persists.

The logical sequence of my argument, however, does not imply the corresponding temporal sequence. It is not necessarily true that power relations produce asset specific conditions and then a discursive structure. The productive processes are much more diffuse, occurring in multiple sites and affecting other layers in multiple ways at the same time. To stylize and simplify my model, I present a three-stage image of institutionalization that shows that at any given moment state identity is institutionalized in three layers through international practices: the state is conceived of as a juxtaposition of power, interests, and discursive structures where each layer interacts with the other two, as Table 4.1 illustrates.

In explaining alliance persistence, I presented the three stages as if they were implicated in a positive-feedback loop. Indeed, such a loop exists in the case of the U.S.-ROK alliance, and it is precisely the positive nature of the feedback that explains the alliance persistence. Although there is in general a feedback loop among the three, I emphasize that the circuit is not necessarily positive; it is equally likely to be negative. When there is a negative feedback, the disjuncture will make space for political struggles between those who want to maintain the alliance and those who are opposed to it. One can only empirically determine whether the alliance will remain in place. In other words, there may be a cleavage between the three stages, setting off a series of actions and reactions that may ultimately lead to the termination of the alliance. Viewed in this manner, an alliance termination is a special case of the institutionalization of alliances.

A cleavage itself might emerge out of political struggle. For example, a disjoint between the power and identity stages might result from a radical transformation of identity that is usually associated with social movements. The South Korean peace movement attempted to achieve just that in the mid-1980s although it ultimately failed for a number of reasons, not least of which is that the movement exhibited many of the discursive elements, such as militarism, that it purportedly tried to resist

TABLE 4.1

Three-Stage Model of Institutionalization

Stage	Interaction
Power	Perceived by states whose identities and interests are constituted by social practices
Interests	Specificities generated by power and interests derived from identity
Identity	Constituted by power practices and constrained by specificities

and overcome. Iran's termination of its alliance with the United States in 1979 can be explained in terms of identity transformation that was brought about by the Islamic revolution. One might also conceive of a disjuncture between the power and interests stages and between the interests and identity stages. An example of the latter would be the, at times, tenuous relations between the United States and its European allies in NATO, particularly in the 1980s when the deployment of American tactical nuclear missiles on European soil caused an uproar.

Many international relations theorists, particularly neorealists and neoliberals, share the assumption that a state is like a billiard ball in that it does not change its properties after it has made contact with another ball. My argument suggests that states are more like sticky molecules that bond together when they make contact with each other, with a sufficient force, for a sufficient duration of time. Once they are joined, they exhibit characteristics they did not have before the bonding just as water molecules display chemical properties different from hydrogen and oxygen atoms. To use an analogy familiar in Asia, states may look like grains of rice but they can, when properly "cooked," make a rice ball.

In a similar vein, some scholars are beginning to look at the surviving security arrangements as an embryonic form of security community. They suggest that a new community has been born in the "West" through military alliance, economic exchanges, and shared norms in which the traditional realist power balancing has been replaced with "binding" (Deudney and Ikenberry 1993). They suggest that the relationship among states within this community is less conflictual than realists might predict, as differences and disputes are resolved or at least channeled through institutionalized mechanisms. A logical inference that might be drawn from such arguments is that a security community where states share a collective identity is likely to attenuate militarized behavior and to increase transparency, confidence-building measures, arms control, arms reduction, and so on.

My argument, however, points in the other direction: the surviving security arrangements, such as the U.S.-Korea alliance, may represent an "insecurity community," a community indeed but one whose existence is predicated on and implicated in the reproduction of danger.[17] The multiple asset specificities built into the existing arrangements and the discursive space produced by them have a good potential to bind all the members of the arrangements in a continual reproduction of insecurity. The rice ball of states may not necessarily be sweet; it can be sour.

Hence the alliance goes on, but this does not mean all is well. Its persistence, whether because of asset specificities or hegemonic discourses, does not preclude disagreements or disputes about the configuration of the allied militaries, burden sharing, social conflicts, and other issues that arise out of alliance operations, as the history of military alliances attests. The South Korean and the U.S. militaries are currently engaged in an intense negotiation about the realignment of U.S. forces and bases in Korea while they manage to keep on the backburner the more contentious issues such as the transfer of the operational command control of the Korean military and the revision of the Status of Forces Agreement. But these technical difficulties do not pose an insurmountable obstacle for the alliance so long as it enjoys a common social reality and draws material benefits from its asset specificities.

Social identities pose a deeper challenge to the alliance. South Korea is currently caught between two conflicting identities: the alliance identity that sees the United States as a friendly security provider and the nationalist identity that pits Korean identity against the United States. It has thus far tried to maintain a delicate balance between the conflicting identities by containing each in its own domain: the United States in national security; and North Korea in culture and economy. As the events of 2002–3 illustrate, this is a balance that is difficult to maintain for long. As the dividing line becomes thin and blurred with the rising tension over the North's nuclear capabilities and with the deepening intercourse between the Koreas, the delicate balance will become increasingly untenable. In the months ahead, such security issues as nuclear weapons and missiles are likely to continue to confront the United States and Korea, but in the long run the clash of identities might represent the more intractable, more fundamental challenge that the United States is likely to face in Korea. The strength of the alliance bond will be tested in the tug of war between the nationalistic bond between the two Koreas and the alliance security bond between the United States and South Korea.

Notes

1. Victor Cha (2001) prefers to call such a phenomenon "alliance resilience."

2. Yi Yŏng-Hŭi presented an argument at a parliamentary hearing that there is parity in the military balance in Korea, an argument that Yi said the Korean Ministry of Defense later acknowledged to be correct. See Yi Yŏng-Hŭi (1992). Stephen Goose (1987) argued in the 1980s that the military balance on the peninsula is at a parity.

3. A similar point is made by Victor Cha (1997). In the United States, a curious mixture of right- and left-wing intellectuals have voiced opposition to the continued U.S. military presence in Korea, but their voice remains marginalized.

4. For example, Dunnigan (1988) shows that F16 Falcons exceed the capabilities of MiG-29s in air interception. In a similar comparison, the MiG-23 displayed an inferior ability to conduct air intercept missions, strike ground targets, and perform reconnaissance missions. A Department of Defense study corroborates Dunnigan's assessment. The 1990 edition of *Soviet Military Power* argues that the MiG-29s "lag behind their U.S. counterpart aircraft in avionics, weapons, and certain other features, but they are a much closer match than previous generations of Soviet aircraft" (Department of Defense, 1990: 294–96).

5. For example, Kim Il-Sung proclaimed in his address to the Supreme People's Assembly in 1993 that "North and South should not threaten or invade the other. Nor should either side impose its system on the other or attempt to absorb the other," a proclamation that subsequently became a foundation of Pyongyang's reunification policies.

6. For this analysis, I compared Kim Il-Sung's New Year's speeches from 1991 to 1994 with those from 1981 to 1984. In the 1980s the United States was always associated with negative adjectives (such as imperialist, hostile, aggressive, etc.); in the 1990s such value-laden words were not used as often. Most dramatic is the change in Pyongyang's preferred means of dealing with Washington: from military confrontation in the 1980s, to peaceful diplomatic negotiations in the 1990s. For texts of Kim's speeches, see Foreign Broadcast Information Service-East Asia (*FBIS-EAS*), various years.

7. Examples include the "submarine incursion" of 1996, skirmishes in the West Sea in 2001 and 2002, and the "Seoul will be engulfed in the sea of fire" remark in 1994. The North Koreans also expelled IAEA inspectors and restarted their nuclear activities without IAEA's monitoring in 2002.

8. Since President Bush removed all tactical nuclear warheads from South Korea in 1991 as part of a worldwide withdrawal of U.S. tactical nuclear weapons, the standard operating procedure no longer applies. The example is used for illustrative purposes only.

9. For a detailed, and by far the best, discussion of the operational plans to use Korean weapons systems and forces to deliver U.S. nuclear weapons, see Hayes (1991: esp. 105–22).

10. As indicated by the Memorandum of Understanding on Technology Use Fees for Defense Material Production in Korea, signed in July 1989, there are close to 140 items that are exempt from the technology fee when used domestically or exported, and additional items, not covered by the memorandum, for which a technical fee is charged.

11. Organizational charts and rules lay out who is supposed to do what in which way. As it is infeasible to imagine and plan for all possible contingencies, however, the formal structure leaves room for adaptation, opening the door to organizational idiosyncrasies. People who actually occupy the dots in the charts and carry out the missions have a tendency to develop their own ways of accomplishing their mission by adapting the charts and rules to their specific circumstances. Personalities also play a role in producing organizational idiosyncrasies. Team specificity refers to durable investment made in people to help them adapt to specific circumstances and organizational idiosyncrasies. See Williamson (1987).

12. The Federation of American Scientists, Arms Sales Monitoring Project, *Official Arms Transfers Statistics*, www.fas.org/asmp/profiles/sales_db.htm. In 2002, Korea was the largest importer under the Foreign Military Sales program. See United States, Department of State, *FY 2004 Congressional Budget Justification for Foreign Operations* (Washington, DC: Department of State, February 2003), www.state.gov/m/rm/rls/cbj/2004/. In March 1991 the Bush administration proposed legislation to establish a $1 billion program to allow the U.S. Export-Import

Bank to guarantee loans to aid the sale of U.S. military products. The Department of Defense runs such programs as the Foreign Military Financing Program to help weapons exporters. Of all U.S. military exports in FY 1991 (total of $42 billion), government sales accounted for 45 percent with private sales accounting for the rest. Government sales include Foreign Military Sales and Foreign Military Construction Sales (Lumpe and Donarski 1998).

13. I thank Victor Cha for bringing the relevant passages to my attention.

14. David Wright (1998) makes a similar argument.

15. According to the *Military Balance*, North Korea possesses 24 FROG missiles and "some 30 Scud-C" missiles (International Institute for Strategic Studies 1999: 194).

16. Woo-Cumings notes, correctly, that 1994, when the Clinton administration considered a military strike against North Korean nuclear facilities, was another year when many Koreans felt the United States could undermine their security. However, such a perception was not publicly expressed in the same way as in the candlelight vigils of 2002.

17. David Campbell (1992) makes a similar argument with respect to U.S. foreign policy.

5

Coping with Strategic Uncertainty

The Role of Institutions and Soft Balancing in Southeast Asia's Post–Cold War Strategy

YUEN FOONG KHONG

> The Foreign Ministers noted the profound impact of the end of the
> Cold War and of East-West confrontation in terms of new strategic
> uncertainties and fresh opportunities.
>
> —*Joint Communiqué, 25th ASEAN Ministerial Meeting, 1992*

A key idea has infused the strategic discourse of the small to medium powers of the Association of Southeast Asian Nations (ASEAN) since the end of the Cold War: the idea of uncertainty.[1] Uncertainty and its conceptual analogues—lack of predictability, flux, fluidity—have been the (mental) constructions of choice to characterize Southeast and East Asia's security environment.[2] Southeast Asia's politicians, policy makers, and scholars seem both transfixed and mortified by this uncertainty. Mitigating this constructed uncertainty has been a critical strand of Southeast Asia's post–Cold War security strategy. Southeast Asian strategic planners, I argue, have resorted to two principal strategies to alleviate this perceived uncertainty: a frenzy of institution building and expansion that began in the late 1980s and continues till the present; and a soft form of balancing behavior that was especially evident in the early as well as late 1990s. These strategies were helpful in bringing about greater certainty on those issues—such as the American military presence, China's intentions, and Japan's military trajectory—on which ASEAN security planners wanted "closure." Post–September 11, the security environment in Southeast Asia is more, not less, cer-

I would like to thank the participants of the Asian Security Workshop in March 2002 at Cornell University for their comments and suggestions on an earlier draft. I am especially indebted to Itty Abraham, Amitav Acharya, Muthiah Alagappa, Allen Carlson, Peter Katzenstein, Rudra Sil, and J. J. Suh for critical feedback; any remaining errors are mine.

tain in that the challenge posed by Al Qaeda's affiliates in the region has become clearer and more threatening. Dealing with these threats will be a major preoccupation of the ASEAN states in the foreseeable future. This battle against terrorism on the Southeast Asian front is likely to enhance the significance of the two ASEAN strategies—institution building and soft balancing—identified in this essay, although it will entail some transformation of their roles. If the major purpose of these two strategies was to help reduce uncertainty in the 1990s, their purpose after September 11 must be adapted to ensuring effective cooperation—among ASEAN members and with others—to defeat terrorism. The process of adapting these strategies—especially soft balancing—to meet Southeast Asia's contemporary security challenges will be neither smooth nor obvious, but chances are good that a solution acceptable to ASEAN and its interlocutors will be found.

A promise of analytical eclecticism is its agnosticism about "metatheoretical battles" and "programmatic debates." Instead, it focuses on "the identification of politically important and analytically interesting [empirical] problems that reflect the complexity of international life" (Katzenstein and Sil, this volume). What then is the problematique addressed in this chapter? It consists of the three empirical observations contained in the opening paragraph: the perception and construction of uncertainty, the expansion and proliferation of regional institutions, and the soft-balancing behavior exhibited by some of the key ASEAN states. Each of these is a "politically important and analytically interesting" problem that might not have been observed or admitted into the analysis had one not been eclectic. Uncertainty, for example, is considered by some as "natural" fact or a constant in international life (Waltz 1979). Yet familiarity with the post–Cold War discourse of ASEAN's elites and analysts suggests that the term had entered the working vocabulary of officials and scholars with a frequency—accompanied by consternation—that was absent during the heyday of the Cold War. Although constructivists, liberals, and realists all have a place for "uncertainty" in their analytic schemes, the salience of the uncertainty discourse could also have been picked up by Southeast Asian area specialists or for that matter, avid readers of ASEAN documents or newspapers. What analytical eclecticism permits, in my view, is to give vent to those sensibilities that, say, "problematize" or "denaturalize" it (uncertainty), inviting us out of a frame of mind that, for whatever reason (for instance, theoretical elegance), might prefer to treat uncertainty as something natural and constant. Herein lies the promise as well as the pitfall of analytical eclecticism: although in inviting the analyst to problematize (explore, dissect, and explain) hitherto unproblematized or taken-for-granted observations or concepts, it holds out the possibility of producing fresh insights and new discoveries, it also risks the danger of being too eclectic, that is, of being too accommodating to too many potential variables, and/or being too analytic, problematizing everything in sight. The result could be as inchoate as it could be unconvincing. These dangers notwithstanding, an approach that encourages analytic openness and playfulness is worth trying: the proof of the pudding must be in the eating.

The post–Cold War proliferation of regional institutions is another "fact" of Asia's landscape that should be obvious to all. Analytical eclecticism points to this development as being potentially important in any post–Cold War portrait of Southeast Asia's security dynamics but it is agnostic about how important it is or what exactly it does. The latter is something to be discovered through empirical research. Liberals emphasize the "demand" for such regimes and institutions in lowering transaction costs and fostering cooperation. Constructivists focus on the identity-building and preference-changing potential of these institutions. Realists, on the other hand, are likely to be less impressed, pointing to the relative youth of such institutions and viewing them primarily as talk shops. Again, to be analytically eclectic is to be open to the possibility that regional institutions such as the ASEAN Regional Forum (ARF) may be important to understanding Southeast Asia's post–Cold War security trajectory; it also means being open to the possibility that such institutions may assume roles not specified or expected by the research tradition with which they have the most affinity. As I shall suggest later, institutions such as the ARF do not just help lower transaction costs as liberals would expect, they perform balancing and identity-forming roles as well.

The third development this chapter describes and privileges is the balancing behavior of the major ASEAN states: by offering the United States use of their facilities as it was leaving Clark and Subic bases in the Philippines, these ASEAN states seem to be engaging in a form of balancing against a rising China. Would the significance of these rather subtle moves have been recognized and incorporated (into one's explanatory sketch) by research traditions that deny the causal significance of hard military power? I believe not. The analytic challenge, as I see it, is to characterize this behavior and for the purposes of this chapter, I have settled on the notion of "soft balancing" as a way of capturing the phenomenon. Soft balancing remains distinct from "hard balancing" or the formation of formal military alliances; but it describes the behavior of those ASEAN states with a clear desire for the United States to remain in the region (at least until September 11). Offering the United States use of their naval bases and ports goes against the official ASEAN mantra of working toward cordoning off Southeast Asia as a "Zone of Peace, Freedom, and Neutrality" (ZOPFAN) where the great powers were to be gradually weaned from their bases in the region. This behavior also suggests that the key ASEAN states are aligning themselves with the preponderant power; that is, they are not balancing against power, they are balancing against a perceived potential threat (see Walt 1987).

It follows that the account of Southeast Asia's post–Cold War security strategy presented in this chapter is an eclectic one. The analysis is not wedded to any one research tradition, but instead brings together "variables" dear to liberals (institutions), realists (balancing), and Southeast Asian specialists (uncertainty) to characterize and explain Southeast Asia's security strategies.[3] The posited link between these three main features of the Southeast Asian landscape—and the main thesis of this chapter—is as follows: The expansion and proliferation of regional institutions and soft balancing may be seen as strategies of ASEAN's security planners to induce greater certainty into the strategic environment.

Below, I begin by exploring the post–Cold War security anxieties of the key ASEAN states. These anxieties can be discerned by examining and unpacking ASEAN's discourse of "strategic uncertainty." Examining the latter reveals four major concerns: the American military presence, Japan's military trajectory, China's future demeanor, and ASEAN's continued relevance. Each of these concerns is discussed in some detail in the next section in order to arrive at an understanding of why they are "security concerns" or uncertainties that ASEAN would like removed. This will be followed by a brief analysis of strategies that ASEAN could conceivably have adopted, but did not, to mitigate these concerns. The strategies that ASEAN did adopt—soft balancing and institution building—are discussed next, with the emphasis on demonstrating how these strategies work to reduce uncertainty. The conclusion assesses the success of these strategies while pointing to the selective nature of ASEAN's conception of uncertainty and its consequences.

ASEAN's Discourse of Uncertainty

As the Foreign Ministers' Joint Communiqué issued at the end of the 1992 Manila ASEAN Ministerial Meeting (AMM) put it, a profound impact of the end of the Cold War was the creation of "new strategic uncertainties" as well as "fresh opportunities" (ASEAN Secretariat 1992: 34). "Uncertainty" has been the construct most frequently used by Southeast Asia's leaders and thinkers to characterize the post–Cold War security environment. In July 1995, Malaysia's Mahatir Mohamad argued that "We live in a world that is still full of surprises and uncertainties"; three months later, at the 1995 Non-Aligned Countries Heads of State meeting in Colombia, he reiterated his view of how the post–Cold War international situation had "relapsed into the old state of uncertainty" (Mahatir 1995). In 1997, the Vietnamese foreign minister, Nguyen Manh Cam, apprised the international situation as one experiencing "swift changes" with "no few uncertain factors which may generate instability" (Nguyen 1997).

Similarly, the chairman's statement issued at the end of the 1998 ASEAN Regional Forum in Manila, "recognized the significant contribution of the ARF to the establishment of a strong foundation of trust and confidence among its participants" and judged this as "essential in confronting the existing uncertainties in the Asia-Pacific region" (ASEAN Secretariat 1999: 120). Singapore's president S. R. Nathan, in his 1999 address to Parliament, assessed the regional and global situation in the following terms:

> Our strategic environment has become more uncertain and complex. In the region, ASEAN's standing has been weakened. . . . Indonesia is undergoing a wrenching political transition, which is not yet complete. Malaysia's economy is recovering, while its government faces political challenges. . . .

> Globally, the major powers are grappling with the political and strategic implications of a globalised economy and the post Cold War power balance. They are tentatively exploring new configurations among themselves and with regional states (Singapore Government Press Release 1999).

Descriptions of the Asia-Pacific strategic environment as "complex and fluid," or "as yet indefinable," or assessments emphasizing the "strategic uncertainties of post–Cold War Asia Pacific," are recurring themes in the nine chapters of the Institute of Southeast Asian Studies' perceptive compendium on *Southeast Asian Perspectives on Security* (Da Cuhna 2000).

Carlson and Suh (2002: 1) suggest that a discourse can be thought of "as a collection of words, statements and representations put forth by political actors on a specific issue." Discourse can have instrumental, communicative, and constitutive uses, and each of these uses matters because ultimately, it can affect behavior. ASEAN's depiction of its strategic environment as "uncertain" is a constitutive discourse: ASEAN's strategic environment—"the material reality"—is, to use Carlson and Suh's words, "imbued with a particular meaning," in this case, uncertainty. This particular meaning or representation, in my view, captures a key aspect of ASEAN's material reality. For neorealists, this recognition of uncertainty is to be expected and hence is unproblematic. With the end of the Cold War, the certainties associated with bipolarity vanished, and an international system in transition by definition is characterized by uncertainty.

ASEAN's discourse of uncertainty does seem to be heavily tinged with neorealist concerns. To begin with, ASEAN's security planners were more interested in grappling with the "strategic uncertainties" than in grasping the "fresh opportunities."[4] Their implicit or explicit reference point was the Cold War, when the general pattern of Southeast Asian international politics was recognizable and predictable. The key actors were constant for forty years: the United States, China, Russia, and Japan. The identities of these actors, as well as their regional "others" were also clear: liberal democracies versus Communist dictatorships. The security dynamics were predictable: the two blocs competed with each other for friends and allies in Southeast Asia and also tried to check the perceived advances of the other (for example, the United States saw itself as checking China's advance in Vietnam). The Sino-Soviet split complicated the picture for the Communist parties in Indochina, but the more shrewd among them seized the opportunity to play the two sides against each other in order to advance their own strategic goals. The Sino-Soviet split did not alter the strategic allegiances of Indonesia, Malaysia, the Philippines, Singapore, and Thailand, which were basically constant throughout this period: with the exception of Indonesia during the Sukarno period, all were formal or informal allies of the United States. And although the Vietnam War—from the perspective of the United States and its allies—was mainly about preventing South Vietnam from falling to the Communist side, by the late 1960s the ASEAN 5 were resigned to an American defeat and eventual withdrawal from Vietnam. A Communist-dominated Indochina was something ASEAN was prepared with live with; ASEAN's 1976 Treaty of Amity and Cooperation hinted at the possibility of accession by other states.

By comparison, the post-1989 period was strewn with uncertainties. One of the key players—the Soviet Union—disappeared from the (East and Southeast Asian) scene; Russia was forced to refocus its energies on its domestic front and its near abroad. In and of itself, the removal of the Soviet Union from the East Asian strategic equation was not a source of consternation for most in ASEAN. It was the strategic implications of that development that proved unnerving. Analysis after analysis in the early 1990s assumed that absent the Russians, the United States would have strong incentives to withdraw militarily from East Asia (Weatherbee 1995; Buzan and Segal 1994; Friedberg 1993/94). Think-tank analysts and international relations theorists tended to be surer than policy makers that the United States would be making a gradual exit. Southeast Asian policy makers, perhaps reflecting their belief in agency instead of "the structure of the situation," tended to be more cautious about the certainty of a U.S. military drawdown; their approach was to factor in U.S. intentions about its forward military presence as one of the key uncertainties permeating the region.

But uncertainty about America's staying power engendered a host of other uncertainties. With the Russians gone and uncertainty about how long and how many Americans would stay, the question of who would fill the regional vacuum became urgent. The leading contenders were thought to be Japan, China, and India (Jeshurun 1993). Echoing the debate in the United States in the late 1980s and early 1990s about Japan as the new contender, some in Southeast Asia also worried about Japan filling the power vacuum. By the mid-1990s however, the focus shifted to China. China's spectacular economic growth would make it over time into a formidable military power and the question in Southeast Asian minds was what kind of power —a responsible one playing by the rules of the game or a regional bully—China would be as it assumed great-power status (Commission on America's National Interests 1996; Johnston, this volume).

The final uncertainty concerned the political clout and relevance of ASEAN itself. The high point of ASEAN cohesion was the 1980s when the ASEAN 5 worked together—with friends and allies in international forums—to pressure Vietnam to leave Cambodia, which it had occupied since 1978. How crucial ASEAN was in bringing about the Paris Agreements of 1991 remains a matter of debate, but ASEAN's self-perception was that without its collective stance and insistence on putting the Cambodia issue high on the international agenda, the international community would have acquiesced to Vietnam's occupation of Cambodia. The resolution of the Vietnam-Cambodian issue in the late 1980s removed the external bugbear that had helped ASEAN coalesce; absent that common external danger, ASEAN's cohesion and clout in the post–Cold War era would be seriously challenged.

The air had hardly cleared when Thailand announced, without consulting its ASEAN allies, its vision of turning the "battlefields" of Indochina into "marketplaces" (with Thailand as the market leader of course). This attempt to refocus Thai priorities in the direction of Indochina was read by the other ASEAN members as an attempt to capitalize on Thailand's geographic propinquity at the expense of its (southward) ASEAN connections. External commentators saw this as the first step in the regionalization of Southeast Asia's security, anticipating the formation of a continental and a maritime Southeast Asia complex (Simon 1992). Moreover, the most worrisome security predicaments of Asia centered in Northeast rather than Southeast Asia. The former focused on a newly belligerent North Korea intent on manufacturing nuclear weapons, the reemergence of the Taiwan issue, the rise of China (and its impact on Japan), while the latter's main issue was the South China Sea. The loci of the most critical post–Cold War security issues, in other words, seemed to be shifting away from Southeast Asia. On the one hand, this was a positive development in terms of the lower probability of major conflict in Southeast Asia, but it did give rise to questions about ASEAN's continuing prominence and clout, unless of course ASEAN found a way to insert itself into the new security equation of Asia.

This portrait of ASEAN's uncertainty discourse is a rough approximation. It is derived from the various statements or speech-acts of the more articulate Southeast Asian policy makers and analysts. Not everyone will agree with the specifics. Some newer ASEAN members, for example, may be less sure about the desirability of the U.S. military presence; by the same token, states such as Myanmar, Laos, and Cambodia may also be less worried about China's future intentions than are the Philippines or Indonesia (Muni 2002). Hence these uncertainties about the intentions of the United States and China may not be as salient to the newer ASEAN members in the way they are to the older members. However, since most of the Indochinese states did not join ASEAN until the mid- or late 1990s, and since these new members are still relying on the more experienced ones in concocting ASEAN's corporate strategy, the focus on the original ASEAN 5's uncertainty discourse remains appropriate. Equally important, our portrait does not deal with the domestic uncertainties—succession, secession, economic revitalization, the forces unleashed by democratization, to name a few—that probably keep ASEAN's leaders awake at night more often than "external" or regional uncertainties. Thus Indonesian president Megawati Sukarnoputri's number one security nightmare might be secession (of Acheh and Irian Jaya), followed closely by worries about economic stagnation and its propensity to generate ethnic violence. In the late 1990s, Malaysian prime minister Mahatir Mohamad's number one nightmare was the political instability associated with the competition among his potential successors. In October 2003, however, Malaysia witnessed the smooth transfer of power from Mahatir to his deputy, Abdullah Badawi. For Vietnam, the chief uncertainty might be its ability to join the bandwagon of rapid economic growth, while for the Myanmar generals, the chief worry is likely to be how long they can continue to usurp power. In other words, these domestic worries vary in content, salience, and intensity from country to country. This chapter cannot do justice to the subtleties and variations in the internal security concerns of each of the ASEAN states. It will therefore not try to do so; rather, the focus will be on those security worries that are common to (most in) ASEAN and that admit of a collective solution. Such security concerns tend to concern the external environment, although a few of them—such as economic revitalization and terrorism—span the internal-external divide. In the months after 9/11, for example, virtually all the ASEAN states with a sizable Muslim population have had to confront the threat posed by Al Qaeda's followers in the region. Only a minute number among Southeast Asia's Muslims are sympathetic to Al Qaeda's tactics, and an even more minute number are extremist enough to do Al Qaeda's bidding in the region. This, however, does not make the terrorist threat any less formidable. The responses of the ASEAN states to the terrorist threat will be discussed later.

Acknowledging these caveats allows us to proceed to "denaturalize" ASEAN's discourse of uncertainty (Carlson and Suh, this volume). The discourse privileged some elements while it remained silent on others. In other words, the uncertainties ASEAN's security planners identified, and saw themselves as grappling with, were not some "objective reality." They were constructed or selected out of a myriad of uncertainties. The political-military intentions of the United States, Japan, and China were construed as "uncertain," while ASEAN's own economic resilience, its way of doing things ("the ASEAN way"), or the threat of terrorism were construed as unproblematic. ASEAN took its high growth rates as a certainty and assumed such growth would persist. It also assumed that its approach to security cooperation, known as "the ASEAN way," would continue to be relevant. And despite being home to the largest Muslim population in the world, ASEAN registered no uncertainty about the "moderateness" of Southeast Asia's Muslims. The discourse of uncertainty was therefore a construction, and not just a reflection of material reality as neorealists assume: certain features of the strategic environment were recognized or left in, while others were unrecognized or left out. The significance of this, as Carlson and Suh point out in this volume, is that such a representation of reality has implications for behavior: in focusing its efforts on reducing the uncertainties it highlighted via regional institutions and soft balancing, ASEAN failed to attend to the uncertainties it had bracketed such as the basis of its impressive economic performance and the emergence of radical Islam. Thus discourse is important in that by selecting aspects of reality and constituting them as the key uncertainties in need of policy attention, it also relegates other (omitted) aspects to the back burner. The problem is, these neglected aspects of reality have of way of returning to surprise policy makers, as the Asian financial crisis and the terrorist bombing of Bali in October 2002 suggest.

To summarize, in the early aftermath of the Cold War, Southeast Asia's security planners framed the security challenges of their region and beyond in terms of four uncertainties. The first centered on the forward military posture of the United States in East and Southeast Asia. Would U.S. force levels descend to where the United States would be no longer palpable or credible? The second uncertainty centered on fears about Japan pursuing an independent military strategy. In the event of U.S. withdrawal from East Asia, would Japan militarize and perhaps even go nuclear? Third was the anxiety about rising Chinese power and its filling the power vacuum left behind by the withdrawing Americans. Would China be a responsible power and a good neighbor? And finally, there was the uncertainty about the clout and relevance of ASEAN the collective. Would ASEAN continue to punch above its weight?

An analysis of ASEAN's discourse of uncertainty is useful in two ways. First, it allows us to derive ASEAN's strategic preferences, or the manner in which ASEAN would like to "resolve" the uncertainty confronting it. If we reverse the "uncertainty" question and ask what certainties ASEAN would most like to see, we arrive at the following: knowledge that (1) the United States intends to maintain a credible military presence in Asia; (2) Japan will remain a great economic but not military power; (3) China will assume its role as a great but responsible power; (4) ASEAN will remain relevant to the East Asian strategic equation. These then are the ends or strategic objectives that ASEAN most prefers. If these elements were in place and would stay in place for ten to fifteen years, ASEAN would be greatly reassured.

Second, examining the discourse of uncertainty also encourages us to detect how ASEAN (or any set of states) might respond to such a situation. It is possible that ASEAN may choose to do nothing, either because it has a high tolerance for uncertainty, or because it believes that there is nothing it can do to alter the situation. In such a case, it would be difficult to speak of an ASEAN strategy; one would have to admit that ASEAN's strategy was one of doing nothing. On the other hand, ASEAN may be proactive in seeking to alleviate this uncertainty and doing what is within its power to alter the probabilities of attaining the outcomes it prefers. As this chapter argues, this was the strategy adopted by ASEAN: a proactive strategy aimed at not only achieving greater certainty, but also of increasing the odds of achieving ASEAN's strategic goals discussed below.

A Continuing American Military Presence?

Of the four uncertainties that worried ASEAN's leaders, uncertainty about the United States military presence in East Asia was probably the most important. It was important in and of itself, but also for the repercussions it would have on other actors if that uncertainty persisted or were to be resolved in the form of a U.S. withdrawal. In what follows, I analyze ASEAN's consternation about the possibility of an American withdrawal, the reactions of some of its key members, and the eventual resolution of the issue.

The role of the United States in East Asia has not been uncontroversial. During the Cold War, anti-Communist states like Indonesia, Malaysia, the Philippines, Singapore, and Thailand—the original ASEAN 5—were largely supportive of the U.S. interventions in Korea and Vietnam. The latter was seen as an attempt to stem the spread of

Communism; some in Southeast Asia have also argued that the U.S. intervention in Vietnam bought Southeast Asia states time to get their houses in order and strengthened their own abilities to deal with indigenous versions of the Communist threat (Lee 2001: 539). When it appeared that the United States was likely to lose the Vietnam War, and when Britain announced its military withdrawal east of Suez, the five most anti-Communist Southeast Asian states came together as ASEAN.

For much of the 1970s, the ASEAN 5 were left to their own devices as the United States sought to distance itself from the painful memories of a war (Vietnam) lost in Southeast Asia. Even when a unified Vietnam invaded Cambodia in 1978, the United States was unmoved. It was the efforts of the ASEAN 5, acting in unison and through ASEAN, that kept the pressure on Vietnam in international forums like the United Nations. ASEAN's aim was to make Vietnam pay a price for violating one of its cherished norms (respect for territorial integrity) and its hope was that over time, Vietnam would accommodate ASEAN's wishes. In the early 1980s, Malaysia and Indonesia worried that excessive ASEAN and international pressure on Vietnam would play into China's hand and increase its influence in Southeast Asia. Since both Indonesia and Malaysia feared China more than Vietnam, they contemplated defecting from the ASEAN's common strategy. In the event however, the arrogance of Vietnam and calls for ASEAN solidarity persuaded the two ASEAN members to adhere to the corporate line. ASEAN's joint effort against Vietnam contributed to Vietnam's decision to withdraw from Cambodia in 1989; today, it is seen as perhaps ASEAN's finest moment—by acting in unison, it succeeded in keeping the issue alive and high on the international agenda, with the assistance of the United States, China, and Japan when necessary.

When the Cold War ended, there was consternation among some in Southeast Asia that the United States would drawdown its military presence in the region. The Department of Defense's 1990 East Asia Strategic Initiative (EASI) called for the withdrawal of 15,000 U.S. military personnel from the Asia-Pacific between 1990 and 1993, to be followed by further withdrawals in 1994–95 and 1995–2000 (Ang 1997). The disintegration of the Soviet Union in 1991 removed another major rationale for the continued forward deployment of U.S. troops in the region. Policy makers in East Asia, as well as analysts worldwide, took these developments seriously and factored the anticipated U.S. withdrawal into their calculations.

In Southeast Asia, Singapore led the pack in anticipating the U.S. military retrenchment, in articulating its consequences, and in expressing its apprehension. In 1989, as the negotiations between the Philippines and the United States on the lease renewal for Clark and Subic bases became bogged down, Singapore was approached by the United States about the possibility of using Singapore's bases. Prime Minister Lee Kuan Yew was forthcoming and in August 1989 Singapore went public about allowing the United States to use its bases (Lee 2001: 537–38). In one of his last acts as prime minister, Lee signed a memorandum of understanding (MOU) with Vice-

President Dan Quayle in November 1990 allowing the United States access to Singapore's facilities, thus giving the "US forces a toehold in Southeast Asia" upon their departure from the Philippines (Lee 2001: 538). In a 1991 interview explaining why the American presence was vital, Lee argued that "Nature does not like a vacuum. And if there is a vacuum, we can be sure somebody will fill it." In 1991, that "somebody" in Lee's mind was Japan, but the competitive logic he saw in such situations holds regardless of who might fill the vacuum: "If the Americans are not around, they (the Japanese) cannot be sure who will protect their oil tankers. So they have to do something themselves. That will trigger the Koreans, who fear the Japanese, then the Chinese. Will India then come down to our seas with two aircraft carriers?" (*Straits Times* 17 Dec. 1991: 27). Hence Lee wanted to "stick with what has worked so far," that is, the American military presence, which he saw as "*essential* for the continuation of international law and order in East Asia" (ibid., emphasis added).

Malaysia's case is especially interesting because as the advocate of the concept of the Zone of Peace, Freedom, and Neutrality (ZOPFAN), it should have welcomed the U.S. departure from the Philippines, especially since the Russians were no longer a threat. The ZOPFAN principle called for the eventual neutralization of Southeast Asia, with guarantees provided by the major powers. The U.S. departure from the Philippines would have been a first step in that direction. But as David Camroux (1994: 17) has argued, Malaysia viewed the drawdown of U.S. military forces in the region in the early 1990s with apprehension. As he puts it, "Mahatir would have preferred the United States to maintain its military bases in the Philippines. . . . Once the decision was made to withdraw, Malaysia both acquiesced in the Singaporean decision to provide repair and other facilities to the United States and offered access to certain Malaysian facilities." Similarly, Amitav Acharya (1999a: 140) has also pointed to a 1990 statement by Malaysia's armed forces director of intelligence that "America's presence is certainly needed, at least to balance other powers with contrasting ideology in this region. . . . The power balance is needed . . . to ensure that other powers that have far-reaching ambitions in Southeast Asia will not find it easy to act against countries in the region."

For Malaysia, Singapore, and Indonesia, the most troublesome evidence in support of the projections of the EASI were the tough negotiations between the Philippines and the United States over the new lease permitting the stationing of U.S. troops at Clark Air Force Base and Subic Bay Naval Base. By 1989 it became obvious that the negotiations had become entangled with a fierce domestic political debate within the Philippines. The surge in Filipino nationalism derailed the negotiations; nature also intervened in the form of the Mount Pinatubo volcanic eruption, which rendered Clark Air Base unusable, thus giving the United States even more incentive to withdraw from the Philippines.

Individual states in ASEAN and ASEAN the organization searched for a strategy to forestall the total withdrawal of the United States from Southeast Asia. Put differently, they acted to alleviate the uncertainty about the U.S. military presence. The strategies they used will be discussed in the next section; what needs to be noted here is that ASEAN's worries about U.S. staying power should have largely dissipated by the mid-1990s. In 1995, the Department of Defense issued the East Asian Strategy Review, committing the United States to a forward military presence of 100,000 troops in the region. What was new about this so-called Nye report, named after its author, Assistant Secretary of Defense for International Security Affairs Joseph Nye, was that it reversed the two previous reports' recommendation of gradual troop reductions through the year 2000. In the press conference explaining the reversal, Nye suggested that the U.S. presence in East Asia was instrumental in maintaining stability, and the relative peace enjoyed by the region between the end of the Vietnam War and the mid-1990s was attributable to the American forward military presence. He emphasized that this military presence, together with America's bilateral security treaties with Japan, South Korea, Thailand, and the Philippines, remained the linchpin of stability in East Asia. Nye did however highlight for his audience a second departure in the report: the United States now saw regional multilateral institutions as playing important supplementary roles in increasing transparency and confidence building in East Asia (United States Department of Defense 1995).

The U.S. decision to maintain 100,000 troops in East Asia, roughly similar to the numbers it has left in Europe, is explicable largely in terms of U.S. calculations of its geopolitical and economic interests. As Nye put it, "the United States maintains a strong interest in East Asia, not only because of . . . geopolitical reasons . . . but also because . . . Asia today is the most rapidly growing economic area in the world" (ibid.). What ASEAN could do, given its limited influence, was to help articulate what those interests were, reinforcing U.S. perceptions of East Asia's geostrategic importance and economic dynamism, and warning the United States about new threats on the horizon. In articulating their views and in trying to persuade the United States that it had crucial interests in Southeast Asia, small powers like the ASEAN states would find regional forums extremely advantageous. The more of them, the more cross-cutting (in terms of issue areas), the better, so long as the United States and the other major powers attend. This search for venues to verbally engage the major powers in general, and the United States in particular, helps explain why regional institutions became a growth industry in East Asia in the 1990s. In that sense, ASEAN's leaders were more optimistic about the powers of agency than their realist chroniclers: the latter, informed by realism, were content to predict a massive U.S. retrenchment from East Asia, thereby bringing about all the instabilities and conflicts they foresaw (Buzan and Segal 1994). ASEAN's leaders were perhaps ignorant of the finer points of realism but they acted within the limits of their capacities to persuade the United States to stay. Their efforts did not come to naught.

Analysts writing in the early 1990s who forecasted conflict in East Asia were right to point to the existence of flashpoints in the region, but they were less perceptive about the United States (see esp. Buzan and Segal 1994, also Friedberg 1993/94). Realists like Buzan and Segal assumed a gradual drawdown of America's military presence in East Asia. Although few of them specified a time frame, the expectation was soon, especially after the implosion of the Soviet Union. Where analysts like Buzan and Segal went astray was in their analysis—or lack thereof—of these U.S. calculations. Even those who argued against the wisdom of such a drawdown, pointed to U.S.-Japan economic quarrels, domestic U.S. politics, and crises in Eastern Europe as factors that, in the words of Aaron Friedberg, "could combine to cause the United States to pull back more sharply from Asia than it is currently doing"; for him, "the fact that such a course of action would be mistaken and dangerous affords no guarantee that it will not be followed" (1993/94: 32). The point is that it was not followed, and the tensions and conflicts predicted by Buzan, Segal, and Friedberg have not materialized. For Southeast Asia's strategic planners at least, the continued presence of 100,000 U.S. military personnel in East Asia is a major reason for the relative calm in the region.

To be sure, there is nothing magical about the figure of 100,000 U.S. troops, but it is symbolically important. Asia has the same number of U.S. military personnel as Europe; in effect, the U.S. withdrew 35,000 troops from East Asia in 1990–94. Fifteen thousand of these were personnel who left with the closure of Clark and Subic bases in the Philippines. Timing also matters in that every additional year of a strong U.S. presence is an additional year for the nascent regional institutions to gather strength and momentum. If the decisions of 1995 delayed a significant U.S. withdrawal by ten to fifteen years, they would give that many extra years for institutions such as the ARF, already in place, to grow, and for processes such as democratization (Thailand and Indonesia became democracies in the 1990s) and increased economic interdependence to work their pacifying effects. Friedberg was on the right track when he surmised that American power "delays the full transition to an independent Asian sub-system and allows time for forces that can mitigate the effects of multipolarity to gain in strength" (1993/94: 32). Where we disagree is that I believe America, for reasons alluded to above, sees itself as part of the Asian subsystem—an Asian-Pacific power—and hence is likely to remain on the scene for quite a while. If my assumption is right, the pacifying effects that Friedberg attributes to regional institutions, economic interdependence, and democratization, will have ample time to mature and exercise their impact. The chances of Asia being the cockpit of great-power rivalry will accordingly be significantly lower.

Will Japan Continue to be Abnormal?

A Japan enmeshed in its bilateral security treaty with the United States is an objective dear to the hearts of ASEAN's strategic planners (see *Straits Times* 17 Dec. 1991: 27). A Japan so enmeshed is "abnormal" in the sense of the great disjuncture between its economic prowess (as the second largest economy in the world) and its military capabilities. To be sure, as Katzenstein and Okawara in this volume remind us, this disjuncture is only "abnormal" from the perspective of research traditions such as realism that sees the correlation between economic and military power as "natural." Constructivists may consider it perfectly normal for Japan to maintain that disjuncture as a result of its changing identity and preferences. Normal or not, ASEAN strategic preference is to see this "disjuncture" continue and the key to that is the military presence of the United States. The presence of the U.S. Seventh Fleet in Okinawa gives America the power projection it wants; but equally critical for Japan and its southern neighbors, it also underpins the credibility of U.S. commitments to the region. For Japan, and for ASEAN, the credibility of these commitments would be undermined were the United States to scale down its military presence to a token. A minimal U.S. presence or the abrogation of the U.S.-Japan Security Treaty would leave Japan vulnerable, and a vulnerable Japan would go "normal," that is, rearm on a massive scale, including going nuclear. This explains why uncertainties about U.S. staying power in East Asia were thought to have negative reverberations for ASEAN.

Southeast Asian sensitivities to a normal Japan are based on the legacies of World War II and lingering suspicions about the extent to which the (Japanese) tiger has lost its stripes. The experience of Japanese rule was traumatic for many in Southeast Asia; only Thailand escaped being occupied by Japan. Southeast Asian attitudes toward Japan are in a state of flux. Although the generation of Southeast Asian leaders with direct experience of Japanese rule has passed from the scene, their successors have inherited many of their fears and attitudes. Newspapers in ASEAN routinely highlight the yearly outcries by China and South Korea about the attempt by Japanese textbooks to sanitize accounts of the rape of Nanjing or the forcible use of South Korean "comfort women" to provide sexual services for Japanese troops. When Japan sent troops as part of the United Nations peacekeeping force in Cambodia, Singapore's Lee Kuan Yew was sufficiently exercised to quip that allowing Japanese peacekeepers to serve in Cambodia was like "giving chocolate liqueur to an alcoholic" (*Straits Times* 17 Dec. 1991: 27) This fear of the Japanese is common in Southeast Asia, in part because of Japan's reluctance, unlike Germany, to own up to the aggression and atrocities of World War II.

But it is also the case that many of ASEAN's younger leaders are not as apprehensive as their elders about Japan's increasing its political and military profile in the region and beyond. The dispatch of Japanese peacekeepers to Cambodia in 1991 may have elicited the famous liquor chocolates comment from Lee Kuan Yew, but other Southeast Asian elites did not raise an outcry. Some analysts have suggested that consternation about Japanese military prowess is greatest in once-occupied countries with a predominantly Chinese population (China and Singapore) because the ethnic Chinese were singled out for especially brutal treatment. The Malays in Malaysia were treated comparatively better, and hence the more relaxed attitude of countries like Malaysia to the use of Japan's Self-Defence Forces overseas. As Malaysian prime minister Mahatir Mohamad told his Japanese counterpart Junichiro Koizumi, he (Mahatir) could not understand why Japan has to go on apologizing for such historical misdeeds (Singh 2002).

The change in Southeast Asian attitudes can also be explained by the deftness of Japanese foreign policy since the mid-1970s. Japanese prime minister Kakuei Tanaka's visits to Thailand and Indonesia in 1974 were marred by violent demonstrations. Instead of welcoming Japanese investment in their countries, Thai and Indonesian protestors accused Japan of "economic imperialism." Tanaka's reception in Southeast Asia led to a shift in Japanese foreign policy toward the region. Japan saw that the separation of economics from politics was not working and revised its strategy by taking ASEAN more seriously. In the late 1970s and early 1980s, Japan gave ASEAN diplomatic backing in its (ASEAN's) efforts to isolate Vietnam after its invasion and occupation of Cambodia. As a result of this cooperative stance on the part of Japan, ASEAN grew less wary of a political-diplomatic role for Japan in Southeast Asia. Since the end of the Cold War, Japan has been keen to encourage the development of a multilateral security architecture for the Asia-Pacific and some analysts have suggested that Japan was among one of the first to float the idea of an ASEAN-based multilateral security forum that eventually took shape as the ARF.

Whether ASEAN would be as relaxed as it is now if there had been no revision of the U.S.-Japan security treaty guidelines is harder to say. But the revision binds Japan more tightly and explicitly to the United States (see Katzenstein and Okawara in this volume, for a different perspective on how much it binds), and a Japan so enmeshed brings comfort to most in ASEAN. Hence it is not surprisingly that Japan's contribution to the war against terror—dispatching six ships and 1,200 crew members to the Indian Ocean—was received favorably by ASEAN (Singh 2002: 294 n88). As Bhubinder Singh suggests in a recent overview of ASEAN's post–Cold War perceptions of Japan, "Kozumi came away from the recent ASEAN Meeting in Brunei in November 2001 convinced that Asian leaders (ASEAN, South Korea and China) 'understand' Japan's intentions in dispatching troops to support the US-led campaign against terrorism" (pp. 294–95). Japan's economic and diplomatic activism in the ASEAN region in the last twenty years has done much to reassure the region's leaders, but as Prime Minister Kozumi's experience suggests, the "understanding" of its northern and southern neighbors is always an issue whenever Japan uses its military power.

A Responsible China?

The discussion so far indicates that a perennial question for ASEAN is whether the United States will remain an Asian-Pacific power. This question does not arise for ASEAN's neighbor to the north, China. Geography, history, and culture—and now economics—tie China to Southeast Asia such that it will always loom large in the latter's strategic calculations. In the past, a poor or weak China meant mass migration southward, with all its attendant problems; further back in history, a rich and mighty China meant the establishment of tributary relations that weakened the sovereign equality of the Southeast Asian states. Today, few in ASEAN wish for a weak or poor China; the assumption is China will grow stronger and mightier and the question is what will its regional demeanor be when that happens. The latter is the key uncertainty the ASEAN states would like to have clarified so that they can plan accordingly.

Meanwhile, most in ASEAN are giving China the benefit of the doubt, though there are shades of differences among the key states. A good indication of the various ASEAN positions can be seen in the attitudes of some of the ASEAN 5 on the "contain-engage" China debate of the 1990s. This debate was largely conducted in the United States between hawks, worried about China's growing power and geopolitical rivalry with America, and liberals who saw a less threatening China with the potential to develop strong economic-political stakes in the status quo (Johnston, this volume).

Although most in ASEAN were uncertain about China's intentions, the public discourse of its elites was solidly on the side of engagement. Within ASEAN, the most articulate and explicit proponent of engagement was Lee Kuan Yew of Singapore. Lee acknowledged that within thirty years China could challenge America's preeminence, but he cautioned (America and others) against pursuing a containment strategy because it would have few backers in East Asia. Lee acknowledged that he did not know which way China would go: a great power that throws its weight around or a great power that acts with restraint. Containing China now, Lee surmised, was likely to make China xenophobic and insecure. Singapore's policy was to engage China on the economic and diplomatic fronts; the former involved encouraging China's full integration into the regional and world economy and the latter meant accepting it as a legitimate and major player in the Asia-Pacific. A China that is accorded such treatment by the international community is likely to prosper as well as feel secure, thereby increasing the probability that it will refrain from upsetting or revising the "rules of the game" through conflict or war (Khong 1999a: 110).

Like Singapore, Malaysia wants to see China take its place "as a peaceful and responsible member of the regional and international system" (Acharya 1999a: 130). Malaysian prime minister Mahatir Mohamad is impatient with the advocates of containment and has argued in public that engagement is the more appropriate policy. Mahatir's proengagement position is significant because China was probably Malaysia's chief strategic threat until recently. The Communist guerrillas who sought to win power by force in 1948–60—the "Emergency" period in Malayan history—were backed by China. Even though the Malayan Emergency ended in 1960, Mahatir's predecessors had always had to worry about the remnants of the threat, in part because of China's refusal to cease its support for the Malayan Communist Party (MCP). In 1989, however, China publicly renounced its support from the MCP, by which time it had become a ragtag crew of disillusioned veterans. However, this disavowal of support remains important for Malaysia. Together with the enormous economic opportunities that seem to beckon, China, in Mahatir's eyes, was transformed from strategic threat to a business opportunity in the 1990s. Throughout the 1990s, planeloads of Malaysian businessmen, sometimes led by Mahatir himself, descended on Guangdong and Shanghai, in search of investment opportunities. Thus the economic and political incentives trumped historical legacies in the shaping of Malaysia's proengagement policy.

Malaysia's approach to China also emphasizes the role of regional and international institutions such as the ARF and the United Nations in socializing China to behave responsibly, although in private some of its leaders have doubts as to whether it will work. Acharya argues that the Malaysian military is especially worried about China's military modernization, its claims to the Spratly Islands, and its future intentions (Acharya 1999a: 132–34). These worries notwithstanding, Malaysia is in no position to adopt a containment strategy, in part because it is a small power and in part because it is equally fearful of moving too close to the United States. As Acharya puts it, "while Malaysia may favor an 'engagement strategy,' it does not wish to be identified with an *American* engagement strategy" (p. 146).

Compared to Malaysia and Singapore, Indonesia is probably most ambivalent about engaging China, in part because of its past encounters with China and in part because of what Michael Leifer called Indonesia's sense of its "regional entitlement" (1999: 87). This "incipient geopolitical rivalry" constrains the extent to which Indonesia can be wholehearted about its engagement policy. Its 1995 security cooperation agreement with Australia (abrogated in 1999) is indicative of its ambivalence about China's long-term intentions. But like Malaysia and Singapore, Indonesia is willing to use bilateral and multilateral processes to impress upon China the importance of its being a good citizen of the region, one who is able to cooperate with its smaller neighbors (p. 88).

Judging from the position of the key ASEAN states on the "engage-contain" China debate in the 1990s, it is safe to say that ASEAN would be content with a China that occupies its place as one of East Asia's great powers, but one that exerts its power responsibly. A China that respects the norms and principles enshrined in ASEAN's Treaty of Amity and Cooperation would reassure ASEAN. Richard Betts warned in the early 1990s that if "polite containment" of China was not possible, realists would have to countenance living with Beijing in Asia as others in the Western hemisphere had learned to live with the U.S. colossus (Betts 1993/94: 54). In fact, what Southeast Asia would most like to avoid is to be lorded over by China. For the moment at least, their preferred strategy seems closer to cautious engagement than "polite containment."

ASEAN's Relevance and Clout?

When ASEAN the institution celebrated its twentieth birthday in 1987, the common refrain among analysts was that it was the most successful regional organization of its kind in the third world (Frost 1990: 28). Among its major achievements were the successful forging of diplomatic reconciliation among its members, the Treaty of Amity and Cooperation of 1976, and its members' ability to act jointly as well as persevere in the 1980s in constructing Vietnam as an international pariah for its invasion of Cambodia. Developments in the late 1980s and early 1990s seemed to lend weight to the accolades heaped on ASEAN. Vietnam, ASEAN's antagonist for more than a decade, finally withdrew from Cambodia in 1989; six years later, it would be welcomed into the fold of ASEAN, an organization it had derided during the Cold War years as a capitalist front for the Americans. These successes on the diplomatic front, together with the impressive economic performance racked up by Singapore, Malaysia, Thailand, and Indonesia, made ASEAN confident and gave it a modicum of diplomatic-political clout in East Asia. The high point was the creation in 1994 of the ASEAN Regional Forum, the only forum to bring together the major and minor powers of the Asia-Pacific to discuss security issues of common concern.

To be feted as "economic tigers" and to be "in the driver's seat" of the Asia-Pacific's only security forum that includes the United States, the European Union, China, Russia, Japan, and India, must have been a heady mixture for ASEAN. In the mid-1990s, therefore, ASEAN appeared close to "having arrived." A transformation of its identity, one might say, occurred: ASEAN was transformed from an institution that was meant to insulate its members from a violent region (as in the 1960s and 1970s) so that they could learn to live with each other to an institution that was given an opportunity by history to reach out to, and help shape, its regional security and economic environment. In short, by the early 1990s ASEAN no longer saw itself as a powerless bystander in regional developments. ASEAN saw an opportunity to be a player in the regional strategic picture and it was keen to grasp it. It was relevant and it had clout, or at least as much clout as a group of small to middle powers can conceivably have. ASEAN's insistence on being in the ARF's "driver's seat," its fear of the advent of a rival Northeast Asian Security Dialogue, and its activism in spawning institutions in which it would be at the center of attention, such as the Asia-Europe Meeting (ASEM) and the ASEAN+3 (China, Japan, and South Korea), all suggest that one of ASEAN's strategic ends was to remain relevant and important to East Asia's strategic equation.

The Asian financial crisis of 1997–98, however, diminished ASEAN's relevance and clout. The crisis revealed the fragility of many of its "tiger" economies and the extent to which corruption and cronyism were undermining sound economic practices. The crisis, the domestic repercussions and intra-ASEAN tensions it generated, has also diminished the political standing of more than a few ASEAN states. The national resilience of Indonesia, Malaysia, Thailand, and the Philippines has been called into question. Distracted by its economic troubles, ethnic riots, and secession threats, Indonesia has not been able to play its traditional role as ASEAN's primus inter pares. ASEAN does seem rudderless and adrift in the last few years (Khong 1999b). Soberheaded analysts like the late Michael Leifer were always skeptical about the "anomaly" of a group of small to middle powers, however up and coming economically, arrogating to themselves the prerogative of helping shape their regional environment and discourse. For such analysts, institutions like the ARF are unlikely to go forward unless there exists a balance of power in the region. In the machinations leading to such a balance, ASEAN is at best a minor player. Today it is probably fair to say that of the four uncertainties that ASEAN would most like to eradicate, it is the uncertainty about its continued relevance and clout that is proving most intractable.

Reducing Strategic Uncertainties: Options and Choices

An analysis of ASEAN's discourse of uncertainty has allowed us to derive its strategic preferences. We basically asked: what uncertainties troubled ASEAN security planners most, and if they could have greater certainty, what would that consist of? It would consist of trying to increase the probabilities of (1) the United States maintaining a credible military presence in East Asia, (2) a Japan that does not rearm independently, (3) a responsible China, and (4) an ASEAN with clout. It is now possible to ask, what strategies did ASEAN adopt to increase the probabilities of achieving (1)–(4)? The behavior of individual states and of ASEAN as a collective indicates that they settled on two strategies, institution building and soft balancing, to help achieve these ends. At a minimum, these strategies sought to elicit credible information about the key players and their intentions, but they also went beyond information gathering and provision by encouraging concrete acts by the ASEAN states that would facilitate the participation of the great powers in the regional balance and regional institutions.

There were also two strategies that ASEAN could have followed—at least according to theory—but did not. The ensuing discussion of ASEAN's strategies begins with an analysis of these rejected options; the discussion then moves from the less to the more important strategies chosen, culminating in an analysis of the institutional strategy. We will also leave aside the question, for the time being, of whether ASEAN's strategy worked.

Mainstream balance-of-power theory, emphasizing the importance of equilibrium so that no preponderant power emerges, would suggest that ASEAN would side with the weak to balance the strong. Yet ASEAN did not act this way; it rejected the strategy of balancing against the stronger power because it saw the stronger power (the United States) as less of a threat than the weaker but rising power (China or Japan). There is a consensus today that the United States is the unipolar power, and it is also the case that it is the preponderant power in East Asia (Mastanduno 1999; Wohlforth 1999; MacGregor 1993). And if China is the rising but much weaker power, ASEAN should have aligned itself with China to balance the power of the United States.[5] According to this view, "a true believer in the balance of power should welcome the (expected) drawdown of America's military presence and the (expected) rise of Chinese or Japanese power because at some point in the distant future, a balance—instead of the current American preponderance—would obtain" (Khong 1997b: 297). Yet the exact opposite happened in the 1990s. Most of the ASEAN states aligned themselves with the United States against China. The manner in which the ASEAN states aligned themselves with the United States will be elaborated below, in the section on "soft balancing."

A second option that ASEAN could have conceivably followed is to deepen the feeling of "we-ness" among its members and then extend it writ large to form an Asian-Pacific security community. Although this did not become a major part of ASEAN's post–Cold War security strategy, the security community approach warrants discussion because of its focus on the importance of identity (Acharya 2001; Adler and Barnett 1998). Equally interesting, some policy makers have appropriated the concept and advocated its implementation in the Asia-Pacific.

There is widespread agreement that the European Union is a security community, that is, a group of states that have renounced the use of force in settling disputes among themselves (Acharya 2001; Deutsch 1957). Some analysts have also argued that ASEAN aspires to being a security community or is already a nascent security community (Acharya 2001, 1991; Khong 1997a). A plausible post–Cold War strategy for ASEAN is, in the first instance, to consolidate its status as a security community, so that its members have absolute confidence that intra-ASEAN disputes will be settled peacefully, and in the second instance, to extend the idea and its practices outward to East Asia. This idea of a peaceful East Asian community is often implicit in discourses about an "Asian renaissance" or an "Asian-Pacific community" that became popular with ASEAN leaders in the days of rapid economic growth (Anwar 1996; Mahbubani 1995). Arguing against the clash of civilizations thesis, Anwar Ibrahim saw the possibility of an Asian cultural and ethical renaissance that would bind Asia and allow it to relate symbiotically with the West. Similarly, Kishore Mahbubani (1995) foresaw the fusion of the best Eastern and Western traditions in the creation of what he called the Pacific Community, a consortium of economically vibrant and militarily secure states.

Perhaps the most explicit appropriation of the security community idea was the call of the commander in chief of the United States Pacific Command (CINPAC), Dennis Blair, for the creation of an Asian-Pacific security community in a series of speeches he made from 1999 to 2001. Blair credited Karl Deutsch as the inspiration behind the notion, listed the attributes of security communities, with the first being nations that genuinely do not plan or intend to fight each other, and promoted the formation of such communities as a strategy for dealing with the challenges of the twenty-first century (United States Pacific Command 2000).

More than anybody else, Amitav Acharya has helped us apply and assess the security community concept in Southeast Asia. In his recent book-length rendition of the concept, Acharya wisely sidesteps the question of whether ASEAN is a security community, preferring instead to use the concept as "a framework for analyzing the process and dynamics of peaceful change" in ASEAN (Acharya 2001: 194). In terms of a security community, he sees ASEAN as a work-in-progress; the strongest evidence for this includes the absence of war among the ASEAN states since the mid-1960s, the acceptance of the norms enshrined in the Treaty on Amity and Cooperation, banding together to oppose and reverse Vietnam's invasion of Cambodia, and the growth of ASEAN-sponsored regional institutions. Acharya's approach gives his analysis a dynamic dimension and allows him to be more circumspect about ASEAN's progress as a security community in the late 1990s: he sees important signs of reversal and decay in the aftermath of the financial crisis. As he puts it, "While [ASEAN] had developed some of the attributes of a nascent security community by the early 1990s . . . such communities can decline as a result of both internal burdens and external challenges." He identifies the internal burdens as ASEAN's expansion of its membership and the emergence of new intraregional disputes, while the external challenges include maintaining intra-ASEAN cohesion on the South China Sea disputes and ASEAN's leadership of the ARF (pp. 206–8). His analysis ends on a slightly despondent note: "After three decades of progress in promoting peaceful intraregional relations, ASEAN . . . now is in a serious need to reinvent itself" (p. 208).

The above suggests that Blair's call for a security community strategy notwithstanding, ASEAN has not moved very far down the security community path as part of its post–Cold War strategy. The recent call by Indonesia, at the ninth ASEAN summit held in Bali in October 2003, for ASEAN to work toward becoming a security community by 2020, sounds more like an exhortation than a plan for action. Although most of ASEAN's leaders were enthusiastic about making ASEAN into an economic community, few focused on the specifics of the security community idea (Directorate General of ASEAN Cooperation, Department of Foreign Affairs, Republic of Indonesia, www.9aseansummit.com/con_page.php). Insofar as some ASEAN members still base their military doctrines on deterring fellow ASEAN members, and on going to war against each other if necessary, it is difficult to conceive of ASEAN as a security community (Huxley 2000).

Unilateral and "Soft" Balancing

If the security community strategy remained an aspiration, balancing against potential threats was followed quite soon after the end of the Cold War. In the early 1990s, as negotiations between the Philippines and the United States on access to Clark Air Base and Subic Naval Base got bogged down, it became obvious to many in ASEAN that there was a real possibility of the United States not having a physical military presence in Southeast Asia. Into this situation stepped Singapore. It was the first in ASEAN to recognize the strategic implications of a U.S. withdrawal. Singapore offered the United States limited facilities in the old British wharves at Sembawang and an agreement to that effect was formalized in an MOU signed in 1990. Singapore was acting primarily in its own strategic interests, which it saw as synonymous with those of the region's. Singapore would feel considerably safer in a world where the United States maintained a military presence in Southeast Asia. Singapore's unilateral decision to allow enhanced U.S. privileges was initially criticized by Malaysia and Indonesia. Although neither Malaysia nor Indonesia was anti-U.S., they resented the lack of consultation in Singapore's decision to invite "external forces" into their vicinity. It also went against the spirit of ZOPFAN, which has been ostensibly adopted by ASEAN. Yet as pointed out earlier, Malaysia and Indonesia also moved to offer the United States use of their facilities in Lumut and Surabaya respectively.

Sheldon Simon's survey of the security dynamics in Southeast Asia in the mid-1990s led him to the view that, "memoranda of understanding have been signed bilaterally with all ASEAN members—except the Philippines—through which U.S. ships and planes in small numbers have rights of access to specific ports and airfields for repair, provisioning, and joint exercises. Through these arrangements the United States remains the dominant sea and air power throughout the western Pacific, not just in Northeast Asia where its only bases are located" (Simon 1996: 21). Since then, and especially after China's "mischief in the reef" (Segal 1996: 121), even the Philippines concluded a visiting forces agreement (VFA) with the United States in order to ensure a U.S. military presence in its vicinity. The MOUs and VFAs that were negotiated in the 1990s are acts of soft balancing in the sense that they were meant to encourage the United States to maintain a strong presence in Southeast Asia (thus deterring would-be aggressors); they also signaled the intention of the key ASEAN states to align themselves more closely with the United States. The target of that soft balancing was China. "Hard balancing" would occur if these MOUs and VFAs were to be translated into military alliances, or if ASEAN coalesced into an informal or formal military alliance. These are options that most in ASEAN would do their utmost to avoid.

Recent events, some planned, others not, have also acted to strengthen the U.S. presence in Southeast Asia. In March 2001, Singapore completed construction of the Changi Naval Base, which is big and deep enough to accommodate U.S. aircraft carriers. In the first year after it opened, the base hosted the visits of five U.S. aircraft carriers and 100 other ships (*Straits Times* 28 Feb. 2002: H2). Hosting the United States military is not a strategy without cost, as Singapore discovered in 1989 when it incurred the unhappiness of its closest neighbors. Three months after the September 11 terrorist attacks against America, Singapore also found that a small number of its Muslim citizens, some trained in Afghanistan, had identified and monitored potential sites in Singapore for terrorist action against American interests and military personnel. With the help of U.S. intelligence, the Singaporean authorities arrested eleven suspects—all members of the Jemaah Islamiah (JI), which the authorities regarded as linked to Al Qaeda. Further north, the Malaysian authorities also arrested more than a dozen similar suspects. What these arrests revealed was that there was a Southeast Asian network of extremists who were sympathetic to Al Qaeda's ideology and who aspired to turn peninsular Southeast Asia—Indonesia, Malaysia, and the Philippines in particular—into an Islamic crescent. The movement was led by Indonesian cleric Abu Bakar Bashir, who was arrested by Indonesian authorities after the Bali bombing of October 2002, which killed over 200 tourists, most of them Australians. Prior to the Bali bombing, Indonesia had been reluctant to confront Abu Bakar Bashir because of fear of a domestic political backlash. The bombing served as a wake-up call to Indonesia and tipped the scales in favor of arresting Bashir and putting him on trial as the prime suspect. The reach of the JI has recently been extended to Thailand and Cambodia. In June 2003, eight JI members were arrested in Thailand and Cambodia. The Thai arrests—which involved cooperation with Singapore and Malaysia security agencies—were particularly chilling: the arrests foiled plans by the JI to bomb the American and Singapore embassies during the October 2003 Asia Pacific Economic Cooperation (APEC) summit in Bangkok ("Tentacles of Terror," *Straits Times* 18 June 2003, http://straitstimes.asia1.com/storyprintfriendly/0,1887,195294,00.html).

Southeast Asia has been viewed as the second front in the U.S. global war against terrorism not because of the above incidents in Singapore, Malaysia, Indonesia, and Thailand, but because the United States had identified the Abu Say'yaf rebels in the southern Philippines as terrorists linked to Al Qaeda. In February 2002, the United States dispatched 660 troops to the Philippines to "train" and perform "joint exercises" with the Filipino troops fighting the Abu Say'yaf rebels. For those Filipinos, including President Gloria Macapagal-Arroyo, anxious to bring back the United States to their island, this has been a godsend, even though some members of the political establishment continue to have mixed feelings about the return of U.S. troops (*New York Times* 24 Jan. 2002).

There is a discernible pattern in maritime Southeast Asia's attitude toward the United States in the last decade. Upon departing from the Philippines, the U.S. military has found itself welcomed by Singapore, Malaysia, and Indonesia through a series of MOUs that gave the U.S. access to a variety of "places" instead of "bases" for port calls, repairs, and military exercises. U.S. troops continue to participate in Cobra exercises with its ally, Thailand, to which Singaporean troops have been invited to participate, with Malaysia and other states having observer status. The Philippines under Presidents Fidel Ramos and Gloria Macapagal-Arroyo has tried to rectify the mistakes of the early 1990s that saw Filipino nationalism gaining the upper hand in the negotiations with the United States over the lease of Clark and Subic bases. The consequences of the U.S. departure came home to roost in mid-1995 when China occupied Mischief Reef (claimed by the Philippines), and proceeded to build military-like structures on it. With its backer gone from the vicinity, and with the United States still spiteful (and taking the position that the Spratlys were outside the remit of the bilateral security treaty), the Philippines was left to confront China alone. After the Mischief Reef incident and the subsequent failure of bilateral and multilateral diplomacy to dissuade China from further building on the reef, the Philippine government has finally moved—against its own nationalistic impulses—to invite the

United States back in a major way (Mangaoang 2003). Under the guise of advising the Philippines army, U.S. combat troops have been invited back to assist in the fight against the Abu Say'yaf rebels.

September 11 and the discovery of terrorists linked to Al Qaeda in the original ASEAN 5 have propelled Southeast Asia to a higher position in the U.S. security agenda. This was not exactly how the states of the region had planned it, but it is an interesting culmination of maritime Southeast Asia's effort to welcome and facilitate a palpable American presence, often at considerable cost and risk to the governments concerned. The uncertainty about the American presence that confronted ASEAN in the early 1990s was significantly reduced by 1995; September 11 makes it even more certain that the United States is unlikely to withdraw from the region in the foreseeable future.

The above analysis of soft balancing appears to be a straightforward realist narrative. Uncertainty about the staying power and continued military presence of the United States persuaded the key ASEAN states to act so as to increase the probability that the United States would find it worthwhile to maintain a sizable presence in Southeast Asia. The U.S. military presence was thought to be crucial to maintaining peace and stability in the region by deterring potential challengers. Thus concerns about the balance of power seems to inform the actions of ASEAN's policy makers.

But this realist veneer yields to a pressing anomaly: if states balance against power in order to preserve their independence as classical and neorealist theories predict, why are the ASEAN states siding with the preponderant power (the United States) instead of balancing against it? Why are they not siding with the much weaker but rising power, China? The answers to these questions have to do with their threat perceptions, which in turn depend on assessments of "state character"—the intentions, historical proclivities, geographic proximity, and cultural affinities, of the powers involved (Walt 1987). In short, the identities of the "balancer" and "balancee" matter greatly (see Wendt 1999).[6]

What ASEAN's behavior suggests is that the identity of the United States as a distant, democratic, wealthy, and benign power—and one ASEAN is able to identify with—tips the scale in its favor despite its overwhelming military power. Instead of viewing the latter as a threat, as realists expect, ASEAN views America's overwhelming power—because it is wielded by the United States—as conducive to peace and stability. Conversely, despite China's military weakness vis-à-vis the United States, its history of supporting Communist movements in Southeast Asia, its geographic proximity, and its ambitions with respect to the South China Sea, have persuaded most in ASEAN to construe it as a potential threat that needs to be "balanced against," albeit "softly" for the time being. Not all of ASEAN views the United States and China this way, but despite worries about America's reliability, its occasional heavy-handedness, as well as its unilateral tendencies, most prefer it above all others to act as the "regional sheriff." The judgment as to who best fits the regional sheriff role is premised more on character and identity than on power resources. China, Russia, and India are critical of "hegemony" and "power politics" and are anxious to usher in an age of multipolarity. But for all their protestations about the importance of the balance of power, most in ASEAN are prepared to live with American preponderance (Mac-Gregor 1993). ASEAN's strategy of soft balancing therefore supports Stephen Walt's claim that states balance against threats, not power. But ASEAN's behavior also suggests the importance of going beyond Walt's notion of threat: geographic proximity remains important, but in the final analysis the identity and history of the "balancee" (China in our case) trumps power. Our case also shows that it is identity and history (of China) that give content to Walt's notions of "aggressive intentions" and "offensive power" (Walt 1987; and esp. Katzenstein 1996c: 22–26).

   That ASEAN's strategy of soft balancing is a function of its threat perceptions is not surprising. What is surprising is that both analysts and policy makers—Western as well as Asian—continue to portray the security dynamics of East Asia in balance of power terms (see Leifer 1996; and remarks by Lee Kuan Yew, *Straits Times* 17 Dec. 1991: 27). That is, the predominant discourse is about the importance of maintaining a balance of power or equilibrium, whereas the predominant pattern of behavior exhibited by ASEAN (and its neighbors further north and south) is siding with the preponderant power against the potential threat (China). Whether this disjuncture between discourse and behavior suggests that ASEAN is using (the balance of power) discourse instrumentally to "gloss over" its (siding with the strong) behavior is interesting to ponder. Such a constitutive-instrumental approach has two potential policy payoffs. First, if ASEAN's representation of the region's security dynamics as "balancing power" (instead of "balancing threat") becomes the dominant lens or vocabulary through which East Asian strategic planners view or talk about the region, the asymmetry in U.S.-China capabilities will be de-emphasized or obscured. This brings policy advantages to the United States and its allies. Accretions to the power base and network of the United States will be interpreted as "balancing" (China or any other challenger) instead of "augmenting" (the strength of the preponderant power). Yet whether ASEAN has the resources and foresight to conceive, connive, and implement such a sophisticated discursive stratagem is open to debate. More plausibly, ASEAN's use of the balance of power discourse is more a symptom of informal usage of the term than an explicit attempt at "spin." This is unexceptional because most analysts of the region also use the balance of power vocabulary when what they actually mean is balance of threat (Acharya 1999a; Khong 1997b; Leifer 1996).

   It is the second payoff associated with the balance of power discourse that ASEAN is likely to find congenial: power balancing de-emphasizes the identity of the balancee in a way that balance of threat discourse does not. The latter in fact directs the klieg light on the identity, proclivities, and intentions of the balancee (Walt 1987). Power balancing is the more polite discourse because it is (supposed to be) agnostic about the non-power characteristics of the balancee: states balance against whoever becomes too strong. Nothing personal. As Winston Churchill put it, "For four hundred years the foreign policy of England has been to oppose the strongest, most aggressive, most dominant power on the Continent" (cited in Walt 1987: 18).

In contrast, balancing against threats is intensely personal. It requires one to identify the source of the threat, and in this the balancee's historical proclivities and aggressive intentions are usually more decisive than its aggregate power. Any balancee so publicly identified will take severe umbrage at those talking about it this way. At the height of the "contain-engage" China debate in the United States, ASEAN leaders warned against using the containment language because, they argued, to identify and portray China as a threat would increase the likelihood of its becoming one. It would become a self-fulfilling prophecy, to be avoided at all costs (Acharya 1999a; Khong 1999a). ASEAN thus uses the balance of power discourse in constitutive and instrumental ways. In fact, the communicative dimension is also present: in privileging the power discourse, ASEAN is also sending signals about its preferences to China: ASEAN prefers to view China as a rising power capable of playing by the rules of the game. However, should events prove otherwise, that is, should China throw its weight around, ASEAN is likely to ratchet up the shrillness of its discourse about China by portraying it as a threat. Meanwhile, ASEAN's actions—as in soft balancing—outpace its discourse.

This analysis of ASEAN's desire for a U.S. military presence for the purposes of soft balancing remains relevant even though 9/11 and subsequent events have diverted the attention of ASEAN and the United States away from China. However, it might be more difficult for Muslim-majority states like Indonesia and Malaysia to align themselves with the United States in the years ahead because of America's war against terrorism. The foci of America's struggle against terrorism are countries, mostly Islamic states, where Al Qaeda and its sympathizers are to be found. Moreover, the George W. Bush national security doctrine of preemption frightens some in ASEAN. The implementation of that doctrine in the form of regime change and the war against Iraq has touched a raw political nerve in parts of Southeast Asia. Malaysia's Mahatir Mohamad has been ASEAN's most vociferous critic of the war against Iraq, equating it to a new imperialism of the West against Islam. For Mahatir, the issue is both cultural and political: post–9/11 American foreign policy appears to target Muslim states and Mahatir also worries about deputy sheriffs (read Australia) who arrogate to themselves the right to intervene in countries like Malaysia or Indonesia to protect their citizens ("Dr. M Slams Selfish Members," *New Straits Times* 12 May 2003, www.emedia.com.my/Current_News/NST/Monday/Frontpage/20030512073949/Art . . . 5/13/2003). As a result of its discourse about regime change and its actions in the Gulf, the identity of the United States as a benign hegemon has come under scrutiny not only in Southeast Asia, but also elsewhere. In the short to medium term, this is unlikely to cause states such as Malaysia to reconsider the U.S. role as the helpful "balancer"; in the long term, much will depend on U.S. actions as it continues its fight against terrorism.

Dealing with Uncertainty via Regional and Subregional Institutions

The one development that leaps out of the Asian-Pacific landscape in the last decade is the emergence of new, and the expansion and deepening of existing, regional institutions. Among the new institutions are the Asia Pacific Economic Cooperation forum (APEC, 1989), the Council for Security Cooperation in the Asia Pacific (CSCAP, 1993), the ASEAN Free Trade Area (AFTA, 1993), the ASEAN Regional Forum (ARF, 1994), the Asia-Europe Meeting (ASEM, 1995), and ASEAN+3 (1997). Existing institutions that have been expanded or transformed include ASEAN itself, from ASEAN 6 in 1986 to ASEAN 10 in 1997, and the Post-Ministerial Conference (PMC), which provided the institutional inspiration for the ARF. If soft balancing was one way ASEAN dealt with the strategic flux affecting the region, the building of these new institutions and the enhancing of the old ones was the other, equally important strategy. This institutional strategy was extremely significant because it was a corporate strategy (involving all extant members of ASEAN), entailed significant costs, and extended far beyond the geographic footprint of ASEAN. By focusing on the ARF and (to a lesser extent) ASEAN and APEC, I hope to show how the strategy contributed to reducing uncertainty.

The real question is how this impressive array of regional and subregional institutions contributed to the reduction of uncertainty. Neoliberals have a ready answer. In a recent work, Celeste Wallander and Robert O. Keohane explore the issue of how institutions can help mitigate the insecurity of states "bedeviled by the problem of uncertainty." By uncertainty they mean "not having information about other states' intentions and likely choices" (1999: 3), a meaning similar to the one used here. A major way of obtaining information, according to Wallander and Keohane (1999: 4), "is to create institutions that provide it [information]. Institutions can serve as the informational and signaling mechanisms that enable states to get more information about the interests, preferences, and intentions of other states. They reduce uncertainty by providing credible information. Furthermore, successful institutions develop norms and rules that regularize the behavior of states belonging to them, making it more predictable."

The ARF is probably the most important organization in ASEAN's institutional repertoire for dealing with strategic uncertainty. Formed in the aftermath of the Cold War—the first informal meeting was held in 1993, with the inaugural meeting in 1994—the ARF is the Asia-Pacific's only security forum. In his contribution to the Wallander and Keohane volume, Iain Johnston has argued that "there was sufficient uncertainty about the regional security environment to create a demand for some mechanism [the ARF] to increase predictability" (1999b: 290). For Johnston, the "key target" and "source of greatest uncertainty" was China. China's intentions as it grew mighty were indeed questions that ASEAN wanted answers to. ASEAN considered the ARF a good venue for observing and testing Chinese attitudes. Johnston is right about China being a key source of uncertainty and about the ARF as a mechanism to probe China's intentions. However, as I have argued above, ASEAN's security planners in the early 1990s were equally if not more concerned about the uncertainty pertaining to the U.S. military presence. This does not contradict Johnston's argument that the ARF was conceived with a role to reducing uncertainty in mind, in fact it reinforces it; however, it does point to the existence of multiple uncertainties that the ARF had to grapple with.

A major way the ARF goes about reducing uncertainty is by lowering transaction costs, providing information, and preventing cheating. Few analysts have paid attention to these aspects of the ARF (and of Asia's institutions) but I believe there is much room for a systematic analysis of how these functions, emphasized by liberal institutionalists, manifest themselves (Johnston 1999b; Wallander 1999; Keohane 1984). Wallander and Keohane's insights about credible information, norms, and rules and how they enhance predictability are helpful in explaining the proliferation and expansion of regional institutions in East Asia in the last decade. At the governmental or track-one level, the most important of these institutions are ASEAN, the ARF, AFTA, APEC, ASEM, and ASEAN+3.

ASEAN the institution organizes about 300 meetings a year. Other than the biannual heads-of-states summit, the Annual (foreign) Ministerial Meetings (AMM), held annually since 1967, are the most critical. In the 1970s, ASEAN decided to hold a series of consultative meetings—known as the Post-Ministerial Conference (PMC) with its chief non-ASEAN interlocutors, including Australia, Japan, New Zealand, South Korea, the United States, and in recent years, China. The PMC was the locus of some of ASEAN's most productive security and economic discussions, including the strategy of isolating Vietnam in the wake of its invasion and occupation of Cambodia. When the ARF, which may be seen as an outgrowth of the PMC, came into being, ASEAN's officials wisely scheduled it as part of ASEAN's Annual Ministerial Meeting (Khong 1995b).

Scheduling the ARF during the AMM and PMC lowers transaction costs and increases the incentives for the participants to attend the forum. Since ASEAN's major Asian-Pacific interlocutors, including the foreign ministers of Australia, China, the European Union, Japan, South Korea, and the United States, would be attending the PMC, this "killing of two (or even more) birds with one stone" approach increases the likelihood that the key players will show up year after year. If the ARF were scheduled, say six months after the ASEAN's AMM/PMC, the likelihood of the U.S. secretary of state or the Chinese foreign minister returning to Southeast Asia again would be lower. Moreover, a near-perfect attendance record by the key players produces positive interactive effects: key players would not want to be left out of security discussions if they know that their potential rivals or detractors will be at the table. ASEAN counts on this logic to ensure the participation of the United States,

Japan, China, Russia, and India year after year. In early 2002, the Bush administration hinted that it might send a lower-level emissary instead of Secretary of State Colin Powell to ASEAN's PMC and ARF in August. The United States felt that the ARF was not moving forward and Powell had more urgent problems to attend to. In the event, Powell did show up in Brunei for the PMC and ARF, and succeeded in concluding a U.S.-ASEAN declaration on combating terrorism (*Straits Times* 2 Aug. 2002: A6). Whether Powell would have showed up without the antiterrorism accord is hard to tell. But the routinization of meetings such as the PMC and the ARF certainly gave the United States a convenient venue to rally supporters in Asia for its war against terrorism. Consistent and high-level participation by the United States in the ARF since 1994 signals to ASEAN's security planners that the United States remains committed to Southeast Asia. This provision of a venue and forum for the United States to demonstrate its commitment to, and to be reminded of its stakes in, Southeast Asia—at minimal financial or political cost to the United States—is a major function of the ARF.

The ARF also lowers transaction costs and aids in the provision of information in a more policy relevant way. On many occasions, the ARF meeting has provided the venue for "corridor diplomacy" between the United States and China when relations between the two great powers were strained. When Warren Christopher and Qian Qichen had a tête-à-tête during the 1996 ARF in Jakarta (repeated by Madeleine Albright and Qian at the 1997 ARF in Kuala Lumpur), they had a low-cost opportunity to reassure one another, to provide information, and to arrest the deteriorating relations between their countries. It was low cost in the sense of less pressure to produce public results and of not committing the prestige of their bosses or country, as formal meetings would. What is true for Christopher and Qian is also true for numerous other bilateral "corridor" transactions that go on in such track-one meetings. In August 2002, U.S. secretary of state Colin Powell and North Korean foreign minister Paek Nam-Sun met over coffee on the sidelines of the ARF, in what one report called "the first high-level contact between the Bush administration and the hermetic communist nation" (*Straits Times* 2 Aug. 2002: A6). Powell justified his meeting with a representative of an "axis of evil" state on the grounds that Pyongyang had showed signs of being willing "to reach out to Tokyo and Seoul" (ibid.). In four to five working days, the ASEAN AMM, PMC, and ARF become the site of one of the most inclusive and extended gatherings for formal, informal, multilateral, and bilateral consultations for the decision makers of Asia. Information is exchanged during these transactions and such information is no less important than information provided by the publication of defense white papers that has become part of the ARF process.

One reason why analysts have been cautious in applying institutionalist insights to describe the ARF's functioning is the belief that the ARF is not involved in the business of preventing "cheating." But it is. The major form of cheating that institutions like the ARF can prevent is not defection from legal rules, but of public inconsistency between word and deed. That is why China is reluctant to have discussions within the ARF about its disputes with the ASEAN states in the South China Sea. It would be damaging to China's credibility to verbally agree to something in the ARF context and then to be seen doing another on the shoals of the South China Sea. "Verbal cheating" can be as serious as disobeying rules because it exposes one as a liar, permits others to impute bad intentions to one's actions, heightens threat perceptions, and leaves one's credibility in tatters. No great power would want to be caught in such a position. That is perhaps why some of the ARF's summary statements are so bland.

That the ARF does most of the things—provide information, lower transaction costs, and frown upon verbal cheating—that neoliberals claim institutions do is beyond doubt. In that sense, the liberal side of our eclectic triangle has much to say about the post–Cold War proliferation and expansion of institutions in East Asia (see Figure 1.2 in this volume). Neoliberals argue that these processes enhance predictability and credibility, which in turn makes cooperation among self-interested states possible (Wallander and Keohane 1999; Keohane 1984). Note however, that the end point of the analysis presented here concerns the institutions' role in producing the outcomes of predictability and credibility, in other words, reducing uncertainty. The analysis offered here does not extend to explaining the end result of cooperation because of our focus on uncertainty reduction. Many of the ARF activities may be characterized as cooperation, though many also fall short. Documenting the cooperative outcomes of the ARF must be left for another study. Here it suffices to note that antiterrorism is an area where significant cooperation may be obtained through the ARF process. The ARFs of 2002 and 2003 suggest that policy coordination on antiterrorism is gaining momentum: Thirteen of the forty-seven paragraphs of the chairman's statement of the 2003 ARF in Phnom Penh were devoted to describing joint efforts to counter terrorism, from interdicting terrorist financing to conducting intersessional meetings on terrorism and transnational crime, with the first of such meetings being cochaired by Malaysia and the United States (Chairman's statement, Tenth ASEAN Regional Forum, Phnom Penh, 18 June 2003, www.aseansec.org/14846).

Neoliberal institutionalism, however, does not exhaust the functional possibilities attached to the ARF. Balancing is also built into the ARF's architecture and processes. As Michael Leifer and other realist scholars have pointed out, one of ASEAN's main motives in creating the ARF was to enmesh the United States in a series of bilateral and multilateral contexts: a United States so enmeshed, the reasoning goes, is a United States that is "committed" to East Asia. The timing of the advent of the ARF—1994—supports this enmeshing thesis because the early post–Cold War period was one of great uncertainty for the region. The prevailing assumption in the early 1990s was that the United States had a strong incentive to withdraw from the region. The U.S. Department of Defense East Asia Strategy Initiatives of 1990 and 1992 recommending a phased drawdown of the U.S. military presence through 2000 injected a heavy dose of uncertainty into the East Asian strategic equation. Iain Johnston's argument that the ARF had China as the "key target" and that it was meant to reduce uncertainty about China hones in on an important mission of the ARF. My analysis suggests, however, that for Southeast Asia's security planners, U.S. intentions were as great, if not a greater source of uncertainty than China. For them, even if the "key target" was China, the way of resolving that uncertainty was to remove the uncertainty about the U.S. military presence. If the United States could be persuaded to stay, it would be able to "balance other powers . . . that have far-reaching ambitions in Southeast Asia" (cited in Acharya 1999a: 140). The ARF was one of several nets cast by the ASEAN states to enmesh the United States ever more tightly in the region (Emmers 2001; Khong 1997b: 297; Khong 1995b: 52).

APEC would be the economic analogue of another of these nets, while the bilateral security arrangements—ranging from alliances to repair facilities for U.S. ships—constitute the military nets. Insofar as these institutions "trap" the United States in the region by requiring it to attend meetings (ARF and APEC), make ports of call, engage in military exercises, and the like, they signal the continued presence and engagement of the United States. Moreover, they also give the Southeast Asians numerous opportunities to impress upon the United States the importance of its being around. Once the uncertainty about the U.S. military presence is reduced, the other pieces of the strategic equation fall into place: Japan will feel secure and refrain from unilateral rearmament, China will tread cautiously, and ASEAN will be reassured. In other words, the ARF is one of those stratagems that seeks to (and here I am paraphrasing Lord Ismay's remark about NATO) keep the United States in, China and Japan down, and ASEAN relevant. In a recent article, Ralf Emmers (2001: 281) has also argued that "the creation of the [ASEAN Regional] Forum was regarded by ASEAN as a diplomatic instrument to promote a continuing U.S. involvement in the region, thus avoiding the need for an independent Japanese security role, and to encourage the PRC in the practice of good international behaviour."

What about the post–Cold War role of ASEAN the institution, minus its outgrowths (such as the ARF)? The literature on ASEAN the subregional institution is voluminous; it is beyond the scope of this essay to survey it here (Acharya 2001; Antolik 1990; Leifer 1989; Emmerson 1987; Jorgensen-Dahl 1982). Suffice it to say that the literature does not portray ASEAN as an institution for reducing uncertainty, although many of the institution's activities may be thought of as doing precisely that.

The main reason why the information-providing, uncertainty-reducing, and contractual-regulating aspects of ASEAN the institution have not been emphasized is because they have been viewed by some as less central to ASEAN's success than its confidence-, community-, and norm-building activities. ASEAN's most perceptive interpreter, the late Michael Leifer, portrayed it as a "diplomatic community" (1989). It was a diplomatic community formed out of the initial purpose of reconciling former adversaries such as Malaysia and Indonesia. In the early 1990s, the label of a security community began to be applied to ASEAN, and although the thinking today is that ASEAN is not yet a security community, most would agree that it has played a critical role in decreasing the probability of war between its members (Acharya 2001: 203–4). That is another way of saying that the ASEAN states can be rather certain about the low probability of war among themselves. ASEAN arrived at this state not so much through transparency, information provision, or contractual regulations as through confidence, trust, and norm building. Through repeated interactions and frequent dialogue over the years, ASEAN officials and leaders developed an understanding of the ways and habits of each other. The processes used by ASEAN to discourage armed conflict among its members include the Treaty of Amity and Cooperation (TAC) discussed earlier. All signatories of the TAC agree, among other stipulations, to respect the territorial integrity and political sovereignty of fellow members and to renounce the use of force in the settlement of disputes. These are both regulatory and constitutive norms—they do regulate intra-ASEAN diplomacy, but when member states subscribe to them they become the core of what it means to be an ASEAN member.

Perhaps even more significant than accession to formal treaties such as the TAC are the norm building, consensual decision making, and frequent consultations that have been part of ASEAN's modus operandi since its inception. This approach to regional problems, often characterized as "the ASEAN way," has helped build confidence, increased trust, and even created a nascent sense of "we-ness" or ASEAN solidarity (Acharya 2001). The salience of the latter can be seen in the dynamics of many bilateral disputes: either a third ASEAN member steps in and asks for a "cooling off" period in the name of ASEAN solidarity, or politicians on either (or both) side(s) of the dispute call for a "lowering of the temperature" on the grounds that in the final analysis "we are all part of ASEAN." This does not include the discreet telephone calls that civil servants from both sides might make to one another for purposes of clarification and depoliticizing the dispute. These civil servants probably know one another on a first-name basis, having attended hundreds of ASEAN meetings over the years.

To be sure, ASEAN's processes of avoiding military conflict between its members would also have to include deterrence. Thailand and the Philippines are military allies of the United States; Malaysia and Singapore are part of the Five Power Defense Agreement with Britain, Australia, and New Zealand; and in recent years Singapore has successfully cultivated the United States as a quasi-military ally. The existence of these alliances and quasi-alliances suggests that many in ASEAN are not yet ready to wean themselves from the military protection of the major Western powers.

Conclusion

This chapter has identified and characterized Southeast Asia's post–Cold War security strategy as two-pronged: the first consists in building and expanding regional security and economic institutions, and the second consists in the soft balancing behavior of offering "places" instead of "bases" to the United States so as to facilitate its balancing role in the region. The adoption of this two-pronged strategy is explained in terms of the need of Southeast Asia's security planners to alleviate the strategic uncertainty they saw as pervading their environment. The explanatory sketch offered, focusing as it does on the construction and alleviation of uncertainty, suggests the importance of delving into, and unpacking, their conception of strategic uncertainty, for only in so doing can we comprehend the form and content of their response (security strategy). Moreover, although the explanatory sketch provided above appears to be nominally based on the liberal research tradition, its elaboration (in the spirit of analytical eclecticism) reveals the crucial importance of identity and power considerations emphasized by the constructivist and realist research traditions respectively. The expansion of ASEAN (to include Myanmar and Indochina), the advent of the ARF, ASEM, and even the ASEAN+3 was motivated as much by balancing considerations as by efficiency considerations. Similarly, in order to understand the soft balancing behavior of some of the key ASEAN states—why they chose to side with the preponderant power against the much weaker power—it is necessary to consider the identities of the powers involved. Absent knowledge of their identities and of ASEAN's historical and geographic links with them, mainstream realism would lead one to expect ASEAN to side with the weaker power (China) against the preponderant power (the United States). In short, adopting an analytically eclectic approach has allowed us to appreciate the controlling importance of identity in the ASEAN states' balancing strategies, as well as the crucial importance of balancing considerations in the institutional strategies of ASEAN. Along the way, we have also tried to recognize the importance of ASEAN's discourse about "uncertainty" and "balancing" and how they impacted its strategy.

A final question remains: to what extent has ASEAN's strategies of reducing uncertainty, focusing on institutions and soft balancing, worked? Of the four uncertainties that troubled ASEAN in the early 1990s, it is probably fair to say that ASEAN is reassured about three of them today. ASEAN's strategies contributed to these outcomes, but the calculations of the United States, Japan, and China were undoubtedly more critical. To be sure, part of ASEAN's strategy was to influence the variables that each of these great powers had to take into consideration in their calculations, but in the final analysis, ASEAN's role cannot have been decisive.

Ironically, the three areas in which there is less uncertainty today compared to the early 1990s are the U.S. presence, Japan's military role, and China's intentions; the areas with greater uncertainty (compared to the early 1990s) are ASEAN's economic future and regional clout. The U.S. presence in Southeast Asia is palpable and real, and recent events—the opening of Singapore's Changi Naval Base and the dispatch of U.S. combat troops to help the Philippines fight the Al Qaeda–linked Abu Say'yaf rebels—have only served to reinforce this situation. Japan remains enmeshed in a strengthened U.S.-Japan security treaty, banishing fears of an insecure Japan pursuing unilateral rearmament. China yearns for a more multipolar Asia, but meanwhile it seems content to occupy its spot—where its voice often has weight—in all the regional tables that matter. The ARF, for example, allowed China to dictate the pace of moving from stage 1 (confidence building) to stage 2 (preventive diplomacy), but the payoff was it increased China's comfort level with the ARF, and allowed Chinese diplomats involved in the process to begin to see advantages in the ARF's form of multilateralism (Johnston 1999b: 304–10). Since 1996—when the Clinton administration dispatched two carrier groups to the Taiwan Strait in the wake of China's saber rattling during the Taiwanese elections—China has also adopted a low military profile in Northeast and Southeast Asia. There has been no repeat of Mischief Reef–type operations and during the financial crisis China went out of its way to reassure ASEAN that it would not devalue the yuan. For almost a decade, China also refused to sign an ASEAN-inspired code of conduct on the South China Sea that, among other things, prohibits the use of force in settling rival claims. In November 2002, China finally put its signature to a modified version of the code called the Declaration on the Conduct of Parties in the South China Sea (Chairman's statement, Tenth ASEAN Regional Forum, Phnom Penh, 18 June 2003, www.aseansec.org/14846). In other words, China appears to be a better neighbor today than it appeared to be in 1995 or 1989.

Ironically, the uncertainty that has haunted ASEAN since 1997 is one that it omitted from its uncertainty discourse of the early 1990s: its ability to sustain the high economic growth of the 1970s and 1980s. ASEAN's strategists took high and sustained economic growth as a given or certainty. The financial crisis of 1997–99 shattered this illusion. As advocates of comprehensive security, ASEAN's leaders have always emphasized the importance of the economic dimension of security. Economic growth and prosperity were seen as critical—and more pressing than civil and political liberties—to political legitimacy and regime security. On that score, Indonesia, Malaysia, Singapore, and Thailand were doing remarkably well. Ever since they jumped on the export-led growth bandwagon in the 1970s, they had not looked back. For twenty years from the late 1970s to the late 1990s, they enjoyed strong economic growth, allowing them to double the per capita income in one generation. Feted as the emerging tigers of East Asia—following on the industrial successes of Japan, South Korea, and Taiwan—these countries and their security planners took for granted their unimpeded economic growth.

When the Asian financial crisis struck in 1997—beginning in Thailand, and spreading to Malaysia, Singapore, and Indonesia—it pulled the rug of economic prosperity from under these ASEAN states, and since then, a new strategic uncertainty has descended on the region's security planners: the uncertainty of economic recovery and the return of sustained economic growth. Although strictly speaking this uncertainty relates to the economic potential and resilience of individual ASEAN countries and of the region as a whole, the security dimension is never far from the surface:

economic hardship aggravates bilateral disagreements or disputes; an impoverished Indonesia that has yet to recover detracts seriously from its playing a lead role in ASEAN, and lethargic economic growth heightens domestic political contestation which in turn leads to political instability as well as exacerbates the potential for internal crises to be deflected externally.

Although the economic situation has stabilized somewhat since 1999, few in ASEAN think that they are out of the woods. It is unclear if Indonesia's economy, after such a massive flight of local (Chinese) and foreign capital, will ever recover. The rest of ASEAN may also find it more difficult to attract the volume of foreign direct investment they are used to, in part because the region's reputation had been dented by the financial crisis, and in part because of looming competition further north. The availability of cheaper labor in China and China's enormous market make it an increasingly attractive destination for investors' funds. In this sense, the uncertainties of the late 1990s are more directly economic than they are strategic. Consistent with the argument of this chapter, ASEAN and its East Asian neighbors are also seeking to reduce such economic uncertainties by building new institutions. A new institution, ASEAN+3 (China, Japan, and South Korea), is gaining momentum as an institution emphasizing intra–East Asian cooperation to avert, or to mitigate the impact of, a financial crisis similar to that of 1997–98. The United States, Australia, and New Zealand are excluded from ASEAN+3, and this in part because of the perception among some key ASEAN countries—especially Thailand, Malaysia, and Indonesia—that the United States was tardy and heavy handed in its response to the crisis of 1997–98. Moreover, the exclusion of the United States also suggests that some "economic balancing" is going on: the ASEAN+3 are keen to consolidate intraregional trade, to demonstrate that Southeast Asia is a region with economic weight that the United States and "the West" ought to notice. Finally, there is also a nascent identity dimension to the ASEAN+3. The financial crisis led some East Asians to question America's commitment to the economic well being of the region and that in turn helped bring about what the Malaysian prime minister had trouble realizing previously: an East Asian Economic Grouping (EAEG). U.S. policy—both directly and through the International Monetary Fund—during the financial crisis persuaded most in ASEAN that it was also essential to consider how the states of the region— defined as excluding the United States, Australia, and New Zealand—might organize to help themselves.

ASEAN is acutely aware that an inability to return to steady economic growth has short- and medium-term security implications. First, regime legitimacy and political stability will be endangered, especially in Indonesia, Malaysia, and the Philippines. Second, when regime legitimacy and political stability are in question, intra-ASEAN relations tend to suffer. The financial crisis seriously strained Malaysian-Singaporean and Singaporean-Indonesian relations. Third, when key ASEAN members such as Indonesia and Malaysia are preoccupied with internal issues, ASEAN the organization is distracted and less able to act cohesively, with a consequent negative impact on its standing and clout.

These challenges have convinced many in Southeast Asia and beyond that it is imperative for ASEAN to reinvent itself. The irony appears to be that ASEAN is more effective in cooperating to facilitate the shaping of its desired regional security environment than in cooperating to create the economic environment it wants. Yet this should not come as a surprise to those familiar with ASEAN's record in security and economic issues. Formed ostensibly to foster economic, social, and cultural cooperation, ASEAN has always been lackluster in its economic achievements. Its successes have almost always been in the security arena. Still, a strategy that contributes to alleviating unwanted uncertainties in three out of four areas cannot be considered a failure in contributing to regional order. Imagine a situation where the realists' predictions came true: massive U.S. military retrenchment from East Asia, an insecure Japan that rearms, an assertive China that seeks to replace the United States, no meaningful regional institutions, and no MOUs between anticipatory ASEAN states and the United States on naval facilities. Then inject the Asian financial crisis into such a security environment: Southeast Asia would find itself very much in the Hobbesian woods indeed. Luckily for ASEAN, this scenario has not come to pass. In ASEAN's eyes, the East Asian strategic environment today seems calmer and more predictable than in the 1990s. With the larger strategic picture under control, the states of ASEAN can hopefully devote their resources to getting their individual acts together.

Notes

1. Throughout this chapter I use the terms "ASEAN" and "Southeast Asia" interchangeably to refer to the collection of states that includes Indonesia, Malaysia, the Philippines, Singapore, and Thailand (also known as the original ASEAN 5), and Brunei, Cambodia, Laos, Myanmar, and Vietnam. "ASEAN" is thus a more felicitous way to denote the ten states than it is a term for the regional organization or institution (with its secretariat in Jakarta). When used in the latter sense, it will always be followed by "organization" or "institution." By "East Asia" I refer to ASEAN plus the Northeast Asian states of China, Japan, Taiwan, North Korea, and South Korea.

2. In formal social science, uncertainty refers to conditions where it is impossible to assign probabilities to outcomes. As the first part of the chapter indicates, the notion is not used in such a formal sense here; "inability to predict with strong confidence" approximates the way the term is used in this chapter.

3. Although the notion of uncertainty also has a place in realist and liberal thought, it is categorized here—for the sake of argument—as a discovery of the area specialist comparing ASEAN's Cold War and post–Cold War documents/speeches.

4. By security planners I mean those involved in interpreting, deciding, and implementing their respective countries' foreign and defense policies. Prime ministers or presidents, their foreign and defense ministers, civil servants in the foreign and security ministries constitute the

first tier of security planners. Analysts, academics, and participants in the track-two processes may be considered second tier security planners since they help interpret the security environment for the politicians and they also float/propose new ideas in track-two forums that may filter up to the first tier for the track-one policy process.

5. Such an alignment might consist in distancing oneself militarily from the United States, as in, say the Philippines' pricing of the renewal of Clark and Subic bases so high that the United States was unlikely to accept, or Thailand's rejection of a U.S. request for a permanent platform in the Gulf of Siam for fear of displeasing China.

6. By "balancee" I mean the state that is being balanced against.

The Value of Rethinking East Asian Security
Denaturalizing and Explaining a Complex Security Dynamic

ALLEN CARLSON AND J. J. SUH

The description and analysis forwarded in this volume, a product of analytical eclecticism, poses three basic challenges to alternative styles of analysis of Asian security. First, it raises serious questions about the accuracy of widely accepted descriptions of the region. Eclecticism generates new perspectives about "natural expectations" for Asia by highlighting blind spots left unilluminated in paradigmatic perspectives. Second, eclecticism challenges predominant explanations of Asian security and creates intellectual space for arguments not easily sustained within any single analytic frame. Finally, eclecticism sheds new light on America's Asian presence. It reveals the vastly different ways in which the United States is understood within the region, belying the utility of analyzing America's role—or, for that matter, choosing policy options —from within the prison of any singular research tradition.

We substantiate such claims in the following sections by first reviewing how the individual chapters succeed in denaturalizing the natural in Asian security. In the second section, we take up the question of whether the individual authors provide a satisfactory answer to the puzzle they formulate with the aid of analytical eclecticism, and explore the contrasting styles of eclecticism they employ. In the third section, we apply analytical eclecticism to the questions of the roles and positions of the United States in Asia. The United States is the "indispensable nation" in the region, as indirectly reflected in the fact that all the country case chapters allocate a significant amount of attention to the United States. What it may do under the Bush administration remains perhaps the single most important factor in determining the future of the Asian security dynamic. Finally, we consider the broader theoretical implications of analytical eclecticism for the study of Asian security within the context of the recent literature on Asian security.

Denaturalizing Asian Security

The turn toward eclecticism grows out of weariness with the increasingly intellectually unproductive paradigmatic debates that have divided international relations and security studies for some time now, as well as disappointment with analyses self-consciously conducted within the context of competing research traditions. This type of research tends to produce natural expectations—the proverbial conventional wisdom—about the variables that are relevant to any given research project, placing highly artificial (yet real) constraints on subsequent studies. Such blinders encourage research agendas that impede considering anything beyond a given paradigm's conventional research tradition. Thus, in the introduction to this volume, Katzenstein and Sil argue that by divorcing explanatory sketches from such constraints, analytical eclecticism creates space for the discovery of puzzles and problems that have gone unexamined and unexplored within existing research frames. In reflecting on the previous chapters, we can then ask whether each of them did in fact generate new research questions, and, crucially, illustrate the centrality of such inquiries to Asian security.

For example, Katzenstein and Okawara's chapter on Japan's role in the Asia-Pacific succeeds on both fronts. It argues that the conventional wisdom about Japan leads to a persistent misidentification of basic aspects of its national security strategy. In support of this claim, the authors methodically expose the tendency within a wide variety of recent studies of Japanese security to draw upon a set of assumptions about Japan's "natural" security state. To escape the constraining effects of such assumptions, they advocate reorienting analysis around a consideration of "new political constellations and policies that will resist analytic capture by ahistorical conceptions of a 'normal' Japan." This move enables them to identify three significant features of Japanese security that have persistently fallen outside the survey of conventional analysis. First, the comprehensive notion of security in Japan expands well beyond the external realm that is the focus of most security studies. Second, this understanding of security is so deeply embedded in Japanese social and political institutions that it constitutes what is considered "normal" in a markedly different fashion in Tokyo than in Washington. Third, and most prominently, there is a union, rather than competition, between bilateralism and multilateralism in Japan's security relations over the last two decades. Indeed, Katzenstein and Okawara argue that the pairing of these two approaches is the central feature of Japanese security strategy. The question then becomes what factors underlie this development, and how durable is it?

Although Johnston less explicitly emphasizes denaturalization and question generation, he also shows how exposing silences within existing research paradigms can produce new questions and create novel research agendas. Where Katzenstein and Okawara explore the assumption of "peacefulness" in Japan's security policies, Johnston examines the almost universal acceptance in American foreign policy and national security circles of China's role as a threat to the status quo in Asia. Troubled by the flimsy foundation of this widely accepted assumption, Johnston asks us first to re-consider how we think about identifying both status quo and revisionist security strategies in international politics, and then turns our attention to Beijing. Within this context, he then directly asks the question that has been surprisingly absent in the wide-ranging debate about engaging versus containing China: to what extent is China a status quo or a revisionist power? His critical inquiry then treats China's po-sition along the status quo / revisionist spectrum as a puzzle rather than a theoretical assumption or product of analytic assertion. This allows him to shift away from cate-gorizing China as status quo via assertion, in order to empirically investigate the ex-tent of its revisionist intentions and capabilities.

Just as Katzenstein and Okawara start their analysis with an observation about "normalcy" and Johnston notes the taken-for-grantedness of China's revisionist iden-tity, Suh finds that the U.S. presence in Korea has attained a "natural" status that rivals the assumptions in the region about China's threat. He attributes this presupposition to the tendency for analysis of military alliances to be monopolized by research tradi-tions that give pride of place to material capabilities as they are conventionally ana-lyzed in terms of balancing, bandwagoning, or deterrence. Within such a framework, the formal alliance between the United States and Korea is unproblematically taken as a natural outcome of power balancing, and its existence is unreflectively credited with the fifty years' peace on the Korean Peninsula. Suh exposes the shortcomings of such a view through demonstrating that despite great variations in the opposing parties' military capabilities on the peninsula over the last four decades and a qualitative de-cline in behavioral "threats" during the 1990s, the alliance structure itself has remained remarkably untouched. Thus, what seems natural within the realist tradition becomes in Suh's analysis an anomaly in search of an explanation. He then turns to the neo-institutionalist explanation of the U.S. role in Korea and argues that its analytic power is also quite limited. In short, he finds that efficiency gains emphasized within neo-institutionalism do play an important role in both Seoul's and Washington's motiva-tions for holding on to the alliance, but also discovers that neither side made their de-cision to adhere to the alliance solely on the basis of rational calculations. Finally, Suh argues that those working within the constructivist research tradition would quite simply fail to see the U.S. presence in Korea as particularly interesting or compelling, as there appears to be very little in the way of socially constructed collective identity on the peninsula. Yet, he notes that on the contrary, identity concerns (alongside power and efficiency) are central to the current security dynamic in Korea.

In other words, Suh argues that the persistence of the U.S.-Korea security alliance has to date only been "seen" by analysts in the same way that the "three blind men" of lore saw their elephant. Security studies have gotten each of the parts right, but in the process have missed the complete picture on the peninsula, in much the same way that the "three blind men" mistook their "elephant." It is only when the "three blind men" compare notes that they can surpass their individual limitations and develop a more comprehensive "vision" of the terrain before them. In this sense, Suh argues that by putting together the three unproblematic facts generated within each of the main research traditions in the field about the situation in Korea, we are left with a problematic and puzzling reality. Moreover, this puzzle generates the following compelling research question: why has the U.S.-Korea security alliance been so persistent over time?

In the final empirical chapter, Khong also positions his analysis within the context of an initial inquiry into the limitations imposed by paradigmatic research traditions. He begins by identifying uncertainty as a central analytic given for structural theorists. Scholars working in this research tradition have rarely considered the meaning of such a concept, let alone how it is constituted in specific security spheres. Yet, he also finds fault with institutional analysis that would treat uncertainty solely in terms of minimizing inefficiencies, and reports that such work rarely considers the possibility that uncertainty may be an expression of strategic objectives—in other words, a collective good (not a collective failure). He also locates "uncertainty" within the discursive domain that tends to feature so prominently in constructivist analysis of the region, illustrating how representative practices linked to the "politics of naming" play a role in shaping understandings of the term within the region. However, Khong cautions that language does not float freely in a frictionless discursive space, but is constrained, facilitated, or channeled by material conditions and institutional structures (Risse-Kappen 1994). Political entrepreneurs choose from the available material possibilities and take advantage of political institutions—and the political capital they confer on them—to make one construct more salient in a given domain than other possible constructions. In short, the content of uncertainty itself becomes a key line of critical inquiry: what does "uncertainty" mean to different actors in the region and how is it linked to regional security strategies?

In sum, the chapters are unified in their demonstration that analysis bound within separate research traditions creates costly silences in the study of Asian security. The authors find a Japan that is both less and more pacific than is commonly assumed; a China whose revisionism, although widely assumed, is poorly understood; a U.S.-Korean alliance whose persistence is a given but whose longevity cannot be described within a single research frame; and a group of Southeast Asian states for whom uncertainty has meant more, and varied more widely, than conventional wisdom would expect. Not surprisingly, the questions generated by such a wide-ranging set of discoveries are quite diverse as well. What is the source of Japan's integrative approach to security issues? Why are both the United States and China increasingly skeptical of each other's security agendas in Asia despite multiple empirical indicators of China's increasingly status quo behavior and intentions? Why does the U.S.-Korean security alliance persist? What type of instutionalization/regionalization is evolving in ASEAN?

In each case, such queries are held together by the fact that they grow out of the utilization of eclectic lenses to reexamine terrain that appeared to be well mapped out by existing analysis. Thus, they demonstrate just how valuable it is to retrace with a critical eye the well-traveled paths created by the main research traditions. Doing so allows for the development of new lines of inquiry that have been neglected by those who, out of conviction, habit, or simple convenience, placed their confidence in the ready-made intellectual maps provided by the dominant paradigms within the security field.

Explaining Asian Security

The eclectic frame should provide scholars with increased "problem solving" capabilities for understanding "the complex ways power, interests, and identities affect each other and combine to shape Asian states' behaviors and relationships" (Katzenstein and Sil, this volume). In a general sense, the preceding chapters fulfill the promise of such a claim through a dual process. First, they expose the weaknesses of arguments bound within singular research traditions. Second, they effectively demonstrate that including each corner of the power, interest, and identity trialectic allows analysis to move beyond such limitations. However, the chapters are also marked by two significant differences over how to substantiate the eclectic turn. First, the way individual authors seek to integrate explanations differ, and do so in a manner that roughly corresponds with the stylized categories of eclectic theorizing sketched out in the introduction. Second, analysis does not converge around a single point within the eclectic triangle, but rather tends to give particular weight to distinct pairs of causal variables. In this section, we briefly review the contrasting explanatory logics developed in the substantive chapters in order to highlight the common traits and distinguishing features in the strand of eclectic theorizing promoted in this volume.

Just as Chairman Deng counseled pragmatism by valuing a cat's ability to catch mice over its color, we see the merits of analytical eclecticism in its pragmatic ability to solve problems. Moreover, there are two important ways in which our pragmatism goes beyond the simple appeal to remain blind to the different colors of research traditions and to focus on problem solving. First, as the previous section demonstrates, analytical eclecticism enables "a progressive problem shift" in that it helps the researcher find new problems to solve by problematizing what is taken as given within each of the research traditions. Explanation necessarily supervenes upon problem recognition, and the first function of theories in any scientific field is the description of the problem. Moreover, analytical eclecticism suggests that by triangulating elements of different research traditions to explore a single phenomenon, one can identify new problems that can go beyond the scope of those embedded within the existing traditions. Second, eclecticism helps the researcher see connections among variables emphasized by various research traditions. In eclectic explanatory sketches, explanatory variables favored by each of the three research traditions are recast in

ways that emphasize the linkages among them. It is the different ways in which identity, efficiency, and power are linked, not how one of them trumps the others, that is
the focus of analytical eclecticism in constructing explanatory sketches.

Building on Jepperson's work (1998), we argue that such juxtapositions create at
least two different types of complementarity among research traditions: problem
recognition complementarity, and modular complementarity. The former leads us to
view systemic outcomes and state behavior as part and parcel of the same problem in
Asian affairs. For example, China's sensitivity on Taiwan, ASEAN members' interest
in a continued U.S. role in the region, and Tokyo's multistranded relationship with
Beijing can be viewed as interrelated trends tending towards regional stability or instability. In the same vein, one can look at the ties between American troop deploy-
ments, Korean nationalism, and the opening of new fronts in the "war on terrorism."

Modular complementarity consists of two distinct frames. In one frame, each
of the different research traditions supplies compelling explanatory variables and
causal mechanisms about a particular phase of institutional development, "stage-
complementarity." For example, explanatory sketches drawing on realism can quite
adequately cover one phase of institutional development, as the origins of bilateral
and multilateral security institutions in Asia are explained in terms of the need to
counterbalance the power of the Communist bloc in the early days of the Cold War.
In this sense, the origins of U.S. bilateral alliances with Japan and South Korea, as
well as ASEAN, fall within the purview of the realist research tradition. In another
phase of institutional development, particularly when established institutions enhance
efficiency in interstate transactions, the liberal research tradition provides conceptual
tools and causal logics that better capture state behavior. Hence, the rise of ASEAN
is explained with reference to reducing uncertainty about actors' intentions and material conditions, while the bilateral alliances produce asset specificities that reduce
transaction costs. In yet another phase, when institutions function as a social space
where actors negotiate their identities, the constructivist tradition proves more useful. For example, Japan's mixture of bilateralism and multilateralism produces a degree of ambiguity where Tokyo can address U.S. and Asian concerns about its identity without necessarily antagonizing one or the other.

A second type of modular complementarity involves nesting one research tradition
within another as it provides a contextualization or scope condition for the latter. For
example, constructivist explanatory sketches can be used to specify the conditions under which realist interactions between states result, while realist sketches can provide
a material contextualization for institution-based coordination among states. Thus, a
security dilemma where states are driven to act as realist actors concerned about relative gains is a condition generated not by the material structure of anarchy, but by the
social interaction between states initially more concerned about identity needs (Johnston, this volume). In addition, the context within which ASEAN countries are engaged in institution building and soft balancing is more explainable with reference to

the profound shift in material capabilities caused by China's rapid rise and by U.S. plans to withdraw its forward presence (Khong, this volume).

Just as researchers may choose among different styles of complementarity within analytical eclecticism, they may also place contrasting levels of emphasis on each of the three points of the eclectic triangle. Along these lines, as Katzenstein and Sil argue in Chapter 1, the three main research traditions in American international relations scholarship constitute three sides of a triangle that take for granted the centrality of some core assumptions of international life in their respective focus on identity, efficiency, and power (see Figure 1.1). Occasionally, some scholars start from one particular side of the triangle and, as they construct explanatory sketches that fill the gap left by their starting tradition, they converge with one or the other research tradition's ontology, epistemology, or methodology, ending up near one of the triangle's other corners. Analytical eclecticism pushes this kind of unwitting and unacknowledged convergence further, without privileging any one type of combinatorial formula or proclaiming a unified theory encompassing every variable identified in competing research traditions. That is, analytical eclecticism regards existing research traditions fluidly and is willing to borrow selectively from each to construct accounts that travel across the sides of the triangle representing constructivism, realism, and liberalism (see Figure 1.2).

In other words, analytical eclecticism opens the possibility that what seems incommensurable is in fact interrelated. For example, the rational calculation of costs and benefits, on which neoliberal tradition relies, can be seen as embedded in a discursive structure that skews perception and interest calculation in a specific way. Thus, the same cost can be seen as being acceptable or too high, depending on the meaning structure within which the cost is understood. Alternatively, institutions may be seen as mechanisms for decreasing uncertainty and enhancing efficiency, thus reducing the overall cost of interactions among states. Such material benefits can then facilitate the development of affective feelings toward the source of such largesse.

Moreover, this process may have transformative effects on state identities. For example, international alliance, being an international security exchange relationship, may generate interests in maintaining the enmity and amity that can then provide a powerful discursive tool for constituting and privileging identity. This last effect is driven by privileging the identities that are compatible with the premises of the institution, to the extent that an organization generates a self-legitimizing identity structure. In short, institutions do more than reduce transaction costs and increase transparency and efficiency, as neoliberals have argued; they are also constructions that reflect and affect shared identities. Understood in this way, institutions produce shifts in actors' interests and identities, and can in turn be transformed by changing configurations of interest and identity, as constructivists suggest.

In accord with such an approach, the substantive chapters outline the complex ways in which identity, efficiency, and power interact in producing state actors' behavior. Yet in light of the contrasting outcomes they analyze and the different styles of eclecticism they develop, it is not at all surprising that they emphasize different sides of the triangle in Figure 1.2. For some authors, material capabilities are significant, not as final arbiters or determinants of behavior, but as something that is constrained or amplified by institutional structures and as something that is made meaningful within an identity structure. For other authors, identities matter significantly, not as ever-fleeting structures of meanings, but as things that are appropriated or denied by power and as things whose influence is facilitated or impeded by institutions. For still others, institutions affect not only efficiency in state interactions, but also the ways states perceive others' identities, as well as the ways they exercise power. Were we to adhere strictly to any one of the three research traditions, these analytic possibilities would fall by the wayside or be viewed as epiphenomenal.

It is precisely along these lines that Khong (this volume) both offers strikingly neoliberal discussions of ASEAN and remains attentive to two different conceptions of institutions. He suggests that ASEAN has reduced transaction costs while at the same time it has helped constitute a new regional identity. But there is a difference in the degree to which the institution succeeds in accomplishing these two very different tasks. Khong concludes that ASEAN has, on balance, scored more points in improving the efficiency of regional interaction than in promoting a cooperative identity. Nevertheless, the two do not necessarily exist independently, as there are interaction effects between institutional efficiency and identity constitution. In other words, ASEAN-style institutions may generate positive feedbacks between the two, in the sense that cost reduction helps promote "we-feeling," which then helps reduce transaction costs further.

Katzenstein and Okawara illustrate yet another way institutions mediate between identities and power. According to them, one of the most important effects of international institutions in Asia is to maintain ambiguity about collective purpose while creating a sense of commonality, rather than to promote transparency of objectives while enhancing efficiency (Katzenstein and Okawara, this volume). As the Japanese adapt to the changed strategic circumstances of the twenty-first century, their relationships with their bilateral alliance and multilateral institutions, they have created a purposeful ambiguity about their intentions and the collective purposes of these institutions. The ensemble of institutions no doubt serves the purpose of enhancing the efficiency of transactions among states, but the ambiguity in them also functions as a tool to manage power distributions.

Suh is less intent on coming to terms with ambiguity than with the persistent cooperation between the United States and South Korea. He does so in a way that also shows the explanatory power of eclecticism. Echoing Khong, he begins with a strikingly realist argument but ends with an argument that resonates with constructivism. Not only does power create an institution, it also affects how identities are constituted. The origin of the U.S.-Korea alliance is proof that Waltz and Walt had a correct, important insight. The Korean War most clearly demonstrated the power disparity in the Korean Peninsula and reminded the two countries of the threat posed by the North. The alliance represented the security measure that the two countries took to counterbalance the power imbalance and the threat. At the time of the alliance formation, power was the independent variable that caused its establishment. Moreover, the institution, started as a tool of realpolitik, left a lasting imprint on how Korean and American identities are constituted.

The ways in which identity, efficiency, and power are linked in producing political outcomes can also be illustrated with a focus on discourse. As the previous chapters illustrate, language and discourse play a central role in mediating the impact of power and efficiency on the security dynamic in the region. The effect words have on Asian security is repeatedly emphasized throughout the book. The authors conceptualize the effects of discursive influence in a notably inclusive fashion that goes well beyond the confines of any one research tradition. On one level, discourse is treated as *instrumental*: it serves as a means to achieving a specific objective. In this conceptualization, discourse represents one of the tools actors rely on to achieve their goals (Krasner 1999). On a second level, actors produce discourse as a way to *communicate* and may as a result come to a common understanding (Risse 2000, 1999; Habermas 1984). In the face of uncertainties and ambiguities inherent in political reality, actors negotiate their understandings of reality through the medium of discourse. Whereas instrumental conceptualization presumes stability in actors' identity and interest throughout the interaction process, a communicative conceptualization leaves open the possibility of interest change and identity reconstitution as a result of discursive interaction. On a third level, discursive politics are treated as *constitutive* (Weldes 1999; Campbell 1992). Discursive politics provides a social structure of meaning to material reality. It serves as a medium through which actors are "identified" and such identities are stabilized. Material reality is thus imbued with a particular meaning through a constitutive discourse. Although discourse has a fluidity that lends itself to an instrumental use, it also has a structural property that cannot be easily changed by willful actions of an individual. Finally, it is also *moving*. In other words, a discourse that began as an instrumental tool can in time become naturalized to constitute a social reality. A communicative discourse can likewise be denaturalized by exogenous factors to function as an instrumental discourse.

The key to such a move is located in the conceptualization of discourse as a political site where actors debate the meanings of power, interests, and identity. More specifically, it is through discourse, or the politics of naming, that politicians construct bridges between their words and actions. Because of the multiplicity of audiences that hear such discursive practices, this process is often fraught with difficulties and perils. In the Japanese case, navigating such terrain is particularly complicated because of the sharply differing attunements of domestic and international listeners. The Japanese ear is understood as being accustomed to tuning into subtle differences between formal statements and evolving interpretations of their meaning. In contrast, international listeners (read Americans) are portrayed as largely tone deaf to such nuances. As a result, where the international audience hears disconcerting dissonance and disingenuity in Japanese statements, its Japanese counterpart appreciates harmony in them.

Such an understanding of discursive practices moves us from a fixation on the distinction between "real" versus "cheap talk," toward a consideration of the role of language in informing and shaping security strategies. In this sense, we see that track-two diplomacy in the region is not simply contentless talk shops, but a potential avenue for new identity formation. In addition, constitutional debates in Japan over Article 9 are weighted with a new significance, as the way in which audiences listen and respond to Japanese statements on defense strategy has varied significantly and substantially during recent debates about Japan's defense policies and military modernization.

Language and discourse can also play a prominent role in constructing "realist" politics. For Johnston, discourse refers to how those in China (and elsewhere) talk about China's rise. Discourse is talk, but represents more than "cheap talk," as it is separate from, but tends to inform, behavior. It imbues the material world with a particular meaning, which then makes certain reactions seem appropriate and others out of the question. However, at the same time, policy actions tend to reinforce certain facets of discursive politics. Indeed, for Johnston it is this interaction between international discourse (constructivist), domestic perceptions (liberal), and "concrete PRC behavior" (realist) variables that is generating a new security dilemma in the region. It is often the most provocative, confrontational analysis by elites on all sides that garners the most attention, both at home and abroad. By calling attention to this process, Johnston's analysis throws new light on the rising tide of name-calling in the United States and China since the mid-1990s, and the extent to which rhetorical "stones" are more than just talk. Although he concedes that rigorous testing with the available events data sets is difficult, he also suggests that both Beijing and Washington have become more impatient, less willing to cooperate, and less willing to acknowledge the potential for benign interaction as a result (Johnston, this volume).

Just as an institution may become independent of the power that created it, identity may become dissociated from the institution. Where Johnston examines the intersection between malign discourses, identities, and security strategies in Sino-U.S. relations, Suh analyzes how a naturalized distribution of identities imbues the power balance and institutional context with a particular meaning. In Korea, power balancing and institutional building occur within the social space constituted by identity. In making this claim, Suh develops a broad conceptualization of discursive politics. He emphasizes throughout his chapter the role of discourse in constraining state behavior. For him, discursive politics is about how to affect a "conventional matrix of interpretations within which some states are identified as allies and others as adversaries" (Suh, this volume).

In contrast, Khong begins his chapter with an emphasis on the instrumental roles of discourse. He opens with an observation of a disjoint between facts on the ground and discourse, noting an interest in "strategic discourse" and "discourses of uncertainty" in the first sections of his chapter. He then argues that only through an examination of the language used by the Southeast Asian states is it possible to understand the differing perceptions of power politics within the region: contrasting ASEAN comfort levels with U.S. presence in the region, acquiescence to Japanese economic power, and misgivings about China as a responsible (not revisionist) power. Later in the chapter, Khong uses discourse in yet another way, by examining how it constitutes regional and national identities in the region. In short, for Khong discourse moves back and forth between each of the conceptualizations outlined above.

In sum, throughout the volume, the contributors reemphasize that words and discourses play a significant role in shaping security outcomes. They can serve as a tool to manage security concerns, create room for political maneuvering, impute a particular meaning to material capability and security institutions, or constitute a social reality within which states identify friends and enemies. The contributors also repeatedly argue that discursive actions are always embedded within a political context that is shaped by material influence and institutional efficiency (Evangelista 1999; Risse et al. 1999; Risse-Kappen 1994). Such a political context can serve to constrain discourses inconsistent with such a setting while facilitating others that are in accord with it. Furthermore, the contributors show that a shift in any corner of the power-identity-institutions triumvirate tends to have a far-reaching, if varied, impact on the security outlook in the region. Such an observation suggests that stability and instability in Asia are not built upon a single foundation, but rather grow out of a configuration of identity, institutions (efficiency), and power. Apparently insignificant modifications in national and regional identities have facilitated and complemented emerging institutional structures. Incremental adjustments in the defense policies of major players have been interpreted in vastly different ways, and for substantively different reasons, in each of the capitals in the region. It is this complexity that leads us to turn our attention to the role of America in the region.

America's Asian Presence

In this book, the United States is conspicuous both by its absence and by its ubiquity. It is absent, as none of the chapters deals with America as the primary object of analysis. And yet it makes up an important part of the story in every chapter. This treatment is deserving of some reflection. On the one hand, the decision to exclude a chapter dealing exclusively with the United States was made with a keen awareness that its presence could not be ignored. On the other hand, it was clear from the start that America is less a part of Asia than any of the states in the region. We also concurred that it was a cliché to simply state that the U.S. presence is tied to stability and prosperity of the region. Indeed, we were committed to moving beyond such conventional wisdom to more specifically locate the ways America's position has shaped the security order in Asia, and convinced that the way to do so was to focus on America's place within each of the case studies.

To begin with, certain aspects of America's role in the region can be understood via each of the dominant research traditions within the field. For example, within the realist paradigm, one sees that the United States is the sole hegemon in Asia by virtue of possessing the dominant military capabilities within the region. This being said, it is also obvious that there are vastly differing views within the realist camp on the desired level of U.S. military presence there. In contrast, in the realm of liberal theorizing, America's pervasive economic influence is given pride of place, while the weakness of regional multilateral institutions is bemoaned. In this sense, America is again a dominant, yet somewhat remote force within the region, one that provides at best a limited foundation for stability. Such a role is seen as even more fragile in light of the (at best) ambiguous support America has given to the development of multilateral institutions within the region—institutions that could serve as vehicles for enhancing trust and cooperation through a process of increasing transparency and changing interests. Finally, within the confines of the constructivist research tradition, one is made aware of America's problematic identity as a part of Asia. National identities within the region are largely defined with reference to U.S. constructs (democracy, free markets, Western pop culture) and the attempt to square such imported normative structures with local culture and tradition.

Each of these frames brings to the fore crucial facets of America's position in Asia and the extent to which it provides order within the region. Yet, as the previous chapters of this book illustrate, such singular takes on the U.S. role in the region remain incomplete at best, for it is in the synergy between each of these frames (rather than the specifics within any one of them) that the U.S. presence is best understood. American power is never just an issue of military force, it is also one of economic and cultural influence. The U.S.-created market efficiencies and institutional structures are as deeply penetrated by considerations of both dual-use technology and comprehensive security as they are by socially constructed ideas about how to run an economy. American power is understood differently within Asia by actors who hold contrasting conceptions of American identity: To ASEAN, America's presence is a source of stability; to China, it remains a concern; to North Korea, it represents a main threat. Also, the United States can amplify its power with institutional efficiency or reap from its bilateral alliances—while it may also find the exercise of its power complicated by, for example, Tokyo's concerns about its neighbors' perception of Japan's identity. In addition, identity politics is not just about defining the self; it is also about identifying friends, partners, and enemies, a social structure that imputes meanings to material capabilities and institutional efficiency. In short, eclecticism provides us with a more comprehensive picture of America's central presence in Asia.

This understanding of the U.S. role in the region stems from the individual portraits the authors in this volume have painted. The authors all agree that American military capability has had a decisive impact on the security environment of Asian countries; they also share the view that America's bilateral and multilateral relationships are largely attributable to the current state of institutional development in the region. To the power and efficiency dimensions, the authors add the issue of how America's role in the region relates to the evolution of national identities there. Within this eclectic framework, it is possible to understand and explain the diverse ways the United States is understood and reacted to by Asian countries.

In its view of the United States, Korea stands out in its extremism. On the one hand, it seems to be gripped by a blind faith in the United States as its liberator, savior, and protector, all drawn from its recent historical experiences with Japanese colonialism, the Korean War, and the Cold War. Korea's faith is so strong—"hegemonic," to use Suh's expression—that an absolute majority of South Korea's population wants to hold on to American military protection even though it is difficult to justify that protection in simple military terms. On the other hand, South Korean's pervasive love for the hegemon stands in a tenuous relationship with its hegemonic love for its own nation. It is a deeply held "fact" that the "imagined community" of the Korean nation is the real thing, preserved in this corner of the Asian continent for the past five thousand years by the common language, culture, and blood of the Korean people. As Suh has shown, such bifurcated identity politics play out within the context of Korea's military and economic relationship with the United States, and in the process help to substantiate the American-Korean alliance even as it creates new resentments of the American role on the peninsula.

Southeast Asia is a region where several countries have had a disastrous liaison with the United States, a few have expelled the U.S. military by force or by treaty, and yet, after the Cold War, many view the possibility of American military withdrawal with consternation. Just as the surge of Filipino nationalism was putting an end to the two U.S. bases in the Philippines, utilitarian rationality convinced not only Singapore but also Malaysia, which had been advocating the neutralization of Southeast Asia, to offer the U.S. military access to their naval facilities. Their rationale had a realist overtone as they all emphasized the need to "balance other powers" (Khong, this volume). As Khong quickly notes, however, "balance" is a misnomer designed to anchor the United States in the area as a benevolent offshore hegemon, without upsetting the sensitivity of Asian countries to American domination. America's hegemonic power—using "hegemonic" in a pure material-capability sense—represents a public good to ASEAN countries as it balances a "rising" China and contains a potentially resurgent Japan. This power imbalancing act and the politics of naming can only be understood when ASEAN's behaviors are juxtaposed with how the identities of the United States, China, and Japan are constituted in Southeast Asia. China is construed, despite its limited and weak military capabilities, as a potentially overbearing bully on the block, whereas Japan is conceived of, despite its institutional constraints, as an "alcoholic" addicted to militarism. Despite its actual overbearing capabilities and the absence of similar institutional constraints—and despite its history of aggression—the United States is generally accepted as a pacifying actor. Yet, this identification of the United States stands in a tenuous relationship with identities that are more based on "Asian values": Mahatir, for example, allows the U.S. military access to Malaysia's ports while advocating the creation of an Asia-only club and emphasizing "Asian values."

Since the end of World War II, Japan has remained firmly under the U.S. security umbrella and within one side of an Asia bifurcated by the Cold War (Cumings 1984, 1983). But at the same time, Japan has struggled to define who it is while being so closely tied to the United States. Not only was the pro-U.S. identity challenged by nationalist right-wingers and internationalist left-wingers throughout the Cold War, but it also coexisted uneasily with Japan's "Asian identity." Japan's attempt to return to Asia in the early twentieth century was disastrous for Japan as well as for Asia as a whole; but for the past two decades Japan has again been drawn to Asia through economic networks and peacekeeping operations (Pyle 1992). Tokyo's recent Asia turn has sometimes manifested itself in the form of cautious exploration of various forms of an Asian club or through anger at U.S. troops in Okinawa. The balancing of East and West in Japan is further complicated by the resurgence of Japanese nationalism in the 1980s and 1990s—a development that has plagued trade relations with the United States and spills over into territorial disputes with Japan's Asian neighbors: Diaoyu (Senkaku), Takeshima (Tokto), and the Northern Territories (Southern Kuriles). The inherent tension is reflected in Tokyo's careful recalibration of the ambiguity in its bilateral relationship with the United States, as well as in its cautious exploration of a multilateral institutional arrangement, as Katzenstein and Okawara illustrate (this volume).

Although Japan has struggled with the challenge of maintaining an "Asian" identity at the same time that it has allied itself so closely (economically, militarily, politically, even culturally) with the United States, Beijing's unrelenting condemnation of American capitalism and imperialism precluded such ambiguities from emerging in China through the early 1980s. However, following the normalization of U.S.-China relations and the incremental opening of the Chinese economy, it became much more difficult for China's leaders to simply categorize the West (and America) as an enemy to be guarded against. Indeed, Deng Xiaoping's reforms have not only strengthened China economically and militarily (as they were intended), but also made room (as some opponents to the reforms initially feared) for a flood of new images of the United States and a greater plurality of views on America. Advocates of engaging China believe it is through such a process that the United States can manage China's rise, but as Johnston points out in his chapter in this volume, such a policy overlooks the extent to which derogatory portrayals of America have worked their way into recent Chinese security discourses. However, the demonization of the United States in China has its counterweights too. First, on both the elite and popular level there is a fascination with the West, especially America. As well as the rejection of America sells in China, Beijing's main bookstores dedicate more space to the sensational memoirs of those who have spent time in the United States and to books advising would-be American visa applicants. Second, in elite circles, there are limited indications of a growing commitment to being part of international society and an understanding that within such a community, China's role should be that of a responsible, mature power (Carlson 2002; Zhang 1998). In short, the American identity issue in China has become more complex and more contested since the start of the reform era; such a development is both embedded within, and contributes to, the pattern of complex economic integration and national security strategies that have emerged over the last two decades.

America has succeeded in stabilizing Asia's security order during the 1990s, in large part because of two relatively novel aspects of American policy during this period. First, the U.S. government allowed for the coexistence of such contradictory interpretations of the United States within the region and tolerated the deep-seated ambiguities within each of the Asian states about their relationship with the United States. Thus, in terms of identity politics, the United States was viewed simultaneously within the region as a threat, a competitor, a land of opportunity, and a source of new norms and ideas. Its economic role was that of a provider of market outlets, a source of investment capital, and a supplier of military hardware, management expertise, and information technology. Finally, in the security realm, it was at the same time an anchor, a bottle cap, and a force to be balanced against. In other words, during the last decade, America's Asian presence was made more palatable (and influential) within the region by its largely tacit acquiescence to Asian discursive efforts and policy decisions that created myriad interpretations of America's role in the region. Second, American policy, although grounded in realist sensibilities about military power's role as an anchor of U.S. influence in the region, also made room for the emergence of incipient multilateralism there.

In short, it was within this multiplicity of images, grounded by the increasingly complex economic and military realities in the region, that America's Asian presence was able to contribute to the fragile peace that prevailed in the region over the last decade. Indeed, one of the policy implications to be derived from the eclectic analysis conducted in this volume is that the strategic stability of the region is weakened by American policies that let either material capabilities or unidimensional identity projections dominate other considerations.

The significance of such a finding is readily apparent when we look back to the unsettled situation in Asia throughout much of the Cold War. Then, in contrast to the 1990s, Washington demonstrated a remarkable indifference to the multiplicity of ways U.S. power was read and interpreted within the region. Quite simply, America was the defender of the free world, and within such a context it imposed a set of simplifying dichotomies on Asia, coding states as Communist or anti-Communist. The political establishments in Japan, South Korea, and the Republic of China benefited from this turn, while the political elites in North Korea, the People's Republic of China, and Vietnam were harmed by it. America's single-minded anti-Communism erased complex realities within each Asian country and expunged differences between them, producing an overarching anti-Communist containment that was indiscriminately applied across the region and created great instability within Asia. First Korea and then China were partitioned in order to contain Communists, to stop the spread of the red disease in Asia following the Communist victory in the Chinese civil war. Then, the United States resorted to the "reversal" of democratic reforms in Japan before getting entangled in the first hot war of the Cold War on the Korean Peninsula. Complex postcolonial societies, viewed through the Manichean prism of free-market democracy versus Communism, were reduced to a mere binary compound from which "impure elements" had to be expunged. The oversimplified reality made it possible—and legitimate in American eyes—for successive U.S. administrations to adopt security policies that contributed to catastrophic outcomes in the Philippines, Korea, Indonesia, and ultimately in Indochina.

Although the relative calm of the 1990s is uncritically attributed either to America's overwhelming power or to Asia's zeal for material gains seen as obtainable through efficiency enhancement, here again we see a fortuitous conjuncture of identity, efficiency, and power that helped stabilize interstate relationships in Asia. As Katzenstein and Okawara argue in their chapter in this volume, the blending of bilateralism and multilateralism in Japan's security strategies—which contributed significantly to the strategic stability—was in part made possible by a recalibration of ambiguity in the institutional arrangements between Tokyo and Washington. In the same vein, when looking at the U.S.-China relationship, one can see a coupling of realist and liberal thinking in the Clinton administration's balancing of power politics and economic engagement, as exemplified by the 1995 Nye report and Washington's later shift on China's ascension to the WTO. At the same time, the Chinese leadership emphasized both the importance of China's economic integration with the rest of the world and the need to strengthen Beijing's material capabilities. On the Korean Peninsula, the first Bush and the Clinton administrations identified North Korea as "a rogue nation" and held on to the U.S. identity as a protector of South Korea, but within this structure room was still left for American diplomatic initiatives and the sunshine policy. This transformative possibility was even more evident in Southeast Asia, where various institutional linkages were contributing to the emergence of a nascent collective identity in the region.

In contrast, in the post–September 11 era, a danger emerged, the danger of a simplifying turn in the U.S. presence within the region. American positioning in Asia once more seems to hinge largely on a binary vision (this time with good and evil framed with reference to terrorism), paired with a preponderant emphasis on the utility of material power (thus slighting the roles of economic and institutional factors within the region). In other words, a realist worldview, refracted through the identity prism, divides the region into two camps. Asian states are either terrorist or not terrorist, or as President George W. Bush asserted in a broader categorization of the world, "with us or against us." Such an "us against them" bifurcation echoes the earlier ideological straightjacket imposed on the region during the Cold War, and constrains the space given to those in Asia to conceive of themselves and the United States in a much more complex and mutually acceptable way. This development has the potential to undermine the current multifaceted peace within the region and pull Asia back in the direction of heated confrontations and even open wars.

The North Korean crisis also shows that Washington's tacking hard in such a direction can result in short-term, expedient agreements among the major players that on the surface may appear to secure an even more stable Asian security dynamic. Bilateral relations between the United States and Japan have improved significantly over the last two years. Although the relationship between Beijing and Washington remains tenuous, it is notably better than it was during President Bush's first few months in office. Moreover, the Southeast Asian acceptance of U.S. military presence in the region has grown since the 2001 terrorist attacks on the United States. In addition, Bush's counterproliferation policies, spelled out in National Security Presidential Directive 17 and Homeland Security Presidential Directive 4, may provide a framework within which China and Japan could cooperate with the United States against potential proliferators like North Korea. Indeed, many countries in Asia, from Australia to the Philippines, share a common interest in nonproliferation, laying a basis on which the United States could consolidate its relations with them. In other words, one could argue that America has through its fight against terrorism consolidated its acceptance in the region, and done so in a way that has also made Asia more stable for state actors.

There have, however, been some costs, and they have already begun to be felt in a manner that seems to be detrimental to maintaining the existing order in the region. Thus, while the initial war on terrorism enjoyed some popular support within Asia, the expansion of U.S. global military power that has followed in its wake has evoked fairly strong domestic opposition in each of the states considered in this book. Moreover, the expansion of the conflict to Asia has already produced ominous reverberations within the region.

To begin with, the U.S.-led global war on terrorism has narrowed the political space within which Tokyo could exercise its "political caution [that] so far has always succeeded in minimizing the risk of being drawn into the far-flung and occasionally imprudent military actions of the U.S." (Katzenstein and Okawara, this volume). For example, in the initial phase of the war on terrorism, Tokyo maintained a delicate balance between its commitment to support the U.S. war against terrorism and its sensitivity to its Asian neighbors' concerns about its military might. Initially, Prime Minister Koizumi had committed Japan to a seven-point emergency plan and sent units of the Maritime Self-Defense Force but not Aegis, the most powerful units. As the expansion of the anti-terror war into Iraq and Washington's increasing pressure on Japan began to undermine the delicate balance, however, Tokyo sent its Aegis-class warships to the Indian Sea to support American forces operating in Iraq in December 2002. Furthermore, this step was followed in 2003 by the adoption of contingency measures that gave Tokyo wide-ranging powers in case of a national emergency. Such actions raise concerns among its neighbors that Japan's pacifist identity is being eroded. These worries about Japan are further exacerbated by a general apprehension that the United States is not only encouraging Japan's identity shift, but asserting its own unilateralist and realpolitik identity in a particularly virulent fashion. Thus, although there has been little dramatic change in the material capabilities of the United States and Japan, a subtle shift in Tokyo's posture, facilitated by the institution of the U.S.-Japan alliance, has exacerbated regional actors' preexisting sensitivities about Japan's role in Asia.

Yet, as Katzenstein and Okawara rightly note, it is premature to declare that Tokyo's political caution has been exhausted. Japan, for example, has maintained a degree of ambiguity in its definition of "emergency" or "areas surrounding Japan" that continues to allow for the pursuit of comprehensive security without alienating the East or the West. Such ambiguity, built into the institutional foundations of Japan's security policies, necessitates a constant negotiation with the United States as well as Asian neighbors over Japan's identity, and Tokyo has handled the negotiation with the political caution accounted for by Katzenstein and Okawara's eclectic approach.

While this new dynamic is slowly falling into place, Korea has been caught in a rapidly escalating crisis that may erupt into an open conflict. Here again, we observe a move in the conjuncture of power, institution, and identity in a direction that weakens stability. The 2000 summit meeting between Kim Dae-Jung and Kim Jong-Il had portended a new possibility for the two Koreas to move beyond the "kill or be killed" logic to a more benign conceptualization of each other's identity. That possibility was undermined by the post–9/11 Manichean framework promoted by the Bush administration, which squarely placed North Korea on the "axis of evil," coupled with new revelations about the North's limited nuclear weapons capabilities. That new worldview pushed North Korea's identity back to that of evil, reversing the transformative process that had begun to weaken the enmity over the Korean Peninsula. Such drastic changes in identity perception and social structure were accompanied by the termination of efforts to build institutional linkages, exemplified by the Korea Peninsula Energy Development Organization (KEDO), and the resurgence of efforts to increase military might. The rise of military tension caused by these developments also produced an unintended consequence—most dramatically seen in the mass candlelight vigils of 2002—of a profound reassessment of U.S. identity by the South Koreans.

The level of danger within the limited shift in North Korean material capabilities has been amplified by the hostile rhetoric produced in both the North and Washington. In other words, to a degree it is only within the social context of enmity that the North's limited nuclear capacity becomes so fraught with danger. The Agreed Framework of 1994 and the summit meeting of 2000 had the potential to turn the enmity into amity, which would have preempted Pyongyang's need to pursue its nuclear option and thus Washington's security concerns. But President Bush's axis of evil speech restored, if not re-created, the enmity, setting the two on a collision course. In other words, a particularly pointed constellation of power and identity has pushed the euphoric Korea of 2000 to the precarious one of 2003. Where the Korean Peninsula is headed is dependent as much on the power distribution among the two Koreas and the United States as on the configuration of identity needs. The North Korean regime needs to maintain poor relations with its adversaries so as to maintain its own internal coherence and sense of self while it desires an improvement for material gains; the South Korean government is torn between its nationalist identity that embraces the North as its brother, and the alliance identity that sees the United States as the only conceivable protector against the North; and the U.S. government's decisions are informed by its contradictory conceptualizations of its own identity as the protector of a small and vulnerable allied nation, and as the injured nation that must take unilateral actions to protect itself against potential threats from the likes of North Korea.

The shift in Sino-U.S. relations is cause for much less consternation—indeed, cooperation between Beijing and Washington appears to be on the rise—but within such a frame we also see worrying indications of the persistence of deeper tensions. In this sense, China's initial post–September 11 rhetorical support to the U.S.-led war against terrorism (via votes in favor of the two main UNGA resolutions condemning terrorism and limited policy efforts to substantiate such a position), as well as Chinese acquiescence to the U.S.-led war in Iraq, should not be allowed to obscure the signs of possible future conflict. The issue here is not one of China's increasing economic and military strength inevitably leading to a revisionist collision course with the United States. Rather, we are concerned by the debate within China over the extent to which the war on terrorism and in the Middle East is being used by Washington to consolidate American hegemony, and the degree to which Chinese elites view such a move as a threat to China. While it is clear that most elites in Beijing argued for China to work with the United States to support the war on terrorism, others expressed grave doubts about such a development. In the lead-up to the war on Iraq, the latter of these two sets of views appeared to gain prominence within China. Thus, although Beijing deferred from leading the opposition to the war, the Chinese media consistently dwelled more on the U.S. insistence on armed con-

frontation rather than on Iraqi misdeeds. In addition, Chinese leaders persistently expressed concern over the U.S. decision to wage the war outside of the UN framework. Moreover, in a return to the language used to denigrate America's 1999 involvement in the Kosovo War, policy journals in Beijing were again filled with
warnings of the dangers of U.S. unilateralism (*dandaozhuyi*) and new ideology of in-
terference (*xin ganshezhuyi*). This being said, the expression of such doubts about
U.S. actions quickly exited the public sphere following early American military success in Iraq. In other words, Chinese leaders and policy makers thought better of opposing the U.S. initiative (especially once Washington's initial victory in the region
appeared to be in hand). Nonetheless, the problematic U.S. occupation has been the
subject of repeated Chinese consternation.

Within such a context, the threat to enhanced Sino-American ties goes beyond the
insightful caution Johnston makes in this volume about the dangers of false expectations being created on both sides. Indeed, we would contend that the greater worry
relates to his broader point about the possibility of a relapse in China's commitment
to the status quo within the region, or more pointedly a reaction against perceived
American efforts to alter the security situation in the region in a way that is detrimental to fundamental Chinese interests and identities. Chinese elites may read shifts
in America's presence in Asia as being distinctly directed against China, constituting a
basic threat to its survival and Beijing's ability to maintain Chinese national unity. To
be clear, such a trend is at best inchoate and is given voice largely at the margins of
China's security discourse. However, even limited indications of such a development
are deserving of close attention. Any reorientation of Chinese strategic thinking and
national security policies in this direction will feed the spirals of "malign amplification" (Johnston, this volume) that are already creating a security dilemma between the
two sides, and lead to intensified confrontation between the two strongest military
powers within Asia. Moreover, in the latter part of 2003 such a destabilizing prospect
again began to loom large as tensions between Beijing and Washington grew vis-à-vis
Taiwan, and renewed questions about its status as a part of China that arose in the
lead-up to the island's March 2004 presidential election. Although Beijing has so far
largely blamed political figures in Taiwan for what is denigrated as "splittist activities"
(*fenlie huodong*), implicit anger over Washington's perceived support for such actions
(despite President Bush's public dressing down of Taiwan during Hu Jintao's December 2003 visit to Washington) is also readily apparent. In the event of more pro-
nounced Taiwanese moves toward independence it would certainly boil over.

As Khong notes, September 11 also had a profound impact on the security situation in Southeast Asia. In an immediate sense, it created new opportunities for the
expansion of American influence there within the context of the expanded war on
terrorism, creating a new terrain for regional institution building. However, such an
expanded role for the United States, ASEAN, and the states of Southeast Asia also has
its own costs. First, in the short term, a more prominent U.S. presence in Southeast

Asia is likely to actually increase the terrorist threat there (to both the United States and states within the region) by creating more targets and aggravating preexisting anti-U.S. sentiment. Second, as Khong touches upon in his chapter in this volume, there exist real questions about the extent ASEAN can adapt its agenda to the transnational nature of the war against terrorism. While he is optimistic about the "chances" of ASEAN and its members showing the flexibility to adapt to such a new set of challenges, his aside that such a process "will be neither smooth nor obvious" gives us pause, especially as ASEAN states have had real difficulties in dealing with other boundary-transgressing threats. Finally, as Khong also notes, the war on terrorism is forcing the states of Southeast Asia to confront the conventional wisdom within the region about the moderate nature of Muslims residing there. Over the long term, such a turn can only add to the already long list of challenges facing each of the states in the region. Indeed, it may well be that states in Southeast Asia have been emboldened in their own fights with separatists, and in the process the hope for negotiated settlements of such issues, and constructive U.S. pressure for such outcomes, has dissipated. In other words, the likelihood for intensified internal conflict has increased since September 11.

In sum, contrary to the expectations of neoliberals who exorcise uncertainty as an evil impediment to international cooperation, in Asia it was ambiguity that contributed to the relatively high level of stability in the region during the last decade. It allowed for multiple interpretations of the U.S. position, gives friends and enemies opportunities to maximize the underlying common strategic interests within the region (in peace and stability), minimizes potential controversy over insignificant differences (ones not strategically important to either side), and perhaps most importantly, provides face-saving ways for states within the region to accept the American position on issues on which the United States has no room for compromise. Contrary to realists who see uncertainty as a cause of security dilemma and war, states in East and Southeast Asia managed to take advantage of it through soft balancing, institution building, and identity negotiations. Moreover, contrary to constructivists who were concerned about negative consequences of conflictual identity configurations rooted in deeply held historical memories, Asian nations created a degree of ambiguity about their identities and used it as a public sphere where they could negotiate the meanings of their actions as well as their identities.

In short, the United States is indispensable to Asia's stability and peace, and for this reason the American presence is widely accepted within the region. In each of the countries we have analyzed in this volume, however, this is at best an ambivalent acceptance. Asians' ambivalence stems from their awareness that the stability and peace is significantly affected by the ways American leaders work with their Asian counterparts to create or recalibrate ambiguity. This task has proven difficult for successive American administrations, all the more so when they have attempted to impose upon ambiguous and complex reality a narrow binary framework by force.[1] Indeed, it is an increased awareness of both the necessity and elusiveness of maintaining such ambiguity that makes us less sanguine about the future than we were two years ago. Although we acknowledge the possibility that such policies can lead to short-term strategic cooperation, the stability won this way stands on a precarious, unidimensional foundation that negates such ambiguity, and thus will likely be short-lived. Failure to acknowledge the simple, albeit subtle, sources of Asian stability is a recipe for disaster in the region.

Conclusion

The book illustrates the pragmatism and prudence of analytical eclecticism. Its pragmatism is evident in its call for problem recognition and solving that motivates the studies in this volume. Its prudence is reflected in the care that eclectic sketches take to avoid the shortcomings of simplifying the complex reality of the contemporary Asian security dynamic within the confines of any one of the established research traditions. With a better understanding of the interaction between identity, power, and efficiency, the eclectic analyst provides not only a fuller explanation of Asian security, but also a warning of the danger that attends undermining the configuration of the three that currently supports stability and peace in Asia.

Analytical eclecticism's call for pragmatism and prudence is shared by many of the recent academic analyses of Asian security. This scholarship made conscious efforts to move beyond paradigmatic battles in its descriptions and explanations of the persistence of stability in Asia, while broadly agreeing that tranquility was the product of a complex set of influences (Alagappa 2003a, 1998a; Ikenberry and Mastanduno 2003; Kang 2003a; Friedberg 2002; Simon 2001). We acknowledge the compatibility between the themes within such work and the observations and arguments made in this volume. However, such general agreement notwithstanding, there are three important ways our eclectic approach parts company with other scholarly approaches.

First, in contrast to the majority of other recent edited volumes, the conceptual anchor of this book is not a call to broaden the way we think about security (Simon 2001; Alagappa 1998a), or to explain the surprisingly high degree of stability in Asia (Alagappa 2003a; Ikenberry and Mastanduno 2003). Rather, this book is grounded by our interest in exploring the source of the widely divergent prognoses for the region generated by different research traditions during the 1990s. This book was based upon a hunch that those who saw emerging order, as well as those who perceived enduring chaos, had shared a common tendency to accept as natural some of the basic features of the Asian security dynamic. This tendency was not so much the result of a researcher's oversight or to a poor research design, as it was the outcome of an explanatory sketch framed within one of research traditions that takes as given too many basic assumptions about actors and the world.

Second, and more importantly, we hear the refrain of inclusiveness that runs through so much of the new Asian security literature as a tune that tends to ring hollow for some of those singing it. In such cases, close listening reveals that the analysis that is "inclusive" actually consists of little more than the addition of a few superficial notes to scores that were completed long ago. Aaron Friedberg's (2002, 2000) recent reappraisals of his mid-1990s prediction about Asia's dire future exemplify this type of limited inclusiveness. Looking back at the past decade, Friedberg acknowledges that the quietude in Asia's present security dynamic exceeded his earlier expectations. However, he remains profoundly skeptical about the longevity of such calm. Moreover, despite conceding that a wide variety of material, institutional, and ideational sources support the current order (Friedberg and Ellings 2001: 8), he continues to privilege those variables that fit most comfortably within his preexisting view of the region (Friedberg 2002). In other words, Friedberg's vision of Asia remains rooted within a classical realist paradigm that prevents him from fully appreciating the diverse set of factors that this volume shows are currently shaping the Asian security dynamic. Such tendencies, as David Kang has noted, lead realists both to fall back on a "just wait" thesis about the region (imbalance in material power within Asia will lead to instability), and to hedge quite a bit on the time frame of, and evidentiary standards for, such a development (Kang 2003a: 63–65). In this sense, any criticism of the volume generated within such a thinly veiled paradigm-driven analysis is countered by several of the arguments advanced in the preceding chapters. At the same time, in light of the continuing influence of such assessments of the Asian security order in both academic and policy circles, we contend that it is now as imperative, if not more so, to point to the serious limitations of such a line of argument as it was more than a decade ago.

It is precisely such an aim that appears to have motivated the editors of three recent projects on Asian security (Alagappa 2003a, 1998a; Ikenberry and Mastanduno 2003) whose arguments are more genuinely inclusive and as such largely in accord with the claims forwarded in this book. However, in each case, the editors have attempted to fit too many explanatory variables under one cover, without an overarching intellectual theme that ties the variables together. Although some of these volumes argue for multivariate approaches, they tend to merely list explanatory variables or analytic frames that are deemed useful. They stop short of considering how an interaction among variables is attributable to the political phenomena they try to explain. This tendency constitutes another point of difference between this volume and the new Asian security literature.

Such a difference is first evident in G. John Ikenberry and Michael Mastanduno's volume (2003), which constructs a broad framework for the study of Asian security by outlining five distinct frames for analyzing the current security situation within the "Asia-Pacific." However, such frames are simply listed in the volume's introduction, with little attention given to how the causal factors emphasized within each one intersect and converge to produce particular outcomes within the region. Along these lines, the editors state in a blanket fashion that "the sources of stability and in-stability in the Asia-Pacific are found in security relations, economic relations, and in the intersection of the two" (Ikenberry and Mastanduno 2003: 3). Beyond such a generality, Ikenberry and Mastanduno hint that it is in turning to the U.S. role in the region that one may find the "crucial variable that will determine whether security conflicts are managed effectively and whether stability endures" (Ikenberry and Mas-tanduno 2003: 3). However, the concluding chapter of the volume picks up this theme, only via a series of four stylized scenarios of the future of Asian-Pacific secu-rity order and a focus on the prospects for shifts in the U.S. presence in the region (largely within the context of American domestic political variables).

    We agree that what happens in the United States is likely to have a profound im-pact on the type of hegemonic presence America projects in Asia. However, eclecti-cism has also shown that the most important point of analysis here is not to concen-trate primarily on Washington's moves. Rather, it is only when the projection of U.S. power in the region is placed within the context of embryonic institutions and shift-ing identities there that it is possible to develop compelling explanations of how the Asian security dynamic is evolving. In other words, the future of Asian security is not, as Ikenberry and Mastanduno suggest, primarily about the "critical choices" fac-ing the United States. It lies in how the decisions made along each of these lines will play out in the region within the triumvirate of variables emphasized in these pages.

    In contrast, Muthiah Alagappa's series of edited volumes on Asian security places a clear emphasis on precisely this type of eclectic analysis. The inaugural volume of the series (1998b) convincingly outlines the importance of developing a broad defi-nition of security and forwards the argument that it is essential to move beyond treat-ing ideational and material influences as mutually exclusive explanations of security outcomes in the region. In the 1998 volume, not only does Alagappa call attention to the "interplay of ideas, interest and power" in producing particular security out-comes, but he also argues that locating the relationship among them requires com-bining "the insights of related paradigms and theories, especially those of realism and constructivism" (p. 675). In the 2003 volume, he refers directly to the necessity of uti-lizing "eclectic theorizing in understanding and explaining Asian security behavior" (Alagappa 2003a: xii). He also emphasizes the weakness of "single general theory" and the need to frame problems within the interface between such theories and the power of eclecticism to build "on the insights of other theories" (p. xiii). In short, Alagappa practices what analytical eclecticism preaches.

    Despite the value of his approach, Alagappa's works illustrate both the utility and the limitations of additive complementarity. Although the case studies in his volumes present fuller accounts of security phenomena in Asia, they pay little attention to the process of generating questions or detecting distinct phases of complementarity, pre-ferring instead to focus on the task of identifying which outcomes match best with which theoretical frame. Often the exercise is little more than starting with realism, adding a dose of liberalism and a helping of constructivism, and in the process hoping to gain a more comprehensive understanding of the issues at hand. Although such additive complementarity can contribute significantly to our understanding of Asian security, it falls short of other forms of the complex complementarities explored in this volume. Indeed, throughout Alagappa's project, more attention is paid to shedding light on the aspects of security that have been overlooked (human security, internal security, regional order) than to specifying the independent variables at play in the region (the relationship between power, institutions, and ideas). This volume has attempted to avoid such pitfalls by focusing more intently on generating compelling explanations for security puzzles in the region, grounding analysis within the broader eclectic tradition in the social sciences, and explicitly outlining the multiplicity of ways such theorizing may be operationalized.

Not only does analytical eclecticism productively engage the recent scholarship on Asian security, it also provides an effective tool kit for analyzing Asian regionalism. Thus far, Asian regionalism has been analyzed within one of the three research traditions, resulting in partial and incomplete understandings of the status and process of regionalization. Explanatory sketches that emphasize material structural conditions portray Asia as a series of power balancing states caught in security dilemmas (Ng-Quinn 1986). Yet they fail to understand that security dilemmas between some states—for example, between North and South Korea, China and Taiwan, and Japan and its neighbors—stem from more fundamental competition for legitimate statehood. Other explanatory sketches zero in on the absence or relative weakness of formal institutions that help Asian states manage their relationships, even if some of them acknowledge that Asian states are enmeshed in informal and personalized "networks" (Ikenberry 2001; Katzenstein 1997). Those who worry about the absence of formal multilateral institutions fail to recognize the ways in which competing states are engaged in institutionalized identity negotiation in public spheres. Finally, a small but growing number of scholars who underline the importance of shared values and ideas claim that some subregions, if not all of Asia, are emerging as a security community (Acharya 2001, 1998; Busse 1999). Yet they neglect the extent to which the process of common identity production is impeded, or facilitated, by the distribution of material capability and by the presence of institutionalized fora of interaction. In order to understand the current status of Asian regionalization and to explain the process of Asia-making, we need explanatory sketches that frame power competition within the context of identity negotiation in institutionalized spheres of interaction.

Furthermore, we suspect that the utility of eclectic theorizing extends beyond Asia. The trialectics of identity, power, and efficiency may well produce different "constitutional structures" in other world regions (Reus-Smit 1999). For example, the axis between identity and power may be most salient in Asia; the one between identity and efficiency, in Europe; and the one between power and efficiency, in the United States. As all the authors in this volume argue, the politics of naming and power politics play a particularly prominent role in Asia, perhaps more so than in Europe and the United States. Although we are not in a position to venture an answer as to why this may be true, we can conjecture that how states construe moral purposes and procedural justices have conditioned the evolution of cooperation and competition prevalent within and between contemporary state and society, just as in Asia.

Finally, analytical eclecticism may be used to shed new light on the writings of classical scholars who have often been thought of as founding or belonging to particular research traditions (Kubálková 1998; Lebow 2001). Rereading some of the classics reminds us that eclectic theorizing is not new; it is arguably as old as the study of international relations. From Thucydides to Carr, many were preoccupied with understanding the complex interaction among three concepts—power, market, and ideas—as they tried to explain the causes of war and peace. Some scholars narrowed their focus to an investigation of the dialectics between military power and economic capability, between power and idea, or between market and idea. Others criticized contemporary theories for overemphasizing one of the three. But such criticism was rarely meant to provide justification for exclusive reliance on only one of the three concepts to the exclusion of the other two. As Albert Hirschman points out, it is inherently more difficult to be eclectic, all the more so when the analyst is dealing with issues of life and death (Hirschman 1982). Yet, as we have argued here, by moving beyond paradigmatic debates we can hope to recognize research problems that have eluded scholars in the past and better understand how the interactions between identity, power, and efficiency are shaping Asian security.

Note

1. For example, Frum and Perle (2003) advocate precisely this kind of policy: the United States must bring its superior material capability to bear upon "evil" in order to end it.

Bibliography

Acharya, Amitav. 2003. "Regional Institutions and Asian Security Order: Norms, Power, and Prospects for Peaceful Change." In Alagappa, ed., 2003a, *Asian Security Order*, 210–40.

———. 2001. *Constructing a Security Community in Southeast Asia: ASEAN and the Problem of Regional Order*. New York: Routledge.

———. 2000a. *The Quest for Identity: International Relations of Southeast Asia*. Oxford: Oxford University Press.

———. 2000b. "Regional Institutions and Security Order in Asia." Paper prepared for the second workshop on Security Order in the Asia-Pacific, Bali, Indonesia (29 May–2 June).

———. 1999a. "Containment, Engagement, or Counter-dominance? Malaysia's Response to the Rise of China." In Johnston and Ross, eds., 1999, *Engaging China*, 129–51.

———. 1999b. "Institutionalism and Balancing in the Asia Pacific Region: ASEAN, U.S. Strategic Frameworks, and the ASEAN Regional Forum." Unpublished paper.

———. 1999c. "Realism, Institutionalism, and the Asian Economic Crisis." *Contemporary Southeast Asia* 21, 1 (Apr.): 1–29.

———. 1999d. "Regionalism and the Emerging (Intrusive) World Order: Sovereignty, Autonomy, Identity." CSGR 3rd annual conference, After the Global Crises: What Next for Regionalism? Scarman House, University of Warwick (16–18 Sept.).

———. 1998. "Collective Identity and Conflict Management in Southeast Asia." In Adler and Barnett, eds., 1998, *Security Communities*, 198–227.

———. 1995. "A Regional Security Community in Southeast Asia?" *Journal of Strategic Studies* 18, 3 (Sept.): 175–200.

———. 1991. "The Association of Southeast Asian Nations: 'Security Community' or 'Defense Community'?" *Pacific Affairs* 64, 2 (Summer): 159–77.

———. 1990. *A Survey of Military Cooperation among the ASEAN States: Bilateralism or Alliance?* Occasional Paper no. 14. Toronto: Centre for International and Strategic Studies.

Adler, Emanuel, and Michael Barnett, eds. 1998. *Security Communities*. New York: Cambridge University Press.

Advisory Group on Defense Issues. 1994. *The Modality of the Security and Defense Capability of Japan: The Outlook for the Twenty-first Century* (12 Aug.). Tokyo.

Agence France Press. 2001. "Asean Security Group to Evolve into Asia-Pacific Mediator." Manila (20 July).

———. 1999. "U.S., Japan and South Korea Use Carrot and Stick on North Korea." Singapore (27 July).

Alagappa, Muthiah, ed. 2003a. *Asian Security Order: Instrumental with Normative Contractual Features.* Stanford, CA: Stanford University Press.

———. 2003b. "Introduction: Predictability and Stability Despite Challenges." In Alagappa, ed., 2003a, *Asian Security Order*, 1–32.

———. 2001a. "Investigating and Explaining Change: An Analytical Framework." In Alagappa, ed., 2001b, *Coercion and Governance*, 29–66.

———, ed. 2001b. *Coercion and Governance: the Declining Political Role of the Military in Asia.* Stanford, CA: Stanford University Press.

———. 2000. "Asia-Pacific Regional Security Order: Introduction and Analytical Framework." Paper prepared for the second workshop on Security Order in the Asia-Pacific, Bali, Indonesia (29 May–2 June).

———, ed. 1998a. *Asian Security Practice: Material and Ideational Influences.* Stanford, CA: Stanford University Press.

———. 1998b. "Conceptualizing Security: Hierarchy and Conceptual Traveling." In Alagappa, ed., 1998a, *Asian Security Practice*, 677–700.

Alford, Robert R. 1998. *The Craft of Inquiry: Theories, Methods, Evidence.* Oxford: Oxford University Press.

Alker, Hayward. 1996. "Beneath Tit for Tat." In Hayward Alker, *Rediscoveries and Reformulations: Humanistic Methodologies for International Studies*, 303–31. Cambridge, UK: Cambridge University Press.

Allen, Ken. 2001. "PLA Navy Building at the Start of a New Century." *C.N.A. Corporation, Conference Report* (July). Alexandria, VA.

AMS [Academy of Military Sciences Strategy Department]. 2000. *2000–2001 nian zhanlüe pinggu* [2000–2001 strategic assessments]. Beijing: Military Sciences Press.

Ang, Cheng Guan. 1997. "United States East Asian Strategy Initiatives." *Pointer* 23, 4: 65–74.

Antolik, Michael. 1990. *ASEAN and the Diplomacy of Accommodation.* Armonk, NY: M. E. Sharpe.

Araki, Junichi. 2000. *Japan's Security Strategy and the Relevance and Difficulties of New Roles for the Japan Self-Defense Force.* USJP Occasional Paper 00–01. Program on U.S.-Japan Relations, Harvard University.

Armacost, Michael H., and Kenneth B. Pyle. 2001. "Japan and the Engagement of China: Challenges for U.S. Policy Coordination." *NBR Analysis* 12, 5 (Dec.): 1–62.

Armitage, Richard, and Joseph S. Nye, Jr. 2000. *The United States and Japan: Advancing toward a Mature Partnership* (Oct.). Washington, D.C.: National Defense University, Institute for National Strategic Studies.

Art, R. J. 2003. *A Grand Strategy for America.* Ithaca, NY: Cornell University Press.

Asagumo shimbun-sha. 1998. *Bōei hando bukku* [Defense handbook]. Tokyo: Asagumo shimbun-sha.

Asahi Evening News. 2000. "Asia-Pacific States Vow to Combat Drugs." (28 Jan.).

———. 1999. "Tokyo to Buy U.S. Satellite Parts." (30 Sept.).

Asahi shimbun. 2003. "Cabinet Extends MSDF Refueling Duties." (10–11 May).

———. 2002a. "MSDF Ships Leave for Indian Ocean." (13 Feb.).

———. 2002b. "Time to Come Home." (11–12 May).

———. 2002c. "Tai tero shien: Hantoshi enchō wo kakugi de kettei" [Cabinet decides on half-year extension of support for antiterrorism operations]. (17 May) evening, 4th ed.

————. 2002d. "Six More Months for Anti-terror Aid." (20 Nov.).

————. 2001a. "MSDF Heads for Indian Ocean." (10–11 Nov.).

————. 2001b. "Aegis kan haken miokuri" [Aegis ship will not be dispatched]. (17 Nov.), 14th ed.

————. 2001c. "Three MSDF Ships Bound for Diego Garcia." (20 Nov.).

————. 2001d. "Boeing Wins Nod as SDF Refueler." (15–16 Dec.).

————. 1999a. "Shūhen jitai: chiriteki yōso fukumu" [Situation in areas surrounding Japan includes geographic factor]. (27 Jan.), 14th ed.

————. 1999b. "Sensei kōgeki: 'Kenpō jō mitomerarezu'" [Preemptive attack: "unconstitutional"]. (5 Mar.), 14th ed.

————. 1998a. "Shūhen jitai no chiriteki han'i: Kyokutō to sono shūhen" [Geographic scope of situation in areas surrounding Japan: the Far East and its surrounding areas]. (23 May), 14th ed.

————. 1998b. "Seifu hokubei kyokuchō wo kōtetsu" [Government removes director of North American Affairs Bureau from post]. (7 July) evening, 4th ed.

————. 1998c. "Shūhen jitai ni aimaisa" [Situation in areas surrounding Japan is ambiguous]. (8 July), 14th ed.

————. 1997. "'Sentō kuiki to issen': Kaijō kuwake muzukashii" ["Away from combat zone": Drawing line in ocean difficult]. (29 Oct.), 14th ed.

ASEAN Secretariat. 1999. *ASEAN Regional Forum: Document Series 1994–1998*. Jakarta.

————. 1992. The Twenty-fifth ASEAN Ministerial Meeting and Post Ministerial Conferences with the Dialogue Partners, Manila (21–26 July). Jakarta.

Ashley, Richard K. 1995. "The Powers of Anarchy: Theory, Sovereignty, and the Domestication of Global Life." In James Der Derian, ed., *International Relations: Critical Investigations*, 94–128. New York: New York University Press.

Auer, James E. 1998. "A Win-Win Alliance for Asia." *Japan Times* (8 Aug.).

Baek, Kwang-Il, Ronald D. McLaurin, and Chung-In Moon. 1989. *The Dilemma of Third World Defense Industries: Supplier Control or Recipient Autonomy?* Boulder, CO: Westview Press.

Ball, Desmond. 2000. "Military Balance in the Asia Pacific: Trends and Implications." Paper prepared for the 14th Asia-Pacific Roundtable, Kuala Lumpur (3–7 June).

Ball, Desmond, and Amitav Acharya, eds. 1999. *The Next Stage: Preventive Diplomacy and Security Cooperation in the Asia-Pacific*. Canberra: Strategic and Defence Studies Centre, Australian National University and Singapore, Institute of Defence and Strategic Studies, Nanyang Technical University.

Bandow, Doug. 1999. "Old Wine in New Bottles: The Pentagon's East Asia Security Strategy Report." *Policy Analysis* 344 (18 May). Cato Institute.

————. 1996. *Tripwire: Korea and U.S. Foreign Policy in a Changed World*. Washington, D.C.: Cato Institute.

Barnett, Michael N. 1996. "Identity and Alliances in the Middle East." In Katzenstein, ed., 1996c, *The Culture of National Security*, 400–47.

Bates, Robert, Avner Greif, Margaret Levi, Jean-Laurent Rosenthal, and Barry Weingast. 1998. *Analytic Narratives*. Princeton, NJ: Princeton University Press.

BBC. 2000. "South Daily Views Direction of Pyongyang-Russia Relations." *BBC Summary of World Broadcasts* (9 Feb.).

Beldecos, Nick, and Eric Heginbotham. 1995. "The Conventional Military Balance in Korea." *Breakthroughs* 4, 1 (Spring): 1–8.

Ben-David, Joseph. 1978. "Progress and Its Problems: Toward a Theory of Scientific Growth." *American Journal of Sociology* 84, 3 (Nov.): 743–45.

Berger, Peter. L., and Thomas Luckmann. 1966. *The Social Construction of Reality: A Treatise in the Sociology of Knowledge*. New York: Anchor Books.

Berger, Samuel. 1997. "A Foreign Policy Agenda for the Second Term" (27 Mar.). Washington, D.C.: Center for Strategic and International Studies.

Berger, Thomas. 2000. "Set for Stability? Prospects for Conflict and Cooperation in East Asia." *Review of International Studies* 26,3: 405–28.

Bessho, Koro. 1999. *Identities and Security in East Asia*. Adelphi Paper 325. Oxford: International Institute for Strategic Studies.

Betts, Richard. 1993/94. "Wealth, Power and Instability: East Asia and the United States after the Cold War." *International Security* 18, 3 (Winter): 34–77.

Blair, Dennis C., and John T. Hanley, Jr. 2001. "From Wheels to Webs: Reconstructing Asia-Pacific Security Arrangements." *Washington Quarterly* 24, 1 (Winter): 7–17.

Bleiker, R. 2001. "Identity and Security in Korea." *Pacific Review* 14, 1: 121–48.

Bōeichō [Defense Agency]. 2000. *Bōei hakusho* [Defense white paper]. Tokyo: Okurashō Insatsu-kyoku.

———. 1999. *Bōei hakusho* [Defense white paper]. Tokyo: Okurashō Insatsu-kyoku.

Bourdieu, Pierre. 1977. *Outline of a Theory of Practice*. Trans. Richard Nice. New York: Cambridge University Press.

Bracken, Paul. 1999. *Fire in the East*. New York: Harper Collins.

Brooke, James. 2002. "Japanese Wage Peace with Talks and Money, Pleasing Asians." *New York Times* (8 Dec.): A15.

———. 2001. "Koizumi Calls for Vigilance after Japan Sinks Suspicious Boat." *New York Times* (24 Dec.): A9.

Bruce, Katherine. 1996. "Fighter Jet Makers Compete at Seoul Air Show." *Reuter Asia-Pacific Business Report* (21 Oct.).

Bueno de Mesquita, Bruce, and James D. Morrow. 1999. "Sorting through the Wealth of Notions." *International Security* 24, 2 (Fall): 56–73.

Busse, Nikolas. 2000. *Die Entstehung von kollektiven Identitäten: Das Beispiel der ASEAN-Staaten* [The rise of collective identity: The example of the ASEAN states]. Baden-Baden: Nomos.

———. 1999. "Constructivism and Southeast Asian Security." *Pacific Review* 12, 1: 39–60.

———. 1998. "Sicherheitspolitik und Identität: Das Beispiel der ASEAN-Staaten" [Security Policy and Identity: The Example of the ASEAN States]. Thesis presented in the field of Political Science at the Free University of Berlin (10 July).

Buzan, Barry, and Gerald Segal. 1994. "Rethinking East Asian Security." *Survival* 36, 2: 3–21.

Campbell, David. 1992. *Writing Security: United States Foreign Policy and the Politics of Identity*. Minneapolis: University of Minnesota Press.

Campbell, John L., and Ove K. Pedersen. 2001. "The Second Movement in Institutional Analysis." In John L. Campbell and Ove K. Pedersen, eds., *The Rise of Neoliberalism and Institutional Analysis*, 249–81. Princeton, NJ: Princeton University Press.

Camroux, David. 1994. *"Looking East" . . . and Inwards: Internal Factors in Malaysian Foreign Relations during the Mahatir Era, 1981–1994*. Australia-Asia Paper no. 72. Brisbane, Australia: Griffith University.

Capie, David H., Paul M. Evans, and Aikiko Fukushima. 1998. "Speaking Asian Pacific Security: A Lexicon of English Terms with Chinese and Japanese Translations and a Note on the Japanese Translation." Working paper, University of Toronto–York University, Joint Centre for Asia Pacific Studies, Toronto, Canada.

Carlson, Allen. 2002. *Protecting Sovereignty, Accepting Intervention: The Dilemma of Chinese Foreign*

Relations in the 1990s. China Policy Series no. 18. Washington D.C.: National Committee on United States-China Relations.

———. 2000. "The Lock on China's Door: Chinese Foreign Policy and the Sovereignty Norm." Ph.D. dissertation, Yale University.

Carlson, Allen, and J. J. Suh. 2002. "Discourse on Discourse." Unpublished note to authors, Cornell Security Workshop on Rethinking Security in East Asia (21 May).

Carr, E. H. 1940. *The Twenty Years Crisis, 1919–1939.* London: Macmillan.

Cha, Victor. 2001. *The Future of America's Alliances in Asia: The Importance of Enemies or Ideas?* (Aug.) Paper for Georgetown Project on the Future of America's Alliances in Asia.

———. 2000. "Abandonment, Entrapment, and Neoclassical Realism in Asia: The United States, Japan, and Korea." *International Studies Quarterly* 44: 261–91.

———. 1999. "Engaging China: The View from Korea." In Johnston and Ross, eds., 1999, *Engaging China*, 32–56.

———. 1997. "Realism, Liberalism, and the Durability of the U.S.-South Korean Alliance." *Asian Survey* 37, 7 (July): 609–23.

Cheng, Joseph Y. S. N.d. "China's ASEAN Policy in the 1990s: Pushing for Multipolarity in the Regional Context." Unpublished paper. Contemporary China Centre, City University of Hong Kong.

Christensen, Thomas J. 2001a. "China." In Ellings and Friedberg, eds., 2001, *Strategic Asia*, 39–47.

———. 2001b. "Posing Problems without Catching Up: China's Rise and Challenges for U.S. Security Policy." *International Security* 25, 4 (Spring): 5–40.

———. 1999. "China, the U.S.-Japan Alliance, and the Security Dilemma in East Asia." *International Security* 23, 4 (Spring): 49–80.

CICIR [China Institute of Contemporary International Relations]. 2000. *Zonghe guoli pinggu xitong: Yanjiu baogao* [System for estimating comprehensive national strength: Research report]. Beijing: China Institute of Contemporary International Relations.

Clarke, Donald C. 2002. Statement Before the Congressional Executive Commission on China (6 June). www.cecc.gov/pages/hearings/060602/clarke.php3.

Cohen, Paul A. 1997. *History in Three Keys: The Boxers as Event, Experience, and Myth.* New York: Columbia University Press.

Collier, Kit. 1999. *The Armed Forces and Internal Security in Asia: Preventing the Abuse of Power.* Occasional Papers, Politics and Security Series no. 2. (Dec.). Honolulu: East-West Center.

Commission on America's National Interests. 1996. *America's National Interests.* Cambridge, MA.

"Competing Claims: Self-Determination, Security and the United Nations." 2000. Rapporteurs' report, University of Denver conference (29 Nov.–1 Dec.). www.ipacademy.org/Publications/Reports/Research/PublRepoReseCompClaims_body.htm.

Conybeare, John A. C. 1994. "Arms versus Alliances: The Capital Structure of Military Enterprise." *Journal of Conflict Resolution* 38, 2 (June): 215–35.

Copper, John F. 2002. "The 'Glue' That Holds China Together." *The World and I* 7 (July): 20–25.

Cossa, Ralph A. 1996. "Multilateralism, Regional Security, and the Prospects for Track II in East Asia." *NBR Analysis* 7, 5 (Dec.): 25–38.

Council on Foreign Relations. 1998. *The U.S.-Japan Security Alliance in the Twenty-first Century: Prospects for Incremental Change.* Study Group Papers by Michael J. Green and Mike M. Mochizuki. New York: Council on Foreign Relations.

Council on Foreign Relations Independent Study Group. 1998. *The Tests of War and the Strains of Peace: The U.S.-Japan Security Relationship.* New York: Council on Foreign Relations.

Cox, Robert. 1981. "Social Forces, States, and World Orders: Beyond International Relations Theory." *Millennium: Journal of International Studies* 10, 2 (Summer): 126–55.

Crenshaw, Martha. 2002. "Terrorism, Strategies, and Grand Strategies: Domestic or Structural Constraints?" Paper prepared for the 43rd annual convention of the International Studies Association, New Orleans (24–27 Mar.).

Cumings, Bruce. 1997. "Time to End the Korean War." *Atlantic Monthly* 279 (Feb.): 71–76.

———. 1984. "The Origins and Development of the Northeast Asian Political Economy: Industrial Sectors, Product Cycles, and Political Consequences." *International Organization* 38, 1: 1–40.

———. 1983. "American Hegemony in Northeast Asia: Security and Development." In Morris H. Morley, ed., *Crisis and Confrontation*, 80–106. New York: Columbia University Press.

Da Cunha, Derek, ed. 2000. *Southeast Asian Perspectives on Security*. Singapore: Institute of Southeast Asian Studies.

"Declaration on the Granting of Independence to Colonial Countries and Peoples." 1961. General Assembly res. 1514 (XV), 15 U.N. GAOR Supp. (No. 16) at 66, United Nations doc. A/4684.

Defense Agency. 2000. *Defense of Japan 1999*. Tokyo: Japan Times.

Defense Monitor. 1991. "We Arm the World: U.S. Is Number One Weapons Dealer." 20, 4: 3.

Deng Yong. 2001. "Hegemon on the Offensive: Chinese Perspectives on U.S. Global Strategy." *Political Science Quarterly* 116, 3 (Fall): 343–65.

Department of Defense. 2001. *Quadrennial Defense Review Report* (30 Sept.). http://www.defenselink.mil/pubs/qdr2001.pdf.

———. 1998. Report to Congress Pursuant to Section 1226 of the FY98 National Defense Authorization Act, *Future Military Capabilities and Strategy of the People's Republic of China*.

———. 1990. *Soviet Military Power 1990*. Washington, D.C.: U.S. Government Printing Office.

Desch, Michael C. 1998. "Culture Clash: Assessing the Importance of Ideas in Security Studies." *International Security* 23, 1 (Summer): 141–70.

Dessler, David. 1999. "Constructivism within a Positivist Social Science." *Review of International Studies* 25 (Jan.): 123–37.

Deudney, Daniel H. 1995. "The Philadelphia System: Sovereignty, Arms Control, and Balance of Power in the American States-Union, 1787–1861." *International Organization* 49 (Spring): 191–228.

Deudney, Daniel H., and G. John Ikenberry. 1993. "The Logic of the West." *World Policy Journal* 10, 4 (Winter): 17–26.

Deutsch, Karl W., et al. 1957. *Political Community and the North Atlantic Area*. Princeton, NJ: Princeton University Press.

Diesing, Paul. 1991. *How Does Social Science Work? Reflections on Practice*. Pittsburgh: University of Pittsburgh Press.

DiFilippo, Anthony. 2002. *The Challenges of the U.S.-Japan Military Arrangement: Competing Security Transitions in a Changing International Environment*. Armonk, NY: M. E. Sharpe.

Donnelly, Jack. 1986. "International Human Rights: A Regime Analysis." *International Organization* 40, 3 (Summer): 599–642.

Downs, George W., David M. Rocke, and Peter N. Barsoom. 1998. "Managing the Evolution of Multilateralism." *International Organization* 52, 2 (Spring): 397–419.

Duffield, John S. 1994/95. "NATO's Functions after the Cold War." *Political Science Quarterly* 109, 5: 763–87.

Duffield, John S., Theo Farrell, Richard Price, and Michael C. Desch. 1999. "Correspondence: Isms and Schisms—Culturalism versus Realism in Security Studies." *International Security* 24, 1 (Summer): 156–80.

Dunnigan, James F. 1993. *How to Make War*. 3rd ed. New York: Quill.

———. 1988. *How to Make War*. New York: Quill.

Economist. 1994. "ASEAN's Failure: The Limits of Politeness." (28 Feb.): 43–44.

Eikenberry, Karl W. 1995. "Does China Threaten Asia-Pacific Regional Stability?" *Parameters* (Spring): 82–99.

Einhorn, Robert. 2002. "Proliferation Challenges in Asia." Comments at the IISS Asia Security Conference, Singapore (31 May–2 June). www.IISs.org/news.php?PHPSESSID=447d91d08506c2aa8d001033daf29c2b.

Ellings, Richard J., and Aaron L. Friedberg, eds. 2001. *Strategic Asia, 2001–02: Power and Purpose*. Seattle: National Bureau of Asian Research.

Elman, Colin, and Miriam Fendius Elman. 2003a. "Introduction: Appraising Progress in International Relations Theory." In Elman and Elman, eds., 2003c, *Progress in International Relations Theory*, 1–20.

———. 2003b. "Lessons From Lakatos." In Elman and Elman, eds., 2003c, *Progress in International Relations Theory*, 21–68.

———, eds. 2003c. *Progress in International Relations Theory: Metrics and Methods of Scientific Change*. Cambridge, MA: MIT Press.

———. 2002. "How Not To Be Lakatos Intolerant: Appraising Progress in IR Research." *International Studies Quarterly* 46, 2 (June): 231–62.

Emmers, Ralf. 2001. "The Influence of the Balance of Power Factor within the ASEAN Regional Forum." *Contemporary Southeast Asia* 23, 2: 275–91.

Emmerson, Donald. 1987. "ASEAN as an International Regime." *Journal of International Affairs* 41, 1 (Summer/Fall): 1–16.

Epps, Valerie. 1998. "Self-Determination in the China/Taiwan Context." *New England Law Review* 32, 3 (Spring). www.nesl.edu/lawrev/vol32/vol32–3/epps.htm.

Ertman, Michael. 1993. "North Korean Arms Capabilities and Implications: Nuclear, Chemical, and Ballistic Missiles." *Korea and World Affairs* 17, 4 (Winter): 605–26.

Evangelista, Matthew. 1999. *Unarmed Forces: The Transnational Movement to End the Cold War*. Ithaca, NY: Cornell University Press.

Evans, Paul M. 2003. "Between Regionalization and Regionalism: Policy Networks and Nascent East Asian Institutional Identity." In T. J. Pempel, ed., *Remapping East Asia: Deepening Regional Connectedness* (under review).

———. 1994. "The Dialogue Process on Asia Pacific Security Issues: Inventory and Analysis." In Paul M. Evans, ed., *Studying Asia Pacific Security: The Future of Research Training and Dialogue Activities*, 297–318. Toronto: University of Toronto and York University Joint Centre for Asia Pacific Studies.

Eyre, Dana P., and Mark C. Suchman. 1996. "Status, Norms, and the Proliferation of Conventional Weapons: An Institutional Theory Approach." In Katzenstein, ed., 1996c, *The Culture of National Security*, 79–113.

Fairbank, John, ed. 1968. *The Chinese World Order*. Cambridge, MA: Harvard University Press.

Fan Shaojun. 2002. "Canyu he peiyu guoji guanxi de zhidu jianshe" [Participate in and cultivate the institutional construction of international relations]. *Guoji guanxi xueyuan xuebao* [Journal of the School of International Studies] (Shenzhen) 2: 16–26.

Fang Ning, Wang Xiaodong, and Song Qiang. 1999. *Quanqiuhua yinying xia de Zhongguo zhi lu* [China's road under the shadow of globalization]. Beijing: Chinese Academy of Social Sciences Press.

Fararo, Thomas J. 1989. "The Spirit of Unification in Sociological Theory." *Sociological Theory* 7, 2 (Fall): 175–90.

Fearon, James, and Alexander Wendt. 2002. "Rationalism and Constructivism in International

Relations Theory." In Walter Carlsnaes, Thomas Risse, and Beth Simmons, eds., *Handbook of International Relations*, 52–72. Beverly Hills: Sage.

Feaver, Peter D., Gunther Hellmann, Randall L. Schweller, Jeffrey W. Taliaferro, William C. Wohlforth, Jeffrey W. Legro, and Andrew Moravcsik. 2000. "Correspondence: Brother, Can You Spare a Paradigm? (Or Was Anybody Ever a Realist?)." *International Security* 25, 1 (Summer): 165–93.

Feigenbaum, Evan A. 2001. "China's Challenge to Pax Americana." *Washington Quarterly* 24, 3 (Summer): 31–43.

Feng Zhaokui. 2000. "Guanyu ZhongRi guanxi de zhanlüe sikao" [Strategic thoughts on Sino-Japanese relations]. *Shijie jingji yu zhengzhi* [World economics and politics] 11.

Feske, Susanne. 1997. "Japan und die USA: Zivilmächte im asiatisch-pazifischen Raum?" [Japan and the U.S.: civilian powers in Asia-Pacific?]. Trier Arbeitspapiere zum DFG-Forschungsprojekt Zivilmächte in der internationalen Politik [Trier working papers for the DFG project Civilian Powers in International Politics]. Trier, Germany (July).

Fierke, K. M. 2002. "Links across the Abyss: Language and Logic in International Relations." *International Studies Quarterly* 46, 3 (Sept.): 331–54.

Finel, Bernard I. 2001/02. "Black Box or Pandora's Box: State Level Variables and Progressivity in Realist Research Programs." *Security Studies* 11, 2 (Winter): 187–227.

Finklestein, David M. 2001. "Chinese Perceptions of the Costs of a Conflict." In Andrew Scobell, ed., *The Costs of Conflict: The Impact on China of a Future War* (Oct.), 9–27. Carlisle, PA: Strategic Studies Institute.

———. 2000. "China's National Military Strategy" (Jan.). Alexandria, VA: C.N.A. Corporation.

Finnemore, Martha. 1996. *National Interests in International Society*. Ithaca, NY: Cornell University Press.

Fisher, Richard D., Jr. 2001. "China Not Yet an Ally." *China Brief* 1, 6 (27 Sept.). http://china. jamestown.org/pubs/view/cwe_001_006_002.htm.

Foot, Rosemary. 2000. "Global Institutions and the Management of Regional Security in the Asia Pacific." Paper prepared for the second workshop on Security Order in the Asia-Pacific, Bali, Indonesia (29 May–2 June).

Ford, Carl. 1992. Under Secretary of Defense, Testimony before U.S. House of Representatives, Committee on Foreign Affairs, Subcommittee on Arms Control and Subcommittee on Europe and the Middle East (23 Sept.).

Freeman, Michael. 1998. "National Self-Determination, Peace, and Human Rights." *Peace Review* 10, 2 (June): 157–63.

French, Howard W. 2002. "Koizumi's Visit to War Shrine Angers Japan's Neighbors." *New York Times* (22 Apr.): A13.

———. 2001. "Top Bush Aide Urges Japan to Form In-Depth Ties with U.S." *New York Times* (9 May): A10.

———. 2000. "U.S. Copters? No, No, No. Not in Their Backyard." *New York Times* (20 Jan.): A4.

Friedberg, Aaron L. 2002. "11 September and the Future of Sino-American Relations." *Survival* 44, 1: 33–50.

———. 2000. "The Struggle for Mastery in Asia." *Commentary* 110, 4 (Nov.): 17–27.

———. 1993/94. "Ripe for Rivalry: Prospects for Peace in a Multipolar Asia." *International Security* 18, 3 (Winter): 5–33.

Friman, H. Richard. 1999. "International Drug Control Policies: Variations and Effectiveness." Unpublished paper. Marquette University, Department of Political Science.

Frost, Frank. 1990. "Introduction: ASEAN since 1967—Origins, Evolution and Recent Developments." In Alison Broinowski, ed., *ASEAN into the 1990s*, 1–31. London: Macmillan.

Frühstück, Sabine, and Eyal Ben-Ari. 2002. "'Now We Show It All!' Normalization and the Management of Violence in Japan's Armed Forces." *Journal of Japanese Studies* 28, 1: 1–39.

Frum, David, and Richard Perle. 2003. *An End to Evil: How to Win the War on Terror*. New York: Random House.

Fukushima, Akiko. 1999a. *Japanese Foreign Policy: The Emerging Logic of Multilateralism*. Basingstoke: Macmillan.

———. 1999b. *Japan's Emerging View of Security Multilateralism in Asia*. Policy Paper no. 51 (June). Berkeley, CA: University of California Institute on Global Conflict and Cooperation.

Gaikō Forum (Foreign Affairs Forum). 1999. Special issue (Nov.).

Gaimushō [Ministry of Foreign Affairs]. 1999. *Gaikō seisho 1999* [Foreign affairs blue book 1999]. Vol. 1. Tokyo: Okurashō Insatsu-kyoku.

———. 1998. *Gaikō seisho 1998* [Foreign affairs blue book 1998]. Tokyo: Okurashō Insatsu-kyoku.

Ganesan, N. 2000. "ASEAN's Relations with Major External Powers." *Contemporary Southeast Asia* 22, 2: 258–78.

———. 1999. *Bilateral Tensions in Post-Cold War ASEAN*. Pacific Strategic Paper 9. Singapore: Institute of Southeast Asian Studies.

GAO [Government Accounting Office]. 2002. "World Trade Organization: Observations on China's Rule of Law Reforms." GAO-02–812T (6 June).

Gershman, John. 2002. "Is Southeast Asia the Second Front?" *Foreign Affairs* (July/Aug.): 60–74.

Gill, Bates. 2001. "Contrasting Visions: China, the United States, and World Order." Remarks to the U.S.-China Security Review Commission, Washington, D.C. (3 Aug.). www.uscc.gov/tesgil.htm.

Gilpin, Robert. 1981. *War and Change in World Politics*. Cambridge, UK: Cambridge University Press.

Glaser, Charles L. 1997. "The Security Dilemma Revisited." *World Politics* 50, 1: 177–81.

———. 1994/95. "Realists as Optimists: Cooperation as Self Help." *International Security* (Winter): 50–90.

Goldstein, Avery. 2002. "Across the Yalu: China's Interest and the Korean Peninsula in a Changing World." Paper prepared for New Directions in Chinese Foreign Policy: A Conference in Honor of Allen S. Whiting, Fairbank Center for East Asian Research, Harvard University (Nov.).

———. 2001a. *Deterrence and Security in the Twenty-first Century: China, Britain, France, and the Enduring Legacy of the Nuclear Revolution*. Stanford, CA: Stanford University Press.

———. 2001b. "The Diplomatic Face of China's Grand Strategy: A Rising Power's Emerging Choice." *China Quarterly* 168 (Dec.): 835–64.

Goldstein, Judith, and Robert Keohane. 1993. "Ideas and Foreign Policy: An Analytic Framework." In Robert Keohane and Judith Goldstein, eds., *Ideas and Foreign Policy*, 3–30. Ithaca, NY: Cornell University Press.

Goldstein, Steven, and Randall Schriver. 2001. "An Uncertain Relationship: The United States, Taiwan and the Taiwan Relations Act." *China Quarterly* 165 (Mar.): 147–72.

Goose, Stephen. 1987. "The Military Situation on the Korean Peninsula." In John Sullivan and Roberta Foss, eds., *Two Koreas, One Future*, 55–93. Lanham, MD: University Press of America.

Gordon, M. R. 2002. "U.S. Nuclear Plan Sees New Weapons and New Targets." *New York Times* (10 Mar.): 1.

Gourevitch, Peter Alexis. 1999. "The Governance Problem in International Relations." In David A. Lake and Robert Powell, eds., *Strategic Choice and International Relations*, 137–64. Princeton, NJ: Princeton University Press.

Gourevitch, Peter, Takashi Inoguchi, and Courtney Purrington, eds. 1995. *United States–Japan Relations and International Institutions after the Cold War.* La Jolla, CA: Graduate School of International Relations and Pacific Studies, University of California, San Diego.

Graves, Ernest. 1989. "ROK-U.S. Security Cooperation: Current Status." In William J. Taylor, Young Koo Cha, and John Q. Blodgett, eds., *The Future of South Korean–U.S. Security Relations*, 13–26. Boulder, CO: Westview Press.

Green, Michael J. 2001. *Japan's Reluctant Realism: Foreign Policy Challenges in an Era of Uncertain Power.* New York: Palgrave.

———. 1999. "Managing Chinese Power: The View From Japan." In Johnston and Ross, eds., 1999, *Engaging China*, 152–75.

———. 1998. "State of the Field Report: Research on Japanese Security Policy." *Access Asia Review* 2, 1 (Sept.): 5–39.

Grieco, Joseph M. 1990. *Cooperation among Nations: Europe, America, and Non-Tariff Barriers to Trade.* Ithaca, NY: Cornell University Press.

Grinker, Roy. 1998. *Korea and Its Futures: Unification and the Unfinished War.* New York: St. Martin's Press.

Gurtov, Melvin. 2002. *Pacific Asia? Prospects for Security and Cooperation in East Asia.* Lanham, MD: Rowman and Littlefield.

Ha, Young-Sun. 1984. "South Korea." In James Everett Katz, ed., *Arms Production in Developing Countries: An Analysis of Decision Making*, 225–33. Lexington, MA: Lexington Books.

Haas, Ernst B. 2001. "Does Constructivism Subsume Neo-functionalism?" In Thomas Christiansen, Knud Erik Jørgensen, and Antje Wiener, eds., *The Social Construction of Europe*, 22–31. London: Sage.

Haas, Peter M., and Ernst B. Haas. 2002. "Pragmatic Constructivism and the Study of International Institutions." *Millennium* 31, 3: 573–601.

Habermas, Jürgen. 1984. *The Theory of Communicative Action.* Boston: Beacon Press.

Hall, John A., and T. V. Paul. 1999. "Preconditions for Prudence: A Sociological Synthesis of Realism and Liberalism." In T. V. Paul and John A. Hall, eds., *International Order and the Future of World Politics*, 67–77. Cambridge, UK: Cambridge University Press.

Hall, Peter A. 2003. "Adapting Methodology to Ontology in Comparative Politics." In James Mahoney and Dietrich Rueschemeyer, eds., *Comparative Historical Analysis in the Social Sciences*, 373–404. Cambridge, UK: Cambridge University Press.

Hamm, Taik-young. 1999. *Arming the Two Koreas: State, Capital, and Military Power.* New York: Routledge.

Haraguchi, Jiro. 1999. "Yakubutsu taisaku no genjō to kadai" [Current state of and problems concerning drug control]. *Keisatsu-gaku ronshū* [Journal of police science] 52, 7 (July): 20–37.

Harrison, Selig. 1994. "The United States and North Korea: The Nuclear Issue and Beyond." Paper prepared for the conference Korea in Transition: New Challenges and U.S. Policy, University of Bridgeport, Bridgeport, CT and Professors' World Peace Academy (16 Apr.).

Hartung, William D. 1994. *And Weapons for All.* New York: HarperCollins.

Hawkins, Charles. 2000. "The Peoples Liberation Army Looks to the Future." *Joint Forces Quarterly* 2 (Summer 2000): 12–16.

Hayes, Peter. 1994. "Hanging in the Balance: North-South Korean Military Capabilities."

Northeast Asia Peace and Security Network (25 Feb.). www.nautilus.org/pub/ftp/napsnet /papers/hayeso294b.txt.

——. 1991. *Pacific Powderkeg: American Nuclear Dilemmas in Korea.* Lexington, KY: Lexington Books.

He Xin. 1993. "Guanyu dangqian guonei xingshi de yi feng xin" [A letter concerning the current domestic situation] (4 May 1992), in He Xin, ed., *He Xin zhengzhi jingji lunwen ji* [He Xin's collected essays on politics and economics], 167–80. Harbin: Heilongjiang Education Press.

He Yinan. 1998. "The Effect of Historical Memories on Chinese Strategic Perception of Japan." Paper presented at the 94th annual meeting of American Political Science Association, Boston (Sept.).

Hearings on Proposed Sale of F-15 Aircraft to Saudi Arabia and U.S.-Saudi Commercial Disputes. 1992. Committee on Foreign Affairs, U.S. House of Representatives, Subcommittee on Arms Control and Subcommittee on Europe and the Middle East. Federal News Service transcript (23 Sept.).

Hedman, Eva-Lotta. 2002. "The Threat of 'Islamic Terrorism'? A View from Southeast Asia." *Harvard Asia Quarterly* 6, 2 (Spring): 38–43.

Heginbotham, Eric, and Richard J. Samuels. 1998. "Mercantile Realism and Japanese Foreign Policy." *International Security* 22, 4: 171–203.

Hellmann, Gunther, et al. 2003. "Are Dialogue and Synthesis Possible in International Relations?" *International Studies Review* 5, 1 (Mar.): 123–53.

Hemmer, Christopher, and Peter J. Katzenstein. 2002. "Why Is There No NATO in Asia? Collective Identity, Regionalism, and the Origins of Multilateralism." *International Organization* 56, 3: 575–607.

——. 2000. "Collective Identities and the Origins of Multilateralism in Europe But not in Asia in the Early Cold War." Paper prepared for the annual meeting of the American Political Science Association, Washington, D.C. (31 Aug.–3 Sept.).

Hirano, Kazuharu. 1998. "Hito no mitsuyu? Kokusai soshiki hanzai no genjō to gaiji keisatsu no taiō" [Alien smuggling? Current state of transnational organized crime and police countermeasures]. *Keisatsu-gaku ronshū* [Journal of police science] 51, 9 (Sept.): 33–51.

Hirschman, Albert O. 1982. "Rival Interpretations of Market Society: Civilizing, Destructive, or Feeble?" *Journal of Economic Literature* 20, 4: 1463–83.

——. 1981. *Essays in Trespassing.* New York: Cambridge University Press.

——. 1970. "The Search for Paradigms as a Hindrance to Understanding." *World Politics* 22, 2 (Apr.): 329–43.

Hishinuma, Takao. 1997. "Japan to Propose Antiterrorism Meeting at G-7 Summit." *Daily Yomiuri* (9 May).

Hong Yuan. 1999. "*Chaoxian zhan* shuping hui ceji" [Notes on the book review meeting on *Unrestricted Warfare*]. *Shijie jingji yu zhengzhi* [World economics and politics] 10: 76–79.

Hopf, Ted. 1998. "The Promise of Constructivism in International Relations Theory." *International Security* 23, 1 (Summer): 171–200.

Hoshino, Toshiya. 1999. "Nichi-Bei dōmei to Asia Taiheiyō no takoku-kan anzen hoshō: Nihon no shiten" [The Japan-U.S. alliance and multilateral security in the Asia-Pacific: A Japanese perspective]. In Hideki Kan, Glenn D. Hook, and Stephanie A. Weston, eds., *Asia Taiheiyō no chiiki chitsujo to anzen hoshō* [Regional order and security in the Asia-Pacific], 166–85. Kyoto: Minerva shobō.

Hosoya, Chihiro, and Tomohito Shinoda, eds. 1998. *Redefining the Partnership: The United States and Japan in East Asia.* Lanham, MD: University Press of America.

Huang Shixi. 2000. "Quanqiuhua dui guoji fa de yingxiang" [The influence of globalization on international law]. *Shijie jingji yu zhengzhi* [World economics and politics] 11: 28–33.

Huang Yuzhi, and Ma Fengqi. 1999. "21 shiji chu Zhongguo gaodeng jiaoyu fazhan de hongguan beijing" [The macro background to the development of China's higher education in the early twenty-first century]. *Liaoning gaodeng jiaoyu yanjiu* [Liaoning higher education studies] 1: 51–57.

Hughes, Christopher. 1997. *Taiwan and Chinese Nationalism: National Identity and Status in International Society*. London: Routledge.

———. 1996. "The North Korean Nuclear Crisis and Japanese Security." *Survival* 38, 2 (Summer): 79–103.

Huntsman, Jon M., Jr. 2002. Testimony to the Congressional-Executive Commission on China (6 June). http://usinfo.state.gov/regional/ea/uschina/huntsman.htm.

Huth, Paul. 1996. *Standing Your Ground: Territorial Disputes and International Conflict*. Ann Arbor: University of Michigan Press.

Huxley, Tim. 2000. *Defending the Lion City: The Armed Forces of Singapore*. Sydney: Allen and Unwin.

———. 1996. "Southeast Asia in the Study of International Relations: The Rise and Decline of a Region." *Pacific Review* 9, 2: 199–228.

Huxley, Tim, and Susan Willett. 1999. *Arming East Asia*. Adelphi Paper 329. Oxford: International Institute for Strategic Studies.

Ibrahim, Anwar. 1996. *The Asian Renaissance*. Singapore: Times Books International.

Igarashi, Takeshi, and Akio Watanabe. 1997. "Beyond the Defense Guidelines." *Japan Echo* (Dec.): 34–37.

Iitake, Koichi. 1999. "Air Refueling Project Postponed." *Asahi Evening News* (18 Dec.).

Ikenberry, G. John. 2001. *After Victory: Institutions, Strategic Restraint, and the Rebuilding of Order after Major Wars*. Princeton, NJ: Princeton University Press.

———, ed. 2002. *America Unrivaled: The Future of the Balance of Power*. Ithaca, NY: Cornell University Press.

Ikenberry, G. John, and Michael Mastanduno, eds. 2003. *International Relations Theory and the Asia-Pacific*. New York: Columbia University Press.

Ina, Hisayoshi. 1997. "An Inside Look at the Defense Guidelines Review: Tanaka Hitoshi Interviewed." *Japan Echo* (Dec.): 30–33.

Inoguchi, Takashi. 1996. "The New Security Setup and Japan's Options." *Japan Echo* (Autumn): 36–39.

Inoguchi, Takashi, and Grant B. Stillman, eds. 1997. *North-East Asian Regional Security*. Tokyo: United Nations University Press.

International Herald Tribune. 2000. "North Korea Power 'Growing.'" Seoul (17 Feb.).

International Institute for Strategic Studies. 1999. *The Military Balance 1999–2000*. London: International Institute for Strategic Studies.

———. 1997. *The Military Balance, 1997/98*. Oxford: Oxford University Press.

International Monetary Fund. 1997a. *Good Governance: The IMF's Role*. Washington, D.C.: International Monetary Fund.

———. 1997b. "IMF Wins Mandate to Cover Capital Accounts, Debt Initiative Put in Motion." *IMF Survey* (12 May): 129–33.

———. 1996. "ASEAN's Sound Fundamentals Bode Well for Sustained Growth." *IMF Survey* (25 Nov.): 377–78.

International Operations and Human Rights Subcommittee, House International Relations

Committee. 1996. Congressional testimony; Hearing of the International Operations and Human Rights Subcommittee (18 Dec.).

Jackson, Patrick Thaddeus. N.d. "Defending the West: Occidentalism and the Formation of NATO." Unpublished paper. Washington, D.C.: American University.

Japan Times. 2000. "Japan to Seek Asia-Centered Free Trade Zone." (9 Jan.): 1, 9.

Jepperson, Ronald L. 1998. "Relations among Different Theoretical Imageries." Paper presented at the annual meeting of the American Sociological Association, Boston.

Jervis, Robert. 2001. "Was the Cold War a Security Dilemma?" *Journal of Cold War Studies* 3, 1 (Winter): 36–60.

————. 1999. "Realism, Neoliberalism, and Cooperation: Understanding the Debate." *International Security* 24, 1 (Summer): 42–63.

————. 1997. *System Effects: Complexity in Political and Social Life.* Princeton, NJ: Princeton University Press.

————. 1978. "Cooperation Under the Security Dilemma." *World Politics* 30, 2 (Jan.): 167–214.

Jeshurun, Chandran, ed. 1993. *China, India, Japan and the Security of Southeast Asia.* Singapore: Institute of Southeast Asian Studies.

Jick, Todd D. 1979. "Mixing Qualitative and Quantitative Methods: Triangulation in Action." *Administrative Science Quarterly* 24, 4: 602–11.

Jin Xide. 2000a. "MeiRi tongmeng guanxi." In Zhang Yunling, ed., 2000a, *Huoban haishi duishou,* 253–304.

————. 2000b. "ZhongRi huoban guanxi de queli he weilai fazhan" [The establishment and future development of Sino-Japanese partnership relations]. In Zhang Yunling, ed., 2000a, *Huoban haishi duishou,* 202–51.

Jo, Toshio. 1999. "Tokyo Pledges to Finance U.N. Anti-Drug Plan." *Asahi Evening News* (3 Feb.).

Job, Brian. 2002. "Track 2 Diplomacy: Ideational Contribution to the Evolving Asian Security Order." In Alagappa, ed., 2003a, *Asian Security Order,* 241–79.

————. 2000. "Non-Governmental Regional Institutions in the Evolving Asia Pacific Security Order." Paper prepared for the second workshop on Security Order in the Asia-Pacific, Bali, Indonesia (29 May–2 June).

Johnson, Chalmers. 2000a. *Blowback: The Costs and Consequences of American Empire.* New York: Henry Holt.

————, ed. 2000b. "Dysfunctional Japan: At Home and in the World." Special issue of *Asian Perspective* 24, 4.

Johnson, James. 2002. "How Conceptual Problems Migrate: Rational Choice, Interpretation and the Hazards of Pluralism." *Annual Review of Political Science* 5: 223–48.

Johnston, Alastair Iain. Forthcoming. "Chinese Middle Class Attitudes towards International Affairs: Nascent Liberalization?" *China Quarterly.*

————. 2001. "Treating International Institutions as Social Environments." *International Studies Quarterly* 45, 4: 487–501.

————. 1999a. "Realism(s) and Chinese Security Policy in the Post–Cold War Period." In Ethan B. Kapstein and Michael Mastanduno, eds., *Unipolar Politics: Realism and State Strategies after the Cold War,* 261–318. New York: Columbia University Press.

————. 1999b. "The Myth of the ASEAN Way? Explaining the Evolution of the ASEAN Regional Forum." In Helga Haftendorn, Robert O. Keohane, and Celeste Wallander, eds., *Imperfect Unions: Security Institutions Over Time and Space,* 287–324. New York: Oxford University Press.

————. 1995. *Cultural Realism: Strategic Culture and Grand Strategy in Chinese History.* Princeton, NJ: Princeton University Press.

Johnston, Alastair Iain, and Robert S. Ross, eds. 1999. *Engaging China: The Management of an Emerging Power.* London: Routledge.

Jorgensen-Dahl, Arnfinn. 1982. *Regional Organization and Regional Order in Southeast Asia.* New York: St. Martin's Press.

Joyner, Sheryl D. 1983. *Pre and Post Marital Chaplain Ministry to Military Personnel and Korean Nations.* Washington, D.C.: Triton.

Kagan, Robert. 1997. "What China Knows That We Don't: The Case for a New Strategy of Containment." *Weekly Standard* (20 Jan.).

Kahler, Miles. 1995. *International Institutions and the Political Economy of Integration.* Washington, D.C.: Brookings Institution.

Kamiya, Matake. 1997. "The U.S.-Japan Alliance and Regional Security Cooperation: Toward a Double-Layered Security System." In Ralph A. Cossa, ed., *Restructuring the U.S.-Japan Alliance: Toward a More Equal Partnership,* 19–28. Washington, D.C.: CSIS Press.

Kang, David C. 2003a. "Getting Asia Wrong: The Need for New Analytic Frameworks." *International Security* 27, 4 (Spring): 57–85.

————. 2003b. "Hierarchy and Stability in Asian International Relations." In Ikenberry and Mastanduno, eds., 2003, *International Relations Theory and the Asia-Pacific,* 163–89.

Kapstein, Ethan B. 1999. "Does Unipolarity Have a Future?" In Ethan B. Kapstein and Michael Mastanduno, eds., *Unipolar Politics: Realism and State Strategies after the Cold War,* 464–90. New York: Columbia University Press.

Kartman, Charles. 1998. "Recent Developments in North Korea." Special Envoy for the Korean Peace Process, Testimony before the Senate Foreign Relations Committee, Subcommittee on East Asia and the Pacific, Washington, D.C. (10 Sept.).

Kato, Hisanori. 1999. *China's Military Modernization and Japan-China Relations.* IIPS Policy Paper 209E (June). Tokyo: Institute for International Policy Studies.

Katzenstein, Mary Fainsod. 1998. *Faithful and Fearless: Moving Feminist Protest inside the Church and Military.* Princeton, NJ: Princeton University Press.

Katzenstein, Peter J. 2003. "Same War—Different Views: Germany, Japan, and Counter-Terrorism." *International Organization* 57, 4 (Fall): 731–60.

————. 2000. "Regionalism and Asia." *New Political Economy* 5, 3: 353–68.

————. 1997. "Introduction: Asian Regionalism in Comparative Perspective." In Peter J. Katzenstein and Takashi Shiraishi, eds., *Network Power: Japan and Asia,* 1–44. Ithaca, NY: Cornell University Press.

————. 1996a. *Cultural Norms and National Security: Police and Military in Postwar Japan.* Ithaca, NY: Cornell University Press.

————. 1996b. "Regionalism in Comparative Perspective." *Cooperation and Conflict* 31, 2 (June): 123–59.

————, ed. 1996c. *The Culture of National Security: Norms and Identity in World Politics.* New York: Columbia University Press.

Katzenstein, Peter J., Robert O. Keohane, and Stephen D. Krasner. 1999a. "International Organization and the Study of World Politics." In Katzenstein, Keohane, and Krasner, eds., 1999b, *International Organization at Fifty,* 5–46.

————, eds. 1999b. *International Organization at Fifty: Exploration and Contestation in the Study of International Politics.* Cambridge, MA: MIT Press.

Katzenstein, Peter J., and Nobuo Okawara. 2001/02. "Japan, Asian-Pacific Security, and the Case for Analytical Eclecticism." *International Security* 26, 3: 153–85.

————. 1993. *Japan's National Security: Structures, Norms and Policy Responses in a Changing World*. Ithaca, NY: Cornell University, East Asia Program, Cornell East Asia Series.

Kawasaki, Tsuyoshi. 2001. "Postclassical Realism and Japanese Security Policy." *Pacific Review* 14, 2: 221–40.

Kegley, Charles W., Jr., Gregory A. Raymond, and Donald J. Puchala. 1990. *When Trust Breaks Down: Alliance Norms and World Politics*. Columbia: University of South Carolina Press.

Keisatsuchō. 1999. *Keisatsu hakusho* [Police white paper]. Tokyo: Okurashō Insatsu-kyoku.

————. 1997. *Keisatsu hakusho* [Police white paper]. Tokyo: Okurashō Insatsu-kyoku.

Kelly, James A. 2001. Assistant Secretary of State for East Asian and Pacific Affairs, Testimony before the Senate Foreign Relations Committee, Subcommittee on East Asian and Pacific Affairs, Washington, D.C. (1 May). www.state.gov/p/eap/rls/rm/2001/2697.htm.

Kent, Anne. 1999. *China, The United Nations, and Human Rights*. Philadelphia: University of Pennsylvania Press.

Keohane, Robert O. 1984. *After Hegemony: Cooperation and Discord in the World Political Economy*. Princeton, NJ: Princeton University Press.

Keohane, Robert O., and Lisa Martin. 1995. "The Promise of Institutionalist Theory." *International Security* 20, 1 (Summer): 39–51.

Kerr, Pauline, Andrew Mack, and Paul Evans. 1995. "The Evolving Security Discourse in the Asia-Pacific." In Andrew Mack and John Ravenhill, eds., *Pacific Cooperation: Building Economic and Security Regimes in the Asia-Pacific Region*, 233–55. Boulder, CO: Westview Press.

Khalilzad, Zalmay M., et al. 1999. *The United States and a Rising China: Strategic and Military Implications*. Santa Monica, CA: RAND.

Khong, Yuen Foong. 1999a. "Singapore: A Time for Economic and Political Engagement." In Johnston and Ross, eds., 1999, *Engaging China*, 109–28.

————. 1999b. "Whither ASEAN?" In Giok Ling Ooi and Ramikirsihen Rajan, eds., *Singapore: The Year in Review, 1998*, 88–101. Singapore: Times Academic Press.

————. 1998. "ASEAN's Collective Identity: Sources, Shifts, and Security Consequences." Paper prepared for the 94th annual meeting of the American Political Science Association, Boston (3–6 Sept.).

————. 1997a. "ASEAN and the Southeast Asian Security Complex." In David Lake and Patrick Morgan, eds., *Regional Orders: Building Security in a New World*, 318–39. University Park: Pennsylvania State University Press.

————. 1997b. "Making Bricks Without Straw in the Asia Pacific?" *Pacific Review* 10, 2: 289–300.

————. 1995a. "ASEAN's Post-Ministerial Conference and Regional Forum: A Convergence of Post–Cold War Security Strategies." In Gourevitch, Inoguchi, and Purrington, eds., 1995, *United States–Japan Relations and International Relations after the Cold War*, 37–58.

————. 1995b. "Evolving Security and Economic Institutions." *Southeast Asian Affairs 1995*. Singapore: Institute of Southeast Asian Studies.

Kinsella, David, and Jugdep S. Chima. 2001. "Symbols of Statehood: Military Industrialization and Public Discourse in India." *Review of International Studies* 27: 353–73.

Kissinger, Henry A. 1957. *A World Restored*. London: Weidenfeld and Nicolson.

Klare, Michael. 1984. *American Arms Supermarket*. Austin: University of Texas Press.

Koch, Andrew, and Jeanette Wolf. 1998. "Appendix: Selected Iranian Nuclear Imports." Monterey Center for Nonproliferation Studies.

Korean National Tourism Organization. 2004. "Kŭmgangsan kwan'gwanggaek 60manmyŏng dolp'a" (Mt. Kumgang tourists top 0.6 million). 2 Feb. 2004. www.travel-northkorea.com/s12_notice/notice_view.asp?seq=520&kw=&kw2=&kw3=&page=1&tbname=news_tour.

Krasner, Stephen D. 2001. "Organized Hypocrisy in Nineteenth Century East Asia." *International Relations of the Asia-Pacific* 1, 2: 173–97.

———. 1999. *Sovereignty: Organized Hypocrisy*. Princeton, NJ: Princeton University Press.

Krauss, Ellis S. 2000. *Broadcasting Politics in Japan: NHK Television News*. Ithaca, NY: Cornell University Press.

Kristof, Nicholas D. 1999. "A Would-Be Anthem in Search of a Meaning." *New York Times* (15 July): A7.

Ku Sang-Hoe. 1998. *Han'gukŭi pangwisanŏp: chŏnmangkwa taech'aek* [Korea's defense industry: Prospects and suggestions]. Seoul: Sejong Institute.

Kubálková, Vendulka. 1998. "The Twenty Years' Catharsis: E. H. Carr and IR." In Vendulka Kubálková, Nicholas Onuf, and Paul Kowert, eds., *International Relations in a Constructed World*, 22–57. Armonk, NY: M. E. Sharpe.

Kuhn, Thomas. 1962. *The Structure of Scientific Revolutions*. Chicago: University of Chicago Press.

Kupchan, Charles A., and Clifford A. Kupchan. 1995. "The Promise of Collective Security." *International Security* 20, 1 (Summer): 52–61.

Kurata, Hideya. 1996. "Multilateralism and the Korean Problem with Respect to the Asia-Pacific Region." *Journal of Pacific Asia* 3: 129–47.

Kwon Yŏng-Hyo. 1998. "Kukpangjodal ŏmmujŏlch'awa chedogaesŏn" [Defense procurement procedures and system improvement]. *Kukpangkwa kisul* [National defense and technology] (Jan.): 44.

Laitin, David. 1995. "Disciplining Political Science." *American Political Science Review* 89, 2 (June): 454–56.

Lakatos, Imre. 1970. "Falsification and the Methodology of Scientific Research Programmes." In Imre Lakatos and Alan Musgrave, eds., *Criticism and the Growth of Knowledge*, 91–196. New York: Cambridge University Press.

Lake, David A. 1999. *Entangling Relations: American Foreign Policy in Its Century*. Princeton, NJ: Princeton University Press.

Lardy, Nicholas R. 1999. "China and the International Financial System." In Elizabeth Economy and Michel Oksenberg, eds., *China Joins the World: Progress and Prospects*, 206–30. New York: Council on Foreign Relations.

Laudan, Larry. 1996. *Beyond Positivism and Relativism: Theory, Method, and Evidence*. Boulder, CO: Westview Press.

———. 1990. *Science and Relativism: Some Key Controversies in the Philosophy of Science*. Chicago: University of Chicago Press.

———. 1984. *Science and Values*. Berkeley: University of California Press.

———. 1977. *Progress and Its Problems: Toward a Theory of Scientific Growth*. Berkeley: University of California Press.

Lawrence, Susan V. 2000. "The Say No Club." *Far Eastern Economic Review* 163, 2 (13 Jan.): 16–1.

Layne, Christopher. 1997. "From Preponderance to Offshore Balancing." *International Security* 22, 1: 86–124.

Lebow, Richard Ned. 2001. "Thucydides the Constructivist." *American Political Science Review* 95, 3: 547–60.

Lee, Daniel B. 1997. "Korean Women Married to Servicemen." In Young In Song and Ailee Moon, eds., *Korean American Women Living in Two Cultures*, 94–123. Los Angeles: Academia Koreana, Keimyung-Baylo University Press.

Lee Kuan Yew. 2001. *From Third World to First: The Singapore Story, 1965–2000*. Singapore: Times Editions.

Legro, Jeffrey W., and Andrew Moravcsik. 1999. "Is Anybody Still a Realist?" *International Security* 24, 2 (Fall): 5–55.

Leifer, Michael. 2000. "Regionalism Compared: The Perils and Benefits of Expansion." Paper prepared for the 14th Asia-Pacific Roundtable, Kuala Lumpur (3–7 June).

————. 1999. "Indonesia's Encounters with China and the Dilemmas of Engagement." In Johnston and Ross, eds., 1999, *Engaging China*, 87–108.

————. 1996. *The ASEAN Regional Forum: Extending ASEAN's Model of Regional Security.* Adelphi Paper 302. Oxford: Oxford University Press.

————. 1989. *ASEAN and the Security of South-East Asia.* London: Routledge.

Lewis, Martin W., and Kären E. Wigen. 1997. *The Myth of Continents: A Critique of Metageography.* Berkeley: University of California Press.

Li Shaojun. 1999. "Ping 'Chaoxian zhan'" [Critiquing *Unrestricted Warfare*]. *Shijie jingji yu zhengzhi* [World economics and politics] 10.

Liang Guangyan. 1999. "Quanqiuhua shidai: Dangdai guoji anquan de beijing" [The era of globalization: The international security background]. In Wang Yizhou, ed., *Quanqiuhua shidai de guoji anquan* [International security in the era of globalization], 1–29. Shanghai: People's Publishing House.

Lichbach, Mark. 2003. *Is Rational Choice Theory All of Social Science?* Ann Arbor: University of Michigan Press.

Lim, Robyn. 2002. "So Much for Japan's Nuclear Taboo." *International Herald Tribune* (13 June): 8.

Liska, George. 1968. *Nations in Alliance: The Limits of Interdependence.* Baltimore: Johns Hopkins Press.

Liu Jie. 2001. *Jingji quanqiuhua shidai de guojia zhuquan* [National sovereignty in an era of economic globalization]. Beijing: Long March Publishing.

Lu Jianren. 1996. "Nansha zhengduan ji duice" [Disputes in the Spratlys and countermeasures]. In *Nansha wenti yanjiu ziliao* [Research materials on the Spratly Islands issue], 302–13. Beijing: Chinese Academy of Social Sciences.

Lukin, Alexander. 2001. *Russian Images of China and Russia-China Relations.* Brookings Institution paper. www.brookings.org/fp/cnaps/papers/lukinwp_01.pdf.

Lumpe, Lora, and Jeff Donarski. 1998. *The Arms Trade Revealed: A Guide for Investigators and Activists.* Washington, D.C.: Federation of American Scientists.

Luo Yuru. 1997. "21 shiji huan Taiping yang quyu jingji fazhan qushi yu Xianggang mianlin de jiyu he tiaozhan" [Economic development trends in the Pacific Rim region in the twenty-first century, and the opportunities and challenges facing Hong Kong]. *Guoji jishu jingji yanjiu* [Studies in international technology and economy] 3: 1–11.

Lyall, Jay. 2001. "The Revisionist State: Definitions and Measures." Unpublished paper. Ithaca, NY: Cornell University.

MacGregor, Charles. 1993. "Southeast Asia's New Security Challenges." *Pacific Review* 6, 3: 267–76.

Mack, Andrew. 1994. "A Nuclear North Korea: The Choices Are Narrowing." *World Policy Journal* 11, 2 (Summer 1994): 27–35.

————. 1993. "The Nuclear Crisis on the Korean Peninsula." *Asian Survey* 33, 4 (Apr.): 339–59.

Mahatir bin Mohamad. 1995. Statement. Dinner in Honor of Mohtarma Benazir. The Eleventh Conference of Heads of State of Government of the Non-Aligned Countries (6 July). 18 Oct. www.pmo.gov.my/WebNotesApp/PMMain.nsf.

Mahbubani, Kishore. 1995. "The Pacific Impulse." *Survival* 37, 1: 105–20.

Makinda, Samuel M. 2000. "International Society and Eclecticism in International Relations Theory." *Cooperation and Conflict* 35, 2: 205–16.

Malone, David M., and Yuen Foong Khong, eds. 2003. *Unilateralism and U.S. Foreign Policy: International Perspectives*. Boulder, CO: Lynne Rienner.

Mangaoang, Novicio. 2003. *The South China Sea Dispute in Philippine Foreign Policy*. Monograph no. 5. Singapore: Institute of Defence and Strategic Studies.

Martin, Lisa L. 1999. "The Contributions of Rational Choice: A Defense of Pluralism." *International Security* 24, 2 (Fall): 74–83.

Masaki, Hisane. 1998a. "Japan to Cochair Peacekeeping Group." *Japan Times* (17 July).

———. 1998b. "Seven Nations to Gang Up against Illegal Stimulant Use." *Japan Times* (6 Dec.).

Mastanduno, Michael. 2003. "Incomplete Hegemony: The United States and Security Order in Asia." In Alagappa, ed., 2003a, *Asian Security Order*, 141–70.

———. 1999. "A Realist View: Three Images of the Coming International Order." In T. V. Paul and John A. Hall, eds., *Order and the Future of World Politics*, 19–40. Cambridge, UK: Cambridge University Press.

Mathews, John. 1996. "Holonic Organisational Architectures." *Human Systems Management* 15: 27–54.

Mead, Walter Russell. 2001. *Special Providence: American Foreign Policy and How It Changed the World*. New York: Knopf.

Mearsheimer, John. 2001. *The Tragedy of Great Power Politics*. New York: W. W. Norton.

———. 1995. "A Realist Reply." *International Security* 20, 1 (Summer): 82–93.

———. 1994/95. "The False Promise of International Institutions." *International Security* 19, 3 (Winter): 5–49.

Memorandum of Understanding Concerning Establishing a Permanent Taegu Operation Location. 1981. (Dec). Article 3.

Midford, Paul. 2002. "The Logic of Reassurance and Japan's Grand Strategy." *Security Studies* 11, 3 (Spring): 1–43.

———. 1998. "From Reactive State to Cautious Leader: The Nakayama Proposal, the Miyazawa Doctrine, and Japan's Role in Promoting the Creation of the ASEAN Regional Forum." Paper prepared for the annual conference of the International Studies Association, Minneapolis (17–21 Mar.).

Ministry of National Defense. 1993. *Defense White Paper, 1992–1993*. Seoul: Korea Institute for Defense Analyses.

Ministry of Unification. N.d. "Taebukchŏngch'aek irŏkke ch'ujindoegoitsŭmnida" [Our North Korean policy]. www.unikorea.go.kr/cgi-kr/body.cgi?31C31/C3128.htm.

Mitzen, Jennifer. 2002. "Dangerous Attachments: The Dilemma of Ontological Security." Unpublished paper (Aug.). University of Chicago.

Mochizuki, Mike M. 1997a. "A New Bargain for a Stronger Alliance." In Mike M. Mochizuki, ed., *Toward a True Alliance: Restructuring U.S.-Japan Security Relations*, 5–40. Washington, D.C.: Brookings Institution.

———. 1997b. "American and Japanese Strategic Debates: The Need for a New Synthesis." In Mike M. Mochizuki, ed., *Toward a True Alliance: Restructuring U.S.-Japan Security Relations*, 43–82. Washington, D.C.: Brookings Institution.

Mochizuki, Mike M., and Michael O'Hanlon. 1998. "A Liberal Vision for the U.S.-Japan Alliance." *Survival* 40, 2 (Summer): 127–34.

Moon, Chung-in, and Chaesung Chun. 2003. "Sovereignty: Dominance of the Westphalian

Concept and Implications for Regional Security." In Alagappa, ed., 2003a, *Asian Security Order*, 106–37.

Moore, Thomas. 2000. "China and Globalization." In Samuel S. Kim, ed., *East Asia and Globalization*, 111–18. Lanham, MD: Rowman and Littlefield.

Moravcsik, Andrew. 2003. "Liberal International Relations Theory: A Scientific Assessment." In Elman and Elman, eds., 2003c, *Progress in International Relations Theory*, 159–204.

Morgenthau, Hans J. 1978. *Politics Among Nations*. 5th revised ed. New York: Alfred A. Knopf.

Morrocco, John D. 1989. "South Korea Drives toward Greater Military Autonomy." *Aviation Week and Space Technology* 130 (12 June): 176–79.

Morrow, James D. 2000. "Alliances: Why Write Them Down?" *Annual Review of Political Science* 3: 63–83.

————. 1991. "Alliances and Asymmetry: An Alternative to the Capacity Aggregation Model of Alliances." *American Journal of Political Science* 35, 4: 904–33.

Munakata, Naoko. 2001. "Evolution of Japan's Policy toward Economic Integration." 2001 CNAPS Working Paper. Washington, D.C.: Brookings Institution, Foreign Policy Studies.

Muni, S. D. 2002. *China's Strategic Engagement with the New ASEAN*. Monograph no. 2. Singapore: Institute of Defence and Strategic Studies.

Mutimer, David. 1997. "Reimagining Security: The Metaphors of Proliferation." In Keith Kruse and Michael C. Williams, eds., *Critical Security Studies*, 187–221. Minneapolis: University of Minnesota Press.

Naito, Yosuke. 1999. "Private-Sector Northeast Asia Security Forum Upbeat." *Japan Times* (28 Sept.).

Nakamoto, Michiyo. 1999. "LDP Debates Military Strikes Strategy." *Financial Times* (26 Feb.): 4.

National Institute for Defense Studies. 1999. *East Asian Strategic Review 1998–1999*. Tokyo: National Institute for Defense Studies.

National Police Agency. 1997. *White Paper on Police 1997 (Excerpt)*. Tokyo: National Police Agency.

National Police Agency, International Cooperation Division, International Affairs Department. 1998. *Police of Japan '98*. Tokyo: National Police Agency.

Neumann, Iver, and Jennifer Welsh. 1991. "The Other in European Self-identification." *Review of International Studies* 17: 327–48.

New Straits Times. Malaysia.

Ng-Quinn, Michael. 1986. "The Internationalization of the Region: The Case of Northeast Asian International Relations." *Review of International Studies* 12, 2: 107–25.

Nguyen Man Cam. 1997. Statement (13 Feb.). www.aseansec.org/amm/amm29oss.htm.

Niou, Emerson M. S., and Peter C. Ordeshook. 1999. "Return of the Luddites." *International Security* 24, 2 (Fall): 84–96.

Nisbett, Richard E. 2003. *The Geography of Thought: How Asians and Westerners Think Differently . . . and Why*. New York: Free Press.

Nolan, Janne E. 1991. *Trappings of Power: Ballistic Missiles in the Third World*. Washington, D.C.: Brookings Institution.

————. 1986. *Military Industry in Taiwan and South Korea*. New York: St. Martin's Press.

Noland, Marcus, Sherman Robinson, and Li-gang Liu. 1998. *The Costs and Benefits of Korean Unification* (Mar.). Stanford, CA: Asia Pacific Research Center.

Nye, Joseph S. 2001. "The 'Nye Report': Six Years Later." *International Relations of the Asia-Pacific*, 1, 1: 95–104.

Observer [Guanchajia]. 1995. "Zhongguo fazhan you liyu shijie heping yu jinbu—bo 'Zhongguo weixie lun'" [China's development is advantageous for world peace and progress: Refuting the "China threat theory"]. *People's Daily* (8 Aug.).

O'Hanlon, Michael. 1998. "Stopping a North Korean Invasion: Why Defending South Korea Is Easier Than the Pentagon Thinks." *International Security* 22: 135–70.

Okawara, Nobuo, and Peter J. Katzenstein. 2001. "Japan and Asian-Pacific Security: Regionalization, Entrenched Bilateralism, and Incipient Multilateralism." *Pacific Review* 14, 2: 165–94.

Oksenberg, Michel. 2001. "The Issue of Sovereignty in the Asian Historical Context." In Stephen D. Krasner, ed., *Problematic Sovereignty: Contested Rules and Political Possibilities*, 83–104. New York: Columbia University Press.

Organski, A.F.K., and Jacek Kugler. 1980. *The War Ledger*. Chicago: Chicago University Press.

Pang Zhongying. 1999. "Dui *Chaoxian zhan* yi shu de ruogan fouding yu kending" [Several disagreements and agreements with the book *Unrestricted Warfare*]. *Shijie jingji yu zhengzhi* [World economics and politics] 10: 71–72.

Payne, Keith. 2001. "Action-Reaction Metaphysics and Negligence." *Washington Quarterly* 24, 4 (Autumn): 109–21.

Pearson, Margaret M. 2002. "China's Multiple Personalities in Geneva: Template for Future Research on Chinese Behavior in the WTO." Paper prepared for New Directions in Chinese Foreign Policy: A Conference in Honor of Allen S. Whiting. Fairbank Center for East Asian Research, Harvard University (Nov.).

———. 1999. "China's Integration into the International Trade and Investment Regime." In Elizabeth Economy and Michel Oksenberg, eds., *China Joins the World: Progress and Prospects*, 161–205. New York: Council on Foreign Relations.

Pei, Minxin. 2001. "The Inscrutable Hegemon." *Foreign Policy* (Sept./Oct.): 92–96.

Pillsbury, Michael. 2000. *China Debates the Future Security Environment*. Washington, D.C.: National Defense University Press.

Pollack, Jonathan D., and Young Koo Cha. 1995. *A New Alliance for the Next Century: The Future of U.S.-Korean Security Cooperation*. Santa Monica, CA: RAND.

Pomfret, John. 1999. "China Ponders New Rules of Unrestricted Warfare." *Washington Post* (16 Aug.).

Powell, Colin. 2002. Remarks at Asia Society Annual Dinner. New York (10 June). www.state.gov/secretary/rm/2002/10983.htm.

Powell, Robert. 1999. "The Modeling Enterprise and Security Studies." *International Security* 24, 2 (Fall): 97–106.

Prestowitz, Clyde V. 2003. *Rogue Nation: American Unilateralism and the Failure of Good Intentions*. New York: Basic Books.

Price, Richard M., and Christian Reus-Smit. 1998. "Critical International Theory and Constructivism." *European Journal of International Relations* 4, 3: 259–94.

Procurement Headquarters, Ministry of National Defense. 1996. *Sŏmyŏnjirŭidappyŏnsŏ* [Written answer to questions]. Parliamentary audit (4 Oct.).

Pyle, Kenneth B. 1992. "Can Japan Lead? The New Internationalism and the Burdens of History." In Henry Bienen, ed., *Power, Economics, and Security: The United States and Japan in Focus*, 189–225. Boulder, CO: Westview Press.

Pyle, Kenneth B., and Eric Heginbotham. 2001. "Japan." In Ellings and Friedberg, eds., 2001, *Strategic Asia*, 71–126.

Qian Ning. 1997. *Liuxue Meiguo* [Studying in America]. Nanjing: Jiangsu Fine Arts Publishing House.

Qian Qichen. 2000. "Dangqian guoji guanxi yanjiu zhong de ruogan zhongdian wenti" [Sev eral key issues in current research on international relations]. *Shijie jingji yu zhengzhi* [World economics and politics] 9: 5–8.

Qin Yaqing. 2001. "Response to Yong Deng: Power, Perception and the Cultural Lens." *Asian Affairs* 28, 3 (Fall): 155–58.

Qing Wenhui, and Sun Hui. 2001. "Hou lengzhan shidai de Zhongguo guojia anquan" [China's national security in the post–Cold War era]. *Zhanlüe yu guanli* [Strategy and management] 1: 1–9.

Rapoport, Anatol. 1960. *Fights, Games, and Debates*. Ann Arbor: University of Michigan Press.

Reus-Smit, Christian. 2001. "The Strange Death of Liberal International Theory." *European Journal of International Law* 12, 3: 573–93.

———. 1999. *The Moral Purpose of the State: Culture, Social Identity, and Institutional Rationality in International Relations*. Princeton, NJ: Princeton University Press.

Richardson, Michael. 2000. "Asia's Widening Arms Gap: Uneven Spread of New Weapons Systems May Jeopardize Balance of Power in East." *International Herald Tribune* (7 Jan.).

———. 1998. "Asian Crisis Stills Appetite for Arms." *International Herald Tribune* (23 Apr.).

Rigger, Shelley. 2001. *Taiwan's Democratic Progressive Party: From Opposition to Power*. Boulder, CO: Lynne Reinner.

Riker, William H. 1996. *The Strategy of Rhetoric: Campaigning for the American Constitution*. New Haven, CT: Yale University Press.

Risse, Thomas. 2000. "'Let's Argue!': Communicative Action in World Politics." *International Organization* 54, 1: 1–39.

———. 1999. "International Norms and Domestic Change: Arguing and Communicative Behavior in the Human Rights Area." *Politics and Society* 27, 4: 529–59.

Risse, Thomas, Stephen Ropp, and Kathryn Sikkink. 1999. *The Power of Human Rights: International Norms and Domestic Change*. Cambridge, UK: Cambridge University Press.

Risse-Kappen, Thomas. 1995. *Cooperation among Democracies: The European Influence on U.S. Foreign Policy*. Princeton, NJ: Princeton University Press.

———. 1994. "Ideas Do Not Float Freely: Transnational Coalitions, Domestic Structures, and the End of the Cold War." *International Organization* 48, 2: 185–214.

Romer, Daniel, et al. 1997. "Blame Discourse versus Realistic Conflict as Explanations of Ethnic Tension in Urban Neighborhoods." *Political Communication* 14, 3: 273–91.

Rose, Gideon. 1998. "Neoclassical Realism and Theories of Foreign Policy." *World Politics* 51, 1: 144–72.

Rosecrance, Richard N. 1985. *The Rise of the Trading State: Commerce and Conquest in the Modern World*. New York: Basic Books.

Rousseau, David. 2002. "Constructing Identities and Threats in International Relations." Unpublished manuscript (1 Aug.).

Rozman, Gilbert. 2002a. "China's Changing Images of Japan, 1998–2001: The Struggle to Balance Partnership and Rivalry." *International Relations of the Asia-Pacific* 2: 95–130.

———. 2002b. "Japan's Quest for Great Power Identity." *Orbis* 46, 1 (Winter): 73–91.

———. 2001. "Japan's Images of China in the 1990s: Are They Ready for China's 'Smile Diplomacy' or Bush's 'Strong Diplomacy'?" *Japanese Journal of Political Science* 2, 1: 97–125.

Ruggie, John G. 1998. *Constructing the World Polity: Essays on International Institutionalization*. New York: Routledge.

———. 1995. "The False Premise of Realism." *International Security* 20, 1 (Summer): 62–70.

———. 1992. "Multilateralism: The Anatomy of an Institution." *International Organization* 46: 561–98.

Rüland, Jürgen. 2000. "ASEAN and the Asian Crisis: Theoretical Implications and Practical Consequences for Southeast Asian Regionalism." *Pacific Review* 13, 3: 421–51.

Rule, James B. 1997. *Theory and Progress in Social Science.* Cambridge, UK: Cambridge University Press.

Rynning, Sten, and Stefano Guzzini. 2001. "Realism and Foreign Policy Analysis." Working Paper 21. Copenhagen Peace Research Institute. www.copri.dk/publications/WP/WP%202 001/42-2001.pdf.

Said, Edward W. 1978. *Orientalism.* New York: Vintage Books.

Sanderson, Stephen K. 1987. "Eclecticism and Its Alternatives." *Current Perspectives in Social Theory* 8: 313–45.

Sasaki, Yoshitaka. 1997. "Asian Trilateral Security Talks Debut." *Asahi Evening News* (7 Nov.).

Schroeder, Paul. 1994a. "Historical Reality vs. Neo-realist Theory." *International Security* 19 (Summer): 108–48.

————. 1994b. *The Transformation of European Politics, 1763–1848.* Oxford: Clarendon Press.

Schwartz, Thomas A. 2000. Statement of General Thomas A. Schwartz, Commander-in-Chief United Nations Command/Combined Forces Command and Commander, United States Forces Korea before the Senate Armed Services Committee (7 Mar.).

Schweller, Randall. 1996. "Neorealism's Status-Quo Bias: What Security Dilemma?" *Security Studies* 5, 3 (Spring): 90–121.

————. 1994. "Bandwagoning for Profit: Bringing the Revisionist State Back In." *International Security* 19, 1 (Summer): 72–107.

Scollay, Robert, and John P. Gilbert. 2001. *New Regional Trading Arrangements in the Asia Pacific?* Washington, D.C.: Institute for International Economics.

Security Consultative Meeting. 1999. Statement. (23 Nov.).

————. 1997. *Joint Communiqué, Twenty-ninth Security Consultative Meeting.* Washington, D.C. (9 Dec.).

Segal, Gerald. 1996. "East Asia and the 'Constrainment' of China." *International Security* 20, 4 (Spring): 107–35.

Shambaugh, David. 2001. "Response." *Survival* 43, 3 (Autumn): 25–30.

————. 2000. "Sino-American Strategic Relations: From Partners To Competitors." *Survival* 42, 1 (Summer): 97–115.

Shapiro, Ian. 2002. "Problems, Methods, and Theories in the Study of Politics, or What's Wrong with Political Science and What to Do About It?" *Political Theory* 30, 4 (Aug.): 588–611.

Shen Jiru. 1999. "Heping yu fazhan mianlin yanzhong tiaozhan" [Peace and development face a serious challenge]. In Wang Yizhou, ed., *Danji shijie de yinmai* [The gloom of a unipolar world], 360–98. Beijing: Social Science Documents Press.

————. 1998. *Zhongguo bu dang bu xiansheng* [China will not become "Mr. No"]. Beijing: Jinri Zhongguo Press.

Sheng Ning. 1998. "Houzhimin wenhua piping yu di san shijie de shengyin" [Post-colonial cultural criticism and the voice of the third world]. *Meiguo yanjiu* [American studies] 3: 50–69.

Shi Yinhong. 2003. "Ru he renshi he duidai Chaoxian he weiji" [How to understand and deal with the Korean nuclear crisis]. *Ta Kung Pao* (Hong Kong) (12 Jan.).

————. 2000. "Meiguo guojia daodan fangyu jihua yu Zhongguo ke you de he yinggai you de duice" [U.S. NMD and the countermeasures China could and should take]. *Haerbin gongye daxue xuebao (shehui kexue ban)* [Harbin Industrial College journal (social science)] 2, 3: 12–16.

Shi Yongming. 1997. "YaTai anquan zhong de maodun yu hezuo" [Contradictions and cooperation in Asia-Pacific security]. *Guoji wenti yanjiu* [International studies] 3: 44–49.

Shinn, James. 1998. "American Stakes in Asian Problems." In James Shinn, ed., *Fires across the Water: Transnational Problems in Asia*, 158–74. New York: Council on Foreign Relations.

Shirk, Susan L. 1994. *How China Opened Its Door: The Political Success of the PRC's Foreign Trade and Investment Reforms*. Washington, D.C.: Brookings Institution.

Sigal, Leon V. 1999. "How to End North Korea's Missile Program." Global Beat Syndicate (2 June). www.nyu.edu/globalbeat/syndicate/Sigal060299.html.

———. 1998. *Disarming Strangers: Nuclear Diplomacy with North Korea, 1988–1995*. Princeton, NJ: Princeton University Press.

Signorino, Kurt, and Jeffery Ritter. 1999. "Tau-b Or Not Tau-b: Measuring The Similarity Of Foreign Policy Positions." *International Studies Quarterly* 43, 1: 115–44.

Sil, Rudra. 2000a. "The Foundations of Eclecticism: The Epistemological Status of Agency, Culture, and Structure in Social Theory." *Journal of Theoretical Politics* 12, 3: 353–87.

———. 2000b. "The Division of Labor in Social Science Research: Unified Methodology or 'Organic Solidarity.'" *Polity* 32, 4 (Summer): 499–531.

———. 2000c "Against Epistemological Absolutism: Towards a Pragmatic Center?" In Rudra Sil and Eileen Doherty, eds., *Beyond Boundaries? Disciplines, Paradigms, and Theoretical Integration in International Studies*, 145–75. Albany: State University of New York Press.

———. 2000d. "The Questionable Status of Boundaries: The Need for Integration." In Rudra Sil and Eileen Doherty, eds., *Beyond Boundaries? Disciplines, Paradigms and Theoretical Integration in International Studies*, 1–27. Albany: State University of New York Press.

Simon, Herbert A. 1981. *The Sciences of the Artificial*. 2nd ed. Cambridge, MA: MIT Press.

Simon, Sheldon W., ed. 2001. *The Many Faces of Asian Security*. Lanham, MD: Rowman and Littlefield.

———. 1998. "Security Prospects in Southeast Asia: Collaborative Efforts and the ASEAN Regional Forum." *Pacific Review* 11, 2: 195–212.

———. 1996. "The Parallel Tracks of Asian Multilateralism." In Richard J. Ellings and Sheldon Simon, eds., *Southeast Asian Security in the New Millennium*, 13–33. Armonk, NY: M. E. Sharpe.

———. 1992. "The Regionalization of Defense in Southeast Asia." *Pacific Review* 5, 1: 301–13.

Singapore Government Press Release. 1999. President's Address at the Opening of Parliament (4 Oct.). http://app.sprinter.gov.sg/data/pr/1999100404.htm.

Singh, Bhubinder. 2002. "ASEAN's Perceptions of Japan: Change and Continuity." *Asian Survey* 42, 2: 276–96.

Smith, Tony. 1994. *America's Mission: The United States and the Worldwide Struggle for Democracy in the Twentieth Century*. Princeton, NJ: Princeton University Press.

Snyder, Glenn H. 1997. *Alliance Politics*. Ithaca, NY: Cornell University Press.

Soeya, Yoshihide. 1998. "Japan: Normative Constraints versus Structural Imperatives." In Alagappa, ed., 1998a, *Asian Security Practice*, 198–233.

Song Yimin. 2000. "YaTai diqu de jige xin fazhan qushi" [Several new development trends in the Asia-Pacific region]. *Shijie jingji yu zhengzhi* [World economics and politics] 9: 9–13.

Sorokin, Gerald L. 1994. "Arms, Alliances, and Security Tradeoffs in Enduring Rivalries." *International Studies Quarterly* 38: 421–46.

Spiro, David. 1999. *The Hidden Hand of American Hegemony: Petrodollar Recycling and International Markets*. Ithaca, NY: Cornell University Press.

Stankiewicz, Michael. 1998. "Preface: The Bilateral-Multilateral Context in Northeast Asian

Security." *Korean Peninsula Security and the U.S.-Japan Defense Guidelines.* IGCC Policy Paper no. 45 (Oct.). Northeast Asia Cooperation Dialogue VII.

Stone, Diane. 1997. "Networks, Second Track Diplomacy and Regional Cooperation: The Role of Southeast Asian Think Tanks." Paper presented at the 38th annual International Studies Association convention, Toronto (22–26 Mar.).

———. 1996. *Capturing the Political Imagination: Think Tanks and the Policy Process.* London: Frank Cass.

Straits Times. Singapore.

Su, Kuofeng. 2000. "Taiwan's Democratization and Its Foreign Policy: The Impact of Taiwan's Elections on Its China Policy." Ph.D. dissertation, University of Michigan.

Su Qi. 2002. "Domestic Determinants of Taiwan's Mainland Policy." Paper presented at the Peace Across the Taiwan Strait Conference, Asian Studies Centre, Oxford University (23–25 May). www.taiwansecurity.org/TS/2002/Su-0502.htm.

Suh, Jae-Jung. 1999a. "Blitzkrieg or Sitzkrieg? Assessing a Second Korean War." *Pacifica Review* 11, 2: 151–76.

———. 1999b. "Pukhanmisailŭn mi-ilhubangwihyŏp t'onghan chŏnjaengŏkchiryŏk hwakpoyong" [North Korea's missiles deter war by threatening the U.S. and Japan's rear]. *Wolgan mal* [Monthly words] (Sept.): 92–97.

———. 1996. "North Korean 'Nuclear Threat' and Cold War Hangover: Northern Exposure or Explosion?" *Bulletin of Concerned Asian Scholars* 28, 1: 13–26.

Tainaka, Masato. 2000. "Nations Renew N. Korea Efforts." *Asahi Evening News* (31 Mar.).

Takeda, Yasuhiro. 1997. "Democracy Promotion Policies: Overcoming Japan-U.S. Discord." In Ralph A. Cossa, ed., *Restructuring the U.S.-Japan Alliance: Toward a More Equal Partnership,* 50–62. Washington, D.C.: CSIS Press.

Tan, Andrew. 2000a. *Armed Rebellion in the ASEAN States: Persistence and Implications.* Canberra: Strategic and Defense Studies Centre, Research School of Pacific and Asian Studies, Australian National University.

———. 2000b. "Intra-ASEAN Tensions." Discussion Paper 84. Royal Institute of International Affairs.

Tan, Seng, and Ralph A. Cossa. 2001. "Rescuing Realism from the Realists: A Theoretical Note on East Asian Security." In Simon, ed., 2001, *The Many Faces of Asian Security,* 15–47.

Tang Shiping. 2001. "Zai lun Zhongguo de da zhanlüe" [Once again on China's grand strategy]. *Zhanlüe yu guanli* [Strategy and management] 4: 29–37.

———. 1999. "A Neutral Reunified Korea: A Chinese View." *Journal of East Asian Affairs* (Seoul) 13, 2 (Fall/Winter): 464–83.

Tang Shiping, and Zhou Xiaobing. 2001. "Dongmeng, Zhongguo, Riben de hezuo ji DongYa de weilai" [ASEAN-China-Japan cooperation and the future of East Asia]. *Guoji jingji pinglun* [Commentary on international economics] (Dec.).

Tao Wenzhao. 1998. "Chaozhe jianli changqi wending, jiankang fazhan de ZhongMei guanxi qianjin—jinnian lai ZhongMei guanxi fazhan huigu" [Toward progress in long-term stable and healthy development of Sino-U.S. relations: Reflections on development of Sino-U.S. relations in this year]. *Taiping yang xuebao* [Pacific studies] 2: 20–28.

Tarrow, Sidney. 1995. "Bridging the Quantitative-Qualitative Divide in Political Science." *American Political Science Review* 89, 2 (June): 471–74.

Taylor, William J., Jr. 1989. "Challenges to ROK-U.S. Security Relations." In William J. Taylor, Young Koo Cha, and John Q. Blodgett, eds., *The Future of South Korean–U.S. Security Relations,* 113–26. Boulder, CO: Westview Press.

Terada, Takashi. 1998. "The Origins of Japan's APEC Policy: Foreign Minister Takeo Miki's Asia-Pacific Policy and Current Implications." *Pacific Review* 11, 3: 337–63.

Tsuchiyama, Jitsuo. 2003. "From Balancing to Networking: Models of Regional Security in Asia." In G. John Ikenberry and Takashi Inoguchi, eds., *Reinventing the Alliance: U.S.-Japan Security Partnership in an Era of Change*, 43–61. New York: Palgrave Macmillan.

Twomey, Christopher P. 2000. "Japan, A Circumscribed Balancer: Building on Defensive Realism to Make Predictions about East Asian Security." *Security Studies* 9, 4 (Summer): 167–205.

Tzou, Byron N. 1992. "Does the Principle of Self-Determination Apply to Taiwan?" *Issues and Studies* 28, 6 (June): 70–85.

Umbach, Frank. 2000. "Military Balance in the Asia Pacific: Trends and Implications." Paper prepared for the 14th Asia-Pacific Roundtable, Kuala Lumpur (3–7 June).

United States Department of Defense. 1998. *The United States Security Strategy for the East Asia-Pacific Region*. Washington, D.C.

———. 1995. DoD News Briefing by Joseph Nye, Assistant Secretary of Defense for International Security Affairs (17 Feb.). www.defenselink.mil/news/Feb1995/t022795.t0227asi.html.

United States Pacific Command. 2000. Remarks prepared for Admiral Dennis C. Blair, University of California, San Diego, Graduate School of International Relations (13 Apr.). http://russia.shaps.hawaii.edu/security/us/blair_sandiego.html.

Uriu, Robert M. 1998a. "Domestic-International Interactions and Japanese Security Studies." *Journal of Asian and African Studies* 33, 1: 76–93.

———. 1998b. "Domestic-International Interactions and Japanese Security Studies." In James Sperling, Yogendra Malik, and David Louscher, eds., *Zones of Amity, Zones of Enmity: The Prospects for Economic and Military Security in Asia*, 76–93. Leiden: Brill.

U.S. Department of State. 1999. Trilateral Meeting Joint Press Statement. Washington, D.C., USIA text (27 July).

U.S.-ROK Military Industry Conference. 1990. *Kukpangkwa kisul* [National defense and technology] (Apr.).

USCC [United States China Security Commission]. 2002. "Report to Congress of the U.S.-China Security Review Commission" (July). www.uscc.gov/anrp02.htm.

Valencia, M. J. 1997a. "Energy and Insecurity in Asia." *Survival* 39, 3: 85–106.

———. 1997b. "Troubled Waters." *Bulletin of the Atomic Scientists* 53, 1 (Jan./Feb.): 49–54.

Van Ness, Peter. 2002. "Hegemony, Not Anarchy: Why China and Japan Are Not Balancing U.S. Unipolar Power." *International Relations of the Asia-Pacific* 2: 131–50.

Voeten, Erik. 2002. "Resisting the Lonely Superpower: Responses of States in the United Nations to U.S." Paper presented at the annual meeting of the American Political Science Association, Boston (1 Sept.).

Wachman, Alan M. 1994. *Taiwan, National Identity and Democratization*. Armonk, NY: M. E. Sharpe.

Wada, Jun. 1998. "Applying Track Two to China-Japan-U.S. Relations." In Ryosei Kokubun, ed., *Challenges for China-Japan-U.S. Cooperation*, 154–83. Tokyo: Japan Center for International Exchange.

Wæver, Ole. 1999. "The Sociology of a Not So International Discipline: American and European Developments in International Relations." In Katzenstein, Keohane, and Krasner, eds., 1999b, *International Organization at Fifty*, 47–87.

———. 1996. "The Rise and Fall of the Interparadigm Debate." In Steve Smith, Ken Booth, and Marysia Zalewski, eds., *International Theory: Positivism and Beyond*, 149–85. Cambridge, UK: Cambridge University Press.

Waldron, Arthur N. 1996. "China as an Ascending Power." Testimony before the House National Security Committee on Security Challenges, Cong. 104, sess. 1 (20 Mar.).

Walker, R.B.J. 2000. "Both Globalization and Sovereignty: Re-Imagining the Political." In Paul Wapner and Lester Edwin J. Ruiz, eds., *Principled World Politics: The Challenge of Normative International Relations*, 23–34. Lanham, MD: Rowman and Littlefield.

Walker, Stephen G. 2003. "Operational Code Analysis as a Scientific Research Program: A Cautionary Tale." In Elman and Elman, eds., 2003a, *Progress in International Relations Theory*, 245–76.

Wall Street Journal. 1999. "While Japan Prepares." (11 Mar.): A22.

Wallander, Celeste A. 2002. "Lost and Found: Gorbachev's New Thinking." *Washington Quarterly* 25, 1 (Winter): 117–29.

———. 2000. "Institutional Assets and Adaptability: NATO after the Cold War." *International Organization* 54, 4: 705–35.

———. 1999. *Mortal Friends, Best Enemies: German-Russian Cooperation after the Cold War*. Ithaca, NY: Cornell University Press.

Wallander, Celeste, and Robert O. Keohane. 1999. "Risk, Threat, and Security Institutions." In Helga Haftendorn, Robert O. Keohane, and Celeste Wallander, eds., 1999, *Imperfect Unions: Security Institutions over Time and Space*, 21–47. New York: Oxford University Press.

Walt, Stephen M. 1999a. "Rigor or Rigor Mortis? Rational Choice and Security Studies." *International Security Studies* 23, 4 (Spring): 5–48.

———. 1999b. "A Model Disagreement." *International Security* 24, 2 (Fall): 115–30.

———. 1997. "Why Alliances Endure or Collapse." *Survival* 39, 1 (Spring 1997): 156–79.

———. 1987. *The Origins of Alliances*. Ithaca, NY: Cornell University Press.

Waltz, Kenneth. 2000. "Structural Realism after the Cold War." *International Security* 25, 1 (Summer): 5–41.

———. 1979. *Theory of International Politics*. Reading, MA: Addison-Wesley.

Wang Houqing, and Zhang Xingye, eds. 2000. *Zhanyi xue* [Operational art]. Beijing: National Defense University.

Wang Jianwei. 1999. *Limited Adversaries: Post–Cold War U.S.-China Mutual Images*. New York: Oxford University Press.

Wang Jianwei, and Wu Xinbo. 1998. "Against Us or With Us? The Chinese Perspective of America's Alliances with Japan and Korea" (May). Stanford, CA: Asia Pacific Research Center.

Wang Jisi. 1998. "Guoji guanxi lilun yu Zhongguo waijiao yanjiu" [International relations theory and research on Chinese foreign relations]. In Zi Zhongyun, ed., *Guoji zhengzhi lilun tansuo zai Zhongguo* [Explorations of international politics theory in China], 295–317. Shanghai: People's Publishing House.

———. 1997. "Multipolarity Versus Hegemonism: Chinese Views of International Politics Today." Paper prepared for conference on Conflict or Convergence: Global Perspectives on War, Peace, and International Order, Harvard Academy of International and Area Studies (13–15 Nov.).

Wang Xiaodong. 1999. "Meiguo zhadan Zhongguo zhu Nan shi hou de yi xie sikao" [A few thoughts after the U.S. bombed China's embassy in Yugoslavia]. In Fang, Wang, and Song, eds., 1999, *Quanqiuhua yinying xia de Zhongguo zhi lu*, 3–20.

Wang Xueyu. 2000. "Cong guojihua dao quanqiuhua" [From internationalization to globalization]. *Shijie jingji yu zhengzhi* [World economics and politics] 8: 48–52.

Wang Yizhou. 2001. "Xin shijie de Zhongguo yu duobian waijiao" [China in the new century and multilateral diplomacy]. Paper presented at a research conference on Theory of Multilateralism and Multilateral Diplomacy, Beijing.

——. 1999a. "Zhubian shouji" [Editor's note]. In Wang Yizhou, ed., *Quanqiuhua shidai de guoji anquan* [International security in the era of globalization], 1–14. Shanghai: People's Publishing House.

——. 1999b. "Duojihua bu deng yu fan Mei" [Multipolarity is not equivalent to opposing the United States]. *Huanqiu shibao* [Global times] (6 Aug.).

——. 1998. "Guanyu duojihua de ruogan sikao" [Several thoughts on multipolarity]. Unpublished paper (Apr.–May).

——. 1995. *Dangdai guoji zhengzhi pouxi* [Analysis of contemporary international politics]. Shanghai: People's Publishing House.

Ward, Michael Don. 1982. *Research Gaps in Alliance Dynamics*. Denver: University of Denver Graduate School of International Studies.

Weatherbee, Donald. 1995. "Southeast Asia at Mid-Decade: Independence Through Interdependence." *Southeast Asian Affairs* 1995, 3–27. Singapore: Institute of Southeast Asian Studies.

Weiss, Thomas. 2001. "Researching Humanitarian Intervention." *Journal of Peace Research* 38, 4: 419–28.

Weldes, Jutta. 1999. *Constructing National Interests: The United States and the Cuban Missile Crisis*. Borderlines, vol. 12. Minneapolis: University of Minnesota Press.

Wendt, Alexander. 1999. *Social Theory of International Politics*. New York: Cambridge University Press.

——. 1995. "Constructing International Politics." *International Security* 20, 1 (Summer): 71–81.

Westin, Susan S. 2002. Testimony before the Congressional Executive Commission on China (6 June). www.cecc.gov/pages/hearings/060602/westinTestimony.pdf.

White House. 2002. *National Security Strategy of the United States*. Washington, D.C.

Whiting, Allen S. 1997. "ASEAN Eyes China." *Asian Survey* 37, 4 (Apr.): 299–322.

Williamson, Oliver E. 1987. *The Economic Institutions of Capitalism: Firms, Markets, Relational Contracting*. New York: Free Press.

Wiseman, Geoffrey. 1992. "Common Security in the Asia-Pacific Region." *Pacific Review* 5, 1: 42–59.

Wohlforth, William. 1999. "The Stability of a Unipolar World." *International Security* 24, 1: 5–41.

Wolfowitz, Paul. 1997. "Bridging Centuries: Fin de Siecle All Over Again." *The National Interest* 47 (Spring).

Wolfson, Murray, ed. 1998. *The Political Economy of War and Peace*. Boston: Kluwer.

Woo-Cumings, Meredith. 2004. "Unilateralism and Its Discontents: The Passing of the Cold War Alliance and Changing Public Opinion in the Republic of Korea." In David Steinberg, ed., *Korean Attitudes toward the United States*. Armonk, NY: M. E. Sharpe.

Wortzel, Larry. 1998. *China's Military Potential* (Oct.). Strategic Studies Institute, Army War College.

Wright, David C. 1998. "Will North Korea Negotiate Away Its Missiles?" Union of Concerned Scientists (2 Apr.). www.ucsusa.org/arms/index.html?NKmissiles.exec.html.

Xiang Lanxin. 2001. "Washington's Misguided China Policy." *Survival* 43, 3 (Autumn): 7–33.

Xu Xin. 2003. "China and East Asia: Identity and Power in the Post–Cold War Era." Ph.D. dissertation, Cornell University.

Yan Xuetong. 1999a. *Zhongguo jueqi—guoji huanjing pingu* [An assessment of the international environment for China's rise]. Tianjin: People's Publishing House.

———. 1999b. "Zhongguo lengzhan hou de anquan zhanlüe" [China's post–Cold War security strategy]. In Yan Xuetong, ed., *Zhongguo yu YaTai anquan* [China and Asia-Pacific security], 18–62. Beijing: Shishi Press.

———. 1997. *Zhongguo guojia liyi fenxi* [An analysis of China's national interest]. Tianjin: People's Publishing House.

Yang Bojiang. 1999. "Riben lengzhanhou de anquan zhanlüe" [Japan's post–Cold War security strategy]. In Yan Xuetong, ed., *Zhongguo yu YaTai anquan* [China and Asia-Pacific security]. Beijing: Shishi Press.

Yang Yunzhong. 2001. "Riben jiashu xiang junshi daguo mubiao maijin" [Japan speeds up in forging ahead toward the goal of military great power]. www.cass.net.cn/s28_yts/wordchen/ch-ddyt2002/ch-qkddyt0205yyz.htm.

Ye Zicheng, and Feng Yin. 2002. "ZhongMei guanxi shi lun" [Ten points about Sino-U.S. relations]. *Shijie jingji yu zhengzhi* [World economics and politics] 5: 21–27.

Yi Yŏng-Hŭi. 1993. "Nambuk hwahaewa kunch'ukŭi sinsidaerŭl yŏlja" [Let's open the new era of North-South reconciliation and arms reduction]. *Wolgan mal* [Monthly words] (Oct.): 58–63.

———. 1992. "Nambukhan chonjaengnŭngryŏk pikyoyŏn'gu: Hanbando p'yŏnghwa t'odaeŭi kunch'ukŭl wihan mosaek" [Comparative study of the war-fighting capability of South Korea and North Korea: An exploration to establish a foundation for peace on the Korean peninsula]. In Kyŏngnam University Far East Institute, ed., *Nambukhan kunbigyŏngjaengkwa kunch'uk* [The North Korean–South Korean arms race and disarmament], 117–44. Seoul: Kyŏngnam University Press.

Yu Bin. 1999. "Containment by Stealth: Chinese Views of and Policies toward America's Alliances with Japan and Korea after the Cold War" (Sept.). Stanford, CA: Asia Pacific Research Center.

Yu Chun-Hyŏng. 1990. "Hanmi pangsanhyŏmryŏkŭn chinjŏndoego innŭn'ga" [Is Korea-U.S. defense industry cooperation moving forward?]. *Kukpangkwa kisul* [National defense and technology] (Apr.): 3–7.

Yuh, Ji-Yeon. 1999. "Immigrants on the Front Line: Korean Military Brides in America, 1950–1996." Ph.D. dissertation, University of Pennsylvania.

Zagare, Frank C. 1999. "All Mortis, No Rigor." *International Security* 24, 2 (Fall): 107–14.

Zhang Biwu. 2002. "China's Perception of the United States: An Exploration of China's Foreign Policy Motivations." Ph.D. dissertation, Ohio State University.

Zhang Ruizhuang. 2002. "Bushi dui Hua zhengce zhong de 'lan jun' yinxiang" [The influence of the "blue team" on Bush's China policy]. *Meiguo yanjiu* [American studies] 1: 40–56.

———. 2001. "Chong gu Zhongguo waijiao suo chu zhi guoji huanjing" [Reestimating the international environment in which China's foreign relations are situated]. *Zhanlüe yu guanli* [Strategy and management] 1: 20–30.

Zhang, Yongjin. 1998. *China in International Society since 1949: Alienation and Beyond*. New York: St. Martin's Press.

Zhang Yunling. 2001. "Peace and Security of the Korean Peninsula and China's Role." www.cass.net.cn/s28_yts/wordch-en/en-zyl/en-peace.htm.

———, ed. 2000a. *Huoban haishi duishou: Tiaozheng zhong de Zhong Mei Ri E guanxi* [Partners or adversaries? Sino-U.S.-Japanese-Russian relations in transformation]. Beijing: Social Science Documents Press.

———. 2000b. "Zonghe anquan guan ji dui wo guo anquan de sikao" [The concept of comprehensive security and reflections on China's security]. *Dangdai Ya Tai* [Contemporary Asia-Pacific] 1: 1–16.

Zhang Zhirong, and Wu Chong. 1996. "Jiejue Nansha zhengduan de duice xuanze" [Choices among countermeasures for resolving the Spratly disputes]. In *Nansha wenti yanjiu ziliao* [Research materials on the Spratly Islands issue], 258–72. Beijing: Chinese Academy of Social Sciences.

Zhao Ying. 1999. "Dui yi ge fuza 'wenben' de jiedu—ping 'Chaoxian Zhan'" [Toward a reading of a complicated "text": Critiquing *Unrestricted Warfare*]. *Shijie jingji yu zhengzhi* [World economics and politics] 10: 75–76.

Zhao Zijin. 1998. "ZhongMei guanxi zhong de Riben yinsu" [The Japan element in Sino-U.S. relations]. In Zhu Chenghu, ed., *ZhongMei guanxi de fazhan bianhua ji qi qushi* [Changes in the development of Sino-U.S. relations and their trends], 347–71. Nanjing: Jiangsu People's Press.

Zhu Chenghu. 1999. "ZhongRi guanxi: Liyi yu qinggan" [Sino-Japanese relations: Interest and emotion]. *Huanqiu shibao* [Global times] (30 July).

Zhu Feng. 2002. "Zai lishi gui yi zhong bawo ZhongMei guanxi" [Understanding Sino-U.S. relations in historical perspective]. *Huanqiu shibao guoji luntan* [Global Times international forum] (28 Feb.). http://interforum.xilubbs.com/.

Zhu Yangming, ed. 2000. *Ya Tai anquan zhanlüe lun* [On security strategy in the Asia-Pacific]. Beijing: Military Sciences Press.

Index